Dark Psychosis
Profiling Serial Killers
& Prolific Offenders

Dark Psychosis

Profiling Serial Killers & Prolific Offenders

Inside The Minds of The World's Most Dangerous Offenders

SAMUEL HODGINS

Copyright © 2021 Samuel Hodgins

All rights reserved. No part of this publication may be reproduced or transmitted in any form or by any means, electronic or mechanical including photocopying, recording or any information storage or retrieval system, without prior permission in writing from the publishers.

The right of Samuel Hodgins to be identified as the author of this work has been asserted by him in accordance with the Copyright, Designs and Patents Act 1988

First published in the United Kingdom in 2021 by
The Choir Press

ISBN 978-1-78963-239-2

'It is a frightening thought that man also has a shadow side to him, consisting not just of weaknesses and foibles, but of a positively demonic dynamism. It is quite within the bounds of possibility for a man to recognize the relative evil of his nature, but it is a rare and shattering experience for him to gaze into the face of absolute evil.'

(Carl Jung, The Shadow).

Contents

Introduction and About This Book:	xi

The Formation of Serial Killers — 1

Chapter 1: Introduction	3
Chapter 2: Early Life Experiences	7
Chapter 3: The Triad of Evil and the Development of a Serial Killer	10
Chapter 4: Power, Modus Operandi, and Victimology	14
Chapter 5: Biological Factors	18
Chapter 6: Brain Abnormalities and Serial Killers	23
Chapter 7: The Western World and Its Modern-day Obsession With Fame and Celebrity Culture	28
Chapter 8: Dangerous Ideologies and Subcultures	35
Chapter 9: Socio-economics: Society and Serial Murder	41
Chapter 10: Medical Monsters	46
Chapter 11: Killer Couples and Folie à Deux	49
Chapter 12: Are They Just Psychopaths?	54

Pen Profiles of the Offenders — 57

Cayetano Santos Godino	59
Dr Harold Frederick Shipman	80
Peter Sutcliffe, The Yorkshire Ripper	109
Albert DeSalvo, the Boston Strangler	141
John George Haigh, the Acid Bath Murderer	174
Dennis Nilsen	215
John Wayne Gacy	248
Peter Kurten, the 'Vampire of Dusseldorf'	284

CONTENTS

Thomas Hamilton, the Dunblane Massacre   312
Derrick Bird   339
Raoul Moat   362

Conclusion   397
Further reading and research used for the commission of this book   401

Acknowledgments:

Thank you to everybody who has helped me to achieve this book being published and too all my family and friends, I hope you enjoy reading the book as much as I enjoyed conducting the research and writing the book.

All the best.

Sam Hodgins, July 2021

Introduction and About This Book:

Criminal profiling has been with us for longer than the media has led us to believe, and people have always tried to explain the behaviour of serious offenders or serial killers, as those who possess a normal personality cannot comprehend the heinous actions of those members of society who do not. Criminal profiling has been around long before the first known criminal profiles and people have always tried to explain the heinous behaviour of society's monsters, for example, those who found mutilated bodies of the victims of serial killers in the dark ages explained this type of behaviour by creating monsters such as vampires, werewolves, witches et al. However, these monsters exist, and they look like you and I, they also exist amongst you and I, and here lies the danger as the evil lurks within and amongst us and these people are not some mythical creature that belong to history or the pages of a story book or the silver screen; serial killers and serial offenders exist in the present day and they are not a figment or a creation of our darkest and wildest imaginations.

Criminal and offender profiling is still in its infancy, and the term 'serial killer' was allegedly first coined by the FBI profiler Robert Ressler when interviewing the American serial killer Ted Bundy, however, there have been several recorded items of evidence prior to the crimes of Ted Bundy being known, as psychologists have been attempting to profile unknown serial offenders throughout the course of criminal psychological history. The most notable and a very early attempt of profiling was conducted by Dr Thomas Bond in 1888 during the Whitechapel murders conducted on Jack the Ripper. As Jack the Ripper was never caught, we will never know how accurate the profile was, and many criminologists and amateur sleuths are still profiling Jack the Ripper today. However, in terms of 'unmasking' Jack the Ripper, I believe that it will be a fruitless endeavour as too many fanciful theories have been bandied about and there is no real basis behind them to

INTRODUCTION AND ABOUT THIS BOOK

be taken seriously. One of these theories is that Jack the Ripper was a 'doctor', based on the premise that he knew how to mutilate his victims. We have seen the media propel this myth with a sense of 'absolute certainty', however, serial killers have since mutilated victims and removed body parts and this includes and is not limited to serial killers with a normal-ranging intelligence quotient (IQ), such as Ted Bundy, to those ranging with lower IQs such as Jerry Brudos, who would remove the feet of his victims and create moulds for his own sexual fetish, and Fred West, who removed the bones of his victims, such as fingers, as well as a foetus from one of his victims (the police don't know what West did with these bones). Jack the Ripper, therefore, may well have actually been local to the Whitechapel area, and may well have been a marauding serial killer, e.g. prowling his local community as opposed to being a commuting or nomadic serial killer, and the reason I believe this is because many people in Victorian Britain were very much confined to the areas and communities they were born into, since during the Industrial Revolution many people lived in terraced housing slums to be able to get to work easily enough, as advancements in transport and commuting was in its infancy.

In the studies and discipline of criminal and offender profiling, it is much easier to profile these offenders who have been apprehended due to the raft of psychological information written about them, as opposed to an *unknown subject or unidentified subject of an investigation* (abbreviated to *unsub*) and despite media portrayals of the serial killer or serial offender being a criminal 'mastermind', with the profiler locked in a constant battle of wits against the offender, a battle between good and evil, in which the profiler always joins the dots together with a Sherlock Holmes moment of investigative intuition, this is far from the truth as serial killers usually get caught as they become sloppy the more they get away with crimes. Serial killers usually end up making mistakes that lead to their capture, incarceration, or execution because the more hedonistic and narcissistic they become, the more mistakes they make as they begin to believe that they are 'invincible' and highly intelligent in comparison to the police, law, general society and of course their victims.

The reality and tragic part of all this is sometimes law enforcement needs them to commit another crime to capture them, leaving a forensic clue or risking identification. For example, the British serial killer, Dennis Nilsen, was flushing the remains of his victims into the drains from his top floor flat, which was causing a stench, and other residents were raising complaints. The property's managing agent eventually called upon the services of a

INTRODUCTION AND ABOUT THIS BOOK

plumber, who found the remains lodged in the plumbing and contacted the police, leading to Nilsen's conviction and arrest. Criminal and offender profiling is an investigative tool used to aid law enforcement; it may not always be accurate, and it is purely an investigative assistance tool and has no basis within a court of law.

Criminal and offender profiling of an unsub is purely an investigative tool, and it derives its basis from multi-faceted psychological traits based upon the following areas: *the crime scene, the victimology, victim typology, the use of aggression and language (the latter if the victim survives), modus operandi, the crime scene, geographical profiling, linkage analysis.* These facets will allow a skilled profiler to link everything together and provide a profile of an unknown offender and the best interview methods upon their apprehension, and it is an extremely skilled job as serial killers, like every one of us, each individual offender will possess their own unique psychological characteristics and psychological traits, making profiling extremely difficult because any inaccurate information can unwittingly mislead investigators. For example, in the case of the Washington Sniper attacks in 2002, the FBI's Behavioural Sciences Unit (BSU) believed that they were hunting an ex-army veteran who was suffering from post-traumatic stress disorder (PTSD) and the killings were resultant because he felt 'let down' by the army and his country. The FBI believed that they were hunting a lone white male in his late 40s or 50s. This criminal profile provided by the FBI was highly inaccurate and mislead the investigation as there was two killers, John Allen Muhammed (aged 42) and Lee Boyd Malvo (aged 17) and neither were suffering from any known mental illnesses or mental conditions. The motivation for the crime proved to be highly inaccurate as well, as John Allen Muhammed was aiming to kill his second ex-wife in the series of killings to regain custody of his children, and therefore the other victims were simply 'collateral damage' in the series of murders. Malvo has since claimed that John Allen Muhammed was waging 'jihad' against the United States with the aim of closing entire cities. This is one example, and there are others where offender profiling has proved to be highly inaccurate. However, the media are partly to blame for this as they portray it as a simple tool that 'solves' a series of grisly murders or crimes, which of course piques the public's interest. However, it is a highly inaccurate and incorrect portrayal of the discipline of criminal profiling.

I believe that the victim typology is where a profiler should always begin the deduction of their theories, as the victim is the primary focus of the offender's criminal motivations. After a comprehensive study of the victims, the profiler should work backwards on any other clues to conduct the profile, since this would provide a more 'top-down' approach to profiling and narrow the psychological and routine habits of the offender being hunted. For example, the Yorkshire Ripper, Peter Sutcliffe, targeted sex workers, and lone women. Sutcliffe was therefore suffering from misogyny and satyriasis, and there were several women who survived and gave good descriptions to the police. His victims explained to the police on several occasions that he was from Yorkshire and not Sunderland (due to a tape from 'Wearside Jack' being sent to the police, the investigation was skewed), the killer was also a 'commuting' killer within the local area, so this suggested he was an employee who had to do a lot of travelling in his line of work. One does have to wonder with all the clues pointing towards Peter Sutcliffe, had the police found a skilled profiler at the time could he have been arrested much sooner and saved several innocent lives? We will never know. However, the investigation was all over the place and the police were inundated with leads; a profile may well have narrowed the search and discredited the Wearside Jack hoax, as the surviving victims told the police that their attacker had a 'Yorkshire accent' and the police ignored this vital piece of witness testimony.

The aim of this book is not to solve any unknown investigations of potential serial killings, as all the offenders I have profiled for the purposes of this book have been apprehended. The aim of this book is to provide the public, students of the subject, law enforcement and general readers with a better understanding of how the processes of criminal and offender profiling is conducted, as not all of my chosen offenders are serial killers and some are spree killers, such as Derek Bird, who committed the Cumbria Massacre in 2010, and Raoul Moat, who went on a killing spree in the same year, as the aim is to investigate why serious offenders become motivated to commit the crimes that they ultimately undertake.

The book will be split into two sections, with the first providing an introduction into the *formation of a serial killer*, and the second part will focus on eleven serious offenders, with some being better known than others in the book. The profiles contained within the book will delve into some of the darkest souls in mankind, and sometimes reading what harm one person to do to another can be extremely distressing, however, to understand good people, we also must understand that evil people exist amongst the good. As the Chinese philosopher Laozi once said, *'Darkness within darkness is the gateway to understanding'* and understanding these monsters may be the only way to stopping them and their malevolent behaviours.

The Formation of Serial Killers

CHAPTER 1

Introduction

'The eyes of a psychopath will deceive you; they will destroy you. They will take from you your innocence, your pride and eventually your soul. These eyes do not see what you and I see. Behind these eyes one only finds blackness, the absence of light. These are the eyes of a psychopath. The darkest souls are not those that choose to exist within the hell of the abyss, but those souls which move silently amongst us.'

Although the above quotation is from the 2007 Hollywood horror movie, Rob Zombie's *Halloween*, this actual quotation is stranger than fiction when we are discussing and psychoanalysing a demographic of people who exist in the shadows amongst us within every country and every society, *the serial killer*. Serial killers exist amongst us and from the outset appear extremely normal, and usually it is not until their capture and arrest that prison psychologists and psychiatrists can delve into their warped psychology and deranged psychosis to attempt to discover their drives and motives, which lead to their confession of such horrific and appalling crimes.

The leading British criminal psychologist Professor David Wilson states the 'normality' that serial killers exude to those around them as the '*banality of evil*', as they appear as normal as every other member of society. However, they are anything but a 'normal' member of society. When conducting research into serial killers, from the outset they live like you and I, which confirms Professor Wilson's initial hypothesis. For example, the American serial killer Ted Bundy was a psychology graduate and a Republican party activist who served on the governor of New York, Nelson Rockefeller's presidential campaign in 1968, and Bundy also served on the successful re-election campaign of Governor Dan Evans (Rep) in the same year. Ironically, during this period, Bundy was appointed to the Seattle Crime Prevention Advisory Committee where he was tasked with studying the motivations of rapists and the effects of rape on their victims. With hindsight, Bundy was quite possibly studying himself as he realised that he had a serious psychological problem, and he convinced himself that he would 'stop' after his initial murders. John Wayne Gacy was a local politician and ran several fast-food restaurants in Chicago Illinois. Gacy's line of work in the fast-food industry not only supplied an income for his family, it also provided him access to young men as many students are employed in this industry and young men were to later become Gacy's preferred choice of victim. Dennis Rader was a Lutheran Church minister within his local community, and he was employed as an ADT security services technician. For Rader, like Bundy and Gacy, his employment allowed him easier access to victims because he knew which homes were vulnerable and when women were alone, and he would not be disturbed during the commission of his crimes. Rader also knew how to disable a security system, which allowed him to wait for his victims to return home, forming part of his fantasies in the lead up to his crimes. The Canadian serial killer and serial rapist Paul Bernardo, also known as the 'Scarborough Rapist', was a sales manager for Amway selling health, beauty and care home products, a job which allowed Bernardo the opportunity to commute around the country and commit a series of rapes and brutal assaults against his victims.

Unfortunately, Bernardo was committing his crimes during a period when criminal and offender profiling was still in its infancy within law enforcement, and at the time many law officials believed that rapists where generally geographical stable as opposed to 'nomadic', and this naivety allowed Bernardo and other rapists more freedom to commit their crimes. Paul Bernardo matched every e-fit that was published by the law enforcement who were hunting the Scarborough Rapist. Had there been more knowledge of offender profiling, the police may well have arrested Paul Bernardo sooner before he could escalate his deviant criminal acts, progressing from rape to murder, and potentially saving the lives of at least four victims.

Gerald Schaefer was a police officer who exploited his position of societal trust in 'upholding' the law to perform the murders of at least five young women (it is believed Schaefer killed over 30 women, though there was not enough evidence to link him to the crimes). Schaefer, like the serial killers mentioned thus far, exhibited a similar behavioural pattern, using their employment to actively pursue their crimes and hide in plain sight amongst their respective communities, appearing 'normal'. Professor David Wilson (2010) states the reason serial killers go undetected for so long is due to their

INTRODUCTION

'*striking veneer of normality*'. Serial killers continue to exist amongst us today, as Professor Wilson claimed in 2015 there are at least two active serial killers on the loose in the United Kingdom at present, and it is estimated by the Federal Bureau of Investigation (FBI) that at least 50 serial killers remain at large in the United States of America. Despite advancements in psychology and forensics, serial killers are still a real and present danger to society and although their numbers are small in comparison to other crimes, they strike the most fear in societies whilst they remain unapprehend.

In the following short text, I am trying to establish several hypotheses which may lead to an overall conclusion as to why a person enters a state of metamorphosis to become a serial killer. I aim to do this by looking into the backgrounds of these people and analyse the contributing factors, such as biological, victimology, neurological, genetics, sociological and/or whether it is one factor or a fusion of several factors that causes such a phenomenon to form a dangerous and warped psychosis. I have chosen this experiment as I feel that if we can explain the formation of a serial killer, we may be able to in the future recognise people who are at risk of becoming a serial killer, and therefore hopefully treating them correctly to inhibit their innate desires and warped fantasies and in the process saving the lives of a potential initial victim which the serial killer chooses based on their warped desires and fantasies. If society and medicine can treat a potential serial killer, it would also spare the secondary victims, the family, and friends of the initial victim who in many cases have their lives ruined through the initial heinous acts, the pain and anguish brought on by their crimes. Serial killers also create a climate of fear through their crimes, and this also creates a sub-group of tertiary victims such as neighbours, e.g., in Wichita, when Dennis Rader was active, residents could not rest because they lived in a perpetual state of fear because 'BTK' would kill indiscriminately against men, women and children and across the differing races that made up the community. The other tertiary victims of the heinous acts of criminality are the wider general society who through the judicial system and the media will be ultimately exposed to their horrific crimes, leaving some members of society terrified of becoming a victim, which despite media interest is actually a very rare crime, according to the FBI only constituting less than one percent of all annual murders in the USA. I believe from my previous knowledge of studying serial killers, I, like many before me, will present a plethora of theories and hypotheses and I will ultimately fail to explain what many believe has been a growing menace in the Western world since the end of the Second World War.

THE FORMATION OF SERIAL KILLERS

To acquire the information for this project, I have studied 48 serial killers exactly, with 40 of these being single perpetrators and eight of these being couples who kill (I will attempt to explain the *'Folie a Deux'* hypothesis in chapter 11). The sources I have used have varied from books, magazines, the internet, and television programmes about the serial killers who have lived amongst us in recent times and continue to live amongst us, albeit in a capacitated state. I hope you find the following book informative, and I hope it will provide at least some of the answers we have so desperately searched for over the past decades of how the psychology of the individual metastasises into the formation of a serial killer.

CHAPTER 2
Early Life Experiences

It is unclear in scientific terms whether a person is either born bad, or whether their behaviours are a result of the environment that they were reared in, or if it is a combination of both factors that produces an anti-social personality. This has been debated since the inception of criminal psychology. For example, early criminologists such as Lombroso (1876) published a paper entitled the *'Criminal Man'*, which focused upon the phrenology of a person as an explanation for their criminal behaviour. The study of phrenology focused on the size of a criminal's skull shape and size and concluded the more bumps and indentations in a skull, the more likely this person was to become a criminal, as opposed to somebody who possessed a skull with fewer bumps and indentations. Lombroso's theory had its origins in Darwinist theories based on 'primacy' and early man's animalistic behaviours. Lombroso believed that many criminals did not fully evolve in the developmental stages with other members of that society and hence became the 'criminal underclasses'. The theory of phrenology has since been discredited and is not widely accepted as credible in the studies of modern criminology and criminal profiling as a tool to explain criminal behaviour. Modern criminologists such as Sims and Gray (1993) listed more than 1,000 studies which linked exposure to media violence with aggressive behaviour.

In the 1970s two FBI agents, Robert Ressler and John Douglas were recruited by the FBI to play a significant role in the development of psychologically profiling violent offenders, which led to them interviewing many serial killers (Ressler coined the term after the arrest of Ted Bundy), and what they noticed in the profile of a serial killer was that most of them had suffered traumatic experiences as children which varied from psychological, sexual, physical and emotional abuse, or a combination of them all. Ward, Polaschek and Beech (2006) suggest similarities between sexual offenders and psychopaths, notably that both groups experienced abuse and neglect as children. Henry Lee Lucas's mother would force her son to watch her have drunken sex with strange men, whilst his invalid father would have no choice to witness these strange men having sexual intercourse with his wife. Ottis Toole's parents would abuse him both *physically* and *mentally* and this mental abuse would involve forcing him to dress as a girl and bullying him whilst dressed as a 'girl'. These anti-social early experiences no doubt played a formative paralysis within his sexual psyche, as his mother did not want him and rejected him as she wanted a daughter, and this would have led to confusion in his sexual maturation in his later years. Toole's older sister frequently sexually assaulted him, and these experiences would have created misogyny in his early psyche and his interpretation of women in society, as the two caregivers should have protected him and not abused him. Toole would have also felt rage towards his mother for the treatment his father received, as his sister also physically abused their father in the presence of a young Ottis Toole. The 'foot fetish' serial killer, Jerry Brudos had a similar despairing upbringing, which was very similar to the upbringing of Ottis Toole in the sense that his mother never wanted a third son, as she wanted a daughter. Instead of accepting this and caring for him, Mrs Brudos would frequently remind a young Jerry Brudos of this and exhibit spite towards him with her overzealous disciplinary 'standards' of behaviour, once hitting him hard for taking a piece of fruit. Brudos's mother would belittle him when she once found him in a pair of heels in his bedroom, as Roland (2007) states that his shoe fetish became so all-consuming that it led him to kill four woman and to cut off their feet and keep them as 'trophies'. It can be theorised that the fact his mother was angry with him wearing the high heels led to them becoming a 'forbidden fruit' and, as we all know, at some stage in their development children rebel against their parents. The psychological problem with Brudos was that this foot fetish became fused with his early sexual fantasies and became intertwined with the misogynistic rage that he felt towards his mother, all of which would end in tragic consequences for at least four women as he developed into an adult.

    The serial killer that inspired the author Robert Bloc's 1959 novel *Psycho* was the 'Butcher of Plainfield', Ed Gein, who was another serial killer intertwined within the pattern of suffering a traumatic childhood with an overzealous mother, Augusta Gein, who would not let young Ed Gein socialise with other children for fear he may become 'immoral'. And yet her vicious beatings meant that when Ed was a teenager his feelings of love, anger and lust towards his mother became intertwined with his sexual fantasies, as he was not allowed to develop within the normal stages of psychosocial development which ultimately led to him spiralling into madness upon her death, as Ed Gein was finally 'free' to act upon his instilled desires without fear of any repercussions for the first time in his life. In 1945, this newfound 'freedom' led him to kill two women and dismember exhumed corpses of recently deceased women from the obituary notices in the local newspapers. Ed Gein, unlike most serial killers who end up in prison or on death row, was institutionalised at the Mendota Mental Health Institute, where he would die in 1984 at the age of 77. The staff at Mendota Mental Health Institute claimed that Gein was a 'model patient', and this is possibly a reaction in Gein's psyche as he had regimentation and order for the first time since the death of his overbearing mother.

The question we must ask within the psychological study of criminal psychology and the formation of serial killers is as follows: *'Is childhood abuse a precursor that makes a serial killer commit the atrocities based upon their prepubescent fantasies?'* As serial killers are psychopaths, and one of these traits is manipulating others which can involve some academics seeing them as the 'victims', we also must ask the following question: *'Do they blame it on abuse as a cognitive dissonance mechanism to, in their own warped minds, exonerate themselves from their heinous crimes?'* The National Society of Prevention of Cruelty to Children's (NSPCC) statistics in 2011 stated that 1 in 10 young adults (9%) had been neglected/abused by parents during childhood, yet on the hypothesis of serial killers such as Kemper and Lucas, one of these should become a serial killer and further still, serial killing is an extremely rare crime and not all serial killers come from neglectful families, with Harold Shipman and Ted Bundy as prominent examples, and therefore the results in this area of study are inconclusive and I believe it will be for the foreseeable future, or at least until psychological studies advance yet again. However, there has been previous research conducted in the field of psychiatry that can indicate an anti-social personality and serial offender in the future, which serial killers exhibit all too commonly in the *MacDonald Triad*.

CHAPTER 3

The Triad of Evil and the Development of a Serial Killer

As we have seen in the previous chapter, the early experiences and environment can play a part in the development of the psychology of a serial killer. In this chapter, I will delve further into the *'the triad of evil'*, aka *'triad of sociopathy'*, aka *'the dark triad'*. All these terms are more commonly known as the *'MacDonald Triad'*, which is a set of three behavioural characteristics that are associated with sociopathic behaviour and long-term serial offending. The triad was first identified by the New Zealand psychologist, John Marshall MacDonald, first discussed and proposed in the psychological study paper *'A threat to kill'*, a 1963 paper in the American Journal of Psychiatry to provide linkage analysis between a triad of behavioural statistics and serious criminal offending.

The triad links animal cruelty, pyromania, and persistent bedwetting past the age of five to violent behaviours, homicidal behaviour, and sexual predatory behaviour. It is known from research that not all violent offenders exhibit these behaviours, however, there is one type of offender who exhibits at least one or all three of these behaviours – *the serial killer*. The FBI Behavioural Sciences Unit agents John E Douglas and Robert Ressler used the *'triad of evil'* linkage analysis and they found that the theory did provide substantial evidence that their selected study of serial killers exhibited these traits, and psychiatrists also claimed that this occurred because of parental neglect, as we have seen in the previous chapter about the detrimental effects on the development of the 'self' within the psyche.

Pyromania has been exhibited by some serial killers. However, not all that have been studied have exhibited a fascination with pyromania. Pyromania is a common psychological obsession amongst many serial killers and sexually perverse serial offenders. The FBI believes that the act of pyromania can provide a potential serial killer, serial rapist, or pyromaniac with sexual gratification as it is an extreme expression of sexual frustration being 'released', although it may not appear on the surface, Roland (2007). David Berkowitz (aka the 'Son of Sam') admitted in an interview with Robert Ressler that he would climax at the sight of a fire that he had set. The serial killer and rapist Joseph Kallinger once said, *'Oh what ecstasy setting fires brings to my body'*. Many academics believe that this is the final stage before the act of murder, as they are now committing acts against society and therefore ostracising themselves as members of that society.

The problem that criminal profiling and academics encounter with the study of pyromania is that not all serial killers exhibit the symptom (or at least to the best of our knowledge), for example, Ted Bundy, Fred West, and Aileen Wuornos have no record of this symptom. The MacDonald Triad instantly poses a challenge for anybody studying the development and formation of a serial killer in regards to pyromania, as it is an *impulse control disorder*, and although Bundy and West, for example, did not show any signs of pyromania, they did exhibit other areas of *impulsive control disorders* with the most common being kleptomania (addiction to theft), as Bundy was a habitual thief and even stole a tree from a store for no reason other than the 'thrill' of the act. Bundy would steal a map from the reception case of the Wildwood Inn, Colorado Springs, that would help the state prosecution against him in the murder of Caryn Campbell, and his own narcissistic criminal addiction helped state prosecutors send him to the electric chair. Fred West was also a habitual thief who was sacked from several jobs after being caught. Aileen Wuornos, on the contrary, did not suffer from pyromania. She did, however, suffer from intermittent explosive disorder (IED), which is another psychological impulse disorder, and therefore the early question already is *'does the MacDonald Triad need to be extended to attribute other behavioural characteristics of the serial killer?'* The problem instantly posed by this fervent question is that the psychology of individuals is complex, and simply using a small sample of three characteristic behaviours of a deranged group of people is too small to quantify and use linkage analysis. The other problem we encounter is that we are almost limiting the psychological variables associated with serial killers, as they all exhibit different various psychological behaviours, for example, Richard Ramirez and William Heirens enjoyed leaving messages on the walls of their victims' homes and did not exhibit the use of pyromania, and therefore, although pyromania may psychologically gratify the motivations of one serial killer, the psychological motivations will differ to that of another serial killer and therefore, in my professional opinion, the MacDonald Triad should be reviewed and adapted as modern criminologists and profilers have more research available to them since the inception of this theory, which was devised in 1963.

It is believed many serial killers practice in torturing animals at a young age as rehearsal for murdering a person in later life, and the act of animal cruelty serves their psychology by releasing their innate frustrations as they are not strong enough to retaliate against their own tormentor, and it also provides them with a feeling of regained power and control in their turbulent lives (Wright and Hensley 2003). The corresponding studies on the development of serial killers and animal cruelty have been found to be true for many serial killers, however, once again this is not the case for all serial killers and provides furtherment to the debate that the MacDonald Triad should be expanded and revised to suit modern criminal psychology research. The American serial killer Richard Chase expressed remorse for the animals that he killed but none whatsoever for the six people he killed during his spree in 1978 (Cowley 2010). The Genesee River Killer, Arthur Shawcross, admitted that he enjoyed killing animals, yet there are no records of other serial killers performing zoo-sadism such as Ted Bundy, Myra Hindley and Peter Sutcliffe. Myra Hindley even flew into a rage at Manchester police station when she was advised that her dog had been put down by the police upon her arrest and called the police 'evil bastards'.

Enuresis is the final symptom of the triad, which is unintentional bedwetting during sleep persistently after the age of five, and more than 60% of serial killers suffer from this problem, including the Hillside Strangler, Kenneth Bianchi, and Ted Bundy.

The results overall are inconclusive, and it does not mean that a child suffering from one and/or all of these symptoms is a future serial killer, and therefore as psychology is a complexity that is continuously being studied, professionals, psychological practitioners and amateur sleuths need to approach the study with attentive vigilance, as in simply labelling someone suffering from these symptoms as a 'serial killer' there is a danger this may lead the individual to act upon this label to achieve their own self-fulfilling prophecy. If psychology and psychologists begin labelling a person a 'serial killer' based on the psychological factors contained within the MacDonald

Triad, this could lead a person to craving the notoriety and power over victims and society which is a central facet of the psychological profile of the serial killer. The American sociologist, Howard Becker, has written several papers and theories on the dangers associated with psychological labelling and he once stated, *'Deviancy is not a quality of the act a person commits, but rather a consequence of the application by others of rules and sanctions to an "offender". Deviant behaviour is behaviour that people label so.'* Therefore, before we label another person as a potential 'serial killer' based on the psychological precursors they are outwardly exhibiting, it may be best to approach this with extreme caution and seek professional and psychological assistance, as the aim of any society should be rectifying the psychological imbalances of those members of society who are in possession of them, as unwittingly labelling a person can lead to catastrophic consequences in the future for the individual suffering the psychological problems, and for potential victims and society as a whole at a later date.

CHAPTER 4

Power, Modus Operandi, and Victimology

The word 'power' has a variety of meanings including *'the possession of control, or command over others'*. Power, modus operandi, and victimology are key factors in the formation of serial killers, and I will attempt to explain how these factors fuse together to form the development of a serial killer during this chapter.

'You feel the last bit of breath leaving their body. You are looking into their eyes. A person in that situation is God!' (Ted Bundy, 1980) Ted Bundy had a unique modus operandi amongst serial killers as he used his charisma, charm, and non-threatening demeanour to entice his victims into 'helping' him and he preyed upon their acts of kindness by acting upon his own primitive instincts. Bundy's modus operandi was to wear a cast on his arm, use crutches and drop his books to appear he was struggling, and he would endeavour to ask young pretty women to help him carry books to his car. Once they were under his control, he would strike them from behind with a tyre-iron which he hid under the vehicle's tyre. This act would gain him complete control over his victim, where he would proceed to take them to secluded areas, including the Colorado Mountains, where he would rape, humiliate, and ultimately kill the victim. Bundy admitted his modus operandi to a stunned Robert Ressler, who could not understand how such a person with a pleasant demeanour could apprehend, rape, and kill so many women. However, Bundy would have enjoyed discussing this with Robert Ressler and the FBI because he would have believed that he was showing how 'intelligent' he was in comparison to law enforcement and the victims. Bundy was enjoying the attention and possibly witnessing the facial expressions of the FBI agents when discussing his modus operandi.

In terms of Bundy's modus operandi, if we refer to Professor David Wilson's claim that serial killers exist amongst us and use their 'veneer of normality' to be able to perpetrate their crimes, then Bundy could not have given a more prominent personification this claim. Having extensively studied the crimes of Ted Bundy, I believe that Bundy's modus operandi to appear 'normal' formed a big part of the 'fantasy' in his psychosis before the commission of his crimes that developed over a period, as he knew he blended into the college campus lifestyle in terms of dress, manner and educational standards and he would appear as 'non-threatening'. These traits allowed Bundy to not only carry out his crimes, but to also go undetected and live amongst the student population without arousing any suspicions from his peers that he was even remotely responsible for the disappearances of the young women on campus. When studying serial killers and their crimes it must always be remembered that the modus operandi is only one part of the profile of a serial killer's warped fantasies, and other areas need to intertwine for them to conduct their acts of violence, and every psychological trait and facet needs to be comprehensively studied to provide a more conclusive profile of each respective offender.

Bundy's chosen victim typology was no coincidence, based on his fantasies and later interviews that he provided to the FBI: they were the beginning, middle and final part of his warped desires and deviant fantasies that manifested within his psyche and developed over the course of his lifetime. Bundy's victims were attractive young women, with dark hair parted in the middle. They stemmed from the American middle-class socio-economic background, the class Bundy yearned all his life to be accepted into and he could not attain due to his psychopathic nature; Bundy, like all psychopaths, need constant stimulation, and Bundy's deviant behaviour was causing disruptions to his studies, and this destroyed not only his long-term career opportunities, but also his relationship with a girl that he fell in love with whilst at university. Bundy once had a girlfriend whom he dearly loved by the name of Stephanie Brooks (pseudonym), yet she refused to marry him as she felt he was immature, and he was 'going nowhere in life'. Bundy was obsessed with Brooks, as she was everything he dreamed of in a woman, yet did her rejection become the catalyst for his crimes? I believe that the answer to this question is a resounding 'no' because Bundy would have been developing these warped fantasies during his childhood and adolescence. The myth around Bundy that the rejection by Stephanie Brooks became the catalyst for his crimes is simply just a myth, as relationship breakup is an area of life that many people must contend with daily. Although most people suffer normal human emotions associated with relationship breakups such as stress, anxiety, sadness, loneliness et al., they do not become serial killers as a way of 'coping' with their loss. It is not known exactly how many victims Bundy killed as he liked to play the 'numbers' game with investigators without divulging information. However, Bundy did later ask Brooks to marry him again and when she said 'yes', he abruptly ended the relationship, thus providing his narcissistic personality, as within his psyche he was in 'control' over her, after all, his mother had pretended to be his sister throughout his childhood, which devastated him, and this would have been a catalysing factor in the development of his misogynistic rage.

The British serial killer Dennis Nilsen and the American serial killer Jeffrey Dahmer, both of whom were ritualistic cannibals, both exhibited an extremely similar modus operandi as they would entice young homosexual men back to their flats and proceed to drug their victims by lacing their alcohol, before strangling and engaging in necrophilia, eating parts of their corpse afterwards in some of the cases, an act of which would have acted as a psychological stimulation of an extreme feeling of 'power', and I believe that this would have provided sexual gratification for a while before the fantasy and tension manifested and built up inside their psychosis, until this tension became unbearable, in which case they had to seek out another victim to satisfy their perverse psychological desires and fantasies. Rosman and Resnick (1989) reviewed 34 cases of necrophilia and found that in 68% of these cases the perpetrators were motivated to possess an unresisting and submissive partner. This is the case with many cannibalistic serial killers, as the act of eating the flesh is the final act of 'possession' in their warped fantasies. Necrophiliacs are frightened of abandonment and rejection, and this appears to be the case for both Nilsen and Dahmer according to their own testimonies. Nilsen stated he did not want to be alone, and Dahmer stated that he wanted to create sex zombies who would never leave him, which I believe was Dahmer's psychological reaction, which was an outward behaviour brought on possibly due to rejection by people close to him in his life, which included his mother during his prepubescent years. Nilsen, like Dahmer, also felt abandoned during his prepubescent years as he witnessed his father leave at an early age, and then his grandfather, who almost acted as his surrogate father, with whom Nilsen formed a close bond, died of a heart attack whilst out fishing. Nilsen saw the body of his grandfather in an open casket and claimed to become 'aroused', and Nilsen would have suffered with a sexual attraction towards his grandfather, an attraction that later became intertwined with his internal rages of feelings of loneliness as adult members of his family could not reach out to him after the death of his grandfather, and Nilsen began to become very introverted, and this is also possibly because he did not want to admit to himself or others that he was homosexual, as this was not accepted as 'normal' during this time. Nilsen's confused sexual identity, feelings of abandonment and loneliness all would have manifested themselves within his psyche, forming a rage that would lead to tragic consequences in his later life for many young innocent people whose young lives were cruelly and callously taken by Nilsen because he could not face his own demons and did not feel that he could seek professional medical help to slay those demons.

The places that serial killers choose to kill or dispose of their victims has a psychological purpose for them during the commission of their crimes – *power*. Bundy felt in control on the Colorado Mountains. Nilsen and Dahmer knew they had full power of their male victims once they had drugged them in their flats and were at their 'mercy', an act which would not be forthcoming. The feeling of power that serial killers derive when committing their crimes is a part of a cycle, with the victim being the last part, which has developed in a dark mind over the course of their lives, and thus far, we have largely attempted to explain the phenomena of serial killers in the 'social' aspect of their development. However, are there any clues as to how their biological development can intertwine with the behaviours in their social psyche to become ultimately the sub-humans they develop into throughout the course of their lives? And thus begins the timeless question in the study of criminality, is crime committed because of *'nature or nurture?'*

CHAPTER 5
Biological Factors

Biological factors and theories of criminal acts associated with them were originally used to explain general criminal behaviour. The study of biological factors and criminality has more recently been used to try to explain the phenomenon of serial killing. In the following chapter I will focus on two biological areas, *testosterone,* and *chromosomes*, to provide further research into the area to ascertain whether biological factors do have a part to play in the development of serial killers.

There are many myths associated with serial killers, which include the following widely accepted myths that firstly they are all dysfunctional loners, and secondly, they are all white men with an extremely high IQ. Once we move away from the media created mythology around serial killers, there is one point that is true – the majority of serial killers are male (not necessarily white) and this can be linked to testosterone as most male serial killers are sexually motivated (Roland 2007).

In the 44 male serial killers whom I have studied for the purposes of this book, I have found that the vast majority had sexual motives as the driving factor for the commission of their crimes. The group that did not seem to have sexual motives was the medical serial killers, at least on the surface anyway, and I will expand more on this statement during the criminal profile of Doctor Harold Shipman later in this book. Richard Trenton Chase was known to have high levels of testosterone, as was Ted Bundy, Paul Bernardo, and Michael Bruce-Ross, yet the latter three could perform sexually with their partners. Chase could not, and he suffered from satyriasis and was a chronic masturbator. However, does sexual immaturity or a high testosterone level cause people to rape and kill? There is not enough evidence to say there is a concrete link between high testosterone to lead for the commission or the psychological development of a serial killer as sportsmen, politicians and businessmen exhibit high levels of testosterone and do not commit such deplorable acts.

BIOLOGICAL FACTORS

Criminal psychologists and criminal profilers believe that with serial killers, rape is another form of power control and possession over their victim, and this is a central theme associated with the psyche of serial killers. For example, sexual predators such as Schaefer, Bundy and Gacy all liked to sexually assault their victims, strangle them, and loosen the ligature before murdering them, which shows their obsession with them being in a power-assertive position over their victims. It is also known that Fred West would keep the victims alive in his cellar at 25 Cromwell Street and he would bind and gag the victims for several days before the fantasy reached its peak, and then Fred and Rose would proceed to kill the victim after days of inducing fear. The Wests are particularly interesting when discussing biology and serial killing, because if a woman's testosterone is lower than a male, surely the woman should not wish to commit the acts of sexual sadism as male serial killers sometimes use phallic objects as a 'substitute' to abuse and degrade the victim, and are there any biological studies that can find imbalances in the female serial killers' chromosome genetic influences?

In a 'normal' human being each cell contains 23 pairs of chromosomes, with one pair defining gender, in a female XX and a male XY. In the 48 serial killers I have researched for this book, I have only managed to find chromosome abnormalities in 3 of the 48; only 6.00% of the cases exhibited chromosome abnormalities and none of these abnormalities occurred in the female serial killers that I studied.

The serial killers who have had the abnormal chromosomes from my studies were Richard Speck (XYY), Arthur Shawcross (XYY) and Bobby Joe Long (XYY). The problems I have encountered during this area of research on chromosome studies and serial killers is the lack of study on this group, and the general male population in the United Kingdom do not know their karyotype (97%), which is their own chromosomal makeup. If the condition of chromosomal abnormalities effects 1 in every 1,000 births, then the incidence of serial killings should be a lot higher, as Roland (2007) states that the FBI believe there are 50 active serial killers in the USA (male population estimate 2009, 151.4 million). One of the serial killers I conducted research on did show a biological factor to argue that serial killing is a genetic disorder, as Bobby Joe Long was a cousin of Henry Lee Lucas, therefore as both children were abused it could be a combination of nature and nurture. I do believe that although my research has found a very tentative link in the argument that serial killing occurs due to biological factors, it still does not explain firstly why the remaining 94.00% of serial killers I studied committed their crimes, and secondly, serial killers have siblings and create offspring who lead normal lives and therefore on this basis, one could argue that the argument of nurture in the psychological development of a serial killer is stronger. However, as I have mentioned throughout, I believe that as each serial killer is unique, we may be in a better position to study each one as an 'individual' and each psychological and biological facet to provide a more comprehensive profile of them as an individual criminal as opposed to a one-size-fits-all approach as the biological factors remain inconclusive thus far and this becomes more apparent when studying chromosomes and female serial killers.

The female serial killers that I researched did not show any abnormalities in their chromosomes. If we take the case of Rose West, then we could argue that the development of the female serial killer is purely down to the 'social environment' as it is recorded that Rose and her father had a sexual relationship from when Rose was very young, and her promiscuity led to sexual acts of 'transference' against her brother. Rose was known locally to provide sexual acts for the local male population, and possibly she was enraged with her mother for not protecting her against sexual exploitation from older men who can only be described as paedophiles.

Rose West's father's abnormal behaviour conditioned her from an early age to believe that men are simply interested in sex, and with sexual intercourse violence is also a part of the act, which may provide a small explanation as to the way Rose treated her own daughters, particularly Anne Marie West and Heather West.

The psychology in the relationship between Fred and Rose West was almost a microcosm of the relationship with her father, in the sense that Fred West was twelve years older than Rose. Rose and Fred conducted their relationship when Rose was aged 16 and Fred was aged 28. Fred was sexually obsessed, and, like Rose's father, Fred West would demand sexual intercourse several times a day, a demand that Rose West was used to providing throughout her life and therefore would not have seen as strange, as she was conditioned to believe that this type of sex drive is 'normal' in all men, when in fact her father and Fred were both suffering with satyriasis. Fred and Rose's father were both obsessed with violent pornography and sex, and it is believed that they would both watch each other taking turns in sexual intercourse with Rose. Rose West was possibly conditioned and developed into a serial killer from internal frustrations and rage and used the male, e.g. Fred, as a conduit to act out her murderous rages and fantasies of rape and possession of another woman, an act which would have been the ultimate transference of outwardly displaying rage against another woman, a rage which was instilled within her psyche due to the early developmental years when her mother did not provide the maternal protection against her tyrannical father.

Although there is no evidence to suggest that Rose West suffered from chromosomal abnormalities, I do believe that Rose West suffered from an extreme form of gender dysphoria, and this was due to the treatment she received at the hands of her father. Rose West, I believe due to the abuse she suffered, used sex as a way of protecting herself against her father's rages, which would occur at trivial occurrences, such as a speck of dust being on door after it had been cleaned. Due to her experiences, Rose West, developed a temper and could more than protect herself against other children in her community, and this including attacking another girl who was bullying her younger brother, Graham Letts (despite Rose sexually molesting him). Rose became confused between her role as 'caregiver', a role which is usually associated with the mother, and the role of 'protector' which is usually associated with the male, and on the outset, it could be said that Rose had chromosomal abnormalities. However, her testosterone developed in an abnormal way due to the abuse she suffered, which I believe led to her suffering from gender dysphoria, and this was evident when Fred West was in jail when Rose, although looking after children, would violently lash out against them for minor indiscretions, which would lead to the eventual murder of Charmaine West. I also believe that Rose West was suffering from gender dysphoria because she exhibited many of the psychological symptoms from low self-esteem: she was socially isolated, she suffered from depression, she took unnecessary risks such as becoming a sex worker to simply satisfy her and Fred's sexual desires. Rose West neglected herself and was overweight and generally unkempt in appearance according to neighbours and images of her during the trial. The abuse Rose West suffered and her own sexually abusive behaviour to her brother led to her suffering gender dysphoria, and she became hyper-sexualised too early, and this led to a sexual maturation disorder which led to her psyche forming an ego-dystonic sexual orientation disorder whereby her sexual identity became confused with her own self-identity and self-image, which led to her becoming anxious about how others perceived her. She was also undoubtedly sexually confused as to whether she was straight or a lesbian, and all these factors coupled with her dire upbringing caused rage within her psyche, and Fred West became a conduit in later life for her to act out her inner rage as a desperate attempt to solve her own inner psychological turmoil.

The research for this chapter has proved inconclusive as to whether biology and chromosomes can explain the development of a serial killer. However, we need to study the most powerful muscle in the human body, the brain, to delve further into the argument for the biological development of serial killers.

CHAPTER 6

Brain Abnormalities and Serial Killers

The frontal lobe is the area in the brains of humans and other mammals that contains most of the dopamine-sensitive neurons in the cerebral cortex, which is associated with reward, attention, short-term memory, planning, motivation, and punishment. It is believed that the frontal lobe area of the brain is responsible for much of the behaviour that allows humans to live together in stable relationships and restricts us from acting on our inherent violent tendencies. The frontal lobe is located within the anterior part of the cranium and is therefore susceptible to injuries.

In several high-profile cases of serial killers, there have been recorded studies that have shown brain abnormalities due to events that have occurred earlier in their lives. For example, the American serial killer, kidnapper, and serial rapist Bobby Joe Long had a motorbike accident which he blamed on his hyper-sexuality and claimed that he was a 'normal' human being prior to the occurrence of the accident. The British serial killer Fred West had a motorbike accident aged seventeen and he was left in an eight-day coma, then, at the age of nineteen, he fell from a fire escape, leaving him in a twenty-four-hour coma. Several months later, West was arrested but escaped imprisonment for molesting a thirteen-year-old girl, a crime which occurred immediately after these accidents. We need to ask, is this a coincidence, and/or is there a strong basis for a scientific argument that law enforcement and criminal psychologists need to delve into further to explain the development of a serial killer?

From scientific research into this area, it is scientifically known that once the frontal lobe is damaged that the perceptions of risk-taking and rule-abiding become impaired and Bennet et al. (1964) conducted an experiment on rats aged between 25 and 80 days of age based on rearing them in an 'enriched' environment, and another group in an 'impoverished' environment. The study found that the rats reared in enriched environment had cerebral cortices which were thicker and heavier than the rats reared in an impoverished environment. Therefore, could the mothers who abuse these serial killers during adolescence create damage to the frontal lobe through a lack of maternal attachment? The studies on serial killers do tend to steer the argument in this direction. However, it is not quite the 'nature vs. nurture' debate, it's 'nurture changing nature', and this has been shown throughout the book thus far with serial killers such as Jerry Brudos, Ottis Toole, Henry Lee Lucas et al., and there are others from my research that follow this pattern, most notably Gary Ridgeway, aka the 'Green River Killer'. Gary Ridgeway was persistently abused by his mother and would often be on the end of her violence, which resulted in him suffering from enuresis, for which his mother would belittle him and make him sleep in her bed until he was in his late teens, which many have theorised resulted in attraction and anger towards women, or sexual confusion, which became the motivational drive for his later killing.

Studies in this area again provide us with no definitive answer because both Bobby Joe Long and Fred West, for example, may have had accidents that could have lowered their behavioural inhibitions and blurred the lines between what is both morally and socially acceptable. However, they were both reared in what one can only describe as an abnormal environment whereby moral boundaries between sexual promiscuity and normal sexual behaviour did not exist. As mentioned earlier, with male serial killers their backgrounds tend to show an extremely dysfunctional relationship with their mother, and neither Bobby Joe Long nor Fred West provide any exception to this 'rule'. Long, for example, was forced to sleep in a bed with his mother until he was sixteen, and one can only theorise that there was an unhealthy sexual relationship with his mother. Long's mother also had ample short-term boyfriends which the FBI believed abused Long, who was also forced to watch his mother have intercourse with strange men. However, Long would never clarify on these theories and as he was executed in 2019, we will never be able to confirm them either way.

Fred West was another killer who had an overprotective mother and a disciplinarian father. Prior to his serious accidents, Fred West was introduced to bestiality by his own father and during this period his mother introduced him to 'normal' sexual intercourse at the age of twelve, and Fred believed that incest was 'normal' and 'acceptable behaviour' insofar as much as rebuking an officer who scorned at his comments about this practice when

BRAIN ABNORMALITIES AND SERIAL KILLERS

Fred asked him, *'What do you mean you don't have sex with your daughter?'* Although Bobby Joe Long and Fred West did suffer brain abnormalities brought on from their accidents, there is a strong theory that they were developing into a deviant personality brought about by their home environment, and they may well have committed their series of murders had they not had the accidents, because we are met with another conundrum in the study of the psychological development of the serial killer, *'How do we explain the behaviour of a serial killer who has never suffered from a brain abnormality?'*

Ann Rule (2001), who was a colleague and close friend of Ted Bundy, would write the 1986 bestselling book *"The Stranger Besides Me,"* in which Rule stated that psychologists found Bundy to be neither psychotic, neurotic, the victim of organic brain disease, alcoholic, addicted to drugs, suffering from a character disorder and not a sexual deviant. In other words, Bundy was a 'normal' person like you and I. However, studies have shown that psychopathic personalities can be superficial and manipulate others, and Bundy's veneer of 'normality' duped not only his victims with his superficiality, but he also managed to manipulate the public into 'liking' him during his trial. Bundy had a good upbringing compared to Ridgeway, Joe Long, West et al. and he admitted as much on his last interview before execution (Bundy also coincidently provided the FBI a psychological profile on the Green River Killer, which proved to be highly accurate), and therefore could Bundy have just simply been 'evil'? There was no evidence of chromosomal problems, brain abnormalities and his upbringing, albeit dysfunctional in parts, was loving as he was his mother's favourite. Again, each serial killer has different psychological and genetic makeups, just like all other members of society do from one another.

The problem that we encounter with the studies of brain abnormalities and the development of the serial killer, and the focus in this chapter on the mentioned serial killers, is that it becomes two arguments, the *nature vs. nurture debate*, and the argument from the traditional medico-psychological approach, are serial killers as much a victim as those they kill? Or are serial killers' brain abnormalities caused due to the abnormal environments that they are reared in that creates a sub-personality due to their own sense of helplessness where they believe evil acts of transference are necessary to solve their inner turmoil? The challenge for law enforcement in this area is firstly being allowed to study convicted serial killers' brain wave activity when discussing crimes, and also have commandeer it upon their death and allow neurologists to study abnormalities in order to see if there is a pattern with serial killers, and for possible defuncts in regions of the brain that modern science could rectify, hopefully stopping these deplorable crimes before they arise.

Neurologists, psychologists, criminologists et al. would also need to study the brain abnormalities in correlation of the environment that they are reared in, and how much the two facets combine within the development of a serial killer. If the latter can be found to be conclusive, law enforcement would be relying on the serial killer interviewed being truthful with them, which is an instant challenge as serial killers like to manipulate and retain information as it provides them with a sense of the 'retention of power'. If law enforcement can somehow manage to convince the serial killer to undertake these studies and be completely truthful, the aim for law enforcement and the medical profession would be then to delve to the deepest depths of personality, conscious and subconscious of the serial killer to hopefully develop a greater understanding of their psychological motivations. If law enforcement and the medical profession did manage to achieve this type of practice with serial killers, it may go a long way into better understanding their personalities. The problem we would encounter is that serial killers have not developed in the stages of psychology as you or I have, and although they know they have committed wrong, it is like dealing with a child in the form of an adult as their anti-social personalities repress their inner self and they will attempt to block external stimuli when they feel threatened.

As the Swiss psychologist Carl Jung (1875–1961) stated in his work on the 'shadow' and the conscious and unconscious personality, *'The shadow is a living part of the personality and therefore wants to live with it in some form. It cannot be argued out of existence or rationalized into harmlessness. This problem is exceedingly difficult, because it not only challenges the whole man, but reminds him at the same time of his hopelessness and ineffectuality.'* If we apply Jung's beliefs to the personality of the serial killer, it is quite easy to theorise that if they agreed to be conclusively studied would be a difficult task: as they know their problem, or the *'shadow'*, exists within them, many of them do not want to be cured and they actively enjoy their notoriety and sense of 'power' and 'control', since upon apprehension it's the last thing they have left as they will never be released. Prison will be a dangerous place for them as they become 'scalps' to their fellow inmates, and in some cases the death penalty awaits them. Law enforcement would face several problems when getting them to talk and be truthful as they are not dealing with a stable and rational personality type, and therefore this could lead to the serial killer to begin seeing these types of interviews and studies as a 'game' which they derive a perverse psychological satisfaction from. Despite serial killers showing the 'veneer of normality' to the outside world, deep down they are failures and largely ineffectual. For example, Ted Bundy failed three courses before graduating in psychology and this ultimately dispels the myth of his supposed 'hyper-intelligence', and I believe that if law enforcement and the medical profession did manage to get this far delving into serial killers' destructive and ineffectual personality, this is where the problems would occur, because in their childlike minds they would perceive these efforts by law enforcement and psychologists as an effrontery, all the previous work up to this point could easily become undone and we would be no further in understanding them than we are at present.

In the area of studies and brain abnormalities and their causes with serial killers, a lot more detailed and empirical research in this area will need to be conducted because the results of current studies are inconclusive, and as Denis Nilsen cited to his biographer, Brian Masters, in his 1985 book on the Cranwell Gardens murders *Killing for Company*, 'A brain can be evil without being abnormal'. Therefore, if Nilsen is telling the truth and he believes this statement, then there are more sociological factors at play during the psychological development of the serial killer.

CHAPTER 7

The Western World and Its Modern-day Obsession with Fame and Celebrity Culture

Although fame may be a strange concept and motivational factor when talking about the psychological development of serial killers, I feel it is an area that is unwittingly overlooked and cannot be ignored in the ethos and grip of modern society.

Although there are multiple proposed theories and explanations in relation to the psychological development of serial killers thus far in this book, I have attempted, albeit briefly, to find a conclusive answer. However, thus far each sub-theory has not provided a conclusive answer and therefore we must broaden our horizons to try to explain the phenomena that is serial killing.

Before the advent and mass commercialisation of television, which was originally used as a communication tool for the transmission of information and learning, to become famous people had to both inhibit and exhibit a discernible talent against another member of society to become famous, as their unique talent set them apart from others. However, the invention of reality television in the early 2000s has not only challenged this concept, but it's also completely altered how people can achieve fame and fortune and encouraged the public to become obsessed with what one can only define as Z-list celebrities in which the obsession was once retained for A-list celebrities only.

In the modern-day Western world, fame can be achieved for having no discernible talent whatsoever, for example, plenty of people have achieved

THE WESTERN WORLD AND ITS MODERN-DAY OBSESSION WITH FAME

fame for simply sitting in a house pretending to be completely naïve, which seems to resonate with the public, or singing on a TV show yet having no real outstanding talent. Yet daily, the media sells the obsession to the public in which celebrity culture is oversaturated in front of us in different forms of media which include magazines, TV shows, books, social media platforms and internet sites; even our national newspapers sometimes run with front page news of a celebrity rather than report more serious issues that are happening within a single country or the world. Such is our obsession with celebrity culture the real news is deemed as 'boring' or 'unimportant'. The question we therefore must ask in terms of the psychological development of a serial killer is, *'Can the modern-day obsession with fame unwittingly encourage a potential serial killer to commit their terrible crimes?'*

I can unequivocally state following on from my research that only two serial killers claimed that they killed for 'fame', one of which was Stephen Griffiths, aka 'the Crossbow Cannibal', the other serial killer being Colin Ireland, aka the 'Gay Slayer'. I therefore do not believe that a serial killer commits their barbaric and primitive acts for the primary object of achieving 'fame', as I believe that the motivation for their acts is solely down to the internal psychological frustrations that they are desperately trying to satiate, which they will never be able to do until either apprehended or deceased.

In psychological terms, human beings will develop their own unique psychological makeup and personality based on their own life experiences, experiences which fuse together to form an individual's psyche. A human being will regularly follow a similar pattern routinely and they may not even realise they are doing it, for example, we all follow either a set or similar routine and, within those routines, there will be small things that breed 'mental restoration', and routine creates a semblance of order in our lives and reduces stress. The danger with serial killers is that they too follow patterns in their warped internal world and psychosis, and from time-to-time the urge builds to kill, and their routines are also patterned behaviour. For example, John Reginald Christie knew that abortion was frowned upon in 1940s Britain and used all his routine behavioural patterns of acting meek and mild to convince the women inside 10 Rillington Place into having an 'abortion', with him being the 'doctor'. Despite having no medical qualifications whatsoever, no victim would ask him for proof of his credentials, and Christie's predatory nature was preying upon his victim's desperation. Upon the victim agreeing to the 'abortion' Christie would proceed to gas them and then proceed to strangle them whilst unconscious and commit acts of necrophilia. Peter Sutcliffe's routine from the course of his employment allowed him to solicit sex from sex workers, and this allowed him to kill them and follow other women who were walking the streets of Yorkshire. Sutcliffe's employment allowed him to be a marauding and transient serial killer and his criminal pattern coincided solely with his employment. Colin Ireland's routine social life of meeting other gay men in London's gay quarter gave him access to his victims. Harold Shipman, a well-trusted general practitioner (GP) and his daily routine through the course of his employment brought him into contact with his predominately elderly victims. The danger with serial killers is that their daily routines and activities coincide with the ever-growing urge to kill, an urge that psychologically manifests itself and builds up over a period so that they need to satiate and release their internal psychological frustrations on an external and living victim, and this sadly becomes a constant cycle until they are apprehended.

As I have stated at the beginning of this chapter, I believe that is more than likely that the majority of serial killers don't kill for the pursuit of fame, they kill for their own intrinsic and psychological reasons such as power and need to be in control over their victim for a warped sense of self-reassurance. However, I do believe that once arrested, and due to their warped psyche, they begin courting the attention and enjoy being in the limelight. For example, Ted Bundy actively courted the media and they duly obliged by providing mass airtime to him during his trial. Dennis Rader left a note signed by BTK in a library book in 1974 that he 'craved attention'. However, Rader, unlike Stephen Griffiths, assumed that he would never be caught, whereas the latter actively wanted to be caught and courted 'fame', which he achieved for a very short while in the summer of 2010, the main focus of the media's attention, even removing the news of the 2010 general election and the negotiations between the United Kingdom's Conservative Party and the Liberal Democrats Party that gave the country its first coalition government in 36 years. Griffiths' narcissistic personality was enjoying the attention and the repulsion felt by the public, including the new prime minister, David Cameron, who spoke about the horrific acts of Griffiths as one of his first parliamentary duties. Griffith's 'fame', however, was extremely short-lived, when on June 2nd, 2010, Derek Bird committed the Cumbria Massacre in which thirteen innocent people were killed and eleven seriously injured. According to the police, Griffiths was said to be enraged at the media for not retaining his crimes as the lead news story.

THE WESTERN WORLD AND ITS MODERN-DAY OBSESSION WITH FAME

On the Google internet search engine, if you type in the words 'serial killer' it offers you a choice of 68,000,000 sites. In 2010 Stephen Griffiths (aka the Crossbow Cannibal) terrorised Bradford and told police that he wanted to be caught so the world would know his 'story'. Griffiths was obsessed with Peter Sutcliffe and even believed that Sutcliffe was 'sloppy', and he was a 'professional', however, Griffiths is not the first serial killer in the United Kingdom to kill in the vain hope of being 'famous'. Colin Ireland killed five men in 1993 after reading the FBI books by Robert Ressler and learning that five murderers would label you as a 'serial killer'. I believe that these two killers had learned from other notorious cases that involved serial killers and witnessed the attention they acquired off the press and the public and in some cases Hollywood. For example, there have to date been five films about Ted Bundy (whom Griffiths idolised), yet in court Ramirez and Bundy became like celebrities with a jury member on the case of the latter comparing him to a young Cary Grant (American Actor). The attention on the killers such as Bundy and Ramirez would have become an obsession to both Griffith and Ireland.

Although the theory of a celebrity culture creating a serial killer is extreme, if we review the similarities in the case of Griffiths and Ireland we can see that both men had an awful upbringing: Ireland's father abandoned him; Griffiths mother was a sex worker whom he caught having sex at the bottom of the family garden; both men had previous convictions for violence; both men never had many friends yet both were vain. For example, Griffiths would have professional photographs taken of himself, despite not having any discernible features to be a professional model, and these photos show just how narcissistic he was upon viewing them. Griffiths and Ireland both had normal sexual relationships and yet they both exhibited their sexual tastes to the detriment of their partners, which are a common feature with cases of serial killers as they enjoy humiliating or degrading other human beings to satiate their perverse desires and warped psychosis. Both men were also obsessed with sadomasochistic pornography and again this form of pornography plays into their psyche and dangerous fantasies of domination over a helpless victim, and the fantasy again reverts to the central facet of the psychological obsession of the serial killer – *power*.

As previously stated, I personally do not believe that the main psychological motive for murder by a serial killer is for the pursuit of 'fame', as their motives are deeply rooted psychological problems that they internalise during their prepubescent and adult years. There is a popular myth that the media has helped circumvent is that serial killers 'want to be caught'. The opposite is true as they go to great lengths to avoid detection and capture, and they usually get caught from escalation in their own narcissism as they believe that they will never be caught. For example, Ted Bundy was driving around a neighbourhood with his lights off and the police patrol conducted a routine stop and found suspicious items in his car. Brady and Hindley wanted to excel their murderous fantasies and bring in a third killer in the shape of Hindley's brother-in-law, David Smith, whom Brady had been 'grooming' for several years. However, Brady misjudged Smith's character, and Brady trying to act out his fantasy became their downfall as Smith told the police after witnessing the murder of Edward Evans (17) with an axe. Harold Shipman was not forensically aware of the computer systems that helped prosecute him, as he was amending data on the computer records, and he was unaware that all previous data was stored in the read-only memory (ROM) on his computer.

The media in this respect has also propelled a myth to create a Hollywood fantasy of the 'good guy', e.g., the criminal profiler, against the 'bad guy', e.g., the serial killer, who is an evil 'genius' constantly outwitting the profiler until the case finally joins together in what is portrayed as a great piece of investigative intuitive genius. However, the truth of the matter is that most serial killers are caught usually due to their own failings.

Throughout the course of this chapter, I have unequivocally stated that I don't believe the media is responsible for the role in the development of serial killers, as there are too many psychological variables that work in tandem during the psychological development of a serial killer. However, as we need to analyse each one as an individual, I would never rule it out in its entirety, and I don't believe that law enforcement should either as they aim to combat the menace of serial killing. Although they may not kill initially for fame, there is a possibility that the notoriety and induced fear they create within society can propel and even escalate their acts of violence against innocent people. Kass-Gergi (2012) cites the former FBI Behavioural Sciences Unit forensic psychiatrist and behavioural consultant when Dietz stated in an interview on *The Criminal Mind* that 'The media help disseminate the message that it's good to be a serial killer ... There are rewards to such violent behaviour – loyal fans, marriage proposals, splashy headlines.' Kass-Gergi (2012) is dismissive of Dietz hypothesis, and he states, 'While it is impossible to prove the potential connection that Dietz presents, the behaviour of some serial killers is suggestive in this regard.' The communications that David Berkowitz had with the *New York Post* during his reign of terror in New York City played a pivotal role in Berkowitz's public self-evolution and his decision to keep on killing. Ted Bundy represented himself in his murder trial in Florida. Even though acting as his own counsel would represent in more negative feelings from the jury, this act was perpetuated by Bundy to control his story with his own narrative, and the media became intrigued with him. The best indicator that killing for 'fame' plays a role in these individuals' actions comes from the serial killer BTK, Dennis Rader, who frequently contacted local news media, and in one correspondence complained *'How many times do I have to kill before I get a name in the paper or some national attention?'* Although once they begin acquiring the attentions of the media it may exacerbate their behaviour, due to their psychological processes they will commit their acts of violence with or without the media influence.

The media can also unwittingly play its part in the downfall of a serial killer, as the media provides a grandiose belief to the serial killer that they are *'invincible'*. The most prominent examples are Ted Bundy and Dennis Rader. As Michaud and Aynesworth (1983) interviewed Ted Bundy for their book "*The Only Living Witness*", Michaud stated the following, *'Ted (Bundy) compartmentalised his crimes and created a fantasy that he was winning the court case, contrary to the state's evidence against him and advice from his own lawyers, Ted kept on playing to the press and was enjoying the spotlight.'* In this instance, Bundy did not realise that he was participating albeit unwillingly in his own death sentence and the media were fuelling his egotistic narcissism as, by the end of the trial, Bundy's psychosis had completely become detached from reality and the consequences of what he was facing if found guilty, which he ultimately would be convicted on several accounts. Bundy would eventually die in the electric chair on January 23rd, 1989. Dennis Rader courted the media, and he was duped by the media into sending a floppy disk into the Wichita Eagle newspaper, which had previously advised him that they would not be able to link it back to him, and the metadata showed his name and the words 'Lutheran Church of Christ', which linked him circumstantially to the crimes, and DNA would ultimately provide the link to prosecute him. Rader is now serving ten life terms without the possibility of parole. The media may play a small role in the processes of their actions as opposed to their development. The serial killers mentioned in this chapter were undoubtedly initially driven by their own warped psychological motivations, and the thrill of achieving 'fame' was a reaction to their criminal actions which led to their downfall, as William Shakespeare once wrote, *'Fame lulls the fever of the soul, and makes us feel that we have grasped an immorality.'* In terms of certain serial killers and their perverse interpretation of 'fame', never a truer phase can be attributed to them.

CHAPTER 8

Dangerous Ideologies and Subcultures

In the following chapter I am going to provide analysis to inquire if political, social, or other dangerous ideologies can play a role in forming, shaping, and developing the persona, psychology, and psychosis of a serial killer. In this chapter, I intend to focus upon four serial killers who have previously stated to law enforcement and investigators their crimes were resultant to a degree due to their prior obsessions with sub-culture ideologies which other members of society find reprehensible.

The serial killers that I will predominately focus upon in this section are as follows: Colin Ireland, Ian Brady, David Berkowitz, and Richard Ramirez, aka the Night Stalker. Political and religious ideologies exist in every country in the world, however, many of the political theories that have become globalised have their origins derived from the Western world.

In the Western world in particular, due to its belief in a democratic system of governance for every ideology that exists, such as Christianity for example, there are dark sub-culture ideologies that are anathema to widely followed ideologies, as democratic societies allow each belief to co-exist, for example, a Christian, a Jew and a Muslim are allowed to practice their religious beliefs within the mainstream context, and on the opposite end of the religious spectrum in the darker enclaves of society, a practicing Satanist is also allowed to freely practice their beliefs. In the Western world, although this belief system is frowned upon, it is not illegal to practice Satanism, whereas in the Islamic world aligning oneself with an 'evil' belief system would be punishable by execution.

The first question and possibly the most uncomfortable question that we must ask ourselves is as follows, *'Is western democracy creating the serial killer menace within our midst?'* It does seem an almost unthinkable question to ask, as democracy and Christianity are the cornerstones of

Western societies and their values. However, there is some evidence that this could well be a possibility as America (2,743), Britain (145), South Africa (112), Canada (101), Italy (94). Japan (91), Germany (75), Australia (75), Russia (70) and India (65) make up the top ten countries for producing serial killers. Except for Russia, which is not a democratic state and works on the premise of an 'elected dictatorship', and Japan, India, and South Africa, which are not in the Western world, they all hold democratic elections and allow for freedom of speech.

If we look at the case of America, this country prides itself on the principles, theory and doctrines of the ancient Athenian lawmaker, Cleisthenes, and is proclaimed as the world's beacon of democracy' and yet she produces the most serial killers in the world and some of the most notorious as well for example, David Berkowitz and Richard Ramirez were both obsessed and self-confessed practicing devil worshippers. Ramirez believed that just as Christ was the son of God who was sent to save man from his sinful endeavours and behaviours, he was sent by Satan to destroy man and believed that, upon his death, he would be rewarded by being seated at the right hand of Satan. In the case of Ramirez, his belief systems were completely anathema to mainstream Christian American society and Ramirez's obsession with Satanism allowed him to intertwine this belief system into his psyche and it became all consuming, which would result in fourteen innocent people losing their lives.

I believe that Ramirez's perverse dogmatic beliefs became intertwined with his fantasies of murder during his adolescent years as his older cousin introduced him into satanic practices, during which time Ramirez was also being sexually abused by his teacher and he witnessed his cousin shoot his girlfriend at home. All these factors became fused together in Ramirez's psyche and psychosis, which led to him beginning to see himself as existing on the peripheries of society, and he was already an 'outcast' from society just as his idol, Satan was an outcast from heaven; this is how Ramirez labelled himself and devoted his life to Satan. This created a very confused and dangerous personality, and along with all the adults who were responsible for guiding his development Ramirez showed levels of abnormal violence and sexual abnormalities.

In the decades of the 1970s and the 1980s, America was in a grip of fear over stories about Satanism, and yet this fitted the persona of Ramirez perfectly. For example, Ramirez dressed in all black (a colour that does not reflect light) and could blend into the darkness and become intertwined with it, and this act became a part of his modus operandi, which fused with his satanic fantasies. This became a recipe for disaster for fourteen innocent people and the inhabitants of Los Angeles who believed that they were going to fall prey to the 'Night Stalker'. Ramirez would break into homes in the dead of night to commit some of the most heinous acts by any serial killer, which included rape, torture, killing husbands in front of wives before eventually killing the latter. Ramirez, after his twisted acts, would scrawl pentagrams at the scene and he would remove the victim's eyes (which are believed to be the window to the soul) as his 'symbolic' calling card. Ramirez was stoking mass-induced fear in Los Angeles and this naturally resulted in firearms sales increasing as residents became terrified to exit their homes after dark and they would endeavour to sleep with their windows closed at night-time, despite the intense heat of Los Angeles in the summer, and this no doubt would have pleased Ramirez as finally in his life he had some form of control in an otherwise turbulent existence, and within his warped psychosis he would have believed that he was finally relevant within not only society, but also within his life, which had been turbulent to say the least.

David Berkowitz stated he was part of a satanic cult and he also believed that he was 'killing for Satan' with every murder that he committed in New York City during his reign of terror. As we are aware, serial killers are psychopaths, and one significant trait of the psychopathic personality is that they can manipulate others, and Berkowitz and Ramirez may have used Satan and Satanism to justify their criminal actions. Therefore, when dealing with serial killers, we must ask ourselves, *'Is the use of sub-cultures part of an elaborate defence or an absolute ideological belief held by the serial killer?'* There is a strong possibility neither Berkowitz or Ramirez did not want to use it as a defence and neither did they really believe in the ideology as they may have been 'pimping' the media to keep themselves 'relevant' to ensure that they retained the media and the public's undivided attention. There can be no doubt, however, that when the media were mentioning their crimes they would have felt in complete control and would have enjoyed the fear and panic they were creating, as nobody knew their identities and they were also goading law enforcement by leaving 'signs' at the scenes to let law enforcement and the media know that they had struck again, and they were not going to disappear from the public's and the police's imagination.

Serial killers love being in control and enjoy the public's undivided attention, whilst at the same time ensuring that the public live in a perpetual state of fear that they could become their next victim (the public can be secondary victims of the crimes committed by serial killers). It reverts to the central theme of 'power', as Ramirez asked death row officers if there would be books written about him like there were about Ted Bundy and Jack the Ripper, which can be linked back to Western obsession with fame. Ramirez and Berkowitz, like most serial killers, suffered mentally, physically, psychologically and sexually due to their abnormal upbringings, and like most serial killers, they did not want to get caught; although they were enjoying seeing the media report their crimes, they did not want to be apprehended. There is a myth that serial killers 'want to be caught', however, in the case of Ramirez and Berkowitz, we can see that this is not true as Ramirez stole a car from one of his victims and unwittingly left a fingerprint on the mirror, which the police already held in their database, and Ramirez deliberately went on the run to evade capture. Berkowitz was caught because a witness had seen a car with a parking ticket near to a shooting which, when the police checked their records, led to the realisation that Berkowitz was in and around the area of the shooting of one victim. Both killers would ultimately link their crimes to Satan to garner more media attention, and naturally the media took the bait as it sells airtime and newspapers.

If we cannot blame a metaphysical entity or a belief in a sub-culture being responsible for the motives of a serial killer, when we provide an analysis on the next two serial killers, can we blame a physical being for their vile and heinous acts? After all, it is only the living that can harm another person.

The physical being that I am referring to is in the shape of the National Socialist German Workers' Party, the Nazi leader Adolf Hitler. The serial killers for this section are Ian Brady and Colin Ireland, both of whom were obsessed with the Nazis. On a nightly basis, Brady would listen to recordings of Nazi rallies, and he would also repeatedly encourage his co-killer, Myra Hindley, to do the same. In a similar way to David Smith, Brady was using his psychopathic manipulative influence too 'test' Hindley to see how far she would align into his fantasies, which she eventually did as she dyed her hair peroxide blonde and engaged persistently in sadomasochist sexual acts based on the 'teachings' (as Brady referred to them) from the Marquis de Sade. Myra Hindley admitted that she dyed her hair for Brady to become a 'member' of the 'master race', and to also replicate the female concentration camp guards, an act which Brady would have enjoyed and heightened his sexual intensity with Myra Hindley, as in his warped mind his fantasies were coming to fruition.

From a young age, Colin Ireland collected a variety of Nazi paraphernalia, and it was not collected for educational purposes; Colin Ireland was obsessed with their behaviour, including the mass murders of millions of innocent victims, and again, the problem with the psyche of the serial killer, this obsession all reverts to the central narrative of 'power' and their perverse obsession with this trait. The Nazis committed mass atrocities from invasion, rape, plunder and genocide, and the theory is that serial killers and abnormal personalities become attracted to these groups because it begins to form in their psyche that they can become 'powerful' and exert this control and power over innocent and helpless victims, the contrast is that the serial killer replaces the Jewish people with their fantasy victim, e.g. Brady chose young children, as he hated children due to his fractured upbringing, being moved from home to home before being adopted. Colin Ireland was a homosexual, and at the time of his murder's homosexuality was still not widely accepted by wider society. The power, control, and dominance over the victims he murdered was evident in his crime scenes as he targeted gay men who were into the sadomasochist and bondage scene, using this as a ruse to subdue them and render them powerless before committing acts of depravity including mutilation and torture.

Unlike Ireland and Brady, both of whom have been mentioned in this chapter, Berkowitz, and Ramirez to the best of our knowledge held no obsessions towards Adolf Hitler or the Nazis, however, their fantasies all revolved around a delusion of 'power'. The only difference is that Berkowitz and Ramirez replaced a living physical entity with a metaphysical entity. Berkowitz killed innocent couples because he craved the normal sexual experiences that many take for granted, as he could not acquire an erection through normal measures, and due to his overall appearance as he was highly unattractive. Ramirez killed families and couples possibly due to his perverse upbringing, and he stated that he hated 'normality' as he was looking inward towards society. In turn, he was becoming enraged at his own problems and this rage simmered with jealousy that he never had a normal life, which became a psychological driver in him committing his series of murders.

The link between serial killers being obsessed with sub-culture ideologies is tentative at best as there are many serial killers who do not become obsessed with sub-culture ideologies and still commit some of the most depraved and unimageable acts. The problem that we encounter in this section is that we cannot rule its effects out because psychology at a general level is relative to that individual, and although it is a tentative link, I do believe that it definitely had an effect on the psyche of both Brady and Ireland and it also did with another British serial killer, Patrick Mackay, who murdered five elderly victims in 1960s Britain as he had a shrine in his home to the Nazis. As mentioned, the link between sub-culture ideology is tentative and I believe, due to other factors, when serial killers become transfixed with a dangerous ideology it intertwines with their warped fantasies and becomes engulfing within their psyche. However, there are more factors at work as opposed to being obsessed with a sub-culture ideology. The common denominators in all four killers focused upon in this chapter is that they all had unstable backgrounds, and the argument is stronger for their crimes being committed as a product of their environment as opposed to a tentative singular factor, for example, Ireland, Brady and Berkowitz all had unstable families and were from broken homes, whilst Ramirez, who hated his bullying drunk father, was raised by his cousin, who Ramirez witnessed murder his fiancé at the age of eleven years of age. Therefore, did they align themselves with something more powerful to feel in control? Brady, who had a terrible childhood, murdered five children. Ireland claimed his murders were not sexually orientated, however, it is believed that when he was killing his victims, he was also sub-consciously killing the part of himself that he loathed, because wider British society at the time did not take kindly to sadomasochistic sex between gay couples, which was perceived as 'perverted' at the time. Berkowitz and Ramirez killed men and women, as Berkowitz was rejected by his mother and loathed by his father, whilst Ramirez was abused by his dad and a paedophile teacher. So, in part, did powerful personas such as Satan, who can fight God, or Hitler, who believed he was killing a 'subhuman race', intertwine into the personas of unstable personalities? Or do other ideologies, socioeconomics and poverty play a role in shaping a person into a serial killer and therefore can money really be the root of all evil?

CHAPTER 9

Socioeconomics: Society and Serial Murder

The FBI have identified several myths that have become associated with serial killers because of fictional portrayals and anecdotal information that has been bandied around by the media to integrate these myths into the conscious of the wider public and society, one of these myths being that all serial killers are white men. Although most serial killers in the Western world are white men there are exceptions to the rule: Alton Coleman (Black male), Richard Ramirez (Hispanic male), Wuornos (White female), however, this still leaves the pertinent question: *'Why are the majority of serial killers white men?'* Wilson and Seaman (2007) state that motiveless murder and sex crime increased in the West from 1960 and peaked in the 1980s; motiveless murder in America had risen from 8.5% in 1976 to 22.1% in 1984 at a time when America and Britain had a serial killing epidemic. Wilson (2010) states that in the 1980s Britain convicted five serial killers more than they did in any other decade thus far. Is this a coincidence or can it be linked to socioeconomics and society of the time? Wilson and Seaman (2007) state that in the 1850s working-class men lived in terrible conditions and had rough upbringings, but they were kept in place by society's demand for labour. The labour movement was controlled by the middle and upper classes and therefore the obsession and thought process was geared towards the very basic human instincts of *survival*. If this is to be the case, then we may be able to explain a lack of serial killing due to the following reasons – nobody had heard of a serial killer until Jack the Ripper came along and committed his depraved acts and became the 'first' serial killer (whilst ignoring the likes of Elizabeth Bathory from history prior to Jack the Ripper). If a society is poverty stricken then the focus is not on sexual desire, even though it exists: food and shelter become the prominent focus of the human mind and therefore this becomes more of a will of survival as opposed to seeking sexual gratification away from the home.

Wilson and Seaman believe that in a poor society sex becomes secondary behind wealth, however, they have not considered serial killers who did not kill for sexual gratification, such as Harold Shipman and Donald Harvey. Their theory can be given some credence as there was two riots in Brixton in 1981 and 1985 at the height of Britain's serial killing endemic as five of the six killers convicted were white men (the only Black serial killer was the 'Stockwell Strangler', Kenneth Erskine) whilst the rioters were from the Black community that suffered from extreme poverty at a time when Thatcherism was in its full swing, and the poor in society were becoming left behind to a degree. During the same period, the Scarman Report (1981) blamed the rioting on institutional racism, high unemployment and crime, poor housing in a predominately African–Caribbean community; yet being affluent alone does not create a serial killer as much as being poor does not create a thief.

In Colombia, in 1949, during the Colombian civil war, Pedro Lopez was born, and the country was in turmoil. By the age of eight, Lopez was kicked out of home by his mother, after which he was sodomised on the streets by a man who promised to 'help' him. Lopez began stealing cars and selling them to survive, yet although he lived in poverty, sex and murder was never far from his mind as he was responsible for over three hundred murders. Can we say that poverty created a killer, or was it a genetic trait as he ever knew his father? Therefore, is it genetics, society, or a combination? The answer is inconclusive, and this is the consistent conundrum with trying to establish a concrete and evidential theory of how a serial killer develops, as a psychological, societal, or biological reason for one is completely different to that of another serial killer.

The other problem with the theory of socioeconomics and the formation of a serial killer(s) is that, as a demographic of people, they transcend class barriers and therefore the link is below tentative, because many serial killers we have been able to study have predominately been born after the end of World War Two and therefore we may not be as aware of those that existed prior as society was very confined to where you lived at the time, and there have been historical figures of the upper and middle classes committing serial killings, for example, Countess Elizabeth Bathory was killed in Hungary in the year of 1614 for murdering young peasant girls. Herman Webster Mudget (HH Holmes) was from the middle class, and he would confess to 27 murders. Fred West was a farm hand and a builder who came from a very archetypal working-class family, whilst the likes of Charles Albright and Henry Lee Lucas, for example, were born into the societal underclass, and yet it illustrates that socio-economic theory and its link to serial murder may be just a theory with no real basis, and the argument is much more stronger when studying serial killers from a psychological perspective as opposed to a monetary and class theory perspective.

Since the publishing in Britain of the Bevan Report in 1941, which identified poverty as a driving factor in criminality, according to the Parliament of the United Kingdom, between 1900 and 1920 the police in England and Wales recorded around 90,000 indictable offences each year. This figure would increase to over 500,000 during the 1950s, despite much of the Bevan Report being implemented and equal franchise between the sexes and the classes. The 1960s was the only decade on record in the 20th century were crime doubled, with steady rises in the decades for the remainder of the 20th century. The fact that the Beveridge Report helped improve living standards and alleviate poverty through healthcare and a national pension scheme does give some credence to Wilson and Seaman's theory that the alleviation of poverty can increase crimes as people's focus shifts away from survival to gratifications for one's own gain. However, the problem we still encounter with such a theory is that petty criminality such as public drunkenness rates and shop-theft rates may increase as people have more disposable income, and the latter as the demand for advancement in technological goods increase and/or to pay for a drug habit. I believe that socio-economic theory is extremely unquantifiable to use as a method to discuss and dispute whether it plays a part in the formation of a serial killer. So, for example, did Harold Shipman only begin killing because he was able to transcend from the working to the middle-class due to his profession as a doctor? If the answer is yes, then firstly it ignores the fact that serial killers do not always psychologically open up to investigators, journalists, criminologists et al. as they like the retention of 'power' that withholding information gives them.

The other issue is the theory that serial killers who transcend societal class structures will only kill when they become 'middle class' is simply absurd, and it totally ignores that serial killers derive from all classes in the same way a government that runs a country can have people from all demographics and classes from society in a modern and advanced society, where the transition between the class demographic is more achievable and actively encouraged. However, the psychological motivations of a serial killer will be instilled within their psyche very early on and will remain with them regardless of their socio-economic status.

The third and the most pertinent problem we encounter with this theory is that it widely ignores the psychological motivations of the serial killer and how they have come to form their own psychological fantasies. If we delve into Britain's most prolific serial killer, Harold Shipman, he may have shown traits common with all serial killers and research into his background does suggest that he does. However, he would not open up to anybody whilst in prison to discuss his true motivations for his crime and as he is now deceased, we are left to theorise as to his motivations. As mentioned, Shipman did exhibit the psychological facets that we associate with many serial killers, for example, his mother was domineering, which is a trait shared with others such as Gein and Brudos. And like Gein, when his mother died, he may have felt angry and sad, but also a sense of liberation as he was now 'free', and suddenly that previous domineering control had suddenly ceased in his warped psychosis, finally leaving him free to do and act as he pleased, and whether this was against the normal moral standards of society or not, it didn't matter to Shipman. Shipman, for example, watched his domineering mother die from cancer when he was aged sixteen. Being his mother's 'favourite' child led to him being isolated from his peers and a becoming loner, and the eerie connection between his mother and his victims is that they died from morphine overdoses and therefore, due to his mother's overbearing upbringing, it can be argued that Shipman's murders were an act of 'transference' brought on by the confused feelings of love and hatred he felt towards his mother.

Shipman, like all serial killers, would have undoubtedly derived a sense of 'power' from watching the victims pass away slowly, the other benefit for Shipman during the process of murder was that he was financially gaining by forging their wills to benefit him. I also believe that due to the strange relationship he held with his mother, Shipman may well have also derived sexual stimulation and sexual gratification from his crimes, as many serial killers harbour an over-active sex drive, whereby they find it difficult to maintain an erection during normal sexual intercourse and yet they can usually ejaculate prematurely during a murder, and sometimes on multiple occasions.

The German serial killer, Peter Kurten, admitted that he could not always achieve an erection, and yet he always managed to ejaculate at the sight of blood or during a murder. The psychological aspects in the socio-economic theory and serial murder are too diametrically opposed to be a truly credible theory, however, as I have mentioned, serial killers, like the general population, will each have their unique psychological makeup and the only real link between socio-economics and murder is stemming from excess wealth in the case of Elizabeth Bathory, for example, during the 1600s when peasants were working to survive and crimes by the peasants such as theft, robbery and prostitution were all common problems. Bathory was indoctrinated from an early age to believe that she was ordained by the decree of God's 'will' and people were there to serve her every wish. The sexual desires possibly became intertwined during adolescence, and this gradually became more sadistic as she began to act out her fantasies due to leading an isolated lifestyle and holding excess power from an early age.

The opposite side of the spectrum to Elizabeth Bathory is serial killers from the most deprived backgrounds whereby they live in poverty and, whilst young, are widely ignored by the authorities as they are in the societal out groups, e.g., the 'social underclasses'. So, for example, Ottis Toole and Henry Lee Lucas came from backgrounds of sexual and physical abuse where the authorities did not know they really existed other than from a statistical point of view, and this allowed perverse abuse to continue unabated and created a warped psychosis and ultimately a malevolent monster. Even this economic theory of those serial killers posted at either end of the economic spectrum still does not explain the serial killers who dwell and exist within the working and middle-class socio-economic groups and how they develop into monsters. The other problem we have with this theory is that the media have portrayed a myth that serial killers are 'evil geniuses' and hold middle class and trusted professions. However, as society becomes more transient in terms of class mobility, it was inevitable that members of society would be able to promote themselves in terms of rank and class, and serial killers choose certain professions to firstly live, secondly to paint a picture of 'normality' in order to 'co-exist', and thirdly many of them choose jobs with a form of authority or a sense of power and this also includes the medical profession, in which a serial killer does not abide by their Hippocratic Oath and protect lives, instead they use their position of responsibility to take lives for their own gratification.

CHAPTER 10

Medical Monsters

The medical monsters, more commonly referred to as 'Angels of Death', are a different type of serial killer from the more common names such as Bundy, Bonin, Gein et al. Yet there is not as much focus given to them by the media (until apprehended). There could be reasons for this, for example, Harold Shipman's victims, bar one younger victim, were all in their twilight years, yet the polar opposite to Shipman was Bundy's choice of victims, all of whom were young women who just vanished without a trace, therefore stories of abduction and a 'madman' on the loose piques the public's interest immediately. As Wilson (2009) points out, serial killing has become a commodity and serial killing like any other product can be brought. Medical monsters ironically are there to take care of people when they need care attention due to suffering from a medical ailment. Instead of caring for these people, the medical monsters kill them, and we must ask the simple and pertinent question of why. Beverley Allitt and Genene Jones, when they were young girls, both suffered from Munchausen Syndrome where they would feign illnesses to get the attention that they did not gain from family life or friends. Jones and Allitt made their victims ill, as many have theorised so that they could achieve recognition from colleagues, parents et al. so they could 'save' lives, a phenomenon known as *Munchausen syndrome by proxy* (MSBP).

    The very notion that another human being would make somebody else ill to 'save' them so that they could become the 'hero' and receive peer recognition and accolades, plus the attention that they never had from family or friends, is abhorrent to normal people. When authors and commentators write or speak of Allitt and Jones, the theory is always put forward almost as gospel regarding MSBP. This is amazing in itself that nobody ever considers that they, like most serial killers, could have derived a feeling of 'power' as serial killers like to play 'God', and it is also quite frankly absurd that nobody has ever questioned whether Allitt and Jones ever derived sexual derivation from their crimes; this is always an area of psychosis that is overlooked when discussing medical monsters and should always be considered when authorities interview them, because it is a possible cause for the motivation of murder (I will expand heavily on this issue during the pen profile of Harold Shipman).

The male medical monsters appear to be driven by psychological motivations at least from the outset. For example, Harold Shipman killed for profit. Michael Swango killed because he claimed to have 'enjoyed' it. Donald Harvey claimed he was committing murder as an act of 'mercy', and Efren Saldivar liked playing 'God'. Saldivar, unlike the other medical monsters mentioned, has defined what many criminologists already know is that serial killers kill for power. Shipman, as mentioned previously, most certainly killed for the feeling of 'power' and 'superiority' over what he deemed to be lesser beings in his warped psychosis.

The fact that Shipman benefited financially from his crimes was almost a secondary motivational factor and served his own grandiose belief that he was 'untouchable', however, his own hedonism and narcissism would prove to become his unwitting downfall as one of the victim's daughters began raising suspicions and hired a private investigator, who in turn raised their suspicions and findings with the police.

This type of serial killer is rare, but they do hold many traits as other serial killers with the only difference being that their modus operandi and victim typology differs. The six mentioned serial killers in this chapter throughout their early lives did not manage to build friendships or relationships easily, and this is a trait common of psychopathy in later life. Apart from Shipman, the rest did not manage to hold down jobs for very long periods, which can be another trait in a psychopathic personality as they struggle for stimulation and following orders could be a reason to explain this problem. The most common factor that they all have is the way they need to satiate their narcissistic personalities, for example, Swango, Jones, Saldivar and Allitt all falsified their history and some of their qualifications, which, tragically, nobody seemed to check for authenticity, and in their narcissistic view of the world they believe that getting away with this 'proved' that they were 'smart' in their own warped hubris and would result in the deaths of the innocent. Unfortunately, a serious administrative error allowed these people to kill freely. Allitt, for example, was given a job on ward four in Grantham Hospital due to chronic understaffing at the time. Shipman was falsifying prescriptions for drugs which he was using himself, as he was a methadone addict, and gained himself the sack yet, despite this serious episode of gross misconduct, he would still acquire wilful employment in a medical practice in Hyde. Shipman's fraud and deception at being able to falsify records and data led his narcissistic personality to begin to acquire an unwarranted perception of himself as a computer 'expert', which ultimately was his downfall as he did not realise that data is retained on the read-only memory (ROM) on the computer, which was later used in court against him.

A hospital, however, is the perfect place for a serial killer to act out their perverse and warped desires and fantasies, as we believe that many of them harbour a 'God complex', and when dealing with sick people you are entrusted with an esteemed societal position. If you are ever unlucky enough to find yourself in this position, your very own existence is down to the decision of a serial killer whether to allow you to live or die.

Although killers like West, Bundy, Wournoss et al. use their hands, the medical serial killer will have access to drugs, and nursing is a respected profession where these types of people can play 'God' over who lives and dies. With serial killers it's about power and control over their victims and I do believe that they choose this as a profession for a steady flow and easy access to victims where they can act out their fantasies of 'power and control'; many people would never suspect their doctor or paediatrician to harm them. On the contrary, we all expect them to act as lifesavers and care for us in our time of need.

I am convinced that serial killers in the medical profession do acquire sexual gratification from their crimes as much as the likes of Sutcliffe and Albright when they were killing their victims. For example, Michael Swango stated to a colleague, *'It gives me a hardon to tell the parents their kid has just died.'* Unfortunately, Swango possibly relived these fantasies over and over until the build-up of tension became too much, when his psychosis would have led him to kill and then kill again. The medical monsters, like all serial killers, are power obsessed, placed in a professional environment, and it is the stuff of nightmares to think that they can reach positions of trust and be in control of us in our desperate time of need. Although the medical monsters are supposed to show paternal instincts to all during their employment, whilst it is evident that they do anything but, are there any rational explanations why couples go against paternal instincts and usually harm younger children or extremely vulnerable victims that other normal couples would protect?

CHAPTER 11
Killer Couples and Folie à Deux

The term 'folie à deux' translates from French to English as 'a madness shared by two', medically referred to as 'shared psychosis'. Folie à deux is a psychiatric syndrome in which a person exhibits symptoms of a delusional belief or a set of values and beliefs that are transmitted from one individual to another. In terms of this psychological trait and serial killer couples, the couple creates a fantasy world in which they are in control of everything and they eventually want to turn their fantasies into reality. Their fantasies are usually projected onto women, children, or young adolescents, as we witnessed in the cases of Ian Brady and Myra Hindley and Fred and Rose West.

During the psychological process of folie à deux, there is usually a more dominant partner in the relationship, which is usually the man, however, the woman can also play an active role in the murders, e.g., Rose West killed Fred's daughter, Charmaine, whilst Fred was in prison, the crime which would ultimately prove that Rose West was a willing participant and not a 'victim' of her husband's crimes. Myra Hindley would obtain the victims by pretending to be 'looking' for a glove on the Moors, and appeared to be on her own, only for Brady to suddenly appear to rape, sodomise and ultimately kill their victims. In similar circumstances to the Wests, folie à deux becomes apparent in the case of Lesley Anne Downey and the tape in which Myra Hindley can be heard being abusive to the child and actively encouraging Brady to escalate his barbarous and primitive acts against them. Once played in court, this tape extinguished any lingering doubts that Myra Hindley was an innocent bystander in these heinous crimes.

In the 'Ken and Barbie Murders' in Canada, Karla Holmoka snared a victim for Paul Bernardo's perverted fantasies and 'pleasure', with one of these victims being her fifteen-year-old sister, whom Holmoka drugged as a birthday 'gift' for Bernardo to rape, torture and kill. The couple filmed their act on a camcorder, which is the most extreme form of murder as it was their own family member and an act of sororicide by Holmoka. On the cases mentioned, we can see a clear pattern emerging with the psychology and criminal acts that arise from folie à deux as the victims are all young, and this serves two purposes, with the first being that children are the most vulnerable of victims as they are easy to control and in their innocence they will automatically trust the woman, as the woman in the world of a child is the caregiver and the protector and this is seen in society, for example, the woman as the caregiver and matriarch is evident in forms of religion in the Pieta of Michelangelo, in which the virgin Mary is holding a dying Jesus. Hollywood portrays the female as the matriarch, caregiver, and protector and this is portrayed predominately in such films as Terminator 2 with the sub-protagonist, Sarah Connor, protecting her son John Connor and by proxy protecting mankind by fighting off machines that want to end the world. Society always portrays the female as the fairer sex, and it is believed that children form early bonds with women whilst growing in the womb as the woman is the instantaneous caregiver from the outset. I also believe that these couples actively seek each other out because evidence and psychological evaluations have shown that each party has a high or abnormal sexual libido, and this allows the man to exert their dominance and he will persistently push the boundaries with his willing female partner, until eventually he feels comfortable enough to cross any moral boundaries and realise that the woman is a willing participant and she will go along with anything that he may wish for her to act upon once suggested, and is an act of grooming for the acts of deviancy that will ultimately follow. This act is yet another act of 'power' within the mind of a serial killer.

I have used three murderous couples mentioned above, including Henry Lee Lucas and Ottis Toole. If the madness of one person can be transmitted to another person, it is important to investigate their backgrounds as there may be similar psychological traits that we see are common with other serial killers, and not to just take the theory of folie à deux as 'black and white', as the psychological theory is vague to state that madness can be simply shared or transmitted from one person to another, because as we see many serial killers lead normal lives with unsuspecting partners, e.g. Dennis Rader had a perfectly normal wife and family; Peter Sutcliffe had a normal wife at home and therefore there must be further background investigations before jumping to a simplistic conclusion, as there will be events in the lives of both killers that lead them to commit their heinous acts.

In the case of Paul Bernardo, for example, his early life was one of misery as his father abused him both physically, psychologically, mentally, and sexually abused his younger sister. When Paul Bernardo was aged sixteen, his mother told him the father who had abused him all his life was not actually his paternal father. Paul Bernardo was disgusted and enraged by this revelation, and he began beating and humiliating the women that he dated. Paul Bernardo resented his mother for allowing her partner to commit the heinous acts against him and his sister, and his later criminal acts can be attributed to 'psychological transference' in which he was projecting his own inner rage and misogynist hatred of his mother upon his victims. In Bernardo's warped psyche, these acts allowed him to hold power over his victims as he was trying to compensate for his own psychological inadequacies due to his dysfunctional upbringing. On the contrary, Karla Homolka was raised in what one can only be described as a normal, functional, and loving home in comparison to her later husband, Paul Bernardo. Karla Homolka had a happy middle-class upbringing, yet she encouraged Paul Bernardo's sadistic and sexual practices and actively encouraged his acts as the 'Scarborough Rapist', which at the time the police were baffled as to who was perpetrating these acts, and yet Homolka knew that it was Paul Bernardo and never once contacted the police to aid their investigation. In all cases of rape, the acts were becoming more savage and escalating with each attack and Homolka, instead of talking to the police, allowed Bernardo to continue unabated, destroying the lives of many innocent people in the process.

Although Homolka came from a healthy, functional, and stable home, she may have been a psychopath and maybe nobody in her family realised during her adolescence. The prison psychologists all struggled to form conclusive opinions on her deviant behaviours and crimes as there was a moral vacuity within her, and Paul Bernardo became a vessel for her to act out her psychopathic fantasies of rape, sodomy, control and eventually murder as most women, if they knew their partner was a wanted criminal, would tell the authorities because most normal women would be living in fear of their own life as much as fearing for the lives of others. In this sense, Bernardo was using Homolka as she was a willing participant and accomplice, and she became a conduit for him to discuss and act out his perverse fantasies, and she was also using him as a conduit to push her darkest fantasies into the realms of reality. A good home and decent upbringing don't always mean a person will grow up to be a good and moral person, and this is the grey area when discussing the psychological development of serial killers and why they perpetuate their crimes.

Ian Brady and Myra Hindley, Fred and Rose West, and Henry Lee Lucas and Toole in contrast suffered from deviant and dysfunctional upbringings, which would act as the catalyst for their later crimes. Killer couples create a fantasy world in which they have 'control' over everything, with the victim being the central theme for this act of 'control'. There is also evidence from their testimonies that they do not perceive there to be anything wrong with their sexual behaviour due to being reared and conditioned in home environments where sexual abnormality is 'normal' in their psyche, yet mainstream society is bound by normal societal morals, and behaviour standards are appalled by their sexual deviancy. This was evident upon the arrest and police interviews with Fred West, who couldn't believe it when being interviewed that the male officers never had sex with their daughters as Fred West had sex with his mother during his adolescence, he perceived this act as 'normal' sexual behaviour, to you and me, this is not only immoral, but also completely perverse and vile.

I do believe that each killer in a relationship of folie à deux must exhibit extreme violence and extreme sexual tendencies as their relationship progresses and develops as an act of 'self-preservation'. As the killer couple becomes more depraved and more extreme with their shared behaviours, the one who perceives themselves to be weaker in the relationship must exhibit their deviancy in part to survive by becoming more depraved and extreme than their partner, as they are more than aware that the other is capable of murder and they could easily become a victim if they show any signs of 'weaknesses'. If my hypothesis is correct, then folie à deux may well be just a fanciful psychological theory to explain killer couples as they are both as evil as each other, and both parties are trying to regain control over their fractured psychological and mental states as they see rape, murder and control as an act of 'regaining' control over their fragmented lives, which have been destroyed by others during their formative years, by committing acts of psychological transference by taking the lives of others. The overriding question with the limited psychological testing and research on the theory of folie à deux leaves us with the burning question '*is folie à deux a real symptom?*' Or do these types of people seek each other out as they can find their own deviancy in another person, which is hybristophilia? There is more evidence to suggest it is the latter when researching killer couples.

Hindley became obsessed with the Nazis, and she would dye her hair blonde to suit Brady's perversion of the iconic figure of a 'pure Aryan', they would also practice sexual deviancy and they would recite from the books of the Marquis de Sade. Toole and Lucas began a deviant sexual affair with each other after they met at a devil cult. Fred and Rose West were both sexually abused by parents when they were young and yet they were both obsessed with sexual deviancy, which included Rose's father visiting Cromwell Street to have sex with her as she was a sex worker, and Fred would watch through peepholes.

Rather than the psychosis of one person passed to another, it seems more that these killers, due to being exposed to abhorrent sexual behaviours when young, become hybristophiliacs because both Hindley and Homolka could have informed the police about their partners' crimes, yet they became willing accomplices in the murder of their partners' chosen victims and, as mentioned earlier, I do believe that Homolka was a psychopath as there is nothing on offer to provide any form of explanation for her behaviour, as some people can simply be born with a psychopathic personality and this is an area predominately overlooked with serial killers as we desperately seek answers for the psychological motivations for the catalyst of the commission of their crimes. Simply being born with a psychopathic personality is an area that warrants further research and discussion in the field of criminal psychology as we attempt to find conclusive answers on how a serial killer develops, as they simply may have a predisposition to kill another human being without feelings of guilt or remorse.

CHAPTER 12

Are They Just Psychopaths?

Although there has been a plethora of theories put forward regarding why a serial killer becomes a serial killer, the most obvious question and answer could be in front of us the whole time, *'Are they just psychopaths?'* And whether they are born or created seems like a question that we will never be able to answer conclusively without raging more debate on the subject. However, the problem that we always encounter is that most serial killers derive from dysfunctional backgrounds and yet they have siblings that lead normal lives, despite also suffering chronic physical and sexual abuse, and therefore could the serial killer be born with a psychopathic personality and already have a psychological predisposition to kill other living beings without remorse?

Mitchell and Blair (1999) have suggested that the underlying problems in the personality of a psychopath is a lack of empathy with other living beings, and they are cunning and manipulative. The latter point allows them to co-exist amongst society undetected. They propose that humans, like most social animals, have an inherited mechanism which allows them to terminate aggressive attacks when the victim shows a submissive signal, yet with serial killers they actively go out and seek a victim with the sole intention of humiliating them, frightening them, and toying with them, and in some cases giving a false hope that they will live. This is them exercising their power over that victim before killing them to serve their own psychological desires, whilst ignoring the rights of another person to live.

It has been established by countless academics that most serial killers have suffered trauma in their early years due to the abuse they suffered from an adult, for example, Michael Ross and Edmund Kemper solely blamed their mothers for the diabolical acts of criminality in later life, but then again not all serial killers have experienced a bad upbringing. For example, Jeffrey Dahmer, Steven Wright and Harold Shipman showed no evidence of abuse by their parents or any other adult that we know about, and came from normal homes, and therefore we need to delve deeper into their lives before they came out of the womb. In the case of Jeffrey Dahmer, his mother was taking around 27 pills a day to cope with her depression and anxiety. Could this have influenced his brain and personality, so in effect was Dahmer born evil? Harold Shipman's mother was overprotective and a doting mother to her favourite, 'Fred', however, does having an overprotective mother create a monster? Steven Wright came from a divorced family, however, in 2019, 42.00% of marriages in England and Wales ended in divorce. If we apply this to Wright, then Britain should be facing a serial killer epidemic in the future. However, family breakdown can't be a sole factor in explaining the formation of a serial killer, and we must look then if some of them are just born evil with a warped personality that develops with the bad events in life that happen to them, or when they begin to explore the world around them. For example, Jeffrey Dahmer was ten years old when he was dissolving roadkill. This is not a 'hobby' that a ten-year-old child should be interested or engaging in, and therefore Jeffrey Dahmer felt no empathy to those dead animals as a normal child would, as he would later show no empathy to his victims whom he also believed were his playthings to be used for his leisure and sexual gratification, or his fantasies of creating 'sex zombies' to serve his perverse sexual needs and desires.

Cowley (2010) cites Davies (2005), *'It is true that most serial killers must endure terrible childhoods, but lots of people have terrible childhoods. Serial killers choose to attempt to pass that pain on to somebody else.'* The Crime Survey for England and Wales (CSEW) estimated that one in five adults aged 18 to 74 years experienced at least one form of child abuse, whether emotional abuse, physical abuse, sexual abuse or witnessing domestic violence or abuse before the age of sixteen years (8.5 million people). If this is to be the case, coupled with the divorce rates, the United Kingdom is almost certainly facing a serial killer pandemic in the future. However, most abused children lead normal adult lives and do not commit acts of transference and cruelty onto others, and therefore when discussing the formation and development of serial killers, just being born evil or being pure evil should not be discarded.

Ted Bundy, in his last interview before his execution, tried to shift the blame on to Western society and what he called an 'unhealthy obsession' with pornography. However, yet again if his theory is correct, then we should have many more serial killers as porn has become freely available in the modern age as with the expansion of the internet it is accessible to every household, and yet many people use these sites as sexual relief but don't go out and commit multiple murders. Ted Bundy was simply shifting the blame for his actions on to something else, which was his own state of cognitive dissonance as a way of him coping with his deviant acts, and as a pseudo-academic way of explaining his repugnant crimes. There is also another reason for Bundy blaming pornography in his last interview with Doctor James Dobson, as he was still trying to retain a semblance of power and show his narcissistic character that he was 'smarter' than law enforcement and society. He was also living in the desperate hope of receiving a further stay of execution, which was not granted as he was put to death on the same night, 23rd January 1989. Bundy also apologised to the victims' families, but were the tears he shed during the interview shed for him, as his fate was sealed as he was due to be electrocuted within hours of the conclusion of the interview?

Other serial killers such as John Wayne Gacy said that his victims 'deserved' to die, as he coldly put it, because they were 'little faggots'. Myra Hindley also showed she was not truly sorry, as she made a ridiculous attempt to escape from prison by making a key impression in a bar of soap, which predictively failed, and became a slap in the face for everybody who believed that she was remorseful including Lord Longford. Longford campaigned on Hindley's behalf to various home secretaries for her release, and again Hindley convinced many that she was as much as a victim as the children she and Brady killed. Hindley, like all other serial killers in this act, shows how cold, calculating and manipulative she was, and she never admitted to the murder of Keith Bennett, as she was trying to exonerate herself from the crime until Brady told the authorities everything when he believed that Hindley had a chance of freedom. Yet Bennett's mother has wanted closure for forty-five-years and this shows Myra Hindley possesses all the traits of a psychopathic personality.

In terms of general psychology, the study of serial murder is in its relative infancy, and since Robert Ressler devised the FBI Behavioural Sciences Unit in 1978, criminologists, psychologists and amateur sleuths are still trying to find the empirical answer of how the psychology of a serial killer develops into the criminal that they ultimately become. I dare to dream that in the future, somebody in the field of criminal psychology will achieve the answer to this question, because it will save so many lives if we can treat the serial killer or a potential serial killer early on in their psychological development. However, for the foreseeable future, this small demographic of people will co-exist amongst us and continue to kill until apprehended.

Pen Profiles of the Offenders

Cayetano Santos Godino

Cayetano Santos Godino born, in Uruguay on Halloween in 1896, was a deviant criminal and a feared member of his local community, so much so that the locals nicknamed him *'El Petiso Orejudo' (The Big-Eared Pest)*. Cayetano Santos Godino is not a name widely associated with serial murder as his crimes were shortly after the series of murders committed by Jack the Ripper in Victorian London, and the media tends to focus more on western serial killers that predominately originate from North America and the United Kingdom. Although Cayetano Santos Godino committed persistent acts of antisocial behaviour, I will focus on his overall criminality and criminal acts to be able to provide a psychological profile of the offender in question. As Cayetano Santos Godino killed four victims and attempted to kill five more, Godino committed acts of serial murder and his crimes fit the FBI definition of a serial killer which is as follows: *'The unlawful killing of two or more victims by the same offender(s) in separate events.'* The purpose of this offender profile will be to establish the psychological motivations within his psyche as to why he committed such heinous and deviant acts, and I will begin by delving into his modus operandi as this area will provide the first psychological clues into the psychology behind his crimes.

In the lead up to the commission of Godino's criminal acts, he would lead the child (his chosen victim typology) away to secluded areas or at least out of view and sometimes successfully murder or injure his victims in a variety of violent methods which included beating, strangulation, pyromania, use of weapons that came to hand such as a hammer and nail and stones (the use of murder weapons that are already at the crime scenes suggests he was an impulsive killer) and even burying one victim alive, Maria Roca Foce, who was only three-years-old.

I believe that Godino committed his acts due to being reared and nurtured in an unstable environment as his father was an alcoholic who would beat his wife and children. Godino was constantly suspended from school and his childhood was far from normal. There can be an argument that genetic imbalance also played a part in his criminal behaviours in the sense that before he was born, his father contracted syphilis, causing Godino to experience serious childhood health problems. This would have made Godino feel different from other children at an early age in the sense that he was not loved like many other children; he was ill which may have resulted in teasing, and even to a degree being ostracised by other children. Due to Godino living in this environment, Godino could not *attach* himself to other human beings. Attachment theory by the psychologist John Bowlby focuses upon the importance of open, intimate, and emotionally meaningful relationships. Attachment theory focuses upon the roles of the biological system and the powerful survival impulses that evolve to ensure the survival of the infant. According to Bowlby, a child who is threatened or stressed will move towards caregivers who create a sense of physical, emotional, and psychological safety for the individual. Godino could not find this within his family life, and he could not find solace with other children either. There are four types of attachment styles, and they are as follows: *secure, anxious-avoidant, anxious-resistant* and *disorganised*. Godino developed the last three, and the last one showed in his acts of criminality.

The problems that Godino faced in not being able to form attachments to any other human beings can also stem from another theory from the psychological school, *constructivism*. Constructivism is a paradigm that characterises learning as a process of actively constructing knowledge. Individuals create meanings for oneself or make sense of new information with other knowledge, often in the content of social interactions. The theory of constructivism will occur within individuals in either one of two ways, individually or socially. In the theory of *individual constructivism*, this will occur when a person begins to construct knowledge through their cognitive process of their own experiences rather than by memorising facts provided by others. *Social constructivism* is when the individual begins to construct knowledge through an interaction between the knowledge they bring to a situation and social or cultural changes within that content. As I mentioned earlier in this section, I believe that Godino was a 'disorganised serial killer', and even the types of murders he committed were a result of his inability to *attach*, and therefore empathise with other human beings due to his unstable upbringing where his parents did not really love him as parents should love their own child and secondly, in terms of his own *individual constructivism* he began to cognitively develop hatred and jealousy of other children, and he therefore began to believe that he was 'different' from others and this began his own self-fulfilling prophecy in which he began to believe that the world was against him and therefore he needed to survive: survival for him meant causing pain to others (transference) the internal and external pain that he was suffering.

As Godino could not form social bonds or attachments with others, in terms of his *social constructivism,* he began to construct his own view that other people were out to hurt him as he could not interact like the other children and he could bring no situational or social exchange to the social setting around him. All these problems with *attachment* and *constructivism* lead to resentment and rage within Godino and this is evident in his murders and crimes; crimes that he committed in the vain hope that he may have found solace or closure to his own phychological sufferings. One can only theorise that he killed children because he was resentful that in comparison to him, the children he killed lived normal lives which could explain why his choice of victims were all children. Although only a child himself, Godino was obsessed with fire and quite easily could have killed adults through this method. Although he was a pyromaniac, he only set fire to empty buildings with no adults present at the time of the fires. Godino set fire to a warehouse on the evening of January 17th, 1912 and told the police officers; *'I like to see firemen working. It's nice to see how they fall into the fire.'* I believe that had Godino not been apprehended at an early age, then he would have been a prolific serial killer who would have murdered adults and children in later life. Pyromania is one of the first signs on the 'MacDonald Triad' (the other two symptoms being cruelty to animals, which Godino acted upon, and enuresis). I am stating my hypothesis because many other serial killers, such as David Berkowitz aka 'Son of Sam' was a pyromaniac and Peter Kurten, both of whom derived sexual stimulation for committing the act of arson. David Berkowitz and Peter Kurten were both abandoned by their parents (although Berkowitz was reared in a good foster home) and both committed acts of cruelty upon animals and each killer killed victims of both sexes as did Godino, and therefore I believe that Godino would have become one of the most notorious serial killers with a higher victim count had he not been apprehended at an early age. Did a more comprehensive crime scene analysis of Godino's crimes suggest he was a 'signature' killer? This provides us with clues when profiling serial killers into their forensic and cognitive states on how they may be thinking before enacting upon their warped fantasies and insatiable impulses.

Although Godino did not seem to leave a 'signature', e.g., leaving a body in a crude or posed position, Brown (2008) believes that this is another associated myth with serial killers, as many act on their impulses and killers who do leave signatures are in the rarest groups of serial killers, as they are doing it to fulfil a particular fantasy. I believe that Godino committed his acts due to being reared in an unstable environment as his father was an alcoholic who would beat his wife and children. Godino was constantly suspended from school, and his childhood was far from one what can deem as 'normal'. One can only theorise that he killed children because he was resentful of them in the sense that in comparison to him the children he killed lived normal and happy lives, or at least this was his perception from the outset, which could explain why his choice of victims were all children, and they also gave him the easiest access and opportunity to transfer his rage upon them, as children cannot fight back and Godino was a deviant and a complete coward who targeted one of society's most vulnerable groups, and this statement becomes evident when we begin to analyse the crime scenes and the victimology together, which is shocking beyond human comprehension.

The crime scenes were in various locations to where Godino resided at the time. The crime scenes suggested that Godino left enough psychological clues that leads one to believe that he was a 'disorganised serial killer', as he used weapons that came to hand and that already form part of the scenery, e.g., he tried to use a horse's water trough when he attempted to murder Gonzalez Calo, and a match he found at another scene to attempt to set fire to Reyna Vaincoff.

Further evidence of his disorganised criminal behaviour was evident during the murder of Jesualdo Giordano, when he lured him with the offer of buying sweets and preceded to take the child to an abandoned house, where he tried to choke him with a belt. The belt snapped and Godino had to bind the child's hands and legs and unsuccessfully tried to beat him to death with his bare hands. Godino knew by this point that he was possibly in danger of being caught, or the victim surviving and being able to identify him, and therefore he went in search of a hammer and nail to kill the victim. Upon leaving the property he saw the father of the victim and he had to hide until his father left the scene. Godino did find the hammer and nail, which he used in the eventual demise of the victim. The reason this provides us with an insight into his disorganised nature of offending was firstly he acted on impulse by taking the victim to a random location where he could easily have been caught, and he nearly was. The victim was attacked in a 'blitz' style attack as Godino needed to satisfy his psychological urges very quickly and again he used a weapon that was on hand and all of these key factors when analysing a crime scene would suggest a disorganised offender to a criminal profiler and the victim analysis follows a similar pattern to provide further evidence of his disorganised nature as he could have been spotted any time leading the victims away from where they were, as there were other children and adults around who could have identified him and therefore children became an easy choice of victim for him to transfer his inner rage against.

The crime scenes were in various locations in relation to where Godino resided. The crime scenes suggest a disorganised killer, as he uses weapons that came to hand as they already formed a part of the scenery, e.g., he had tried to use a horse's water trough when he attempted to murder the 22-month-old Severino Gonzalez Calo by asphyxiation by drowning and used a match to set fire to Reyna Vaincoff (aged 5). Although Cayetano Santos Godino only managed to kill children, I have also stated that I believe that had he not been apprehended at a young age, he would have killed across both genders and age groups due to his psychopathology. It must be remembered and reiterated that Godino, being a child himself, would have struggled immensely to overpower an adult due to his age and therefore would not have been mature enough to either overpower an adult, neither had he developed the cognitive skills to trick an adult in order to make them become submissive, for example, John Wayne Gacy was a weak individual who tried to rape a victim who fought back and went to the police, and therefore he used his handcuff 'trick' on his future victims in order to make them become submissive. John Wayne Gacy's American counterpart, Theodore 'Ted' Bundy would pretend to be injured to acquire 'help' from caring and unsuspecting middle-class co-ed women on American university campuses and beaches. Both Gacy and Bundy had different upbringings, Gacy's was more violent and uncaring, whereas Bundy was doted upon by his mother and came from a relatively stable family background, however, both men were cognitively developed enough to use a ruse to capture their prey.

Godino on the other hand had not developed enough cognitive intelligence to become an 'organised' serial killer as he had not developed through the normal stages of sexual and social development due in part to his age and his degenerate family life. The social psychologist Erik Erikson devised a theory on the *psychosocial* stages of development greatly influenced by the work of Sigmund Freud and his theory on the *psychosexual* stages of development. Unlike Freud, Eriksen focused his works more upon the ego and how it was developed and shaped by society and culture and the conflicts that take place within the ego itself, whereas Freud emphasized the conflict between id and superego (McLeod 2008). Eriksen proposed his theory of *psychosocial development* in eight stages with the first being *trust vs. mistrust (infancy zero to one years)* with the basic virtue at this stage being 'hope' and the culminate stage is *ego integrity vs. despair* with the basic virtue at this stage being 'wisdom'. Godino, likely did not properly complete stage one of the development stages in the sense that he did not trust his caregivers and therefore began to hate and mistrust others within society. Stage 3 of Eriksen's theory is *initiative vs. guilt,* (stage 2 is *autonomy vs. shame ages one-and-a-half to three years*); due to Godino not developing past the other stages we can see the only 'initiative' he took was to cause wanton destruction upon society and its members with a complete sociopathic lack of guilt – the basic virtue at this stage is *purpose* and his purpose was to exact his internal misery upon the society and its people that he loathed. Stage 4 is *industry vs. inferiority (ages five to twelve years)* and the basic virtue at this stage of development is *competency.* Godino was not socially or academically competent and this was the stage in his 'development' where he was arrested and as Godino had not reached this stage correctly, life in general was always going to be an uphill task and due to his anger and resentment and being mentally disabled to a degree, he would have continued to commit more serial acts of criminality throughout his life.

Although Godino may have suffered from mental disability, it is not to say that he would not have learnt how to commit crimes and become more aware of covering his tracks to evade capture; human beings learn how to master things over time using repetition and Godino eventually would have become a more organised serial killer as he grew older as he would have evolved into this category of serial killer. Most serial killers do not begin killing human beings at such an early age – they usually begin killing animals as practice which is a pre-cursor to later crimes (Godino was also practicing zoo-sadism whilst killing humans). The disorganised serial killers, Richard Trenton Chase and Ed Gein for example were known to have killed and tortured animals in their varying degrees of zoo-sadism and yet they killed human being in later life. Zoo-sadism is also a common factor amongst their more organised counterparts, for example, Dennis Rader the infamous American *Bind them, Torture them and Kill them 'BTK'* serial killer, and the Genesee River Killer, Arthur Shawcross, were known to have practiced zoo-sadism and yet were known to begin killing in their mid-to-late-twenties, and I am therefore hypothesising that the name of Cayetano Santos Godino could have become a more synonymous name associated with serial murder had he not been apprehended whilst still a child, and the more we delve into his psychology, I believe that he would have become a highly prolific serial rapist and serial killer as he was a very cunning and manipulative criminal as evidenced throughout the course of his crimes.

The victims all followed a pattern in the fact that they were all young children ranging from the ages of eighteen months (youngest) and thirteen years of age (oldest) of known murder victims. The offender did not discriminate against the genders of his victims. The four known murder victims of Cayetano Santos Godino are as follows: *Arturo Laurona (13), Reyna Vaincoff (5), Jesualdo Giordano (18 months) and Maria Roca Foce (3).* The attempted victims of Cayetano Santos Godino are as follows; *Miguel de Paoli (21 months-old), Ana Neri (18 months-old), Severino Gonzalez Calo (22 months-old), Julio Botte (22 months-old), Roberto Russo (8), Carmen Ghittoni (3) and Carolina Neolener (2).* The crimes varied from assault, attempted murder to murder. The victims in total had an age range of just two years and two-months old and all were of Hispanic ethnicity.

The age range of the victims, I believe, were chosen for multiple reasons with the first being that he could not target adults or older pubescent children because they could potentially overpower him. Secondly, younger children were easy targets for him to vent his internal rage upon them as they could not provide much resistance and were easily overpowered by him and thus from this deviant act Godino would have felt in control; control is a key psychological facet when explaining the psychology of violence in serial murderers. Thirdly, as Godino was born deformed and was regularly beaten at home, he would have more than likely become jealous of other children who had loving homes and he could socialise normally with other children, whereas Godino was incapable of such basic human acts and instincts. Fourthly, Godino by the age of ten was a compulsive masturbator and he was already exhibiting a hypersexual drive better known in males as *satyriasis* and *nymphomania* for females.

Godino was more than likely killing children and animals to not only feel empowered, but to also derive and extend sexual stimulation from his cruel and perverse acts. On the 23 December 1911, then aged fifteen, Godino became a reformed school graduate, and worked for three months before quitting and wandering the streets of Buenos Aires again, which led to more wanton destruction and assaults, attempted murder, and murder against fellow human beings. In modern criminal classification terms, Godino would be classed as a *sexual psychopath,* as he bears the characteristics that we have associated with modern day monsters such as Arthur Shawcross and Ted Bundy. Godino showed signs of psychopathic traits when he held down a job for a mere three months, psychopaths struggle to maintain employment as mundane activities do not tend to stimulate them and hence they cannot or at least struggle to conform to rules set out by others or society in general and this was evident in Godino from an early age. In 1906 when Godino was nine years old, his father took him to the local police station and filed charges against him, complaining that he was unruly and rebellious and did not respond to any kind of authority. Psychopaths cannot respond to authority and play their warped games to manipulate others. Edmund. Kemper, then aged sixteen, for example, was incarcerated for murdering his grandparents in 1964 and in Atascadero State Hospital, befriended his psychologist and became his 'assistant' and was later released as he was *'no threat to himself and society'* and yet he was released into his mother's care, the very woman who developed him into a sexual psychopath and misogynist due to her cruel and unusual punishments by belittling, humiliating him (by dressing him as a girl) and by verbally and physically abusing him. Edmund Kemper would go onto kill eight more women including his own mother. The danger with psychopaths is that they fear the strong but learn to manipulate the weak and Godino did just this and it was evident in his victim choice. The American psychiatrist, Hervey Cleckley (1903–1984) in 1946 published a book by the title of the *'Mask of Sanity'* in which he described the common traits of a sexual psychopath as *'incapable of love; they don't experience guilt or remorse, they are impulsive without considering the consequences of their actions; they act on the slightest of their urges; they are not typically put off by things that normal people would find repulsive or repugnant and they often engage in a variety of unsatisfactory behaviors in every field for example, they don't specialize in just one type of crime, they are often involved in different types of illegal acts.'* (Dr David McDermott 2006 citing the works of Cleckley 1941) Godino exhibited all of those mentioned pathological traits and, like Kemper, should never have been released into mainstream society as they were going to target their usual victim groups to derive their form of perverse sexual stimulation.

The other aspect of the victimology linked with Godino's crimes is the following question: *'why did he only choose to target Hispanic children?'* I believe that the answer to this is quite simple. In the early 1900s many countries were more homogenous than they are today, for example the demography of the United States, Lisa Wade PhD for the USA Society Pages (2012) published demographic research for 1960 to 2011 and projected for the year 2050 with the results being for 1960 as follows; *85% White, 3.5% Hispanic, 11% Black and 0.6% Asian.* These results show changes in demography in 2011 and the results are as follows; *63% White, 17% Hispanic, 12% Black and 5% Asian.* The projected demographic changes for the year 2050 are as follows; *White 47%, Hispanic 29%, Black 13%, and Asian 9%.* The changes in world demography are due to the advancement of technology and globalisation and I will attempt to explain why so many serial killers originally killed within their own racial groups according to several studies on the subject.

On the FBI website, under reports and publications, there is a report called *Serial Murder: Multi-Disciplinary Perspectives for Investigators* written for the *Behavioural Analysis Unit (BCU) National Centre for the Analysis of Violent Crime* by Morton, Hilts, Johns, Keel et al (2005). It makes the following claim: *'Serial killers are not limited to any specific demographic group such as their sex, age race or religion.'* The myth that serial killers only kill within their demographic derives from the media and possibly the more 'famous' serial killers such as Ted Bundy, John Wayne Gacy, who all killed white women and men respectively (due to their sexual orientation). World demographics are rapidly changing and therefore societies and countries are becoming less homogenous and beginning to dispell the myth that serial killers kill solely within their own demographic group, for example Arthur Shawcross and Gary Ridgeway killed Black, White and Hispanic prostitutes, whereas Jeffrey Dahmer predominately killed young Black males as well as Hispanic and White males. Godino, as I mentioned previously, would have killed anybody who was unfortunate to cross his path had he not been apprehended, his victim choice ultimately would have become mixed between gender, age and sex as his murderous career developed. Sexual psychopaths like Godino are primitive and opportunistic and are therefore highly dangerous. Godino's victims were all children, and children tend to be more trusting of an older person, whether this be a teenager or an adult, and a sexual psychopath like Godino will exploit these types of situations for their own evil intentions and this is evident within his victimology pattern and offender characteristics.

The victims all followed a pattern in the fact that they were all young children ranging from the ages of eighteen months as the youngest victim and thirteen years of age as the oldest (known victims). The offender did not discriminate against the genders of his victims; he chose them upon 'access' and 'opportunity' as they provided him the easiest opportunity to kill. I believe that when we are assessing the offender characteristics of Cayetano Santos Godino, there are several elements contained within them that provide us with psychological indicators that he was more than capable of committing such heinous criminal acts as the offender from an early age showed all the warning signs of an antisocial personality disorder and I have outlined them as follows:

- *Godino suffered from enuresis up until his late teens (bedwetting, which forms a part of the 'MacDonald Triad').*
- *Godino participated in animal cruelty (again, this cruel behaviour forms part of the 'MacDonald Triad').*
- *Godino was fascinated by pyromania and when he set fire to a building, he told the police 'I like to see fire fighters working' (this forms the final part of the 'MacDonald Triad') and Godino more than likely derived sexual pleasure and stimulation from his pyromaniac acts, which is a common psychological trait amongst serial killers.*
- *Godino lacked an education and dropped out of school, as his psychopathic personality would not have been able to withstand rules and regulations being imposed upon him.*
- *Godino did not integrate with other children in any environment such as community life, sport, or schooling.*
- *He attacked his siblings with overt force and enjoyed doing so and felt no remorse for his actions.*
- *Godino did not respond to treatment in reform school.*
- *He was reared in an environment unfavourable to the formation of acceptable behaviour.*

The above-mentioned factors provide us with the psychological precursors which show us that he is capable and willing to use violence to satisfy his own selfish psychological needs with no regards for the feelings of others. For us to understand the outlined points in more detail, we need to delve further into the psyche and psychosis of Godino to attempt to establish a primary motive or the primary motives for his criminal behaviours.

Godino's first acts of criminality may have been due to a mental disturbance, as the Negri-Lucero report (31st January, 1913) concluded;

'*Godino is mental or insane in the legal sense*'. As he became older and puberty took its natural course the offences would have had a more sexual element as he was known to be a compulsive masturbator according to the same report, and therefore the mental disturbances and antisocial behaviours that he was exhibiting, such as pyromania, were committed to provide his psyche's constant craving for stimulation to quell his sexual paraphilic behaviours. The report conducted by Negri-Lucero (1913) highlights how deviant Godino was and how his victims once he had managed to snare them, experienced unparalleled levels of risk which as innocent children they could not have been prepared for against a callous predator.

The victims experienced a high level of risk when dealing with a merciless criminal like Godino. Godino could lead many of his victims astray from their 'comfort' zones and areas of safety, e.g., near to their home and family. From the outset, Godino appeared 'normal' and he presented no abnormalities to his victims, as he would appear kind and friendly as a ruse to gain their trust. When they agreed to follow Godino and he had them in an area in which he felt comfortable to commit his perverse criminal acts undisturbed, the victim's chance of survival was virtually non-existent as Godino was an adult and they were very young children who would have been terrified at what was befalling them. The level of risk was high due to Godino's antisocial and deviant personality and a constant selfish psychopathic need and desire to stimulate his antisocial personality. Godino shows the psychological traits that we now associate with sufferers of a psychopathic personality disorder in the sense that he manipulated the victims to snare them, he showed a complete disregard for others and violated their human rights, he had recurring problems with the law, and he also exhibited high risk-taking behaviour during his crimes.

Godino, in comparison to some other serial killers such as the Canadian serial killer Robert Pickton, took high levels of risk when selecting his victims and murdering them, as his first attempted murder in 1904 was at the age of just seven years old, when he was caught by a policeman on a wasteland stoning twenty-month-old Miguel de Paoli, and even later in life at the age of twelve, he attempted to drown twenty-two-month-old Gonzalez Calo in a water trough before being interrupted. All Godino's victims were people that others cared about, in comparison with a serial killer such as Robert Pickton, who killed at least 26 sex workers, as Egger (2006) states; '*Prostitutes are easily available to a serial killer, and nobody is going to report a missing sex worker as most have already run away from home.*' Godino was choosing victims that were still functional within society, and their families dearly cared for them due to their ages as is, or at least should be, human nature. When we analyse the sequence of acts that inhibited Godino's psyche prior to his crimes and the acts after the commission of his crimes, we can begin to see a common psychological theme occurring as to why he undertook such risks in killing his victims.

As serial killing was an unheard-of term at the time (it was only coined by Robert Ressler after Ted Bundy was arrested), the study of their behaviour was completely unknown, and no psychological linkage analysis would necessarily have been provided against Godino's crimes. This allowed him to continue to kill unabated. In the case of Godino we can only theorise from studies conducted by the FBI that the fantasy manifests before a serial killer need to go out and kill to 'satisfy' their fantasies and psychological desires. Godino did tell the police that days before he committed a murder, he would suffer from terrible headaches, especially after drinking alcohol (a practice he started from a young age due to his dysfunctional upbringing), which were accompanied by an overpowering compulsion to kill. Godino, like many other serial killers after committing a crime, carried on with mundane life as normal. We know from studies and interviews that serial killers act in this manner as they have confessed to such actions, for example Dennis Rader killed four members of the Otero family on the morning of 15 January 1974, and he went back to work in the afternoon as if nothing had happened. This is done for several reasons, firstly their psychopathic nature does not allow them to feel remorse, secondly, they can compartmentalise their criminal actions and deviant behaviours against their routine and mundane daily activities, and thirdly, it provides them with an alibi, as nobody suspects them of committing such evil acts. As I have established, I believe that Godino was a disorganised serial killer, and I will expand on this hypothesis on the length of time his acts took to commit as this is yet another indicator in the psychology of the organised and disorganised classification typology of serial killers.

The time during the leadup to the killing and the act of killing itself would have been conducted very quickly due to the risks involved for Godino, and due to his antisocial personality disorder, he would have acted on impulse, which meant no prior planning had gone into the murders. Godino was an impulsive killer. They were usually over within a matter of minutes. For example, he set fire to Reyna Vaincoff whilst she was alive and strangled Arturo Laurona with his hands as he needed them killed quickly so he could get away from the crime scene, whereas more organised serial killers, such as Fred West for example, plan their murders as retaining and spending time with the victims becomes the central facet of their fantasy, and an organised serial killer usually has a place where they commit their crimes and feel comfortable, e.g. West had 25 Cromwell Street and Midland Road. Godino found a random place and searched for a victim, and therefore the act of murder needed to be concluded swiftly because of the risk of getting caught. The attempted first murder when he was only seven years old would have had a psychological imprint on the way he killed his victims, because the first time the act of stoning led to the victim surviving and the police apprehending him, which would have caused him early psychological frustrations that his victim survived which would have led to rage in his psyche, and therefore his later victims would be disposed of as quickly as possible.

Godino committed all his crimes close to where he lived and this proved to be his downfall, leading to his arrest for the murder of three-year-old Jesualdo Giordano, when an eyewitness testified, she had seen Godino with the boy and he confessed to his crimes and again as he chose a random place before killing his victim. His psychopathic and impulsive nature would not allow him to re-enter a state of psychological equilibrium as he needed to be psychologically satisfied there and then and this led to his own downfall as he left witnesses and the crime scene was left intact as he had to commit his crimes and he would flee the scene quickly, which is a common trait with all disorganised serial killers, and this is evident as Godino did not move any of the victim's bodies from one location to another, and this is a common psychological trait with disorganised serial killers.

All Godino's victims were murdered and discovered at the same sites. One victim, Maria Roca, was never found as he buried her on a site which was later built over with a two-storey building. I have outlined several reasons as to why I fundamentally believed that Cayetano Santos Godino would fit into the disorganised serial killer typology classification, however, there are other common traits associated with this classification that Godino exhibited, and I will outline his own unique individual characteristics below:

- He had a low level of IQ. (A trait common with disorganised killers.)
- Godino did not follow his crimes in the media.
- He lived near each crime scene.
- All the victims were killed at a site which was there for 'convenience', and he did not use a site where he felt comfortable, which suggests an impulsive serial killer.

- *The corpses of his victims were all left intact, as disorganised killers kill very quickly, whereas more organised killers like to dismember victims to hide them, and sometimes the act of dismembering a body also acts as an opportunity to take a body part as a 'trophy'.*
- *The crime scenes were left in a chaotic state, and he left weapons that he used there to easily be recovered by the police.*
- *He left physical evidence at the crime scenes; however, this was the days before forensic science was used and may explain why he did this as the biggest danger to him was witnesses.*
- *His use of weapons suggests a disorganised killer as he used weapons that came to hand and already formed part of the scenery e.g., rocks, nails, hands, etc.*
- *His last victim, Jesualdo Giordano, struggled and fought back against Godino, which resulted in Godino having to use his belt to control his victim, whereas an organised serial killer would take their own 'murder kit' to the crime scene.*
- *He suffered from mental illness, which is a common theme with disorganised killers, for example, the Vampire of Sacramento, Richard Trenton Chase, who suffered from schizophrenia, and this is common amongst disorganised serial killers as their mental illness damages their ability to conduct longer-term planning.*
- *He attacked the victim in a 'blitz pattern' e.g., he tried to kill them as quickly as possible to minimise the risk of him being caught and apprehended.*

The above-mentioned reasons are outlined as to why I believe that Godino was a disorganised offender and there are further psychological factors that we need to delve into understand his psychological motivations for the commission of his crimes which suggest in more detail that he was a disorganised serial killer.

The cause of death varies between each victim, and this is due to his impulsive behaviour. The act of killing for Godino was the means to an end as he simply enjoyed the power, he gained over killing his victims, and he did not leave a signature as this later act served no psychological purpose for him as he did not follow his crimes in the media. The location of the wounds again varies due to his disorganisation due to his denigrated mental state. The wounds perpetuated against the victims show 'overkill', which suggests that he would have been in a state of rage whilst killing his victims, an act of transference from the rage and anger he inhibited in his psyche from his own childhood.

As mentioned, Godino did not alter the crime scenes at all as once he had committed the crimes, the tension that built up within his psyche over the days, weeks and moths had been 'satisfied' for an interim period and Godino made no attempt to alter the position of the bodies at the crime scenes, again this is a common psychological trait with disorganised serial killers. The positions of the bodies were left as they were slain and were not posed or altered in any way. Therefore, it is hard to induce a theory as to his motivations from the position of the body. This is common with disorganised killers, as usually organised killers, such as the Hillside Stranglers or Ted Bundy, will use a 'signature' which suggests power and control and the victims are usually moved to one location from another to fulfil a pschological and sexual fantasy. The organised serial killer also enjoys the notoriety that the media coverage gives them, which acts as a psychological driver for the commission of their next crime.

Away from his crimes, FBI research and general criminological research provides us with more psychological evidence that Godino was a disorganised offender, for example, Godino was never married, and he was never known to have any form of an intimate relationship. This is another common trait of a disorganised killer as they usually live alone and do not date due to their psychological imbalances and impulsive behaviours. Normal members of society see them as 'odd' or 'dangerous' and they struggle to hide their innate psychological problems, whereas the more organised offenders are better at compartmentalising their innate warped psychological desires which allows them to commit their crimes without the eye of suspicion falling upon them for a longer period. For example, Britain's most prolific serial killer, Dr Harold Shipman, killed unabated for several decades, however, as he had a middleclass profession, was well educated and married, nobody believed that their family physician could be a serial killer as Shipman could compartmentalise his deviant criminal behaviour with normal mundane life and he could intertwine the two, which allowed him to kill unabated for a very long time.

Godino was also unemployed and yet again this is another common occurrence with disorganised killers as their mental illnesses usually mean that they find it extremely difficult to acquire long term and steady employment, possibly due to their impulsive behaviour and need for constant psychological stimulation. Holding down long-term employment would not psychologically stimulate them for long, unless their employment allows them to commit their crimes, for example, Peter Sutcliffe used his job as a lorry driver to be able to commute around the north of England to kill innocent women.

Although Godino was a disorganised serial killer, it does not make him anymore or any less dangerous than his organised counterparts as he inhibited and manifested several dangerous psychological characteristics within his psyche, and these were outlined by several psychologists and psychiatrists during their interviews with him. According to various reports, Godino was driven by a primeval animal instinct with stunted social skills. He was an aggressive type without feelings and inhibition. The Ernesto Nelson report (1 April 1913) states that, *'He (Godino) cannot be held responsible for his crimes as he is a case of degeneration aggravated by his social neglect and his background.'* In terms of his beliefs and values, due to his mental illness he was a conscious impulsive and extremely dangerous to those around him and had no concept of responsibility for his actions, which is observed in many alienated killers (Esteves-Cabred report – May 29th, 1913.)

Godino exhibits further evidence of his dangerous and warped psychosis when he was interviewed by the police as he willingly confessed willingly to the Giordano murder and calmly told police of his modus operandi to get the kids to trust him by offering rewards such as toys and sweets to entice them into a secluded area before killing them. He told the police that he killed purely for 'fun', and this was the motivation for the murders. He also admitted to the police of his obsession with pyromania and his acts of zoo-sadism. He also blamed some of his murders on not being able to secure any form of employment. The pertinent question we must ask here is, had the police used linkage analysis, could they have checked criminal records of local offenders that may have provided several clues to who may have been committing these dreadful series of crimes against children?

Although there were no scientific studies on serial killers back in the early 1900s, Godino had an extensive criminal history to suggest he would commission serious offences later in life in the fact that he attempted to murder twenty-one-month-old Miguel de Paoli by attempting stone him to death and throwing him into a ditch to be left to die. There are other factors which we now know (although not on his criminal record), such as that he practised pyromania and animal cruelty; he did not respond to psychological treatment. If a background check with all the above elements was conducted, Godino, may well have been a prime suspect in the murders. Unfortunately, the FBI Behavioural Sciences Unit was only established in

1972 and this innovation in law enforcement led to the other law enforcements in the world becoming interested in the procedures and methods being used by the FBI in how they detected criminals. Sadly, this was non-existent whilst Godino was an active serial killer.

Pen Profile

Cayetano Santos Godino committed his crimes between the ages of seven to sixteen years of age before his ultimate incarceration, where he was also murdered on November 15th, 1944, at the age of 48, possibly due to killing a fellow inmate's pet. I am therefore unable to offer a psychological profile of an *unknown subject of an investigation (UNSUB)*. In effect I am trying to offer a psychological post-mortem offender profile, based on the information contained herewith in the above offender profile to try to establish the psychological motivations for the criminal acts committed by Cayetano Santos Godino.

1. The criminal acts committed by Godino were of a serial nature as he committed seven known murders, at least three attempted murders and several assaults on young children. Each criminal act followed a 'cooling-off period' before the next criminal act.
2. Cayetano Santos Godino's victims ranged between the ages of eighteen months (youngest) to thirteen years of age (oldest) from the records available to us. Godino's *modus operandi* was to offer the local children sweets, toys etc. as a ruse to acquire their trust and lure them away from safety to commit his criminal acts. I therefore believe that Godino was a deviant and cunning character and preyed upon the innocence and the vulnerability that exists in children.
3. After conducting research on Cayetano Santos Godino, I believe that he suffered from an antisocial personality disorder from an early age as he showed many classic symptoms associated with this mental alignment. For example, he participated in cruelty to animals, he attacked his siblings/other children with overt force, he did not integrate well with other children, he suffered from enuresis, he was fascinated with fire (pyromania) and he did not respond to professional and medical treatment for his disorder. I am therefore led to conclude that Godino suffered from a psychopathic personality disorder.

4. I believe that Godino's problems and criminal acts resulted from him being reared in an unstable environment. Godino's father was an alcoholic who beat his wife and children, sometimes with Cayetano becoming the focus of his father's rage. This affected Godino's school life as he began failing in classes and he began re-enacting the acts of violence towards his classmates. Although not all children act out the violence they see, some children will imitate that violence. Bandura and Ross (1961) conducted an experiment with 36 boys and 36 girls aged between three to six years of age. A doll was at first treated in a gentle and kind way and the children imitated this behaviour. Once the doll was treated aggressively by the man, many of the male children attacked the doll in an aggressive way and in some cases with a hammer, calling for the doll to 'die'. The children in the experiment were the same age as Godino when his psychological problems began to occur.
5. Godino was seven years of age when his problems and crimes began. Godino was in danger of becoming a serious offender at these early formative years of his life and he needed to be psychologically treated and reviewed carefully to stem or stop this destructive behaviour. Godino's later behaviours were due to not having the treatment techniques and medicines available as we do within the modern era. Godino may have lacked the treatment needed to treat his disorder, however, we know from his psychological records that he did have a form of treatment but he did not respond to the treatment, and yet the understanding of psychopathy was not within the knowledge of psychologists and psychiatrists at the time, which meant Godino may have been dismissed simply as a 'difficult' patient.
6. Godino's early criminal acts including the torture of animals, and his pyromania obsession were early warning signs of a dysfunctional personality. Godino showed all three symptoms of the 'MacDonald Triad' aka the 'Triad of Evil'. I believe that the acts of animal cruelty and pyromania involved a sexual element due to problems with maladjustment at home and with society in general. Zoo-sadism and pyromania when dealing with serial killers in particular have sexual connotations conjoined within the act itself, for example Peter Kurten and David Berkowitz both stated that 'the sight of fire and the dangers involved could provide them with multiple orgasms'. Arthur Shawcross and Fred West both enacted bestiality on animals before torturing and killing them. These two types of perverse acts can be associated with

enacting power over a weaker creature that they lack in general family life, and pyromania can be an act of 'revenge' upon society, as Peter Kurten said he wanted to make Dusseldorf 'pay' for the way the city and its inhabitants 'treated' him.

7. I believe that the type of victims that Godino chose stems from rage borne out of his formative life experiences. I deduce my theory on the basis that the victims all came from loving families, or at least had people who cared for them, e.g., Reyna Vaincoff, whom Godino set alight, her grandfather ran across the road to try to save her and was killed by an oncoming vehicle, and thus he became a secondary victim in Godino's crimes. Godino, unlike many serial killers such as Gary Ridgeway, aka the 'Green River Killer', Dennis Nilsen or William Bonin, was not targeting sex workers or runaways, he was targeting people that would be missed. Godino targeted children as his victim typology, as I believe that when he was hurting them and killing them, he finally felt in control and instead of being victimised as he was by his father, he was now the victimiser, and at the same time was killing an innocence, an innocence that he had never known.

8. I believe that the offender in question suffered from several psychological problems which became outwardly evident during the commission of his crimes. I would categorise Godino as a 'disorganised serial killer'. I am deducing my theory on the basis that firstly he committed all his crimes near to where he lived and lingered near, or at the scene after the initial death (an eyewitness saw him at an attempted murder scene and contacted the police, which led to his apprehension), and the acts did not take long to commit and could be over in a matter of minutes. He did not move the body from one place to another, or keep the body, which can act as a form of a perverse possession, as opposed to an organised serial killer who likes to act dismember a victim for a particular body part for a 'trophy' as part of this 'fantasy'. Each victim was killed either by his hands or a weapon of 'convenience', e.g., a rock, a horse's water trough He had to restrain one victim using his own belt, which reflects impulsive behaviour as opposed to an organised assault where a killer will usually take their own 'murder kit' to the crime scene.

9. There is further evidence to suggest that the crime scenes can act almost as a personification of his mental state and his disorganised methods, as he left many clues for an investigator, e.g., his own belt. DNA would have been all over the crime scene and several witnesses saw him leave one

PEN PROFILES OF THE OFFENDERS

crime scene. Unfortunately, they could not provide an accurate description to the police. The geographical profile of the murders suggest that each victim possibly knew their killer and he potentially knew them, or was at least familiar, which may have helped him snare his prey. Godino took high risk in his victim selection, as he was known as the town 'delinquent', and many other older children knew to stay away and not become involved with him. However, the younger children would not have understood he was the local thug, and Godino preyed upon their complete innocence for his own perverted psychological needs.

10. There are further character attributes and the crime characteristics to suggest that Godino was a disorganised serial killer. He had a low level of IQ (a common trait with disorganised killers), he suffered from severe emotional and physical abuse by the hand of a family member, he did not follow his crimes in the media, he suffered from a form of mental illness (according to the reports, please see my conclusion for my theory on this matter), he attacked his victims in a 'blitz pattern' and he aimed to dispose of them as quickly as possible. He did not form any friendships with people and/or intimate relationships throughout the course of his life he could not gain employment for long periods.

11. I believe from my research into the crimes committed by Cayetano Santo Godino that if techniques such as geographical profiling and advanced knowledge of psychology were available, if the police had linked the type of crimes through linkage analysis, extensive research into the victim typology and had they conducted an extensive background check on local offenders, Cayetano Santos Godino would have been apprehended much sooner due to eyewitness accounts. Police deduction could have used 'linkage analysis' to piece together the puzzle and solve the crimes that were being committed.

12. Although the report by Esteves-Cabred (May 29th, 1913) states that Godino suffered from mental alienation that takes the form of imbecility, and that his stupidity was incurable, with this part of the report I concur. In terms of the findings of the report that Godino is totally irresponsible for his actions, and that he had no concept of responsibility for his actions, I do not agree. Godino, I believe that Godino did suffer from an anti-social personality disorder (ASPD), however, I believe that he knew his actions were extremely unlawful as he lured many victims to a secluded place to kill them, and the victims he chose are society's most

vulnerable groups. Later studies on serial killers have shown that this group of people harbour a deviant personality, and they are extremely manipulative, for example, Edmund Kemper convinced the psychiatrists that upon his release he was going to be a 'model citizen' yet went on to become one of Americas worst serial killers. Although Kemper had an IQ of 136 (Russell 2002), there have been cases of serial killers with less intelligence trying to manipulate others, such as Henry Lee Lucas, who enjoyed the notoriety who would take police on false errands to find missing victims. I therefore conclude my profile by stating that when dealing with serial killers, be extremely careful that they are not trying to mislead an investigator, law court, doctor et al., as this may be their last dance as a form of retaining some semblance of power and control over the judicial system and wider society.

Final Synopsis on the Profile of Cayetano Santos Godino:

Cayetano Santos Godino is not a well-known serial killer as he is only known to criminologists, and the possible reasons for this is because his crimes were committed in South America and the media tend to focus on serial killers from Britain, North America, Germany et al. The reason Godino has been used for the purposes of profiling is because Godino was one of the earliest recorded serial killers and we can see that he exhibits many of the classic signs from abusive parents, exhibiting early signs of hybristrophillia and the warning signs of the 'Triad of Evil', and therefore he is an interesting study.

Even upon his apprehension and imprisonment, Godino was still trying to murder other inmates and kill their pets and although he was declared legally insane, as serial killing was completely unknown at the time, based on his behaviour and psychology, had Godino committed his crimes today he would not be declared legally insane as he would be the focus of intense studies by psychologists and law enforcements, and I have no doubt that he would have been branded as a 'serial killer' as the bodies of the children were occurring at regularly alarming rates. The next serial killer profiled is much closer to home, and unlike Godino, he swore an oath to save lives and not take them.

Dr Harold Frederick Shipman

Harold Shipman was born in 1946 on the Bestwood Council Estate, Nottingham, England, just after the conclusion of World War Two, and like many working class families at the time life was difficult, as many people were still on state rations and housing was not particularly great at the time and many council areas would not see living standards improve until the 1960s when the Beveridge Report (1942) would begin to be implemented to its full. Harold Shipman's mother, Vera, always had high hopes for her favourite 'Fred' and she must have been thrilled when he began to live up to her expectations. Unfortunately, he used his profession to become Britain's most prolific serial killer. Harold Shipman is by far Britain's most prolific serial killer, managing to kill a known total of 215 victims between the years of 1975 up until his arrest in 1998, and therefore averaging 9.3 victims per year over a 23-year period.

Shipman is Britain's most prolific serial killer, and his number of victims outweighs that of any other British serial killer, as Peter Dinsdale is second in the list with 26 victims. Due to the previous statement, as there was a 'cooling-off' period between each murder, Shipman would fit into the classification of a serial killer based upon the FBI definition; *'The unlawful killing of two or more victims by the same offender(s) in separate events.'* Due to the number of known victims that Shipman killed, there are no grey areas or ambiguities, and he can therefore quite easily be classed as a 'serial killer', however, we need to firstly assess his modus operandi and work backwards to establish a motivation for his crimes and criminal acts.

I believe that Shipman committed the murders due to his narcissistic personality and the power and authority that his profession afforded to him to commit his crimes. In terms of criminology, there have been several studies on 'white-collar' and 'blue-collar' criminality. The former of the two theorises why those in the higher and upper socio-economic class are not as severely dealt with by the law and are not always suspected to be criminals and are therefore not thought of as committing acts of criminality as much as their blue-collar counterparts. Williams (2005) cites Sutherland (1940 and

1949) when he states that white-collar crime and criminality are 'committed by a person of respectability – someone with no convictions for non-white-collar crimes; and of high social status; and in the course of his/her occupation.' I believe that Sutherland's hypothesis is evident in the case of Dr Harold Shipman when a local Hyde taxi driver, John Shaw, noticed that the elderly women he used to pick up from the surgery had a higher mortality rate than that of another local practice. Shaw, however, was not the only resident to raise suspicions, and Doctor Linda Reynolds reported her suspicions to the police. Detective Inspector David Smith interviewed Dr Reynolds and she confirmed that there were two bodies awaiting cremation. Smith failed to submit a request to the coroner to have the autopsies carried out. Smith then approached the Tameside Register Office and requested copies of all death certificates signed by Shipman in the previous six months. Instead of the 31 he should have been given he accepted twenty. Smith took the certificates to Doctor Alan Banks, the assistant director of primary care and medical advisor to the health authority. Upon receipt of these he examined the medical records and certificates of the patients and advised DI Smith that there were a few deaths where there was insufficient evidence in the records to diagnose the cause of death that should have been referred to the coroner and he did not stress any great failings on the part of Dr Shipman.

Doctors must abide by many codes of practice. The best known of these is the Hippocratic Oath, an undertaking that many think was first laid down by the Greek healer Hippocrates, 500 years before the birth of Christianity. Part of the modern version reads, *'I will respect the privacy of my patients, for the problems are not disclosed to me that the world may know. Most especially must I tread with care the matters of life and death. If it is given to me to save a life, all thanks. But it may also be within my power to take a life; this awesome responsibility must be faced with great humbleness and awareness of my own frailty. Above all, I must not play at God.'* (Leslie 1999)

The problem was that Shipman's motivation for becoming a doctor was not for him to protect and save lives; it became a vessel for him to implement his own grandiose perceptions of 'superiority' by using his intellect against others whom he undoubtedly saw below him (this included the interrogating officers until presented with the computer records evidence) and Shipman enjoyed the fact that he could play God over the life and death of another human being.

Shipman was predominately motivated by power, which would later turn into greed, which would in turn result in his downfall. Shipman harboured a fascination with death from the time when he used to administer morphine to his ill mother and became fascinated the effect morphine could have on a person. Shipman's modus operandi consisted of him visiting a patient's home (sometimes without warrant), upon which he would administer lethal doses of morphine and other concoctions of drugs for sometimes minor complaints, as Shipman believed he was invincible and enjoyed playing 'God' with his victims.

I believe that Shipman convinced his patients that they were suffering from far worse medical ailments than they had initially thought, and this gave him access to his trusting victims. However, many of us in general life will be obedient when we are told to do or listen to advice from another individual who is a figure of authority, and this formed a part of Shipman's *modus operandi*. This is evident when Shipman told several of the victims' relatives when they raised concerns that the victim had died of some severe condition brought about by multiple causes, for example, the murder of Muriel Grimshaw: the patient had only been suffering from a degree of arthritis and high blood pressure, yet Shipman concluded that her death was brought on as a result of a cerebrovascular accident resultant from suffering from a stroke and hypertension with a contributing factor of rheumatoid arthritis – this diagnosis in itself is absurd and one does have to wonder how Shipman managed to dupe his own colleagues within the medical profession.

The deceased was sitting upright in her chair, and Shipman did not even check the deceased's pulse as he simply issued a certificate of death with the previous contributing factors, and yet the family and friends of the victim did not question Shipman about this cold and untoward behaviour from a family doctor. I am under no illusions and or doubt that instances such as this would have provided his psychosis with an immense feeling of superiority and power that he was committing and getting away with murder. When we evaluate the crime scenes of where most victims were killed, many of whom were killed in their own homes, I believe that this was a central facet to Shipman's psychological motivations for the series of murders and therefore, we need to assess the crime scenes against his psyche to try and establish a motivation for his crimes.

Many of Shipman's victims died within their own homes whilst sitting upright in an almost sleep-like position and a comatose state, whilst others died in their own beds. If reports and autopsies had been conducted in the correct manner and had the practice been in place whereby two other practitioners, other than the doctor who issues the death certificate, needed to countersign the document, then Shipman would never have gotten away with his crimes for as long as he did, and lives would have been saved in the process.

The murder of Maureen Ward, an active and healthy fifty-seven-year-old recovering from cancer, had suffered from a bout of migraines, which is nothing unusual. Shipman certified that Mrs Ward had died as a result of carcinomatosis: patients who die as a result of carcinomatosis do not die suddenly and usually suffer for a period prior to death, and again this is another murder that was, I believe, contributing to his own sense of hedonism and providing him with a perverse sense of 'invincibility' as Shipman, would have seen those people taking his word as 'stupid', increasing his own grandiose sense of self-worth.

The murder of Winnie Mellor again shows flaws in Shipman's deduction that she died because of coronary thrombosis, as she died sitting upright in a chair. Coronary thrombosis is more commonly known as a 'heart attack' and people who die of a heart attack usually do not die sitting upright as blockages within the arteries of the heart cause the body to go into shock, which ultimately results in the victim collapsing. However, yet again nobody questioned Shipman's diagnosis. The other specifics of the crime scene(s) involved Shipman taking items of jewellery and photos of the victims, and in this regard, I will explain and expand on my hypothesis in relation to this in greater detail during the profile on Dr Harold Shipman. The victimology is always key to assessing and establishing the psychological motives of serial killers and therefore we need to establish the predominate victimology type associated with Dr Harold Shipman and look for psychological clues as to why he targeted those victims as the victim is the key facet in the psychological motivations that allows a serial killer to be able to commit their crimes that normal members of society are repulsed by.

The youngest victim of Harold Shipman was a four-year-old girl, Susan Garrfit, and his oldest was Ann Cooper, aged 93. The victims were all predominately old and/or at least entering the twilight stages of life and provided a combined age of 15,900 years old and I believe that Shipman targeted the elderly for several reasons, with the first psychological motivation being due to instances in his formative years, and in particular his peculiar relationship with his mother.

In comparison to many other serial killers, Shipman's mother, though domineering and overprotective, did love him dearly and pushed him into 'greatness'; at least that is what she perceived she was doing to her son, however, she was unwittingly creating one of the worst monsters that the annals of British criminal history will ever have the misfortune of having to deal with.

The young Harold Shipman, known as Fred' to avoid confusion with his father, was never allowed to join games of football or tag, etc., on a normal British working-class estate during the 1950s. Fred's mother, Vera, would make him do extra schoolwork, and this also included at the weekends, and instilled a sense of superiority in the young boy which tainted his relationships with other peers, and this would cause problems forming healthy and normal peer relationships throughout his later life as well as his early life.

Shipman was extremely rude to classmates and local children in the neighbourhood; they ultimately turned their guns on him, and he became the victim of their taunts as he dressed in a nice suit in comparison to the way the other children dressed, and therefore from an early age young Harold Shipman was experiencing social ostracization and I believe this may be the first instance in his life that he began to resent his mother. I believe that even in this early instance, Shipman believed, due to indoctrination by his mother, that he was superior to the average 'proletariat' and therefore he was singled out by his peers because he was superior to them, which was a vehemently delusional and grandiose belief that he and his mother created, as it helped them both mentally cope with the aggression shown towards him by other children, which is an act of cognitive dissonance.

I also believe that Shipman suffered from a mild form of *Oedipus complex* in the sense that although he did not hate his father, he loved and enjoyed the attention that he received from his mother and he began to develop sexual feelings and desires towards her, as she was very selective of who he could socialise with, and therefore he did not develop within the normal developmental stages as outlined by Cherry (2009) when she cites the work of the developmental psychologist, Erik Erikson.

The development: *Stage 1: Ego Identity (conscious sense of self that develops through social interaction learning to trust or mistrust); Stage 2: Autonomy vs. Shame and Doubt (Children who successfully complete this stage feel secure and confident, while those who do not are left with a sense of inadequacy and self-doubt); Stage 3: Initiative vs. Guilt (completion of this stage begins to ferment during the preschool years, children begin to assert their power and control over the world through directing play and other social interactions) Shipman was never given the correct environment to complete this stage; Stage 4: industry vs. Inferiority (through social interactions, children begin to develop a sense of pride in their accomplishments and abilities (again Shipman was not given the correct environment to successfully develop past this stage) Stage 5: Identity vs. Confusion (completing this stage successfully leads to fidelity, which Erikson described as an ability to live by society's standards and expectations)* Shipman became a serial killer and therefore broke all the taboos and boundaries set out by society. Due to his mother's domineering persona and attitude, I fundamentally believe that she was the personification of a template for the choice of Shipman's later victim preferences.

Most of his victims were elderly women, and I believe that because Shipman did not develop correctly through each stage of the Erikson psychological stages of development, he became confused sexually and he equally both loathed and loved his mother, and when killing the elderly women he was in effect killing the hated object of anger and warped and confused sexual desires which was his own mother, a mother who doted upon him and was over-zealous in her upbringing of him by overprotecting him and placing him on a higher social pedestal than others as she harboured high hopes for him, unwittingly created the devil incarnate.

Harold Shipman was a narcissist who enjoyed being in control of others from the very outset and I believe that he sought out a profession such as a doctor as this type of profession would have provided him with a feeling of power over others. For the first time in his life, he derived a sense of power over other members of society as he finally became a 'somebody', due to attaining a middle-class and highly respected profession, and this feeling of supremacy was evident by the way he talked rudely to junior members of staff, and again this is Shipman exerting his own dominance over others who he perceived as below him in the societal structure. Shipman also did not like having his authority and judgement questioned by some of the victims' relatives, and again this is evident within the same way he exhibited disdain for junior staff as he saw those below him as irritants and were there to serve him and never question his judgements, as he was of superior intellect to others. This is one of the many traits of a psychopath.

Shipman, surprisingly, during infancy and adolescence, exhibited no outwardly signs of a future serial killer in terms of the MacDonald Triad (bedwetting beyond the age of ten, animal cruelty and pyromania) although it is not to say he did not show antisocial and delinquent behaviour. Shipman did, however, show symptoms associated with other male serial killers in the sense that I believe he suffered from an Oedipal complex as other serial killers tend to exhibit, for example Henry Lee Lucas.

Freud used this term in his theory of the psychosexual stages of development to describe a boy's feelings of desire for his mother and feelings of jealousy and anger towards his father. As already stated, Shipman's mother doted on him and told him he was 'superior' to other children, this would have provided his psychosis with a feeling of empowerment and a grandiose belief that he was more intelligent than others – he was not, however, and had several inadequacies due to being reared in a dysfunctional environment due to the personality of his mother.

Shipman did not have many friends and he would blush when women or other young girls spoke to him, as he was only allowed to socialise with girls his mother specifically picked for him. Until he met his wife, Primrose, his mother was the only woman he really loved as he was not allowed to develop psychologically and socially correctly, and the sexual stages of development became intertwined and confused within his psyche. I believe that over the ensuing years, Shipman eventually began to become jealous of and loathe his own father, who was employed as hosiery warehouseman, as Shipman would have even seen himself intellectually superior to his father due to his profession and see his father as 'inferior'.

Another problem with Shipman's dysfunctional relationship with his mother and father was that his father was perceived as 'weak' and his mother was a dominant matriarch character, and therefore Shipman began to exploit the weak and fear the powerful, and this manifested itself into his psyche and formed a part of his psychosis during his murderous career and his choice of marital partner.

Shipman chose to date and marry the seventeen-year-old, plain, and plump Primrose Oxtoby, who became pregnant. Shipman chose Primrose for several reasons to suit his own psyche and psychological attributes, with the first being that she was an outsider just like him, immature, weak, young and vulnerable. Shipman, possessing flaws within his psyche, knew that somebody such as Primrose was not attractive to other young lads and therefore had no prior sexual relations, and would become wholly reliant upon him once she entered his world, a form of manipulation and control which is a central psychological trait associated with serial killers. Shipman would have enjoyed this as it made him feel 'wanted' and Primrose Oxtoby would serve his psychosis to an even more grandiose narcissistic plane of psychosis. I also believe that Shipman chose Primrose due to the striking similarities between her and his mother, as Primrose looked much older than her seventeen years when they first met, and again she may have been a representation of his mother, and here lies yet another psychological reason for his murders: they provided him with sexual gratification as opposed to a solely financial benefit.

If my hypothesis is correct on the relationship between Shipman and his mother, due to the way she reared him, Shipman may have derived some sexual pleasure from his murders and may have had unnatural sexual desires towards her, and this is further heightened by the following statement from Watson (2004), who mentions an unusual change in Shipman's modus operandi during and after the murder of Kathleen Grundy: *'It is ironic that he was finally brought to justice after he allowed greed to modify his usual modus operandi'*. Shipman began to see the acquisition of wealth as a secondary benefit to his crimes in almost the same way a rapist sees sex as secondary to what they crave the most – *power*.

The primary motive for the crimes committed by Shipman were to exert his power over the victims, for him to try to achieve a sense of equilibrium in his otherwise inadequate psychosis. According to Lynn Scott (2011) when she writes about serial killers and power, she states the following: *'Some serial killers will identify with perceived sources of power, to siphon of some of the feeling of control and omnipotence for themselves. Some will indulge in illusions of religious grandeur, be it Christ or Satan. Others look to the police, and mimic them, as if their borrowed authority gives the killer the authority to kill others.'* In the case of Shipman, he became a doctor as this would provide him with the power and respect that he felt he deserved throughout all his life, which he never achieved through the fault of his mother feeding him a delusional sense of self-worth which led to him ostracising himself from other members of his community during his formative years. The other factor in the case of Shipman is that his mother hated living in working-class areas as she saw the lifestyle below her family, without any real justification why the family should move up the class barriers. Shipman, through his profession, was able to transfer from one social class to the next and again this would have made him feel more important than the average working-class person, who I believe he would have viewed as completely inferior to him, and this is evident when many relatives of the victims said he was rude and aloof with them during their period of grieving, and again this shows

Shipman's psychopathic trait of being completely indifferent to the suffering and pain of others.

Although Shipman may have originally committed his murders predominately to feel 'powerful' over those he was meant to provide a duty of care towards, towards the end of his series of murders he may have wanted more gratification and reward as just the 'thrill' of murder was not enough to gratify his narcissistic personality any longer. Watson (2004) states: *'Shipman was unusual in that his original motive was not money, but those inner demons that drive the serial killer. His choice of profession enhanced his ability to not only to kill, but to remain undetected for so long. It is ironic that he was finally brought to justice after he allowed greed to modify his usual modus operandi.'* The murder that Watson is referring to is the murder of Kathleen Grundy when Shipman tried to forge her will. Shipman was motivated to kill for different reasons, however, as Shipman was killing undetected and with an unusually high frequency, and he was simply getting away with murder, I believe that every patient was a potential victim and once Shipman had them in their own homes and at his mercy the risk to the victim was extremely high as Shipman could simply choose if they lived or died at his own behest.

As Harold Shipman masqueraded as a family practitioner and a caring authority figure within the community, he had acquired the complete trust of each victim. I am therefore concluding that each respective victim suffered from a great deal of risk as Harold Shipman is somebody you would not expect to be a serial killer and in turn, this allowed Shipman to take the risks he did when killing his victims.

Shipman took huge levels of risk in killing his victims for a variety of reasons. Firstly, if an autopsy had been conducted on any of his 215 known victims, then the toxicology reports would have concluded that there was an element of 'foul play' involved, and as Shipman was the doctor issuing the death certificates suspicion would have almost instantly been cast upon him. Shipman also began trying to commit fraud alongside his crimes and therefore this becomes a huge risk, as many people who die usually leave their estates and personal belongings to the surviving relatives and this was evident in the murder of the eighty-one-year-old Kathleen Grundy, whose daughter, Mrs Angela Woodruff, became suspicious when another legal firm contacted her, and they confirmed that they were unhappy with the way they received instructions for probate of Mrs Grundy's estate.

Shipman had forged the will of Mrs Grundy to leave him her estate worth more than £380,000, but he had failed to declare the second property Mrs

DR HAROLD FREDERICK SHIPMAN

Grundy had owned as he was not aware that she had the second estate. This led to the beginnings of building a prosecution case against him, as suspicion for the first time was being cast upon his behaviour. Had the second property not been in the possession of Mrs Grundy, Shipman would have continued to simply kill unabated. The probate instruction led to his own downfall and allowed the police to investigate several other strange deaths associated with Dr Harold Shipman, which became easy to attribute to him as the sequence of acts before the death of a patient were to be too alike to be simply 'coincidental'.

The sequence of the acts before the killings would be that Shipman would visit the victim in their own home and administer deadly doses of morphine or other medicine which would kill the victim. Shipman would then provide a false diagnosis of why the patient died. Shipman would visit some of the patients even if they were not on the home-visit roster, which should have raised concerns when the patient died. Shipman again showed his psychopathic tendencies and his utter contempt for the feelings of others after several of the murders. For example, after the murder of Lizzie Adams, her daughter, Dorothy Thorley had asked Shipman for a post-mortem, which he declined (even though Mrs Adams was in good health and died suddenly) telling her there was no need for a post-mortem as he knew what was wrong with her, and that she 'should have visited her daughter more often', a response which naturally caused Mrs Thorley distress and again displays Shipman's psychopathic and narcissistic personality in full. Shipman would falsify computer records of the patient's illnesses (whilst not realising that computers kept a record of previous data entered).

The acts usually would range from a few minutes to the maximum of one hour to commit the murder. However, Shipman could be at the patient's houses for up to an hour after the murder had been concluded. This may be because Shipman was enjoying his 'work' watching the victim taking their last breaths, as this would have made him feel even more empowered as in this situation he became 'God', and nobody would ever doubt him.

A witness at one of the murders who found Marie West dead (the witness was hiding in the kitchen to not interrupt) stated that Shipman went upstairs and seemed shocked to find her in the kitchen. It was confirmed after his arrest that the police found several items that belonged to the victims, and these would have served a psychological purpose for Shipman as they would have acted as 'trophies'. Many serial killers take trophies to retain a power or form of control over that victim, and they can also help the killer relive the murder and the fantasy again and again. It is not known whether Shipman became sexually stimulated by the murders. However, as Shipman would not open up to the police about the real motivations for his crimes (again this is Shipman trying to remain in control somehow even though he was not) we can never be 100% sure, but we also cannot 100% rule it out either and I do believe that Shipman developed and inhibited sexual desires towards his own mother and the subsequent murders and 'trophies' did indeed provide him with sexual gratification and I believe that the fact that many of the crime scenes were the victims homes, this afforded his psyche and his 'God' complex that he was all powerful, and I believe that this warrants further investigation as to the places where he chose to kill his victims.

Shipman's crimes were committed within the confines of the victims' homes. However, due to Shipman possessing a grandiose narcissistic personality, he killed one patient, Ivy Lomas, in his own surgery because Shipman felt that she was, according to him, a 'nuisance' who originally checked in for symptoms aligning to pains in her arm. Shipman, before calling Mrs Lomas into his practitioner's room, had falsified records of her death before killing her (this would be later used as evidence against him in court). He claimed that Mrs Lomas had died on the electric cardio graph (ECG) table of a heart attack, and he admitted to having made no attempts to resuscitate her as she was already dead. The police questioned him in his surgery about this murder and took his word for it (again, nobody questioned his behaviour or diagnosis due to his authority). This would have again added to his belief that he was superior to others and he could kill anywhere and get away with murder and to not arouse any suspicions, I believe that Shipman did not alter the crime scenes or pose the bodies of his victims as he believed that nobody would ever question him.

The victims were poisoned and died in almost peaceful states where they were at the time of death, usually in bed or sitting in a chair – the places where Shipman administered his deadly doses. Shipman would not have felt the need to move the body (even though he was a highly organised serial killer), as he felt that nobody would question him when he stated the cause of death. After all, many people would not usually question the diagnosis of the family doctor.

Each victim was found where they were murdered by Shipman, as he did not need to move them to serve his own psychological gratification. The removal of the body is more commonly associated with sexually psychopathic serial killers such as Jerry Brudos or Ted Bundy for them to be able act out fantasies with the dead bodies and be in complete control of the victim in death, or in other words possession and power, which are common themes with the motivations of serial killers. Medical serial killers cannot do this with their prey as it would arouse too much suspicion. However, I would never rule out sexual stimulation whilst they watch their patients take their last breaths. As mentioned previously, I do believe that Harold Shipman was an organised serial killer, and I will provide further analysis on this statement below.

The murders of Harold Shipman where highly organised as he acted as the caring doctor and he would even visit patients in their own homes which other doctors would have found annoying and time consuming. However, we are now aware that Shipman was not being altruistic to the needs of his patients as he was visiting their homes to commit premeditated murder. There are several points during the Shipman murder cases where the motivations are unclear and will never be clear as Shipman is now dead. However, I do believe that they were sexually motivated, and he may have just committed others as the need to kill built up and became consuming within his mind and psyche. The other reasons why you can class Shipman as an organised offender are as follows:

- *Shipman had an extremely high IQ (it was rumoured that he was asked by prison officials to stop partaking in the prison quizzes as he was too intelligent in comparison to other prisoners).*
- *To a degree he was socially adequate in terms of being respected, and he was employed in a profession that is given the upmost respect by the members of the public.*
- *Shipman lived with a partner/wife (Primrose Shipman). Again, this helps a serial killer show society their 'mask of sanity' as they appear just as normal as the next person.*
- *Shipman was a stable father figure to his three sons, Sam, Christopher, and David, who believed that he was innocent right until the end.*
- *Shipman was geographically and occupationally mobile in the sense that his profession took him to Wales, Yorkshire, Hyde and Manchester and it is believed that he began killing at the start of his career. Shipman left the largest body count of any British serial killer and was not even suspected of any crimes for a long period of time as he was forging records, and this, coupled with his profession, helped him to get away with his heinous acts of criminality for so long.*

PEN PROFILES OF THE OFFENDERS

- *Organised serial killers are usually college educated, and as we know Shipman became a doctor, which shows he has a high enough IQ.*
- *Shipman had good hygiene skills and again this shows that he did not suffer from mental health problems, as poor hygiene is associated with a variety of mental disorders such as depression and schizophrenia, and again something that appears 'trivial' helped Shipman become Britain's worst serial killer.*
- *Shipman had diurnal (daytime) habits. Shipman also did visit patients in emergencies during the evening, but most of his victims died during the day – when most relatives would have been at work, just as Shipman was.*
- *Shipman did not seek self-help and/or professional help, as he was a grandiose narcissist and he did not recognise that he had a problem (even though he had touched on psychology as a subject during his medical courses).*
- *Many organised serial killers use a ploy or hold a conversation with the victim before the murder as they are not acting as impulsively as a disorganised serial killer. For example, Ted Bundy pretended to be injured to source a conversation with the victim. John Wayne Gacy knew many of his victims and would take them back to his house to kill them. Shipman would build a rapport with his victims without the lure of alcohol or a ploy because he was their doctor, the man they entrusted with their health, and he became the man that ultimately took their lives.*
- *A general person did not think to question the diagnosis, though if the victim had such a terrible death e.g., a heart attack, why were they sitting upright or lying-in bed looking peaceful? To a degree Shipman left a very controlled crime scene and not many questioned him on his diagnosis.*

Harold Shipman did show several associated signs of being a disorganised serial killer due to the following reasons:

- *He killed near his own home and his place of employment all too frequently, which allowed suspicion to be aroused by some of the other members of the community (however, I believe that because Shipman was killing so many and getting away with it, his psychosis and his sense of self-worth was out of control).*

- *Shipman did not understand computers and that they copy everything on the hard-drive, and this was used as evidence against him in court. The murder of Kathleen Grundy showed again that forensically he was not aware, as he left fingerprints over the typewriter and even tried to claim that 'Mrs Grundy borrowed it from time to time' from him, even though her family knew that it was Mrs Grundy's typewriter.*

Although Shipman, did show some signs of being a disorganised serial killer, the reasons outlined above are too few to even classify him as a 'mixed offender' and when we analyse the crime scenes, Shipman has a unique modus operandi against other organised serial killers as the crimes were not so much staged to taunt the police (as we see with some serial killers) and he did not move the body. He did, however, forge the records and issue death certificates to attempt to cover his tracks and avoid detection, all of which later became his downfall.

Further analysis of crime scenes associated with Shipman tend to show that the position of the bodies where never posed, and they were left in the way they died because Shipman, even though he was a doctor, did not think that anybody would question the position of the body and his diagnosis, and many did not. Had Shipman posed the bodies this may have averted some suspicion away from him.

One can only theorise that the reason Shipman left the bodies in their original position of death is that he may have watched them taking their last breaths to stimulate his own psychosis and heighten his sexual experience whilst watching his victim's struggle. Shipman may have killed some of the victims because they simply had 'annoyed' him, and if possibly any of them questioned his diagnosis, which would have questioned his 'authority' and, it sounds cliché, but Shipman truly was evil to commit acts such as this on the premise that a patient simply 'irritated' him, and possibly Shipman may have killed more than the 215 attributed to him. However, some records of his patients were lost from his early career and therefore the 215 attributed victims are possibly a lot higher than we have accounted for.

The Shipman enquiry found that they believed that Shipman began killing around the year 1975 and therefore he would have been aged 28. This fits in with the study *Serial Killing Myths Versus Reality: A Content Analysis of Serial Killer Movies Made Between 1980 and 2001* by Sarah Scott McCready on behalf of the University of North Texas, when she states, '*The majority of serial killers are white males between the ages of 25 to 34.*' (McCready 2002)

She also cites the work of Rossmo (1995), who states, *'Males were involved in over 90% of serial murders. The average age for a serial killer to begin killing is 27.'* (McCready 2002) Shipman fits into the study perfectly conducted by McCready from his gender, ethnicity, to his age being very close to the average as outlined by Rossmo (1995).

The Shipman report, however, makes no reference to Shipman's normal mundane life away from his crimes. Although this may seem relatively unimportant, when dealing with serial killers and why they commit their crimes, it is an area that should never be overlooked as it can provide key psychological insight into their personality and therefore potential information into the motivations for their crimes. Harold Shipman was married to the first women he ever became intimate with, Primrose Shipman (nee Oxtoby), and I believe that she was chosen to be his wife because she was extremely easy to manipulate and control, as many organised serial killers choose meek and mild people as partners because they become subservient to them, and this provides them with a steady psychological stream of feeling 'powerful' and in 'control', for example, in the relationship of Ted Bundy and Liz Keppell, Bundy would manipulate her and he sought her out based on her personality. Keppell only began 'rebelling' against Bundy when she started having suspicions and seeing e-fits of the killer called 'Ted' in the newspapers and Bundy's insatiable demands for kinky sex began raising the alarm bells for Keppell. The employment of organised serial killers also allows them to throw a cloak of 'normality' and 'respectability' over themselves to avert suspicion of their warped psyche and their criminal behaviours.

The general employment of the offender Harold Shipman had always been within the medical profession. Shipman had previously, in 1975, been sacked from a practice in Lancashire when a pharmacy assistant disclosed to the board of directors that Shipman had been prescribing large quantities of pethidine, a synthetic opiate like morphine, which he had been self-administering to feed his own drug addiction. In February 1976 he was found guilty of the forgery of 8 prescriptions with 67 other similar offences considered, and amazingly he was not struck off by the General Medical Council (GMC) as he had voluntarily checked himself into a drug rehabilitation clinic. The fact that Shipman had prior criminal convictions should have raised alarm bells and stopped him practicing medicine, however, the fact he could continue in the medical profession would he reinforced his psychological beliefs that he was more 'intelligent' than anybody else, a grandiose belief system that would have devastating consequence for so many innocent people.

DR HAROLD FREDERICK SHIPMAN

The psychological characteristics of Harold Shipman are similar of that to other serial killers in the sense that he was a grandiose narcissist and a control freak who believed that he was superior to anybody and everybody. I believe that Shipman, like many serial killers, had maturity problems due to his mother's overbearing and domineering personality, in which she would not allow him to socialise and interact with others, thus convincing him he was different from all the others, when in fact Shipman was as ordinary as the next person, if not sub-ordinary due to his resultant psychological problems.

Forensic psychologist Dr Richard Badcock, who interviewed Shipman to provide the police with an insight into why he killed, told the BBC: *'He (Shipman) was not doing it for excitement, far from it. He was doing it mainly to try and resolve something within himself... to get rid of an anxiety but an anxiety which he might not even have let himself think about.'* (2000). I believe that Shipman was doing it for excitement and for some form of sexual and psychological gratification because, to a degree, as he became older and he went onto university where he witnessed many people leading normal lives, he began to realise that the world was not always the scary place his mother indoctrinated him into believing it was, and once again Shipman was in a state of societal ostracization and a state of social confusion. As Shipman became older he was forced to mature, he began to loathe his mother and yet still retained he his love her at the same time, which caused too much confusion in his already dysfunctional psyche. I believe that when Shipman was killing the elderly women, he was in effect exerting his power over them, the power that he could never exert over his mother. Psychopaths are usually neurotic and exhibit less fear than another person within society and I believe that when Shipman was forging the records/death certificates, in effect this was part of the 'excitement' and at the same time he was stimulating his inept personality.

Leslie (1999), when mentioning Shipman's original dismissal from his first job, provides us with an insight into his personality by stating the following: *'Shipman had been caught, but only because he was careless; next time he would be more careful. This power-crazed control-freak set out to take revenge on the society that refused to acknowledge his ideas and superior intellect.'* Shipman was rude to his own staff and the family of his victims with his narcissistic belief in his superior attitude, the same attitude he would later try to exert onto the police when he was questioned for the murders. As with most serial killers, due to their immaturity, they believe law enforcement and courts are not as intelligent as they are and, in many cases, the opposite belief turns out to be the case.

PEN PROFILES OF THE OFFENDERS

Steve Connor (2001) provides an in-depth account of the interviews with the police after his arrest and his complete contempt and arrogance and his narcissistic personality when he states, '*His arrogance was ultimately his downfall when police used a psychological ploy to break his iron-like conceit during one of the taped interviews conducted after his arrest. The senior policeman in charge of the case deliberately handed over the interview to two less experienced officers, one of whom was a young policewoman, who Shipman evidently held in contempt. The tactic was meant to puncture his feeling of self-importance, which he used to defend himself by answering questions in a pedantic manner to control the course of the interrogation. Throughout the interview, Shipman continued to stare at Marie Snitynksi with a condescending countenance. He thought he had an unassailable intellectual superiority over his interrogators until he was suddenly confronted with unequivocal evidence showing that he had forged computer records.*' Shipman spoke to his solicitor and sank to his knees and began to sob uncontrollably, not through guilt or remorse as he was a narcissistic psychopath, but more likely due to the fact that for the first time in his murderous career he was not in control and his grandiose sense of self-worth proved to be 'false' all along and he was not the superior being anymore and all his control of power had evaporated as the police were firmly in control of Shipman's destiny, the delusion of 'superiority' was shattered. There are too many psychological variables when assessing Harold Shipman that now suggest he was a dangerous predator and potentially a sexual psychopath, however, can anybody in the medical profession really be blamed for him being allowed to continue in his profession? The answer is no because Shipman, like many psychopaths, are cunning and manipulative. In terms of the study of serial killers, Shipman is unique because he appears to the best of our knowledge to not have an extensive criminal past or misdemeanours with the law, which is highly unusual.

Pen Profile

I, Samuel Hodgins, can confirm that I have researched and studied the case and the criminal career of the serial killer, Harold Shipman (Caucasian male) in depth. The earliest known murder of Shipman was committed in 1975 (according to the Shipman enquiry) when Shipman would have been twenty-nine-years old.

DR HAROLD FREDERICK SHIPMAN

The crimes committed by Harold Shipman followed a similar and almost rigid pattern for a serial killer, and even his modus operandi did not change until his final murders. I am therefore classifying the offender as Britain's most prolific serial killer who I believe committed his crimes for power, greed, and sexual stimulation and to serve his incomplete psychological development selfishly at the expense of his innocent victims' lives.

As Shipman committed suicide in Wakefield Prison on January 13th, 2004, only he will ever know the true motivations for his crimes, and we can only theorise and debate with reasoning based on sound psychological theory. I am therefore not trying to offer a psychological profile of an *unknown subject of an investigation (UNSUB)*, in effect I am therefore trying to offer a psychological post-mortem of the offender in question.

The pen profile of the offender is based upon the information contained here within the above profile sheet and I will try to explain in detail my hypothesis as to the motivations and innate desires of Harold Shipman, which in turn I hope will shed new light on the psychological motivations for his crimes seventeen years after his death into his motivations for such heinous acts of criminality.

1. As established throughout the course of the profile, the criminal acts committed by Shipman were of a serial nature. Shipman is Britain's most prolific serial killer with a total known amount of 215 victims, maybe many more. Unfortunately, the truth will never be known exactly how many, or what exactly motivated him to commit the crimes that he did.
2. Shipman knew his victims very well due to his profession as a medical doctor and formed a very professional client-doctor relationship over the years and gained the trust of his patients. Leslie (1999) states: '*In 1993 he (Shipman) left (the Donnybrook Practice), claiming that he could not agree with the ideas of his colleagues, and set up his own one-man practice in Hyde, poaching up to 3,000 patients to guarantee a good income.*' This shows several things with Shipman, firstly he wanted to be in complete control of everything; this is not uncommon with narcissistic psychopathic personalities, and it is also a common psychological trait in serial killers. Shipman had gained the trust of his patients, who thought that he was 'caring' and being 'altruistic' towards them during their times of need. However, Shipman due to his psychopathic tendencies, used them as pawns for his own psychological gratification and to exact his revenge on the Donnybrook Practice for

not agreeing with his method of management, which again was a failed method of management, and Shipman shows the inner child inside him due to his failure to develop correctly as an adolescent.

The total combined age of Harold Shipman's victims was an astonishing 15,900 years old and thus the average age of each victim was 73.9 years old. I will mention later in the profile as to what I believe his motivations were for murder, however, the question is how did Shipman get away with it for so long and why did he predominately target the elderly? I believe that Shipman got away with murder for so long because he was in a profession that commands respect, and most people will trust and obey the word of their doctor as they are reliant upon them for help through periods of sickness and illness.

Professor David Wilson (2006) believes that it was the failure of social protections for the elderly by stating: *'So sadly, here we have Shipman revealing a hitherto hidden reality about the place of the elderly, and the inadequacy of the social protections for that group. Serial killers' prey on the vulnerable – those groups that cannot compete within the structural conditions of patriarchal capitalism; those people who do not feel able to answer back to those whom this structure adorns power – often power of life and death.'* To a degree, I agree with Wilson regarding the capitalist system: some members of society are discarded in the United Kingdom, particularly the elderly. The critical aspect of Wilson's hypothesis is that serial killers will kill when the access and opportunity arise, and this is what David Wilson has always claimed and therefore this is almost contradictory of his own hypothesis. Serial killers will kill in any political or religious climate as they have a psychological purpose to be served from the act of murder. For example, Andrei Chikatilo was a serial killer during the post-war era in which Russia was gripped by Communism and the Russian authorities (including the police and the totalitarian government) claimed that serial killers only existed in the capitalist Western countries such as West Germany, Britain and of course the USA. Hitherto to this hypothesis, I believe that due to Communism and its principle of state control, in the case of Chikatilo, idealistic and fatalistic beliefs left them unprepared to deal with the menace of serial killing, whereas in the Western world the authorities were looking into modern sciences and techniques, e.g. geographical profiling, smallest space analysis etc. to try to counteract what we realised was an ever-growing menace within our societies during the

1970s and 1980s in particular. The state of Iran had a series of women being murdered in 1997 in the city of Tehran by Ali Reza Khoshruy Kuran, aka 'the Tehran Vampire', and Tehran is a very strict Islamic state and Kuran was eventually hanged for his crimes. Serial killers will kill when the opportunity arises regardless of the social, political, or religious climate and therefore to blame either a socialist or capitalist state cannot really explain why serial killers choose their victims.

3. Shipman does not show many of the classic symptoms that we have come to associate with serial killers, for example there is no record of him torturing animals, there are no records to suggest that he suffered from enuresis and there are no records to suggest that he had pyromania. Although there are no such records to suggest that Shipman committed/suffered from any of the symptoms from the MacDonald Triad, it does not necessarily mean that he did not have or suffer from one of these symptoms, as serial killers live in a secretive world from others as they do not wish to be caught or arouse any suspicion.

4. Shipman's background does, however, show some signs that are associated with serial killers in the sense that in most cases there is one parent who is overbearing (in this case it was the mother) and the other parent is placid or weak, and the serial killer learns to manipulate the weak parent but fear the more overbearing parent. Shipman's father treated his kids well and was a loving father by any standards, however, Shipman perceived this as a sign of 'weakness'. The other factor is that Shipman did not bond well with other people, and this carried on from his childhood throughout his adult life, and many serial killers are known to have suffered in this way, e.g. Ed Gein, Jerry Brudos and Jeffrey Dahmer was all seen as 'strange' and many of their peers did not associate with them because their bizarre and strange behaviours meant people did not wish to associate with them. The problem in Shipman's case was that his mother instilled in him that he was 'superior' to others, and a deranged personality such as Shipman's would have placed himself on a higher plane than his peers and others in general (even though I do believe that he would later realise in life to a certain degree that this was not true, ultimately destroying his sense of self-worth).

5. I believe that Shipman suffered from a form of Oedipus complex due to his mother being over domineering towards him. As Shipman was not allowed to socialise with others in his local community and he never dated women, I believe that he began developing innate sexual desires

towards his mother, resultant of not being allowed to socialise with others from an early age, causing him to suffer from neurosis later in life. The reason that I am hypothesising the theory that Shipman did indeed suffer from Oedipus complex is because his mother would not let him socialise from the time, he began infant school (aged four). In Sigmund Freud's psychosexual development stages, Freud believed that the Oedipus complex is formed during stage 3, *the phallic stage,* and as Shipman could not successfully complete that stage, he could not complete stage 4, *latency,* successfully and this is the stage from the age of six to puberty in which the erogenous zone allows sexual feelings to become dominant within his psyche and this is also the stage where sexual unfulfillment develops if fixation arises in this stage. The other issue and common denominator with Shipman and Freud's theory is that somebody being 'mother-fixated' during their adult life can lead to a choice of a sexual partner that resembles the parent of fixation, and Primrose Oxtoby looked much older than her seventeen years old when Shipman met her. I believe that Shipman, in a part of his psyche, hated his mother for not allowing him to have a normal childhood (Shipman was actually seen as a loving father to his own children in later life) but at the same time he was obsessed with her, and I also believe that when he was killing the victims (the majority of whom were older women) he was in fact killing his own mother in order to try to resolve the inner conflict within his own psyche and to attain the power that his mother held over him during her life and even after her death. This theory may sound extreme, however, when dealing with serial killers they usually kill the victims based on inadequacies within their own psyche. For example, the sex killer, Ted Bundy, killed mainly middle-class women as this was the social sphere he could never quite achieve, and his girlfriend from this class left him as he was too immature. Dennis Nilsen killed gay men and admitted to Masters (1985) that when he killed them, he was 'killing himself' (as he loathed his sexuality). The problem with serial killers is that they kill the victims of choice to try to cure their inadequate psyche and it does not make them feel any better; the murder makes them feel worse because the act of killing another human being is an emotionally traumatic experience, witheld it makes them feel more empty as they know their ales are perverse.

6. The Swiss psychologist Carl Jung proposed a theory in 1938 known as the 'shadow aspect'. Jung theorised that the shadow is an unconscious

aspect of the personality which the conscious ego does not identify, because one tends to reject or remain ignorant of the least desirable aspects of one's personality and the shadow is largely negative. Jung also theorised that everybody carried a 'shadow' and the less it is embodied in the individual's conscious life, the blacker and denser it will become within one's psyche. The shadow is linked to man's more primitive animal instincts which are superseded in early childhood by the conscious mind.

Shipman carried a 'shadow', and his primitive instincts came out whilst committing the murders because Shipman had an inferiority complex due to not developing within the normal stages as outlined and theorised by both Erikson and Freud. As Shipman was also a narcissistic control freak, he could not accept that he had flaws within his own personality and therefore convinced his own psyche that he was 'above' others within society, and this is what a psychologist would define as *cognitive dissonance*. Shipman's conscious personality knew that he was, in part, very inadequate in comparison to his peers at a very early age and therefore needed to become 'something' to feel accepted. At the same time, I believe that Shipman's 'shadow' made him believe that he was superior to others, and this would have led to a state of 'disequilibrium' within his own psyche as Shipman could not accept his social standing and the expectations mainly set by his own mother and her upmost belief that Harold was something special in comparison to others.

7. The average age of the known 215 victims of Harold Shipman was 73.9 years. Shipman sought this type of victim for several reasons: they were accessible, and he had the opportunity (access and opportunity is crucial to a serial killer deciding the victim); Shipman chose them as they were vulnerable and they trusted him and many people would believe the word of a doctor. Shipman was changing his *modus operandi* towards the end of his criminal career and he was therefore becoming greedy by beginning to forge wills without understanding the law of wills and trust, which ultimately became his downfall. However, most importantly I believe that he killed the choice of victims he did due to his own innate desires to serve a psychological purpose in the sense that he had seen his mother die and had administered the morphine himself whilst she was ill.

8. I believe that due to Shipman being doted upon by his mother and not being able to develop within the developmental stages with other children at a young age, he blamed his mother for his inadequacies as his

psyche would not allow him to realise his own shortcomings as he was a narcissistic control freak. I believe that Shipman had conflicting emotions of both love and hatred towards his mother and I believe that Shipman would have experienced this at a very early age. As Shipman was not allowed to develop within the normal stages of both psychosocial and psychosexual development, I believe that Shipman harboured innate sexual feelings towards his mother and Shipman knew that this was wrong and again his hate began to consume his psyche and this would ultimately lead to his main choice of victim, elderly people – it was a rarity that Shipman killed anybody of a younger age and most of his victims were elderly women.

9. Serial killers choose victims to destroy the thing that they hate the most and blame for their problems as they are trying to resolve the inadequacies within their own psyche. For example, Ted Bundy, who always wanted to achieve middle-class status, killed pretty and well-educated middle-class women; Ed Gein, who, like Shipman, had conflicting emotions towards his mother, killed three women and dug up corpses from the Plainfield Cemetery who resembled Augusta Gein. Ian Brady, who never had a stable childhood and was shipped from home to home, ended up killing five children with Myra Hindley, and John Wayne Gacy killed young men because he hated himself for being homosexual which his father severely disapproved of. With this information, and due to the psychology of Harold Shipman, I believe that the victims and patients in general experienced an extremely high level of risk once with Shipman, and even younger people, as Shipman could kill at any time and due to his psychopathy, he had no qualms about doing it if somebody offended him.

10. In further reference to the above statement, I believe that had Shipman understood law and the registry of probate after death and Shipman had not assumed that Mrs Kathleen Grundy only had one estate (Shipman made no reference to the second estate in the forged will), then I believe that he would have continued to commit murder after murder. The reason I believe that Harold Shipman would have continued to kill is that the known victims he killed from 1993 onwards appear to remain at a steady pace of increase, for example in 1993 he was believed to have taken the lives of fifteen people (including two in one day), and then in 1994 he took eleven lives. After these years we begin to see a larger number of victims, which is unusually high, even for a serial killer. In

1995 he took the lives of 28 people; in 1996 he took the lives of 30; in 1997 he took the lives of 37 people and in 1998 up until June 24th he managed to take the lives of 18 people before his arrest.

The emerging pattern was that Shipman was increasing his number of murders and he was getting away with them, which undoubtedly made him feel empowered and 'invincible' as he was forging death certificates and was literally getting away with murder. As he was a grandiose narcissist he would have believed that he was uncatchable, and as Watson (2004) noted, Shipman altered his *modus operandi* this may well be because he was a psychopath and needed more stimulation from the act of murder, because murder for Shipman was becoming sometimes a daily routine, and therefore the act of murder in itself wasn't stimulating Shipman any longer as it had become as routine as any other mundane task.

Shipman also had a lack of knowledge of forensic science in the sense that the forged will of Kathleen Grundy was typed up on his typewriter, the same typewriter his fingerprints were all over, and he even tried to claim that he borrowed the typewriter to Mrs Grundy. The toxicology reports from the exhumation of Mrs Grundy found that there were fatal overdoses of morphine which indicated that Shipman was the killer, amazingly Shipman tried to claim that Mrs Grundy was a drug addict and yet when the police searched her home there was no drug taking paraphernalia (Whittle and Ritchie 2005). The hard-drive at the surgery also found that Shipman had been forging records and he was unaware that the hard-drive made a backup of every entry on the system. Although Shipman was a highly organised serial killer, he did not research the methods of how his own ilk had been caught by and became extremely careless and sloppy; many serial killers get caught by their own sloppiness, as opposed to some genius police work. For example, Brady and Hindley, after years of Brady grooming David Smith, Brady wanted Smith to partake in the murder of Edward Evans, which Smith ultimately witnessed and unsurprisingly told the police; Ted Bundy was another organised serial killer, who smoked marijuana and drank beer and then decided to drive his car with a broken taillight; the arresting office found Bundy's rape kit in the boot and booked him; Fred and Rose West kept making 'jokes' that their daughter, Heather West, was under the patio, and social services alerted DCI Hazel Savage, who pushed for a warrant for 25 Cromwell Street. All the serial killers mentioned, including Shipman, have one thing in common – the innate desire for the feeling of complete power becomes all-consuming within their psyche. All of them had killed many times before without getting caught and it becomes routine, and they believed that they would continuously get away with murder and they were all wrong.

11. Due to Shipman being a narcissistic control freak and his belief that he was superior to others, I believe that a very important personality variable in his psyche was that he believed that he had a *locus of control*, and therefore he believed that he was always in charge of his own destiny. Putwain and Sammons (2002, p. 24), cite Rotter (1966) when they claim that *'Individuals with an internal locus of control tend to believe that things happen and/or happen to them largely because of their own actions.'* Shipman was that confident he would never be caught, hence the claims that Mrs Grundy was a drug addict and that she borrowed his typewriter. When Shipman was finally confronted with the evidence of forged computer records, he broke down in the interview room, as this was the first time in his whole murderous career that he was no longer in control and his power had been vanquished.

12. It has been established throughout the course of the profile that the crimes committed by Harold Shipman were of a serial nature, that strangely began with the 'thrill' of murder only and progressed to greed. After researching the crimes of Harold Shipman in depth, I believe that his murderous career intertwines within four categories of serial murder as outlined by Lane and Gregg (1992), as I believe that Shipman would fall into the following serial killer categorisations; *hedonistic; power-seeking and gain*, as outlined numerously during this profile.

13. Lane and Gregg (1992) classify the *hedonistic* killers as *'A complex category incorporating the types of killer for whom, in its broadest sense, "pleasure" is the reward of murder.'* I believe that Shipman enjoyed the act of killing firstly through the power he gained from the act due to his narcissistic personality, and the fact that he decided if these patients lived or died. I secondly believe that he enjoyed deceiving the relatives of the victims, as this act became part of the 'enjoyment' of the murder process in the fact that nobody from other medical staff, the police or relatives on most occasions never questioned him, and this would have provided his ego with a sense of 'superiority', as he would have believed that he had outwitted everybody. I also believe that he took pleasure in killing the victims due to his childhood experiences with his mother as

he was killing what he 'hated', but at the same time what he also 'loved', and this was paradoxical throughout Shipman's career in the sense that many of the patients he killed had known and trusted him for years and had even followed him from Donnybrook Practice to his own surgery. The other reason why I believe that he was a *hedonistic* killer is the fact that year upon year his victim count keeps increasing, and this is only what we know of from the Shipman enquiry.

14. Lane and Gregg (1992) define the *power-seeking* killers as; *'A common complication among personalities showing low self-esteem is the desire to have control over the life and death of others to such a degree that it serves as an intrinsic motive to murder.'* I fundamentally believe that Shipman had very low self-esteem, and this was evident in his drug use during the beginning of his career, as it became a way of coping with the inadequacies within his psyche and personality. The act of playing 'God' over a victim was intrinsic to Shipman and we can all theorise as to why he murdered, but we will never fully know the answer as Shipman would not confess and committed suicide, which I believe was his final act of power (I will mention more about his suicide at the end of the profile).

15. Lane and Gregg (1992) define the *gain* killers as; *'Comfort-orientated killers, gain killers exhibit the comparatively rare motive among serial killers of personal, usually financial, acquisition. For this type of killer, the act of killing is an incidental, often irksome, necessity in the pursuit of some other goal. Clearly a sociopathic outlook which has reduced humankind to "objecthood" is a prerequisite for this type of killer, but an outward respectability and believability that will deflect suspicion from a theoretically obvious suspect is essential.'* Shipman only just fits into this category due to the murder of Kathleen Grundy, as he had forged the will to inherit one of her estates. The other two British serial killers who fall into this rare classification are George Hague, aka the 'Acid Bath Killer', and Joseph Smith, aka the 'Brides in the Bath Killer', however, the latter two killed far less than Shipman and were apprehended much quicker due to both failing in their professions and arousing suspicion on themselves. Shipman did arouse suspicion, which was dismissed by fellow medical professionals and the police at the time, and bizarrely it was a taxi driver who first raised concerns about Harold Shipman. Shipman managed to deflect suspicion away from him because of his profession as most people do trust their doctor or another figure of authority, e.g., a policeman, with their lives.

PEN PROFILES OF THE OFFENDERS

16. Lane and Gregg (1992) define the *post-kill phase* as; 'For most serial killers the passing of the experience of killing results in a feeling of emptiness and depression, often aggravated by realization that primary "defect" in the psyche (the restrictive childhood, rejection by female peers etc.) has not been repaired by the act of killing, and the killer will be obliged to take more and more lives in search of temporary relief.' Shipman may have also killed to try to gain some temporary relief as there are instances contained within the Shipman report where he killed more than one person in a day on several occasions.
17. Although it has been established that Shipman was an organised serial killer, I would also classify him as a 'signature killer', even though this does not appear obvious to somebody who is not trained or has no knowledge of the way serial killers operate. Harold Shipman can be classed as a signature killer because his victims were in the majority elderly women; they were predominately Caucasian people; many of them were from the working-class socio-economic group. It must be remembered that in the cycle of serial murder(s) that the victim is the end of the cyclical process that a killer goes through, as the victim will be chosen to serve some psychological purpose for the killer. For Harold Shipman, although he did not pose the bodies like other well-known serial killers such as Albert DeSalvo, his signature was to overdose them with morphine and leave them all sitting in a chair or lying in their beds, in an almost sleep-like comatose state as described by witnesses. I am therefore stating that due to Shipman's narcissism, despite being a doctor, he left the victims in this way after death as he believed that nobody would question him about the way the victim had died, thus in effect becoming his unique 'signature'.
18. Shipman was arrested in 1998, 24 years since Robert Ressler from the FBI first coined the term 'serial killer'. By the time Harold Shipman was arrested, the 'image' of a serial killer had been seared into the minds of people through media portrayals, such as the 1990 blockbuster movie *The Silence of the Lambs*. Many people would have associated serial killers as people who abduct people on the street, for example Ted Bundy, and therefore a doctor would have been the least likely person that would have been categorised or thought of as a serial killer, even though the study of serial murder was a mainstream subject in colleges and universities, and in modern police work was becoming common practice/ knowledge, e.g., criminal profiling and forensic science was used

routinely by police for the purpose of an investigation. I do not believe that Shipman would have been caught if he had not changed his *modus operandi*. Shipman was killing undetected for so long because many people will automatically trust a figure of authority such as a doctor. The other problem with the case of Harold Shipman was the fact that because there were no corpses dumped in a field, for example, nobody suspected that they had a serial killer on their hands, and the taxi driver who raised concerns was dismissively told to not waste police time as Harold Shipman was a respected member of the community and Shipman had even appeared on the ITV show *World in Action*. The other problem was before the Shipman murders became known another doctor did not have to countersign a death certificate, which meant that Shipman could provide any diagnosis he wished. All this, coupled with Shipman's profession, allowed him to kill again and again without arousing much suspicion, and therefore this is the reason I believe that the environment was right for Harold Shipman to kill undetected for so long.

19. After studying the case of Dr Harold Shipman in great depth, I believe that he is possibly the most organised serial killer I have studied over the past several years. Harold Shipman falsified records, he played on people's trust, and despite an obvious lack of medical knowledge to pursue his murderous agenda, he used his esteemed and trusted profession to commit 215 murders and he was above average intelligence. Shipman thought that nobody would ever question him – and very few ever did, and even police officers took his word on the final diagnosis of some patients. It almost sounds paradoxical, but Shipman left the biggest body count of any serial killer in British history and hardly anybody realised, including staff from the medical profession, that they were completely given the wrong diagnosis by Dr Shipman and that he should have warranted further investigation. To quote Charles Bauldelaire; *'The greatest trick the devil ever played was convincing the world that he did not exist.'* I feel this sums up Harold Shipman unequivocally as Shipman was a narcissistic psychopath, who was not suffering from any form of mental illness and killed to serve his own psychological fallacies with complete and utter disregard for his initial victims and their families, and of course he was highly regarded and trusted by many members of his own community.

20. To sum up the profile of Harold Shipman, I am concluding that he was a narcissistic psychopath and killed for 'pleasure', and I do believe that

some of the crimes may have had a sexual element to them and, had he never been caught, I believe that he would have killed many more throughout his career as his murders were escalating year upon year and were becoming more frequent, and sometimes he killed two in one day. This sheds confusion upon the FBI definition that a serial killer will have a 'cooling-off period' in between each murder. However, the complex psychology and motivations of an individual human being will also apply to the complex psychology of an individual serial killer: what motivates one will not necessarily motivate another. Leslie (2004) states: *'At 6:20am on January 13th, 2004, Fred ripped up bed sheets, fashioned them into a rope that he fixed to the bars on the cell window, formed the other end into a noose and hanged himself. He was pronounced dead at 8:10am. He killed himself so Primrose would become entitled to a full National Health Service pension.'* I, on the contrary, believe that Shipman killed himself as a final act of power over the victims, the police, the government, and society. When dealing with serial killers a central part of their psychology is the motive of 'power', and I believe that Primrose receiving a state NHS pension was a convenience as Shipman was a narcissistic control freak both in life and ultimately in death.

Peter Sutcliffe, The Yorkshire Ripper

Peter Sutcliffe was born on the 2 June 1946 into the slums in post-war Britain to an abusive father and a caring mother, and was the eldest of the children, yet the seemingly innocuous child would develop into a monster that Britain had not seen since the series of killings committed by Jack the Ripper. Peter Sutcliffe committed a known thirteen murders and at least seven attempted murders in the north of England between October 1975 and November 1980, averaging four victims per year, therefore based on this knowledge, I believe that Sutcliffe fits into the FBI definition of a serial killer: '*The unlawful killing of two or more victims by the same offender(s) in separate events.*' Sutcliffe is now a reviled monster in the annals of criminal history and Britain hopes and prays that it does not witness anything on this scale again in the future, however, we need to firstly assess his modus operandi and work backwards to establish a motivation for his crimes and criminal acts.

The criminal acts committed by Peter Sutcliffe have already been established as those of a serial nature. The *modus operandi* that he would use is to approach a victim under the pretence that he wants 'business' with the sex worker in the vast majority of cases (excluding some victims, e.g. Jayne MacDonald, who was not a sex worker), after which they would enter his car and he would take them to a secluded spot where he would proceed to strike them from behind, rendering them powerless to fight back or escape from his evil clutches and will. Sutcliffe would proceed to strike them several times until the victims were dead and he would proceed to brutally and excessively stab the already deceased victim. The way Sutcliffe killed his victim is what criminal psychologist and forensic experts brand as 'overkill' and this shows that Sutcliffe harboured misogynistic rage against his helpless victims.

The peculiar part of each crime scene is that Sutcliffe only had penetrative sex with one victim, Helen Rytka, and he would usually pull the victim's bra up above her breasts and lower the clothing, thus exposing the vaginal area.

He would proceed to masturbate over the dead victim, and this was down to Sutcliffe's fantasies of possessing a dead woman as he felt completely inadequate and shy around them, Sutcliffe, I believe, suffered from impotence, and more than likely he had not developed within the normal stages of sexual development, which was a dangerous cocktail when coupled with his misogynistic rage.

I believe that the motivation for his crimes arose within his psyche over a long period of time, since he developed into a social inadequate, which in part was due to the domineering patriarchal lifestyle his father wanted Peter to follow. Peter's personality was nothing like that of his father. During his prepubescent and adolescence stage of development, according to reports from family members, Peter was a quiet, shy boy, who preferred to stay indoors with his mother rather than join in the rough and tumble games of his younger brothers and sisters. He preferred to read than play sport and was greatly intimidated by his father's masculinity. Peter found a haven in his mother, a gentle loving woman who adored all her six children and doted on Peter. This is a common trait amongst many serial killers in the sense that they learn to hate authority and manipulate kindness, and this creates mass confusion within their psychosis as the lines between morality do not become blurred, it ceases to exist in its entirety with ultimately tragic consequences.

Peter Sutcliffe attempted to murder a sex worker in 1973, according to his friend, Trevor Birdsall, when one night Peter left him in the car for a few minutes and, upon his return to the car, Peter informed him that he tried to hit a sex worker with a brick hidden in a sock, however, the brick fell out as he tried to hit her (Steel, 2012). Over the years Peter Sutcliffe has been suspected of more murders, including murders in Tamworth, West Midlands. This is not uncommon with serial killers, because they are always suspected of more murders and never admit them to the police as they like to retain some sense of 'control' even after being incarcerated for life or facing death row. Sutcliffe has possibly killed more than the thirteen victims he was convicted for, as the Yorkshire Ripper murders began in 1975 when Sutcliffe would have been 29 years of age, and a serial killer does not begin killing suddenly as they move towards middle age. The opposite is true as it is believed that as their testosterone slows down, so do the killings, and therefore it would have been worth the police trying to speak to Sutcliffe regarding these murders before his death in November 2020, to try and solve murders that fit his criminal profile in terms of victimology, psychology and modus operandi all fitted Sutcliffe's offender profile perfectly. Unfortunately, as Sutcliffe has now passed, it may well have been the last opportunity to solve these cases and allow the surviving family members some closure after five decades of living in hell.

Sutcliffe's first attempts at murder where unsuccessful, when he tried to kill Anna Rogulskyj and Olive Smelt, as Steel (2012) states; *'Sonia Sutcliffe suffered a miscarriage, and it was not long after this that Peter made his first reported attack.'* I am therefore led to believe that Sutcliffe committed his crimes due to a very severe misogynistic rage against women, in the sense that he felt throughout his life they had failed him, e.g., Sutcliffe was socially inadequate with women and became shy, and did not share any sexual relation with a woman until his early twenties when he met Sonia Szurma (later Sonia Sutcliffe). Sutcliffe would feel more isolated and alone and possibly felt that once again a woman had 'let him down' when his mother died in 1978 from heart disease at the age of 59. Peter became grief stricken and blamed his father for her death, who had many affairs during his marriage to Kathleen Sutcliffe, and I believe that Sutcliffe began to believe that all women were 'evil', and the anger and rage fermented in his psychology to hate women for what they put his mother through. He would have hated his father, and yet due to his childhood experiences he would not have confronted his father. Sonia Sutcliffe having suffered from a miscarriage only heightened Peter's warped psychosis that women were against him and therefore the rage consumed his psyche for him to become a serial killer. I believe that the rage that Sutcliffe inhibited within his psyche was borne out against his victims when evaluating the crime scenes and their grotesque details and specifics.

The actual crime scene(s) would suggest a serial killer acting on impulse rather than an organised offender who would be selecting a victim(s) to fulfil a fantasy, as sex workers and runaways are victims of convenience for serial killers, as these people have dropped out of society.

The way a trained investigator could have established that the killer was disorganised is firstly the way he bludgeoned each victim with a blunt instrument, for example in his first known murder of Wilma McCann, who he struck with a hammer twice and then stabbed fourteen times in the lungs and throat; this shows rage against the victim, and many disorganised serial killers exhibit 'overkill'.

The second murder of Emily Jackson shows a disorganised killer again as she was bludgeoned and stabbed 52 times with a screwdriver, at this crime scene there was also further forensic evidence, such as the size 7 work-boot footprint, and again, in the murder of his third victim, Irene Richardson, there was a tyre mark made by two India Autoway tyres which matched Sutcliffe's work vehicle. Again, this shows the police investigation was in disarray as the police were overworked and were not prepared for the level of interest from the media and public which was the biggest of its kind since the Jack the Ripper slayings in London back in 1888.

The fourth murder (Tina Atkinson) again showed that the killer was disorganised, as a bloody footprint was found at the bottom of the bed, and this murder also suggests that he was now not just marauding in the city of Leeds but he was now commuting outwards, and this is evident again in his seventh murder of Jean Jordan, who he murdered in Manchester, and again in this murder he left a new crisp five-pound note which could be traced back to the bank, who in turn could trace what company it was sent to.

In terms of the murders being away from Leeds, this showed a growing confidence in the criminal's behaviour and that he also knew that he was more likely to be caught if he perpetrated his crimes in one area and, therefore, he was becoming a bit more organised in that sense. The sixth murder of Jayne MacDonald, who he murdered in an open park, changed the public's view on the killings as Jayne MacDonald was not a sex worker, and the public became enraged and fearful now as the sex workers were not seen as 'victims' by the public due to the nature of their trade. However, this is an absurd prejudiced view as they are still human beings that warrant help and support from society.

The murder of Jayne MacDonald suggests further disorganisation, as he could easily have been seen by another member of the public walking through the park, or somebody looking out of a house window could have spotted him from all the houses that surrounded the park, which also suggests that Sutcliffe was a high-risktaker during his crimes, which is also a very common trait with disorganised serial killers.

The ninth murder victim, Josephine Whittaker, had a bite mark on her left breast, which shows signs of sexual sadism and indicates that the killer was highly dangerous and was not forensically aware, as this is further evidence that could be used in gaining a conviction as *forensic odontology* has helped convict serious offenders in other cases – most notably Ted Bundy in the murder cases of Margaret Bowman and Lisa Levy in the Oregon State murders. Although Bundy was highly organised and studied the FBI's techniques on how they attempted to detect and capture serial killers, due to their nature and aggression, they lose control of their impulses and a sense of rationality during their crimes, and with advancements in forensic science it is easier to secure a conviction. Sutcliffe was highly enraged during the murder of Josephine Whittaker, and it was used as evidence against him in the court trial. The rage exhibited against Josephine Whittaker and the other victims is an outwardly manifested behaviour that lived within his psyche and developed over time, and further assessment of the victims of Peter Sutcliffe are completely warranted to gain a greater understanding of his psyche and psychosis, which led to the commission of his heinous crimes.

Many of Sutcliffe's victims were sex workers, however, not all of them were sex workers, as Jayne MacDonald was a sixteen-year-old shop assistant, Josephine Whittaker was a nineteen-year-old building society clerk from Halifax and Barbara Leach was due to begin her third and final year reading social psychology. The majority were sex workers, and yet the common denominator with all the victims (other than gender) is that they were victims of opportunity, and access and opportunity is a factor usually determining whether a serial killer will kill a potential victim.

The victims were not subjected to sexual penetration from the offender, and yet many were posed in a crude way, exposing their breasts and vaginal area, and some of the victims were sexually degraded in the vaginal area with a screwdriver (Josephine Whittaker) or a piece of wood (Emily Jackson). Although to the untrained investigator this will appear to be the act of a warped mind, and to a degree this is a correct assumption, the way he (Sutcliffe) posed the victims after their demise, and the use of such items used to penetrate the victims, shows signs of an Oedipal complex, as the items are of a phallic (penis-shaped) nature, and the fact that he struggled to have sex with them shows that he was substituting actual intercourse with an object, and this act is therefore showing sexual immaturity. It is also a psychological clue that the offender is suffering from a form of severe misogyny within his psychosis if we analyse these types of acts and link it with the excessive overkill of the victim(s) and therefore further investigation of Sutcliffe's offending behaviour is warranted as his victims became the end of a pattern that manifested itself within his psyche over his early life through to the ultimate act of the murders themselves.

Although I have unequivocally stated that I believe that Peter Sutcliffe falls in the bracket of a 'disorganised serial killer', I do, however, believe that Sutcliffe's crimes were entirely calculated and he knew his actions were entirely wrong and he was not suffering mental impairment due to the way he deliberately sought out a vulnerable victim, e.g. he had previously spotted Wilma McCann in a drunken state and knew that she would not offer much resistance; Jayne MacDonald was alone in a dark field in the dead of night, and again this allowed him the two most important factors for a serial killer to be able to conduct their crimes, *access* and *opportunity*.

Although Sutcliffe claimed that 'God' had sent him on a mission to rid the world of sex workers, I believe that the reason he killed them was because he had a paranoid constitution with a personality disorder, formed during his adolescence, impelling him to kill them because of the pain that 'loose women' had brought upon his mother before her death, and the rage became all-consuming within him and he was using a sense of cognitive dissonance to justify his criminal behaviour. I believe that Sutcliffe, despite his claims and his mental alignments, knew what he was doing was wrong.

I also believe that, over time, Sutcliffe began believing that any women he encountered in the north of England was a 'whore' in his warped psychosis, and therefore he began killing (or in some cases attempted to) as an act of 'revenge' on his mother's 'behalf': his mother was the only woman other than Sonia that he dearly loved. Sutcliffe's last victims towards the end of his series of murders/attempted murders were not sex workers, for example the final three murders of Barbara Leach (university student), Marguerite Walls (civil servant) and Jacqueline Hill (student), and therefore I have stated the above hypothesis. I also believe that Sutcliffe was killing indiscriminately due to his hedonism from all the press coverage, and secondly, I believe that he also knew that with persistent interest from the police, the game was almost up, and it was a matter of time before he was finally arrested and caught. Due to the interest from the public, the police, and the media, although the initial fantasies that dwelled within his psyche were the initial motivations for the commission of his crimes, I believe that he became obsessed with the coverage, and this acted as a secondary motivation for him to commit his crimes.

I believe that the murders committed by Peter Sutcliffe were committed primarily from a sexual and a personal motivation. In the sense that each murder was personal, I believe that Sutcliffe felt that killing the women he hated was in his psychosis an act of misguided 'revenge' for all those times he had seen his mother suffer from the love affairs that his father would have with other women, as Sutcliffe developed a world whereby all women were 'whores', which is not the case. However, as Sutcliffe suffered from a personality disorder, mental ailments, his rage fused together to bring death to all those innocent women. Sutcliffe also hated his father and yet he could never express his hatred towards him as he still yearned to impress him.

In terms of the act of masturbating over the corpse whilst exposing the breasts, this was not only an act of sexual desire, it was also a way of exercising his power over the deceased, the power that he had never had in any other part of his life. The murder of Jacqueline Hill does suggest some signs of mental disturbance in the sense that when he was asked by the police why he had stabbed her in the eye, he replied, *'She seemed to be looking at me reproachfully, so I drove the blade into her eye.'* (Wilson and Wilson, 2006). If the eyes are 'the window to the soul', as many religious scholars persistently claim, then Sutcliffe, due to his Catholic upbringing, may have felt some remorse for this murder, or he was paranoid during his evil frenzy, and possibly highly sexually excited at the time, that she was 'watching' his evil and twisted sexual actions, and therefore the act of stabbing the eye could have been (in his mind) a way of diminishing his guilt, or to stop her from 'looking' at him whilst passing into the afterlife.

As Sutcliffe manifested a severe form of misogynistic rage, he would take his chosen victims to isolated spots where it was unlikely, he would be disturbed (although in some instances he was, which this shows another form of disorganisation), and due to the sexual savage nature involved with the crimes, the victims experienced high levels of risk, and this is evident by the grotesquery and savagery that he used against his victims.

I also believe that the victims were exposed to a high level of risk due to the way he subdued them by hitting them with a hammer, and therefore giving them no chance to plead for their lives, as we do see in some cases on the odd occasion the serial killer can feel empathy towards the victim and allow them to live. Sutcliffe had no intention of this, as he desired a subdued and dead victim for his own twisted sexual fantasies and sexual gratification. Although it is highly unlikely a serial killer will allow a victim to live, there have been cases of 'Stockholm Syndrome' working, most recently the case of Carl Powell and Jessica Pryce, in Nottingham, England. Ms Pryce managed to build a repartee with Powell, and it was something as simple as the following: *'I don't usually smoke, but when he lit a cigarette I asked for a drag, if only so he could see I had something in common with him.'* (Mackay, 2013) Ms Pryce's act and quick thinking possibly saved her life, unlike Sutcliffe's victims, whom he rendered defenceless. There would be no chance of dialogue and therefore no opportunity to plead for mercy. I do believe that Sutcliffe needed to render these women unconscious, because a submissive victim was the fantasy that had been building up over time, and therefore he could not allow himself to see them as fellow human beings and this fantasy meant Sutcliffe would undergo great risks to fulfil the fantasies of murder and sexual fantasies that were causing excessive stress and pressure within his psyche.

Sutcliffe took a high level of risk as he killed his victims in very public places, albeit very dark and very secluded. However, they were places that the sex workers were familiar with and would take their clients, and again this shows that he was a highly disorganised serial killer in this respect, as he could easily have been caught and/or recognised with a murdered sex worker, due to his distinctive appearance.

In the murder of Yvonne Pearson, for example, Sutcliffe hit her whilst in his car as she was climbing into the backseat of his car (this act alone is risky due to the amount of forensic evidence left), another car almost immediately pulled up alongside him. The murder of Jean Jordan again shows his risk-taking behaviour, as car headlights appeared in the distance whilst he was bludgeoning her to death all the while his car was on the other side of the road, and again this is high-risk taking behaviour because the police began taking the case more seriously after Jayne MacDonald was murdered, as she was not a sex worker and this caused public outrage and placed pressure on the police to bring the unknown perpetrator to justice for his crimes. In this instance, if the car was a police patrol car and an officer knew this was an area frequented by sex workers and their clients, they could have investigated further, and Sutcliffe may have been apprehended there and then.

Peter Sutcliffe's level of risk is higher than that of an organised serial killer in the sense that an organised serial killer does not usually leave as much evidence at the scene and will sometimes use a 'base of operation', e.g., John Haigh used his 'workshop' in London (which was a rented basement) and John Wayne Gacy killed young boys and buried them under the floorboards of his house. When serial killers are organised, they are very careful of outdoor spots as they know that the chance of them being spotted is virtually zero. For example, Ted Bundy used the Colorado Hills and very rural and isolated areas to perform heinous acts against his victims, and the Moors Murderers used Saddleworth Moor, as they knew that they and their victims would be the only souls on there. Sutcliffe on the other hand was using intersections and areas of land where the public could pass by and the sex workers could perform sex acts on their 'clients', again showing Sutcliffe to be a very impulsive and disorganised serial killer and this is evident when assessing the sequence of acts before and after the killings of his victims.

Sutcliffe would usually drive around the red-light districts of Yorkshire and the north of England in order to find a sex worker on her own, usually in a state of intoxication brought about by substance misuse and lure them into his vehicle under the pretence that he wanted 'business' in the form of a sexual favour. He would proceed to take them to a secluded spot and bludgeon, mutilate and commit perverse sexual acts over their corpses.

Sutcliffe inadvertently created an alibi for himself in the murder of Jayne MacDonald, as he had spent the night drinking in pubs with friends. The murder of Jean Jordan was on the 9 October 1977, and he and his wife Sonia held a party at their house after which Sutcliffe had dropped home friends, and therefore, despite being a suspect and the police being inundated with work and following leads, Sutcliffe was not pursued more vigorously as a suspect in the case. Sutcliffe would go home and clean his blood-stained clothes, and in the murder of Helen Rytka returned the knife to the kitchen draw after cleaning it, as he thought he was 'covering' his tracks, although he had left much more evidence at each respective crime scene. This, I believe, shows that he was not suffering from delusions, and that he was in fact a cold and callous murderer who knew he was committing heinous criminal acts, and although he showed many signs of a *disorganised* serial killer, he did exhibit some signs of the *organised* serial killer, in this instance in terms of showing premeditation and a high degree of calculation prior to his crimes and therefore in the case of Peter Sutcliffe, we need to assess the acts of murder themselves as the times and locations began to vary as he became a more accomplished serial killer.

The acts of murder and mutilation could vary in how long each individual crime took to commit due to mitigating circumstances. For example, sometimes he was disturbed and he would need other members of the public to leave the vicinity before he could continue. Some of the victims took longer to die than the others, and this is the reason why he stabbed Wilma McCann as he thought that she was going to survive his initial attack. I also believe that he stayed with the victim(s) after each murder for a while, as he posed them to expose their breasts for his own sexual gratification and a feeling of power and 'accomplishment', and I believe that whilst he was exposing the corpses he was generating multiple orgasms whilst viewing the victim; Sutcliffe did not develop sexually as an adolescent as he was frigid and the psychosexual stages of development were not achieved, leading to

Sutcliffe suffering from *satyriasis*, and he was finally having the opportunity to satisfy his abnormal sexual urges and fantasies.

Although each act varied in the length of time they took to commit, one of the most alarming and vicious murders during his spree was the murder of Patricia Atkinson, whom he killed in a bedsit. This was the first known time that Sutcliffe managed to catch a victim indoors, giving him more time with the victim in which he bludgeoned her to death and then used the claw of a hammer to graze her body, including her breasts and vaginal area. Sutcliffe stabbed her six times in the abdomen as well as her back, leaving several slash marks on her body. The murder of Patricia Atkinson shows the extreme danger that his victims were placed in. He had more time with the victim, during which I believe his satyriasis would have entered a sexual frenzy, making the stabbing of the womb symbolic in this case. The womb initially preserves and gives life to an unborn child. Sutcliffe, due to his misogynistic rage and the fact that Sonia Sutcliffe had suffered from a miscarriage, was the manifestation of anger in this murder, as in his psyche he saw it as not taking one life but two lives, hence the excessive stabbing of the abdominal area. By now in his series of crimes, it is evident that Sutcliffe was growing in confidence as he was killing indoors where he could easily have been observed and disturbed or heard. Therefore, when a serial killer is becoming confident, investigators need to use all resources available to them, and one of these resources is *geographical profiling*, which is a tool that can potentially tell investigators where the offender may reside by linkage analysis over the areas of where the crimes are being committed.

The crimes were committed in several cities over the north of England, and Dr Stuart Kind, the then director of the Home Office Central Research Establishment (CRE), believed that the killer was living in Bradford City, and that his base of action was in the Manningham/Shipley area of Bradford. Sutcliffe lived in the Heaton district of Bradford, which lies midway between Manningham and Shipley. Canter (1994) states, *'A careful examination of the sequence of offences which led Kind to conclude that the criminal was at pains to avoid returning to the towns of the recent earlier crimes.'* This was how a theory came about where the perpetrator lived at the time of the crimes, as each crime was linked on a computer by adding an eighteenth pin after the seventeenth attack to theorise where the murderer was residing.

The tragedy in the case of the Yorkshire Ripper is that geographical profiling was in its infancy during the 1970s, and the senior police chiefs were mostly dismissive of the tool. If the police had used more intuition and the tools available, along with the E-fits (all of which resembled Sutcliffe), and the fact that he was seen in the red-light areas where many of the victims were going missing, and the fact he had been interviewed several times, Sutcliffe may well have been apprehended much more quickly and lives could have been saved as a result as Sutcliffe was also a very disorganised serial killer, as he did not move the bodies or hide them, he would have left a lot of forensic evidence which could have been used against him if the police investigation had not been in disarray, and I will further assess Sutcliffe's behaviour with the bodies of his victims after the commission of the crime.

In terms of the body being moved from one location to another the answer is a resounding 'no'. This type of behaviour is usually linked to organised serial killers, and Sutcliffe was a predominately disorganised serial killer, and killed his victims in a 'blitz' pattern. Again, this is another characteristic associated with the disorganised serial killer group, as the organised serial killer plans their kills more methodically, as it is part of the fantasy to have a live and terrified victim at their mercy as it gives them a chance to play 'God'. The disorganised serial killer, on the contrary, is much more impulsive.

In terms of the bodies being moved from the initial attack spot to a place very close by, Sutcliffe did do this. For example, in the murder of Jayne MacDonald he moved her away from the main walk path in the park so he could commit his perverse acts upon her corpse for his own sexual gratification. During the murder of Helen Rytka, for example, he moved the body from the back of his car and had to put his hand over her mouth as two taxi drivers pulled up whilst he was in the process of murdering her. Upon the taxi drivers' exit he pulled her from out of the bushes and savagely beat her to death with his hammer. This is yet another example of him falling into the disorganised category, as he could easily have been seen or apprehended, whereas the organised serial killer will pick and choose both their kill sites and dump sites carefully.

In all the murders committed by Peter Sutcliffe, the discovery site and murder site were the same, hence the amount of evidence left at most of the crime scenes. Again, this is another tragedy of the whole case as DNA evidence was still in development, and its first use in an arrest of a serial killer in Britain would not occur until the arrest of Colin Pitchfork in 1987. As Sutcliffe was a disorganised killer, the amount of DNA in terms of hair strands, fingerprints, etc. left at the crime scenes, coupled with the circumstantial evidence such as the footprints and size 7 shoes, and the E-fits would have made it easier for the police to link and match Sutcliffe to the crimes. Sutcliffe was leaving far too many clues for the police and the media and suspicion should have been directed towards him, and I believe that as Sutcliffe was acting very much on his primitive psychological impulses, he would fit the classification of a disorganised serial killer and I will outline my hypothesis in greater detail below.

I do not believe that the murders were organised in the sense that Sutcliffe chose a particular victim to 'fulfil' a particular fantasy; I believe that he was a very opportunistic killer who killed when the chance arose and therefore did not stalk a victim prior to his criminal acts. So, for example, sex workers are victims of 'opportunity and convenience' for a *disorganised* serial killer, whereas an organised serial killer will have a particular victim to fulfil an entrenched psychological fantasy and they will usually use a set modus operandi to lure a victim; for example, John Wayne Gacy lured young boys to his home with the pretence of acquiring employment through his building contract company.

I believe that Sutcliffe has the below listed traits of an organised killer. However, I believe overall he was a disorganised serial killer, and I will outline my hypothesis as to why during the remainder of his profile. I believe the organised traits that are usually associated with an organised serial killer can be linked to Peter Sutcliffe:

- *He was socially adequate and would frequent the pubs with a variety of friends and work colleagues and used this veneer of 'normality' to throw people off his suspicion.*
- *He lived with a partner, who provided the police with an alibi for his whereabouts on some of the nights of the murders, which he had pre-planned.*
- *I believe that he followed his crimes in the media (although this would not have been difficult, as the whole of the country could not escape the stories at the time), however, he went quiet during times, until I believe his urge to kill consumed his thoughts persistently and he had to acquire a form of psychological release to function back within the realms of normal society.*
- *He had good hygiene and housekeeping skills, and although this seems very tentative in the reasoning of what constitutes an organised serial killer, it helps in the fact that they appear to be regular and nothing untoward, or what Professor David Wilson describes as 'the veneer of normality', helping the wolf blend in amongst the sheep.*

- *Despite Sutcliffe claiming to suffer from delusions, there is no record of him prior to the crimes seeking any form of psychiatric help, and many organised serial killers do not seek help as, although they know there is a problem within their psyche, they like the feeling of power and use compartmentalisation as a cognitive mechanism to cope with their crimes.*

From the above psychological key factors, it would be easy for one to state that Sutcliffe was an 'organised' offender, however, I believe that predominately Sutcliffe was a disorganised serial killer due to the below mitigating factors:

- *He had a low IQ, or at best average.*
- *He struggled originally upon acquiring employment, was immature and would annoy colleagues. Sutcliffe also shows immaturity in his sexual development, as he could not speak to women without becoming embarrassed easily.*
- *He lived near the crime scenes; despite commuting around the country, he killed in the north of England only (though there is strong evidence to suggest more murders).*
- *He had nocturnal habits – this is important with disorganised serial killers as they have no plan of action and nightfall is the least likely time they will get caught. Organised serial killers kill in the day time, as they usually concoct a callous plan or have a 'base of operation' in which they feel comfortable, e.g. Ted Bundy abducted two women under false pretences at Lake Sammamish; Dennis Rader murdered women in their homes by cutting alarms and phone lines and waiting for them to arrive home; John Haigh would take them to his 'workshop' in the daytime, in which he would kill his victims and then leave them to disintegrate in an acid bath; and Hindley and Brady would lure their victims to Saddleworth Moors in the daytime.*
- *He killed at one site and killed them savagely and quickly, considering his 'work' is complete despite leaving a lot of forensic evidence and the body exposed to the elements, where the public could easily find the corpse of the dead victim.*
- *He attacked in a 'blitz' pattern, and in the case of Sutcliffe the savagery was excessive, as the misogynistic rage he was suffering from was exhibited during his murders.*

- *The bodies were not dismembered as he knew that he had committed wrong and would want to exit the scene as quickly as possible.*
- *He was known to depersonalise the victims in the sense that in most of the murders he covered their faces, leaving only their breasts exposed, and even clawed his third victim, Patricia Atkinson, with a hammer. The depersonalisation of the victims is because Sutcliffe was turning them into objects in his mind, whereas an organised serial killer chooses a specific victim type to enact out certain fantasies, Sutcliffe picked all his victims on access and opportunity.*
- *He left a chaotic crime scene for the police and there was no evidence of planning, and many of the bodies could easily be found by members of the public going about their routine activities.*
- *Sutcliffe left a lot of physical evidence at the crime scene, including boot marks, hair fibres, a £5 note, and tyre tracks.*

Another psychological indication that Sutcliffe was a disorganised offender was that none of his crimes were staged to mislead the police, apart from the murder of Marguerite Walls, in which he knelt on her chest whilst he strangled her. After she was dead, he stripped her of all her clothing except her tights before leaving her partially covered with grass cuttings and leaves. This led Detective Superintendent James Hobson to announce: '*We do not believe this is the work of the Yorkshire Ripper.*' Sutcliffe later admitted that he had changed his *modus operandi* to mislead the police, regretfully, however, this does show some of the police ineptitude during the entire investigation. Sutcliffe may have changed his *modus operandi* in future murders, as he would have realised from the media interest in the 'Wearside Jack' tape that the police were focusing on men from Sunderland, and if he could convince them there were two serial killers operating in the area, the consistent police pressure he was receiving may have been guided away from him as the police kept visiting him, and this was leading to him being taunted by his work colleagues and friends in the pubs. This was the only time in his modus operandi that he showed any sign of being an organised offender. However, it was by pure chance that it occurred because the Wearside Jack tape threw the police investigation away from him and allowed him to continue to kill unabated. The police ineptitude in the investigation on a simple change of killing technique and a tape that anybody could send in as a 'joke' derailed the investigation in many respects. The police should have been reviewing the psychological indicators, e.g., how the victims were killed, the types of

PETER SUTCLIFFE, THE YORKSHIRE RIPPER

wounds inflicted and detailed crime scene analysis from profilers within the FBI, which could have helped steer the investigation back towards Sutcliffe as the prime suspect by using constrained interviewing techniques which would have eventually led to Sutcliffe unwittingly providing them with more psychological clues and insights into his personality.

As most victims were bludgeoned, the motivation may show that this person harboured a hatred towards women and wanted to kill them quickly as possible, he was angry at them, and this was also evident throughout the excessive stabbing. Serial killers who strangle their victims are usually in control of the situation, and are doing it to fulfil a fantasy, whereas the Yorkshire Ripper was re-enacting 'revenge' upon his victims, and this is evident in the location of wounds that he inflicted against the victims. The wounds to start with were blunt trauma as he struck them on the head. This act shows his motivation that he wanted to render the victim helpless so he could be in complete control of a woman. Several of the victims had suffered laceration wounds to the vaginal area with various items, such as a screwdriver and a log for example, this may suggest that the killer was sexually inadequate, and the use of phallic objects could suggest that the killer had an Oedipal complex and had a bad relationship with a father figure throughout his life.

As mentioned, the police should have actively reviewed the positions of the bodies, as this would have provided a psychological insight into the type of offender that they were hunting for at the time of the murders the bodies were mainly left in fields (Tina Atkinson was the only victim he killed indoors) and we do not fully know if Sutcliffe wanted some of them found, as he may have revelled in the notoriety that the case was generating, and the fact that so many people in Yorkshire were terrified may have given him a sense of power. The paradox of this theory is that we assume serial killers leave bodies in the open because they like to taunt the police and society, however, in the case of Sutcliffe we can see from his own accord and reports since his capture that he came close to being caught on several occasions, and he may well have left the bodies in the open as he was a predominately *disorganised* serial killer and had to quickly flee the crime scene. After all, I believe that serial killers, after the primary victim(s), e.g., the actual victim, the secondary victims will be family and friends, and the tertiary victim will be the local community and society in general, and Sutcliffe would have enjoyed the notoriety and attention his crimes were receiving from the media.

PEN PROFILES OF THE OFFENDERS

Had the police investigation used offender profiling at the time of the murders and used all the evidence from surviving victims, Peter Sutcliffe would undoubtedly have become a prime suspect based on his existing and previous employment record because the profile would have found that firstly disorganised offenders have unskilled manual jobs and generally struggle with discipline, and this can lead to termination of employment. Peter Sutcliffe had a variety of jobs, mainly labouring positions which were tainted by habitual lateness, some of which he had been fired from. We are aware that Sutcliffe gained employment as a gravedigger and at his trial in 1981 claimed that he heard the voice of God telling him to go out and rid the world of sex workers (Cawthorne, 2000). There have been theories since that Sutcliffe committed acts of necrophilia during employment as a gravedigger, however, there has never been any evidence of such acts being committed, however, this should have been thoroughly investigated at the time because it could have provided a psychological clue, if found to be true. Although there is no record of Sutcliffe committing acts of necrophilia during his employment as a gravedigger, when discussing serial killers, I would never rule any such theory out in its entirety. I do believe that due his sexual paraphilia, Sutcliffe began to fantasise about the possession of dead bodies, and within his deranged psychosis his fantasies of murder became intertwined with possessing a dead woman, and this sadly became evident in Sutcliffe's later crimes. Sutcliffe's final employment was as a shift worker and a truck driver for T&WH Clark Holdings Ltd before his incarceration and this was the employer where the police linked the £5 note serial number back to and the police began to put more pressure on Sutcliffe because of this and the fact that his employment allowed him to commute could have made him a person of interest in the investigation.

The psychological characteristics of Sutcliffe were that he was a highly disorganised killer with no understanding of police work, and the evidence he was leaving at the crime scenes are testament to this. Had he been committing his crimes in modern-day Britain; I believe he would have been apprehended much sooner and lives would have been saved.

I believe that he became a serial killer and targeted women in general, and not just sex workers, due to his father's adulterous lifestyle, in which he saw his mother unduly suffer, and as Sutcliffe may have suffered from a form of Oedipal complex due to never being accepted by his father but doted upon by his mother, combined with the misogynistic hate that began fermenting in him due to his father's adulterous relationships, and the fact that Sutcliffe saw women as 'untrustworthy' and 'impure'. Therefore, he could not break down a psychological barrier where he could form a meaningful relationship with women (until Sonia), and therefore he had to reassert his power and take 'revenge' for his mother over these women. In the case of Sonia Sutcliffe, she was a very timid and shy girl who would not answer back and she would be completely adherent to Sutcliffe. This is an interesting aspect with serial killers, as they choose submissive partners in many cases, and again they are exploiting the vulnerability of others to serve their own sociopathic psyche. Harold Shipman knew Primrose Shipman was a meek and mild human being; Jerry Brudos knew his wife feared him and therefore she would obey his command at every turn as he was a patriarchal tyrant, so much so that his wife never went into the family basement, where Brudos was killing innocent women and cutting off their breasts and feet as 'souvenirs', and therefore we can argue that the wives of some of these serial killers are also victims of their warped psychosis.

Although Sonia Sutcliffe would corroborate her husband's alibis, Sutcliffe would eventually be arrested for picking up a sex worker named Olive Reivers and offering her £10 to have sex with him. Near the area at the time, there was two police officers who checked the police national computer and realised the plates were stolen, and again this shows Sutcliffe's disorganisation; even when he believed that he was 'methodological' in his planning to avoid capture, he had no understanding of police procedures. The driver of the vehicle gave his name as Peter Williams and asked the officers if he could relieve himself behind a cabin. The police knew the plates belonged to a Mr Khan and were ultimately suspicious of Peter Sutcliffe. The next day the officers, believing that they had the Ripper in custody, went back to the scene and found a hammer and a sharpened screwdriver in the cistern. When Sutcliffe was informed of the officers' find he finally provided his real name and confessed to thirteen murders and seven attempted murders (Innes 2006), and other than the routine interviews during the investigation, Sutcliffe had never had any contact with the police previously, which made the commission of his series of crimes even more disturbing.

Peter Sutcliffe did not have a criminal record; however, this could have been different if his friend, Trevor Birdsall, informed the police in 1969 that Peter Sutcliffe had confessed to him that he had attempted to hit a sex worker with a brick, and this could have resulted in Sutcliffe gaining a criminal record, which could have been of use in the investigation years later. This is another tragic circumstance of the Yorkshire Ripper murders: had this initial

PEN PROFILES OF THE OFFENDERS

crime been reported, it may well have helped the police use 'linkage analysis', which is the process of linking previous crimes against an unsub. With reports of surviving victims and E-fits etc. Sutcliffe could have been apprehended more quickly. Even when Wearside Jack sent in his tape to the police, surviving victims tried to explain to investigating officers that the Ripper was from Yorkshire as he had a Yorkshire accent, and had the police been shrewder and more organised, in hindsight there was a lot of linkage analysis against Peter Sutcliffe to make him more than just a viable suspect.

Pen Profile

I, Samuel Hodgins can confirm that I have researched the case and the crimes committed by the serial killer, Peter Sutcliffe (Caucasian male), aka the 'Yorkshire Ripper'. Sutcliffe committed his crimes (that we are aware of) between 1969, when he would have been 23 years of age, until his arrest and incarceration in 1981, when he would have been 36 years of age. In view of this I am therefore unable to offer a psychological profile of an unsub. I am therefore in effect trying to offer a psychological post-mortem of the offender in question based upon the information contained within the above offender profile to attempt to establish a motive as to why Peter Sutcliffe committed the heinous crimes, he did in the North-West of England during those twelve dreadful years.

1. The criminal acts committed by Peter Sutcliffe were of a serial nature and were committed over time with a 'cooling off' period in between each attempted murder or murders, which is the FBI's definition of a serial killer. Peter Sutcliffe, from what we are aware of, committed his first attempt at murder in 1969, and he would continue to kill and attack unabated for a period of 21 years until his arrest and imprisonment. I do believe that Sutcliffe would have had many more victims had it not been for a stroke of fortune, as the police investigation was not methodical enough to capture him – despite the amount of forensic evidence that he unwittingly left at the scenes of the crimes, had the police officers who arrested him not used their intuition and returned to the original arrest scene, we would more than likely be discussing scores more victims. Sutcliffe's criminal 'career' of attempted murder/murder began in 1969 and he would continue up until his arrest on January 12th, 1981,

therefore the murders were committed over a period of twelve years and there was a 'cooling-off' period between each murder. Before the murder of Wilma McCann he had already attempted two murders (Anna Rogulskyj and Olive Smelt), all three crimes happened in the space of just over a month of each other and I believe that Wilma McCann became a victim because his two previous attempts at murder had failed and the fantasy to commit a murder was more than likely inhibiting his thoughts and beginning to dictate his psychosis to carry out a murder and achieve what he saw in his mind as the most satisfying climax of sexual gratification.

Sutcliffe then appears to only have committed one murder and one attempted murder in the year of 1976, however, in 1977 he committed three successful murders and two attempted murders between the months of April up until October, thus averaging a victim every 4.8 weeks on average. There is a possible theory to explain why Sutcliffe increased his killing pattern so quickly, if Sutcliffe truly was a 'mission-orientated' killer as he claims to have been, with his 'mission from God', then he would have perceived his criminal actions as 'justified'. However, I don't believe that Sutcliffe was a mission-orientated killer, I believe that the feeling of power and control formed a delusional belief within his psyche that he was 'uncatchable', as the police investigation was in a mess and therefore the feeling of invincibility, he derived was in fact adding to his grotesque narcissistic view of himself. In this sense he is a *hedonistic* serial killer, as he was killing to derive pleasure from these perverse acts. In terms of the *hedonistic* serial killer, there are four sub-categories which are *lust, thrill,* and *comfort*. I believe that Sutcliffe was most definitely a *lust* killer because sex is the primary motive of these types of killers and it does not matter one iota if the victim is dead or alive, and in Sutcliffe's murders, they were all dead by bludgeoning before he would enact sexual intercourse. Lust killers also perform excessive killing and extreme mutilation, which Sutcliffe enacted upon his victims, and this again intertwines within his psychosis of the need and innate desire to exert, power, dominance, and control over his victims, and these are psychological motivations that are attributed to the lust killer. The use of weaponry for Sutcliffe was a claw hammer and a knife after. Lust killers use weapons whereby they need to get close to the victim to make the experience 'personal' to provide sexual intensity and excitement. The other characteristic that Sutcliffe shares with lust killer characteristics is that he chose different races, appearance, classes, and age and killed frequently, and this was because his destructive sexual urges needed constant stimulation. The urge to kill, and the savagery of his crimes were becoming more intense, as was his hedonism, from all the press coverage he was receiving.

I fundamentally believe that the act of murder was purely a means to an end for Sutcliffe as he needed a completely submissive victim for him to be able to perform his heinous acts of sexual gratification, as it would have made him feel powerful, when in fact he was a pathetic individual who targeted vulnerable and lone women. All serial killers are extremely dangerous beings; however, Sutcliffe is one of the most deranged and dangerous criminals that I have ever had to profile thus far.

2. The age range of Peter Sutcliffe's (known) victims range from 16 years old at the youngest (Theresa Sykes) with the oldest being 47 years old (Marguerite Walls), and they varied physically and in socio-economic, ethnic, educational and job backgrounds, and I am therefore led to believe that Sutcliffe would kill any women indiscriminately if the chance arose due to his misogynistic rage brought about by his father's promiscuous relationships whilst married to Sutcliffe's mother (I will refer to this in more detail later in the profile). As Sutcliffe was a *hedonistic* serial killer, the victims' appearance and age was relatively immaterial as he needed to sexually stimulate and gratify the warped fantasies and desires that inhibited his thoughts.

3. Peter Sutcliffe claimed that whilst he was employed as a gravedigger he was led by a voice to the gravestone of a Polish woman, in which the Polish words JEGO, WEHBY and ECHO were written on the tombstone. Sutcliffe claimed that whilst resting by this stone the same voice had told him to kill sex workers, and this became his 'mission' from God (Steel 2012). Sutcliffe had been overheard by a prison guard telling his wife that if he could convince everybody he was mad then he could get a reduced sentence and be out in ten years' time (Steel 2012).

It is known from medical records that Sutcliffe's wife, Sonia, had suffered from mental breakdowns and depression, and therefore Sutcliffe may have recognised the symptoms and used it to his advantage, as serial killers are psychopaths and they are adept at mimicking the behaviour of others around them, and this type of behaviour helps them exist within society and appear outwardly 'normal' to those that they meet. The mere fact that Sutcliffe used this attempt to be exonerated of his crimes under 'diminished responsibility' is an affrontery to all his victims as there is no evidence of Sutcliffe ever suffering from mental health problems, and it was a last desperate attempt to exert his form of power and control, not only against the law enforcement and the legal system but also against the victims and their surviving relatives and against society. As Sutcliffe was a *hedonistic* serial killer, he was continuing to derive pleasure from watching all these intelligent people debate over what he was, and experts trying to argue in his favour, and this is power *by proxy* and Sutcliffe knew deep down that he would never be released, even under the Mental Health Act of 1959 as he was an extreme danger to the public, and possibly for his own safety as well as he would be safer whilst being incarcerated. Sutcliffe was playing a game with the police and the legal system for his own derivation of power.

4. In reference to the above statements, I believe that Sutcliffe suffered from a severe misogynistic rage which became psychologically imprinted within his psyche from an early age due to his father's adulterous behaviours, which severely affected his beloved mother, who would later die at the age of 59 because of her life with Sutcliffe's father. This would lead to a delusional belief in Sutcliffe that all women are 'evil', and although they become the core focus of his fantasies and desires, the comfort and later sexual gratification he desired from women became out of reach from him because of a delusional and dysfunctional belief system, and he couldn't form meaningful relationships and friendships with women, which led to mental frustration for him and he reverted back into his dangerous fantasy world as a form of self-protection. It was also an act of cognitive dissonance as a form of coping with the harsh realities that his psyche was enduring.

Sutcliffe would not just feel let down by his mother, as the only other woman he truly loved in his life also let him down to add further proof to his own warped mental state that all women are 'evil'. His wife, Sonia Sutcliffe, was also unfaithful to Peter, and that she suffered from several miscarriages and could not give Sutcliffe the children that he desired. A month after the first miscarriage he carried out his first known murder. Later the murder of Patricia Atkinson would show signs of excessive rage when he stabbed her abdomen six times in a height of rage and sexual frenzy. Sutcliffe, whilst working as a gravedigger, liked to take 'trophies' from the dead female corpses that he buried and horrified his workmates with constant references to necrophilia (Greig 2009), and although there is no evidence to suggest that he committed these types of acts, I believe that this does show that he was at least fantasising about committing the acts. Due to his later acts of necrophilia, I would not rule out that Sutcliffe did not commit these types of criminal acts prior to his spate of serial murders.

Due to his experiences with women, and how he could not interact with them, I believe that within his psyche he formed a pathological hatred and generalised them all as 'sluts' and 'whores', and this rage and dysfunctional belief fermented within his psyche, and women in general were in extreme danger and not just sex workers. Wherever he was in the country at the time would have been in great jeopardy as Sutcliffe killed whenever the opportunity arose. For example, Jayne McDonald was a student walking through a park after visiting her grandparents, as victims were chosen to satisfy his sexual desires and once access and opportunity arose the victim did not stand a chance against an enraged and sexually excited killer.

Peter Sutcliffe, on the night of his arrest, was wearing a long-sleeved V-neck sweater in place of his underpants with the arms pulled up on his legs and the V-neck allowing his genitals to be exposed (Bilton 2006). I believe that this repulsive garment was created to protect Sutcliffe's knees whilst viewing his dead victims and masturbating over them, and I am theorising this because all but one of the victims had been sexually penetrated by him and all had their shirts pulled up to expose their breasts. As Sutcliffe had a perverse obsession with necrophilia, his method of killing and rendering the victim helpless would have given him the power he never had over women in his life as he was in possession of them, and I believe that misogyny, sex, control, brutality, and power became intertwined in his warped psychosis.

5. It is highly possible that Sutcliffe may have been responsible for many more attacks than the thirteen murders he was convicted for, as we know he made unsuccessful attempts to murder other women during his reign of terror. We are aware from a statement made by his friend that Sutcliffe admitted to an attack on a sex worker in 1969, in which the brick he put in a sock fell out and he fled in panic. Egger and Boyd (2006) state that sex workers are 40 more times likely than other women to be murdered, and sex workers have many reasons for not reporting attacks to the

police. They may be in fear of a pimp, are committing illegal acts such as drug taking, or may also and unsurprisingly wish to keep their secret life hidden from family members, and this occurred in the case of the murdered Suffolk sex worker, Tania Nicol, whose mother told Ipswich crown court that her daughter had been working as a hairdresser and in a bar (Siddique, 2008). Goodchild (1996), in her newspaper article for the *Independent* cites the work carried out by the then West Yorkshire chief constable, Keith Hellawell, who confirmed that he believed Sutcliffe had committed more attacks than he was convicted of, and Sutcliffe has admitted to more attacks as well. However, once again due to his sociopathic personality, he may have been saying this to play games with the police and exhibit his power over the victims of the families who have been searching for answers for decades.

Hellawell based his assumptions on the fact that many of the victims were not linked at the time to the 'Ripper enquiry' as the police believed that he was targeting sex workers only, and again it shows the naivety and the ineptitude of the entire Ripper investigation. Hellawell also states that the modus operandi of the attackers fits that of Sutcliffe from testimonies of surviving victims, in the sense that firstly many of the victims were followed by their attacker, who chatted to them prior to the attack and for all intents and purposes seemed friendly and polite. Secondly, (in most cases) they were battered with a ball-point or claw hammer. And thirdly, the victims who survived his monstrous and depraved acts described their attacker as being swarthy with a dark beard, which fitted Sutcliffe's appearance.

6. I believe that Sutcliffe in part became a serial killer due to his father's overbearing patriarchal dominance over his own family, and in particular Peter and his mother. However, I do also believe that this was only a small part of why Sutcliffe became a serial killer. There are other factors as to why I believe that Sutcliffe became a coldblooded killer that began during his formative years. For example, as a boy Sutcliffe would not partake in sports as he would prefer to read – although there is nothing wrong with reading in the normal context, Sutcliffe was anything but a normal person as he led a very introverted life and read many comic books and more than likely created a fantasy world for himself as a way of coping with the harsh realities of life. A young Peter Sutcliffe was greatly afraid of his father's aggressive masculinity and lived in a constant state of fear of his father's explosive temper and felt helpless against him.

Sutcliffe was also severely bullied at school and played truant for two weeks, hiding in his loft reading comics by torchlight. All these factors appear that Sutcliffe was an introverted and an extremely helpless child, and his shyness would continue until he was sixteen, in which he began partaking in sports including bodybuilding and was soon, to his father's great delight, able to beat both of his brothers at arm wrestling. Sutcliffe, I believe, may have only done this as a way of 'protecting' himself and as means to an end to finally be accepted by his father and his own peers. Sutcliffe later in life would once again feel rejected by women in the sense that his father's polygamous and adulterous lifestyle put mental pressure on his mother, who would have more than likely confided in Peter, as he was always close to her and reciprocated her love. The only woman who he became sexually intimate with was Sonia Szurma, who would cheat on him with other men and Sonia would miscarriage on several occasions, and this again reaffirmed his belief that all women were 'evil' and 'against' him. These instances, I believe, would have made Sutcliffe feel as though women were 'laughing' at him and brought out his misogynistic rage that had developed and manifested within his psychosis for several years.

The strangeness in the case of Sutcliffe is that he did not show any symptoms of the *MacDonald Triad* during adolescence, as he did not (as far as we are aware) commit pyromania, he treated animals gently and he did seem to suffer from enuresis after the age of five, and even in later life he did not possess a criminal record, like many other serial killers at the time of their apprehension. This is a strong argument that he was suffering from mental health problems. However, like all people in society, each person is unique as an individual and we are not fully aware if he did exhibit any of these signs as he was an introvert and no child will admit to torturing an animal for 'pleasure', as serial killers live in a very dark world that they create for themselves and ultimately, once they are found out, they begin to create a dark world for the rest of us.

7. Sutcliffe confessed to the police that he had an early experience with a sex worker in which she 'conned' him out of money and belittled him when he could not maintain an erection. I believe that this experience only added fuel to Sutcliffe's misogynistic rage and, according to Cawthorne (2007), Sutcliffe found out his mother was having an affair with a neighbour, a local policeman, and the only woman Sutcliffe truly loved and held a meaningful relationship with had just destroyed the aura he had created around her and reaffirmed his belief and hatred towards women.

Sutcliffe's father was humiliated by this and arranged for all his children, including Peter, who was accompanied by his bride-to-be, Sonia, to be present at the Bingley hotel. Kathy Sutcliffe turned up to the bar under the pretence she was meeting her boyfriend and was forced to show the nightdress that she had brought for the tryst, and at the same time it transpired that Sonia also had a secret boyfriend not long after Sutcliffe committed his first murder. It is again becoming transparent that Sutcliffe would have felt betrayed by the only two women in his life that he cared for, and this helped to escalate his misogynistic rage in his psychosis. In the next three points I will elaborate on my theory as to the type of killer Peter William Sutcliffe was and the reasons as to why.

8. Lane and Gregg (1992, pp. 10–13) outline seven different types of serial killers under the subheading of *the question of motive*. It has been well established that Peter Sutcliffe was a serial killer and I believe that he can be categorised into the following two typologies of serial killer: *missionary* and *power-seeking*.
    a. Lane and Gregg (1992) describe the missionary killer as the 'clean-up' killers who accept a self-imposed responsibility for improving the quality of life and ridding society of its 'undesirables'. I believe that due to Sutcliffe being let down by both his mother and father and Sonia, his psychosis, and any sense of self-worth he previously held within his psyche completely disintegrated. These occurrences in his life led him to class all women as 'whores' and 'untrustworthy'. I do believe that Sutcliffe had a deep underlying misogynistic hatred of women in general and sex workers because they are actively selling sex to anybody and Sutcliffe in his own delusion of 'grandeur' would have seen this as perversion and yet at the same time be fascinated by them and became easy victims for him to channel and transfer his inner rage against them. I therefore believe that Sutcliffe did not recognise them as victims and he reduced them to mere 'objects' and became wilfully and completely oblivious to their circumstances as to why they were selling themselves which was not through them seeking sexual desire, it was through the necessity and the primitive human instinct of survival which wells within us all.

    The other issue because Sutcliffe predominately selected sex workers was because of 'access and opportunity' as a sex worker will put themselves in very dangerous positions. Lane and Gregg

(1992) when discussing *'missionary'* killers state; *'Almost any category of identifiable appearance, occupation, spiritual or political belief could fall victim to the 'missionary', though most target groups are selected because they are the objects of society's most deep-rooted prejudices – the bugaboos of prostitution, homosexuality and racial minority.* Sutcliffe chose sex workers and the public only become outraged when he murdered the 16-year-old student, Jayne MacDonald. Sutcliffe deluded himself in his warped psychosis when he murdered a sex worker that was in part doing society a favour and again this is his deranged personality 'justifying' his actions and trying to cognitively 'rationalise' his warped sexual psychosis. A secondary motivation for the murders were that he felt that maybe nobody would care about sex workers, despite them being someone's daughter, mother or partner and this is summed up in the following quote to his brother, Carl Sutcliffe, after his arrest; *'I was just cleaning up the streets, our kid. Just cleaning up the streets'* (Lane and Gregg 1992).

b. Lane and Gregg (1992) define the *power-seeking killer* as the following: *'A common complication among personalities showing low self-esteem is the desire to have control over life and death of others to such a degree that it serves an intrinsic motive to murder.'* I believe that Sutcliffe killed the women, and not just sex workers, due to his intrinsic motivation of misogynistic rage that fermented in him over several years, and the only way he could acquire power over women in society was by killing them, and by this act he would have complete control over them.

c. Sutcliffe did show sexual elements in killing these women, e.g., the way he knelt over the bodies to masturbate over his victim's corpse, however, Sutcliffe was an extremely disorganised serial killer, and he does exhibit several psychological characteristics of a 'lust killer'. This type of killer is more associated with organised serial killers as they usually go through the following number of phases; *fantasy, the hunt, the kill,* and *post-kill phases,* and all these phases derive from the main category of the 'hedonistic' serial killer. Sutcliffe did have abnormal fantasies regarding women and the murder victims did show elements of a 'lust killer', however, Sutcliffe was an opportunistic serial killer, better known as a *disorganised* serial killer.

9. The crimes committed by Sutcliffe were predominately that of a disorganised nature as all his victims were borne of 'access and opportunity', and he did not appear to stalk them or pick them based on a warped fantasy.

The disorganisation within his crimes is shown consistently, as firstly each victim was murdered near to where he lived at the time (this helped Dr Stuart Kind build a hypothesis on where the killer lived using geographical profiling). Each victim was killed at one site and not moved; they may have been transported there on the premise that they were going to earn 'business', but this does not mean that Sutcliffe was organised as it was a means to an end for him to enact murder and serves him with a psychological purpose. The victims had suffered from severe 'overkill', and the way he killed at one site and in such an aggressive manner shows that he is an impulsive killer and was not in control of the victims without rendering them unconscious first. For example, he bludgeoned each victim, whereas an organised killer may usually prefer to strangle a victim, as this would act as the ultimate act of power for this type of predator. The bodies of the victims were left intact and not dismembered, and he did not appear to take any 'trophies' from the victims, e.g., in the murder of Emily Jackson he left her handbag nearby with all her possessions at the scene of the crime.

The main factors which show Sutcliffe as a disorganised serial killer is the amount of forensic evidence, he left at the crime scene(s). For example, during the murder of Emily Jackson he left a heavy-ribbed wellington boot mark on her thigh, which was either a size seven or eight – Sutcliffe was a size eight. In the murder of Irene Richardson there were two tyre marks that were made by two India Autoway tyres, which would have also shown Sutcliffe to be at the scene of the crime at some point. In the murder of Patricia Atkinson, he left the same boot mark that was left on Emily Jackson at the foot of the bed, if Sutcliffe had any knowledge of forensic evidence, he would have got rid of the boots in case the police asked to confiscate them under warrant. In the murder of Jean Jordan, he left the newly awarded £5 note which his employers, Clark's Transport, had paid him two days earlier, which raised even more suspicion upon him. During the murder of Josephine Whittaker, Sutcliffe savagely bit her left breast, and it had been made by somebody with a gap between the two upper front teeth (Sutcliffe had this gap but denied biting Whittaker). Many people would assume that Sutcliffe was leaving 'clues'

PEN PROFILES OF THE OFFENDERS

to actively taunt the police. However, it was down to his impulsive criminal and psychotic behaviours that he left them, and this is common with disorganised serial killers that usually kill in a blitz pattern.
10. Peter Sutcliffe does show some characteristics of an organised serial killer, however, there are too few too even pronounce Sutcliffe as a 'mixed offender' let alone an organised serial offender.
11. During the height of the Yorkshire Ripper murders, there were many investigative tools available to the police, and the investigation was criticised in the Byford report (1982) for not corroborating evidence with different police forces over a large area, as the murders were taking place in more than one city. This was sadly policing at the time, as other forces did not trust other forces and some high-ranking police officers wanted their own force to solve high-profile cases as it won political and public accolades. All whilst innocent people were falling prey to a remorseless predator.

Sutcliffe's vehicle had been seen in the red-light districts of several northern cities on several occasions, and he was interviewed by the police at least four times before he was caught. Sutcliffe's friend, Trevor Birdsall, had previously reported his suspicion to the police that Peter was the Yorkshire Ripper, and the police did not follow this up, which is insane with all the witness descriptions and the fact Sutcliffe was interviewed numerous times. Instead, the investigation shifted its focus to the 'Wearside Jack' tape sent to Superintendent George Oldfield, claiming to be the killer, which would ultimately send the investigation on the wrong course as George Oldfield focused the investigation to Sunderland and really focused on anybody with a northern accent. George Oldfield even threatened to sack an officer that was convinced that Sutcliffe was indeed the Yorkshire Ripper based on surviving witness reports, telling him he would be removed from the taskforce if he came up with such a 'ludicrous' theory again. This shows how the police were stretched and there was no real structure or profiling to how the evidence and witness testimonies were managed.

The police should have corroborated their information better, for example, Dr Stuart Kind noted in his profile that the killer had an unusually wide commuting area where the crimes were being committed (this was in fact due to Sutcliffe's job as a lorry driver which allowed him to commute), Dr Kind noted that the killer's base of action was in the Manningham/Shipley area of Bradford. Although Sutcliffe was arrested

PETER SUTCLIFFE, THE YORKSHIRE RIPPER

in Sheffield it was eventually established that he did indeed live in the Heaton district of Bradford. Heaton lies midway between Manningham and Shipley (Canter 2003). If the police had used the spatial analysis and geographical profiling investigative tool and combined with the forensic evidence, they may have narrowed the ever-growing suspect pool of persons of 'interest' into a smaller geographical area, and Sutcliffe may have been apprehended much more quickly, resulting in lives being saved. It is highly unlikely that a serial killer will kill in their own area because of the risk involved, e.g., being recognised, a victim escaping and seeing them on the street for example.

The serial killer, Ian Brady, commented on the case of the Yorkshire Ripper to Professor David Wilson in 2009, a quote that sums up Sutcliffe's disorganisation and the failings within the overall police investigation; *'The fact that Sutcliffe managed to evade capture for five years was not due to his intelligence but rather to an astonishing lack of it on part of the police ... Even more amazing was the fact that detectives had questioned Sutcliffe at his home several times during the five-year hunt as, with his black beard, he fitted almost identically the police artist's portrait of the killer drawn from the description of victims who survived. Why the police never thought to put him in a line-up for the surviving victims to identify defies comprehension.'* (Wilson 2009) Ian Brady was not an intuitive genius, however. When profiling Ian Brady, he would fall under the definition of an *organised* serial killer, and he is correct in this instance that police failures allowed Sutcliffe to not only evade capture but to continue his killing spree.

12. In relation to the above points and in further reference to the profile, even if the police had conducted a criminal records background check on Peter Sutcliffe, they would not have found any previous misdemeanours other than a previous motoring conviction for breaking the speed limit, which would not result in the police warranting further investigation into him as a person of interest.

A criminal records background check on Sutcliffe may have appeared virtually clean, yet it does not provide us with a true picture of the real Peter Sutcliffe, because we know from his friend Trevor Birdsall that he had attacked a sex worker in 1973. He attacked another woman outside her home in Leeds and he was never caught or cautioned for any of these offences. The other issue is that Sutcliffe may have physically attacked sex workers prior to the series of murders, however, sex workers are reluctant to report attacks due to fear of being ignored, because they are committing illicit acts themselves and are trying to feed a drug or alcohol habit, and because some are even hiding their 'double-life' from their own families. Prostitutes are on the 'outgroup' in society and therefore their vulnerability allows for monsters like Gary Heidnik and Peter Sutcliffe to target them at will.

Although this is highly speculative, I believe that Peter Sutcliffe may have committed further offences than he was convicted for, and in the murder of Marguerite Walls he changed his modus operandi by strangling her to deceive the police and it worked, which is incredulous that something so innocuous during the course of a series of murders against women was simply discarded as a 'random' attack, and this once again shows the disorganisation of the police investigation, and it's one of the instances where Sutcliffe did show a sign of being or possibly becoming an *organised* serial killer. I believe that the act of strangling was too personal for Peter Sutcliffe, as he falls into the category of a 'lust killer' his own perverse sexual gratification would have been reliant on the mutilation and excess stabbing of his victims.

The police ruled out Marguerite Walls as a victim based upon forensic evidence, as Detective Chief Superintendent James Hobson announced to the media: '*We do not believe that this is the work of the Yorkshire Ripper.*' Sutcliffe admitted to the police that he changed his MO to mislead them – this was in fact another investigative failure on the investigation's behalf, as Marguerite Walls had a hammer wound and chest wounds which were previous 'signatures' of the Yorkshire Ripper.

13. On May 5th, 1981, the trial of Peter Sutcliffe began at the Central Criminal Court, London, Sutcliffe pleaded guilty to manslaughter on the grounds of diminished responsibility. His defence put the case forward that he was suffering from schizophrenia. Sutcliffe was originally found guilty of all charges and sentenced to life imprisonment. Shortly afterward, prison service psychiatrists pronounced him insane, and he was transferred to Broadmoor Hospital for the criminally insane (Innes 2006).
14. To conclude my profile of Peter Sutcliffe, I do believe (although I initially did not) that he was suffering from paranoid schizophrenia, and a 'paranoid constitution' intertwined with a confused sexual psychosis, in the sense that I believe he was having mental delusions brought about due to the experiences of the women in his life. I believe the experiences he suffered during his formative years and then as an adult did bring

about a paranoid constitution in the sense that originally, he believed that women were all 'evil' and 'against' him. However, although he had these delusions, I do believe that he was more than consciously aware during the commission of his crimes that he knew that he was committing wrong, and therefore I will unequivocally state that I believe he is criminally culpable for his crimes, and he should have been in a prison and not in a secure mental hospital. I state this because I believe that Sutcliffe knew more about mental health due to his wife suffering from the ailment, and as psychopaths are good at mimicking the behaviour of others, I believe that he manipulated the prison psychiatrists, as psychopathic personalities are extremely cunning at manipulating others for their own gain.

Sutcliffe may have shown signs from an early age that he was not developing within the normal stages of sexual development in the sense that he would avoid contact with people and would be shy in front of the opposite sex. Although this can be attributed to puberty development, it could have been in this case an underlying symptom of a greater problem that nobody recognised and was therefore allowed to manifest and become incorporated into his psychosis.

Sutcliffe, as he became older, would have gained a great sense of injustice from the constant cheating and promiscuity happening around him, and this may have caused a form of depression and paranoia that nobody recognised and, therefore, he did not seek help for his problems, e.g., cognitive behavioural therapy (CBT) or counselling and supportive psychotherapy. Sutcliffe used to always complain about the promiscuity of individuals: although he used sex workers himself whilst his wife was at home, he may have also grown to hate himself and the act of murder became an act of transference, in effect he was killing the women who 'betrayed' him and the part of himself that he came to loathe.

15. Although there is no excusing Sutcliffe's heinous crimes, had he been involved with people who were trained in the field of mental health, maybe somebody with a sound knowledge of the subject could have recognised some of his behaviour and thus prevented the tragedies that he later went on to commit, as Sutcliffe had told a colleague previously that God had told him to 'remove the prostitutes from the street' whilst working as a gravedigger, and his remark was seen as 'off the-cuff', and unfortunately it was in hindsight a sinister remark with tragic and deep and everlasting consequences.

In terms of serial killers in general, and Peter Sutcliffe is no exception to the rule, this minority group of people in all societies through their criminal intentions and actions create multiple victims. In the latter many people in the north of England were afraid to leave their homes after dark, and the lead investigator in the case of the Yorkshire Ripper, George Oldfield, could too be classed as a victim of the Yorkshire Ripper and 'Wearside Jack'. Although Oldfield made a severe and fateful oversight upon receiving the tape from 'Wearside Jack', he was putting all his energy into catching the offender and in the process placed his own health in jeopardy. After the 'Wearside Jack' tape was played to the public, the public response was enormous with an extra 50,000 calls received by the police, putting further strain on the already under-staffed West Yorkshire force (Steel, 2001). The strain of the investigation had taken its toll on George Oldfield, who suffered three heart attacks and was hospitalized at the end of July 1979. He would not return to the investigation until the beginning of 1980 (Steel, 2001). George Oldfield would eventually die on the 4 July 1985, which was only his fourth year of retirement, and I believe that George Oldfield became a secondary victim of Peter Sutcliffe.

Albert DeSalvo, the Boston Strangler

Albert DeSalvo was born in 1931 in Chelsea, Massachusetts, and he would eventually gain notoriety for his crimes in the annals of American criminal history and the wider world due to the horrific nature of his criminal acts. As the Boston Strangler committed thirteen murders (known) between the 14 June 1962 and the 4 January 1964, with the murders being committed over a period of 19 months and thus averaging a victim every 1.46 months, with a 'cooling off' period between most of his murders, I believe that he fits in with the FBI definitions of serial murder: *'The unlawful killing of two or more victims by the same offender(s) in separate events.'* Albert DeSalvo also fits in with the other FBI definition: *'The term "serial killings" means a series of three or more killings, not less than one of which was committed within the United States, having common characteristics such as to suggest the reasonable possibility that the crimes were committed by the same actor or actors.'* (Morton, J Robert, 2005) The crimes DeSalvo committed were during the 1960s during the era of the 'flower power' movement and the 'sexual liberation' of women, and DeSalvo possibly used an element of this 'progressive' attitude and the empowerment and liberation of women within his crimes by pretending to be from a 'modelling' agency, and therefore before analysing potential social factors as to why he may have committed his deviant crimes, we need to firstly assess his modus operandi and work backwards to establish a motivation for his crimes and criminal acts.

On the surface Albert DeSalvo did not appear to be a threatening person, and he even admitted to investigators at the time of his arrest that most people who knew him personally did not believe him capable of vicious crimes (Bardsley, 2012). Albert DeSalvo, like most other serial killers, will show you what they want to show you in terms of their 'mask of sanity', before this 'mask' eventually slips and you meet the Hyde, as opposed to the Dr Jekyll, in their character.

DeSalvo's modus operandi was to knock on the doors of lone women and pretend that he was from a modelling agency where he would measure them, and sometimes have consensual sex with them. DeSalvo would proceed to tell them that somebody from the agency would call them; nobody ever did because the agency and 'Mr Johnson' did not exist. Mr Johnson was an alter-ego of Albert DeSalvo, and this is where the pseudonym of the 'Measuring Man' derived from in the case of the Boston Strangler.

When the crimes began to escalate to rape and murder, a man dressed in green work overalls approached the apartment of Mrs Marcella Lulka and advised her that the superintendent from the building maintenance company had sent him to see her about painting her apartment. He also told her that he would need to fix the ceiling and complimented her on her figure, at which point she became suspicious and told him her husband was asleep in the room next door, upon which he left, and then the medical student, Sophie Clark, aged 21, who lived opposite, was found murdered. As it was a failed attempt at murder initially, this would have enraged DeSalvo, and Sophie Clark became a victim of his inner rage and a victim of opportunity, as his previous attempt had failed and serial killers usually state that the urge and desire to kill builds up within them and once there, it becomes an all-consuming process that needs satiating, which can only be achieved through murder (the act of killing itself can sometimes leave them feeling depressed for several days after).

This is where the pseudonym of 'the Green Man' derived from in the case of the Boston Strangler. We know from the attempted murder of Gertrude Gruen that the strangler had told her he had been sent to conduct work on her apartment and he tried to strangle her, but she fiercely thought back, biting, and scratching him before he left. Mrs Gruen's actions would have destroyed the killer's fantasies of a completely submissive victim at his mercy. As Mrs Gruen fought back, the fantasies of the killer would have been destroyed, and he would have been enraged that a so-called 'weaker being' could fight back against him and this would have damaged his sense of self-worth.

The modus operandi in the case of the Boston Strangler is common with many other serial killers in the sense that he uses several aliases, such as 'Mr Thompson' and 'Mr Johnson'. The American serial killer Ted Bundy had several aliases, including 'Officer Roseland' when he tried to kidnap teenager, Carol Da Ronch, by getting her to come into his car under false pretences that her car had been targeted by a thief. I would not rule out the chances that Albert DeSalvo had disguised himself as a law enforcement officer to acquire and gain the trust of the victim(s), as there were no signs of

ALBERT DESALVO, THE BOSTON STRANGLER

forced entry into any of the apartments, and serial killers use professions of authority to gain the trust of their victims, as they are obsessed with professions of authority and the power these professions bring, the power that they crave, as I will explain. In the case of serial killers who pose as a figure of authority, e.g., the medical professional, for example, Beverley Allitt, who failed all her medical examinations and yet still managed to manipulate her way into work at a hospital. John Wayne Gacy was an active and outgoing figure in business and society. David Russell Williams served as a colonel in the Canadian Forces, as did David Berkowitz, who served in the military in the USA. According to Lynn Scott (2011), she states, *"The most coveted role of the psychopath is a position of authority, for example, playing the role of a police officer, however, is the most predictable. Carrying badges and driving cop-like vehicles not only feeds to their need to feel important, but it also allows them access to victims who would otherwise trust their instincts and not talk to strangers".* This is key to Albert DeSalvo's modus operandi for two reasons; he was an inadequate in many ways, including being sexually immature; posing as a workman would not have aroused suspicion, as in developed societies a workman is commonplace. Serial killers kill when they have access and opportunity to victims, DeSalvo had to pose as a trusted person to gain the trust and access of the victim(s) as there was no forced entry as too much noise or suspicious behaviour would have ended his acts in the apartments, and there was a higher risk that he could have been seen and identified.

The actual reason for the act of strangulation is for power and sexual gratification, and this form of murder becomes 'interpersonal' for the killer. I believe that Albert DeSalvo was a sexual sadist who was stimulated by the practice of asphyxiophilia (erotic asphyxiation, breath control play). I believe that, as Albert DeSalvo, even during intercourse with his wife, would have multiple orgasms, this led to him experimenting in other sexual practices to continuously arouse him as his wife would not agree to such practices being conducted upon her body. Geberth (1995) cites Meloy (1992), who defines sexual sadism as *'The conscious experience of pleasurable sexual arousal through the infliction of physical or emotional pain on the actual object.'* Many of the victims of DeSalvo had lacerations in the anus, mouth and the vaginal area, for example in the murder of Evelyn Corbin's friends found her in an upright position on the bed and traces of semen had been left on the corpse, in her mouth and vagina (Wilson and Wilson 2007).

I believe that a sexual sadist such as DeSalvo would have kept bringing the victim back to life, as this would have been the ultimate control over the victim, and later research on serial murder has found that strangulation is a form of control which intertwines with sexual arousal and stimulation. Ted Bundy, who killed his victims in several ways, stated strangulation and bludgeoning were his preferred method to Robert Ressler; *'You feel the last breath leaving their body. You are looking into their eyes. A person in that situation is God.'* Bundy was referring to the victims on the Colorado Mountains, where he would have had complete control over the victims and performed acts of necrophilia, and I believe that as Bundy and DeSalvo where similar personality types, DeSalvo would have been able to commit these types of acts as he had the victims under his control and was unlikely to be caught in the act. I believe that DeSalvo kept them in a semi-state of consciousness and kept performing grotesque sexual acts upon them, and this was central to his psychosis and his modus operandi, and the sheer monstrosity of the murders was that once he felt sexually satisfied, he simply left them and carried on with his duties as normal, and this shows his completely psychopathic personality, and this is evident when we assess the crime scene specifics in greater detail..

The victims in the Boston Strangler murder series had been posed in various ways including being left sitting upright, legs spread, knees bent at a 45-degree angle, one left in the bath on her knees. At the time nobody knew why the perpetrator was leaving the bodies in such lewd poses, as the term 'serial killer' would not be used until the 1970s and the study of these monsters was still in its infancy.

It has been established from interviews with serial killers that the posing of a victim is another form of power and a final act of humiliation towards the victim. Roland (2007) states, *'For killers arranging their lifeless victim like a mannequin can be the sole reason for committing the crime. Many serial killers and sex offenders are inadequate individuals who feel driven to avenge themselves on those they imagine having spurned or humiliated them. In turn, they will pose their victims in a way that degrades and dehumanizes them. It is their one chance to exercise some form of control over others. It becomes the distinguishing feature of their crimes and what is known as their signature.'* Albert DeSalvo would also leave a ligature in a bow shape around his victim's neck, which also formed a part of his signature. I believe that as DeSalvo was an inadequate individual this was his chance to exert power. The 'signature' in terms of serial murder is not just a warped retention of power over the victims, this type of 'signature' will bring them to the attention of the media who will provide them with a moniker, e.g. the Suffolk Strangler (Steve Wright), the Gay Slayer (Colin Ireland), and brings them to the forefront of the public's attention as well as the police, and therefore they can hold power over society that their inadequate personalities have craved and I believe this to be the case with DeSalvo as the media began to undertake an interest in the case, however, and as always with the media, they rarely take an interest in the plight of the victims and they consistently take interest with the perpetrator, when they may obtain more psychological clues as to the offender that they are so transfixed upon if they conducted a comprehensive analysis of the victims, as the victim is always central to the fantasies of a serial killer and the ultimate commission of their crimes.

The victims of Albert DeSalvo ranged between young and old, over different races and differing socio-economic status. The thirteen victims of DeSalvo combine to generate a combined age of 691, and thus an average age of 53.1. Considering this, I believe that the victim typology selected by DeSalvo was selected for psychological and anger purposes unwittingly brought about by his mother during his adolescent formative years. The pseudo-medical analysis of serial murder is to look at why the serial killer kills, and does not focus enough on the victim, who will be the central component of the warped desires and fantasies of serial killers and are purposely chosen for the end of a warped psychological cycle. Albert DeSalvo had developed love, anger and sexual desires for his mother in the sense that he would have had a natural maternal bond to his mother, he would have developed anger towards his mother, as firstly he was reared in an abusive environment with an alcoholic father, who was physically abusive to his wife and the children; the father forced DeSalvo into prostitution at the age of ten and forced the others to steal. His mother then remarried Paul Kinosian, who turned out to be as brutal as his paternal father and vented his temper on the stepchildren. This could have resulted in DeSalvo developing an Oedipal complex towards his mother, whom he dearly loved, but he resented the two father figures in his life and developed a mixed emotion of anger and love towards his mother for putting the DeSalvo children into a second dangerous environment. Albert DeSalvo also saw his mother physically beaten and raped in front of him, and the paternal father used to bring home sex workers and have sex in front of the children. These awful experiences would have had an impact during the development stages of DeSalvo's life, and I am deducing that he developed a misogynistic rage against women, and that is why his victim selection was women from various socio-economic and ethnic backgrounds.

PEN PROFILES OF THE OFFENDERS

As we are aware today due to the advancement of studies in serial killers, abnormal psychology, criminology etc., we know that Albert DeSalvo showed many of the classic signs from a young age, and also had a similar upbringing to a lot of other serial killers in the sense that he came from two abusive homes, he tortured animals, including trapping cats and dogs in milk crates and watching them try to tear each other apart, and this type of behaviour forms a side of the MacDonald Triad. DeSalvo was constantly committing acts of kleptomania (theft); he was heavily sexualised by a young age, e.g. he became a child sex worker at the age of ten; he was violent towards other children in his neighbourhood and was sent to Lyn Reform School for Boys but was back there after stealing a car upon his release; he had a hyper sex drive and would enforce sexual intercourse upon his wife at least five times a day; he had managed to obtain another criminal conviction for the molestation of a nine-year-old girl.

In terms of the characteristics evidenced by DeSalvo, I believe that his hyper-sexuality derived from seeing his violent and abusive father rape his mother and bring home sex workers to have sex with them in front of him and the other children, and this also lead DeSalvo to turn to prostitution at such a young age, possibly to acquire some money that his family never had and to also experiment with the perverse acts that he was forced to watch. DeSalvo was reared in an awful environment. This helped him to form a 'psychopathic personality', and the act of harming other children was a way of DeSalvo mimicking his father's behaviour which gave him a sense of power over others that he could never gain over his father and later his stepfather. Albert DeSalvo also showed other traits of a psychopathic personality in the sense that he did not react to reform treatment, he could not hold a job down and was also released from the army, and this is common with a psychopathic personality as they cannot follow orders and obey rules and laws that other members of society abide by. The characteristics of DeSalvo actually tie in with the following statement by Cleckley (1941) as cited by Montaldo (2013); *'Since the psychopath has no real emotions, they develop their own personality throughout their life by mimicking those around them. Their inability to control inappropriate outbursts of anger and hostility can result in loss of jobs, dissociation with family or friends, and even divorce. This is filtered by the psychopath into a justification process for more aggressive behaviour.'* DeSalvo almost certainly had a psychopathic personality, and this is evident throughout his criminal acts and therefore it is imperative that each potential psychological motive for the commission of his offences is actively assessed to build up a composite psychological profile.

I believe that, as there was nothing taken from the crime scenes in terms of monetary items such as radios, television sets etc., and there were several items of personal belongings taken from the victims, this is classic sign of 'trophy' taking, which is synonymous with serial sexual offenders and serial killers. The crimes scenes also showed evidence of excessive violence and sexual assault and battery against the victims, which included the insertion of 'foreign' objects into the victim's genitalia and anal passages. I believe that as DeSalvo suffered from hyper-sexuality and he was almost certainly a psychopathic personality type, the primary motive was to satisfy his hyper-sexual desires, and he was a *hedonistic* killer and falls into two of the sub-categories in terms of this type of killer in the sense that he was *a lust* and *thrill* killer.

DeSalvo exhibited the signs of a lust killer in the sense that he wanted complete power and control over the victims, which he showed by strangling and stabbing them, as these two methods are extremely interpersonal and serve the lust killer's psychosis, and the victim was played with after death and then posed in obscene fashions to taunt the dead and the police. I also believe that he killed for the 'thrill', as he would have been inflicting the upmost terror and pain upon his victims, which provides intense excitement for a sex killer like DeSalvo, although, initially, it was believed that there is no sexual element for a 'thrill' killer. However, I believe that this has been dismissed too early and I believe has become one of the new 'myths' associated with serial killers. For example, Richard Ramirez enjoyed the thrill of finding a home and potential victim, and there was a heavy sexual element to his crimes, and as psychology is still complex and developing all the time it is quite frankly absurd to simply dismiss that a serial killer cannot intertwine between the different sub-categories as mentioned in a previous chapter. I believed that Harold Shipman was a *hedonistic* killer, and he fitted into the three sub-categories for this killer, *lust, thrill, and comfort*. Shipman killed elderly women, as I believe he derived sexual satisfaction from watching them take their last breaths, and again this is associated with power and control. Shipman exhibited symptoms of the *thrill* killer as I believe that he built up fantasies before visiting a victim and the comfort came from his stealing items from the victims and forging wills, both of which intertwined with his grandiose narcissistic personality. I believe that DeSalvo crossed into two of the *hedonistic* serial killer sub-categories based upon the evidence that we are aware of from his known crimes and therefore his victims were at grave risk once he had manipulated them into allowing entry into their residence.

Albert DeSalvo was what I believe to be an organised serial killer, and his demeanour did not appear threatening and/or untoward to his victims, which provided him with the access and opportunity to commit his crimes. Due to his veneer of normality and meek behaviour, the victims suffered a high level of risk since DeSalvo managed to isolate them from view, and he would have derived the sense of the ultimate power over each victim as he was in complete control as they would have been at his mercy. I believe that this was central to his fantasy and a way of acquiring 'power' over each victim, as DeSalvo was a sexual psychopath. I also believe that he kept them alive for a while before actually killing them as he would have had them under control, and the fact they were killed in their apartments meant he had time with each victim and DeSalvo enjoyed control, which was central to his warped fantasies.

Meloy (1992) explains how dangerous a psychopathic sexual sadist can be when he states the following from the *Diagnostic and Statistical Manual of Mental Disorders, 4th Edition (DSM-IV)*; *'Over a period of at least 6 months, recurrent sexual urges and sexually arousing fantasies involving acts (real, not stimulated) in which the psychological or physical suffering (including humiliation) of the victim is sexually exciting to the person. These behaviours are sadistic fantasies or acts that involve the activities that indicate the dominance of the person over his victim (e.g., forcing the victim to crawl, keeping them in a locked cage), or restraint, blindfolding, paddling, spanking, whipping, pinching, beating, burning, electrical shocks, rape, cutting, stabbing, strangulation, torture, mutilation or killing.'* We know that DeSalvo committed several of these acts, for example he raped and sodomised many of his victims, he stuck a fork into the left breast of Mary Brown (stabbing), Evelyn Corbin was found bound and gagged (restraint), and again this is the exercising of power by a sexually inadequate psychopath, and the victims experienced an extremely high level of risk upon meeting Albert DeSalvo, however, due to DeSalvo's psychopathic nature and his own sense of hedonism, the risk he undertook in killing the victims became part of the fantasy, fantasies which would have built up within his psyche between each murder.

The murder took a high degree of risk when killing his victims for a variety of reasons. However, we need to assess whether this 'risk' was a part of his fantasies and therefore apart of the 'thrill' that he was deriving from his own sexually sadistic fantasies.

The first reason being that the victims were not runaways and/or people on the peripheries of society; they were all people that were cared about by others and lived within what society defines as its 'in-groups'. For example, after the first murder, Anna Slesers, who was murdered on the evening of June 4th 1962, her son, Juris, found her after knocking down the door, and in view of this situation had the murderer been any later he may well have been caught in the act and we may not be discussing the case today, as this could have led to his apprehension very early on during his spate of murders.

He also took high levels of risk in that women may have recognised him in the area after knocking on their doors pretending to be from the 'modelling agency' (the Measuring Man). The other risk for DeSalvo was that he had distinctive features and he was playing a high-risk game, especially as one victim survived his murderous desires. In the case of DeSalvo, as in the case of organised serial killers, there may have been an element of him stalking his victims prior to the actual murder, ensuring that they lived alone and, in a way, reducing his own risk of being caught in the act. I believe that DeSalvo may have stalked the victims prior to their murder as this was a part of his fantasy of committing the 'perfect' murder, and in the murder of Joann Graff he asked her neighbour *'Does Joann Graff live here?'* which suggests that he may have known her personally, and/or he had stalked her prior to her murder. If DeSalvo did indeed stalk his victims then he would be the classification number three, *predatory stalker* as outlined by Ainsworth (2001); *'Such people will stalk a victim prior to the attack. The attack itself is often of a sexual nature. Their stalking allows them to gather information about their intended victim and even to rehearse or fantasize about a future assault. The stalking is usually carried out in a way as to not alert the target. As such it is perhaps best described as an instrumental act, yet for some stalkers the feeling of power and control which their actions produce may be a source of satisfaction in themselves'.*

The fact that it does not seem to appear that there was stalking prior to the murders DeSalvo committed is baffling to say the least, as nobody has asked the question, *'How did he know these women were alone?'* I believe that 'risk' during his crimes manifested itself within his fantasy, as psychopaths desire stimulation and the only way they derive 'stimulation' is through their own 'excitement' and this formed a part of DeSalvo's psychosis before the ultimate acts of murder.

PEN PROFILES OF THE OFFENDERS

The sequence of acts before the killing would be to acquire the victim's trust by posing as somebody in authority and/or somebody with an important job to do, as this would give DeSalvo access to the victims, who would be at his mercy as it was just him and the victim, which is again central to his modus operandi and the feeling of power that he derived from gaining access to the victim's home more than likely stimulated him. The sequence of acts after the killings would be that DeSalvo would ransack the apartment, however, this may have been done as he was looking for some form of trophy from the victim to relive the memory of his crimes afterwards. After each murder he would leave his *'signature,'* which was altering the position of the body, leaving a 'decorative' bow around the neck of the victim and/or sexually assault the victim with a hard and phallic object which came to hand, suggesting that DeSalvo was a sexually impulsive character and may have suffered from erectile dysfunction on occasion, this behaviour became more evident and much more refined as his murders progressed, for example, in the murder of Patricia Bissette (victim number eight) he committed all three heinous acts, and this was because he was growing in confidence and was now beginning to taunt society with his crimes as well as the initial victims. The murderous acts committed by DeSalvo appeared to be of a relatively quick nature initially, however, as he began to feel more confident and assured during the commission of his crimes, the time spent with his victims appeared to increase.

I believe that the acts of murder could have taken longer to commit then just a few minutes, as I believe that as DeSalvo was an organised killer and was there to act upon his fantasies as DeSalvo can be classified into the following serial killer/rapist categories: *power-reassurance* – DeSalvo was an inadequate person in many ways, and Ainsworth (2001) states, *'The main driving force for these types appears to be the removal of doubts and fears about their sexual inadequacy and masculinity, and the offender might thus strike again within a few days or weeks, and probably in the same district.'*

Albert DeSalvo was a sexual sadist and would fit into the *anger-retaliatory type*, as these offenders, according to Ainsworth (2001) *'appear to possess a great deal of anger and animosity towards women in general and use the act of rape as a way of expressing or releasing this anger. He also appears to derive pleasure from degrading his victims.'*

Albert DeSalvo also crosses and intertwines into the *anger-excitement type* in the sense that he would have been aroused by the victim's fear and suffering, stimulating himself both psychologically and sexually. As DeSalvo crossed between these three types of criminals, I believe that the acts would have taken longer than a few minutes as he was acting out his fantasies on a particular victim, as he would have had complete control, something he lacked in early life and his general life thereafter. DeSalvo was reliant upon the victim exuding fear of him as this act would have sexually stimulated him, and unlike many *anger-excitement* rapists, who may attack a random victim in the street, the key to DeSalvo's manifested dark desires meant he needed the victim in his control inside a residence whereby he would not be disturbed, otherwise the fantasy would have collapsed and the tension would have continued to manifest itself and build up inside of his psyche and psychosis.

All the thirteen victims were found in their apartments in nine areas of Boston, USA. DeSalvo was a marauding serial killer as opposed to a commuting serial killer as he targeted one geographical area that fitted in with his daily activities, marauding to one's crimes is much more common with sexual offenders as opposed to commuting, which is much more associated with burglars as they can go further afield and find greater rewards in more affluent areas, therefore with the latter socio-economics and demography can play more of a role in the psychology of their decision-making processes.

The bodies of the victims were not moved away from the original murder site, although he did pose the victims to 'retain' power over them and taunt the police. There are other reasons why the bodies were not moved from their original sites, and this is because firstly there is a huge risk for DeSalvo if he tried to move a body around an apartment block, and secondly, there is no psychological purpose for him to do so because he has satiated his lust whilst he has spent time with the victim, both when they are alive and both when they are dead and as each victim was murdered in their apartments and the bodies were not moved, the murder and discovery sites were the same as this act formed part of DeSalvo's fantasies and there was no need to move the bodies as he wanted the unlucky recipient to witness the full horror of his crimes, which included the posing of the body as he knew the police and media would report their findings, thus providing him with the attention he craved. These acts tend to show a highly organised serial killer; however, it is not always the case to simply classify a serial killer as 'organised' and 'disorganised' as there is also a 'mixed' classification which the media tends to ignore, and I will refer as why I believe that DeSalvo falls into the 'mixed' classification of serial killers.

PEN PROFILES OF THE OFFENDERS

I believe that Albert DeSalvo was what the FBI classify as a 'mixed' serial killer, as opposed to pigeon-holing him into the organised or disorganised category, as he exhibited the psychological traits of both respective categories. I have outlined the reasons why I believe this to be the case previously in the profile and the organised traits that he showed are as follows:

- *Albert DeSalvo lived with a partner. Usually, a disorganised impulsive serial killer such as Cayetano Santos Godino and Benjamin Atkins, the 'Woodward Corridor Killer', act more on their impulses and are unmarried. However, some of them are, e.g., Peter Kurten, aka the 'Vampire of Dusseldorf' had a wife, whereas the organised serial killer, Jeffrey Dahmer, the 'Milwaukee Cannibal' lived alone.*
- *He suffered from family abuse either physically, psychologically, verbally, and mentally during his formative years.*
- *DeSalvo followed the media coverage of the case. I believe that this was also evidenced in the fact that he would leave the victims in crude poses, and this became his 'signature', which no doubt the media would pick up on, and could also act as a catalyst to remind him of the crimes, as opposed to returning to the crime scene to relive the murder. Organised serial killers usually follow their crimes in the media as they enjoy and become excited at the interest, whereas the more disorganised serial killers, due to their more impulsive behaviour and fractured mental state, usually do not follow their crimes in the media. However, again here lies the problem in profiling, Peter Sutcliffe was impulsive with his killings and yet he followed the media coverage of his crimes, whereas DeSalvo would not fit the 'visionary' killer typography, e.g. DeSalvo shows a high degree of planning in his crimes to satisfy his psyche for the usual elements of lust, thrill, power and control, and again these are classic symptoms associated with organised serial killers as they are in complete control of their own morality.*
- *DeSalvo did not seek any self-help for his psychological problems as this which may have brought attention upon him about his crimes, and again this shows that he was more than aware that he was committing wrong and he had enough mental capacity to not wish to stop the crimes, as he was deriving satisfaction, e.g. thrill, lust, power and control, and this was evident with the posing of the bodies, which is a common feature with serial killers who enjoy taunting the police,*

ALBERT DESALVO, THE BOSTON STRANGLER

media, the victims and the families, along with the general public.

- *DeSalvo (there has been some evidence to suggest he stalked his prey prior to the murder) pre-planned exactly what he was going to do and how he was going to do it before arriving at the scene, e.g., pretending to be from the modelling agency, pretending to be in the apartment block to carry out maintenance repairs. He may have also acted as a police officer to acquire the victim's trust. This may be a bit presumptuous, but it could have been a guise to acquire the trust of the victim(s), as a police officer commands respect and again we see organised serial killers using law enforcement as a ruse to gain their victims trust, e.g. Gerard Schaefer was an actual police officer, whereas Bundy and Bianchi pretended to be a police officer to acquire the access and the opportunity to commit their crimes against their chosen victim.*

- *DeSalvo used restraints and ligatures to subdue and control the victims, which can provide evidence of the offender acting out a planned fantasy as opposed to acting solely on impulse.*

- *DeSalvo left the scene on many occasions without any witnesses seeing him, as he was almost chameleon like and blended in, possibly dressed in work attire, and he would be as unassuming as any other person entering the apartment blocks on the days of the murders. Although, to the best of my knowledge, there was blood at several crime scenes, I do believe that DeSalvo may have brought a change of clothes to make his exit much easier, because any ripped clothes or blood on him would raise suspicion from members of the public. Although this may appear very sceptical, DeSalvo was organised in many respects and extremely cold and calculating.*

- *I believe that he ransacked some of the apartments of his victims for the following two reasons; (i) to try to originally make it look like a robbery gone wrong, as this became less common as the murders progressed and he gained more press attention, and the murders became about psychological stimulation in the sense that he was showing he was in control; and, (ii) he may have been looking for a particular 'trophy' for memories and stimulation later on. The taking of 'trophies' is a common trait amongst organised serial killers as they use them to remember their crimes and to achieve sexual gratification thereafter.*

The above are the elements as to why I believe that DeSalvo's crimes showed a degree of 'organisation' and therefore one could simply label him as an 'organised' offender, however, there are elements and psychological traits that he has in common with the disorganised offender classification and they are as follows:

- DeSalvo's IQ was measured at between 60-70. This is below average and is commonly linked with disorganised serial killers, such as Richard Trenton Chase and Cayetano Santos Godino, whereas more organised serial killers exhibit a higher IQ, for example Jeffrey Dahmer, who graduated with ease with qualifications in chemistry from high school.
- DeSalvo was socially inadequate and did not have many friends, and again, this was due to his completely abnormal upbringing, and because to his father's actions and his mother he would not have developed the ability to share the required intimacy to form normal friendship bonds and would have almost certainly struggled to form sexual bonds and experiences with the opposite sex, the latter of which would have enraged him and fuelled his fantasies even further.
- DeSalvo lived near each crime scene, although as mentioned this is a common psychological trait of sex offenders, DeSalvo used his occupation to acquire his victims and he could easily have been caught. The other side to this issue is that as he was a thrill-seeking killer, this could have formed within his psyche as part of his 'game'. Truth be told, during the 1960s, the FBI and police did not have the methods on how to track serial killers or sexual predators, however, serial killers and sex offenders did not have to worry about how the FBI or police may track them. Since the advancement in books and media, serial killers are much more aware about 'commuting' as opposed to 'marauding', and DeSalvo killed after pre-planning his crimes, and this is another area where he crosses between an 'organised' and 'disorganised' serial killer.
- He depersonalises the victims and leaves DNA evidence at each crime scene, whereas more 'organised' serial killers usually go to great lengths to hide their victims and sometimes dismember their victims to take another 'trophy', whereas DeSalvo never exhibited this, and this is possibly because he time he had with the victim and the act of posing may have served his psychological processes better than dismembering them, as he had left his 'signature'. The danger of this, apart from the DNA, is that he may have asked female partners to pose in these positions for him, which can generate suspicion upon him.

- *He attacked some of the victims in a blitz pattern, e.g. in the murder of Mary Brown, he stabbed her in the left breast fourteen times and left the fork in the breast, and her cause of death was by being beaten to death and was not by strangulation, which could suggest that in part he may have become nervous of something and therefore switched his modus operandi, suggesting that this murder and one or two others may have been impulsive that and not all of them were pre-planned, as one victim did manage to fight him off.*

The crimes appeared to be staged originally to look like a burglary gone wrong, and this gradually stopped as each murder progressed, as DeSalvo was receiving more attention from the media he did not need to ransack the apartments of his victims. There are possible explanations for this in the sense that he may have started off his crimes as 'impulsive' or 'disorganised' and, true to human nature, the more a person carries out an act the better and more confident they become. I believe this to be the case with DeSalvo, as it is with many other serial killers. The posing of the bodies and excessive use of force into the vaginal and anal orifices became his 'signature', and he may have taken more trophies such as clothing to stimulate him later, as the acts he was committing psychologically stimulated him, as opposed to trying to hide his crimes by 'faking' a crime scene.

Albert DeSalvo may have ransacked the apartments to firstly find 'trophies', and secondly originally out of fear that he may be caught, and this may have stopped over time as he got away with his crimes and his confidence grew, therefore he did not need to stage a crime to mislead the police, however, we need to assess more areas of his crimes to establish a composite psychological picture for the innate motivations that may have led to him committing such deviant crimes, such as the cause of death, location of wounds and the positions that the bodies were left in.

The cause of death was caused by *asphyxiation* in most cases. The motivation derived by a sexual sadist such as DeSalvo would have been not only an act of power over a victim, but also an act of *erotic asphyxiation* in which the perpetrator may have had an orgasm whilst committing the act of murder. Strangulation is also an intimate form of murder and again this would have acted as a substitute for the 'intimacy' that he could not find in the confines of a normal and healthy sexual relationship.

The location of the wounds on the victims, other than the initial strangulation, shows a man who has many sexual inadequacies with women and is fearful of both women and his own sexual inadequacies, as he needs to 'objectify' them for his own psychological and sexual gratification, and because he hates them and wants to completely dehumanise them.

The act of strangulation was the chosen method of murder for the purposes of intimacy and control, and because for DeSalvo, like many sexual psychopaths, the act of sex or sexual experience is based on impulsivity and aggression due to wanting complete control, and empathy does not form a part of their psyche. DeSalvo used strangulation to kill or at least render the victim into a semi-conscious state for him to have complete control over them to act out his fantasies. Many of the victims had been assaulted with phallic objects such as a wine bottle (Nina Nicholls), the end of a broom (Jane Sullivan), a pipe (Mary Brown), and many of the other victims had similar violent lacerations from unknown objects. This action conducted in the killer's modus operandi suggests that the killer had an Oedipal complex, and as I have mentioned earlier in the profile, I believe this to have been borne out of his mother not protecting him against two violent and promiscuous men during his childhood and adolescence. A young Albert DeSalvo would have hated them both and yearned for his mother's love, and yet despised her at the same time, as a mother should be maternal from the womb to grave for her children. His early childhood and adolescent experience almost certainly entered his psyche into a state of confusion in his *psychosis*, and the sexual acts he had seen and was committed upon him led him to become confused about the normal constitutions of normal and healthy sexual acts/relationships and helped aid and develop his early warped sexual fantasies and desires, which he would act upon due to his abnormal sex drive.

The positions of the bodies where usually posed, and always had a ligature in a bow around the necks of the victims, usually made from their own pantyhose, pillowcases, scarves etc. Albert DeSalvo posed the victims in ludicrous positions, e.g., the legs of the victim were spread wide open in the case of Nina Nicholls, or in the case of Ana Slesers her left leg was stretched straight towards him (her son), the other flung wide, almost at right angles, and bent at the knee so that she was grossly exposed. This became known as the perpetrator's 'signature', and they are psychologically significant acts in the sense that the killer was retaining power over the victim, and those who found them would be haunted by the sight and thus they became 'secondary' victims. The media become interested in high-profile cases and therefore he had a form of control over the tertiary victims – the public. DeSalvo, despite his deviant crimes, did manage to hold down a normal relationship and build a family of his own and was by all accounts a very loving husband and father to his children, despite the dreadful upbringing his father bestowed upon him in his formative years.

Despite DeSalvo having a very bad childhood, later in his life things seemed to take a turn for the better when he met and married a middle-class, Catholic girl by the name of Imgard Beck in 1954 whilst was serving in the army and being posted to Frankfurt, Germany. Unfortunately, Imgard Beck would suffer the innate sexual desires that manifested themselves within DeSalvo's psyche, which I believe was imprinted within his psychosis due to the behaviour he was forced to witness from his father during his formative years.

Albert DeSalvo was a *sexual psychopath* who would demand sexual intercourse from his wife on average five times a day, as her testimony has provided us with this information. DeSalvo again is showing us his true sexual psychopathy, and, in these acts, he is objectifying his own wife to a vessel for his own sexual pleasure, showing truly that sexual psychopaths are incapable of empathy and love. Unfortunately, serial killers are predatory even when courting a partner, and they target those who exhibit empathy, and they become vessels for their partners to provide the 'veneer of normality', which aids them to be able to commit their crimes for so long; after all who really would believe a normal hardworking family man would be a serial killer? We always look for monsters under our beds, however, we never gaze over our fence at the true monsters that lurk within our communities. Serial killers choosing the meek as partners are not uncommon, as previously mentioned, however, the more intertwined with sexual sadism the psyche of the serial killer is, the more the partner is at risk from a lifetime of subjugation.

Serial killers target and choose vulnerable partners as it gives them a sense of domination and control over a willing person, and they will act upon their abnormal sexual whims and desires. These actions are not an isolated in terms of a *sexual sadist* serial killer, and examples include Jerome 'Jerry' Brudos, who married an impressionable young girl when he was discharged from the army and she went along with everything Brudos wanted, including staying naked in the house throughout the day, staying out of his 'workshop' and avoiding the attic (Ramsland 2012). This is another form of power for the sexual and social inadequacies that the likes of Brudos and DeSalvo yearned for in their everyday lives, which was brought about by an abusive father in the case of DeSalvo and an abusive mother in the case of Brudos. Another common factor in each case is that each woman refused to succumb to their sexual desires once they bore children, and this is when the murders of both DeSalvo and Brudos began to escalate as their hyper and abnormal sexual desires and fantasies were no longer being satiated.

When assessing serial killers, it is not just important to psychologically assess their choice of partners, it is also important to assess their employment history, as this can provide us with crucial psychological information on their behaviour with a previous employer. Albert DeSalvo's first known job was as a delivery boy, and later had two stints in the US army, which he was discharged from on both occasions. Again, this is not uncommon with people who have a psychopathic personality as they struggle to adhere to rules as set out by others/society due to a number of reasons as outlined by Cleckley (1941); *'Psychopaths have a grandiose sense of self-worth, a failure to accept responsibility for his/her own actions, they have a need for stimulation as they are prone to boredom, lack of responsibility, poor behavioural controls, impulsivity, irresponsibility, a juvenile delinquency, criminal versatility.'* It is not uncommon for serial killers to struggle in employment, for example John Haigh was released from work for theft, and the German serial killer, Fritz Harman, was discharged from National Service and imprisoned in Germany for being absent without leave (AWOL). Amazingly, and possibly due to his age at the time, Albert DeSalvo only began to respect authority when he confessed his crimes to his wife, who in turn advised him to turn himself into the police.

Albert DeSalvo listened to his wife when the police arrested him, as she unequivocally advised him *'to not hold anything back from them.'* This is key to understanding DeSalvo's personality in the sense that his wife may have been the only woman he truly loved, as she was the only woman who provided him with affection and stability in his life that he felt his mother never provided to him. He admitted to the police that he broke into four hundred apartments and committed a 'couple' of rapes, and that he had assaulted 300 women in a four-state area. If this is true, then it confirms the hypothesis that serial killers do not just start suddenly killing, and that killing becomes the end game which they psychology prepare themselves for by perpetrating other serial acts, for example, many serial killers have admitted to burglary and kleptomania simply for the 'excitement', and this is more than likely their first criminal and deviant venture against mainstream society. DeSalvo may well have also been lying to cause the police more work

ALBERT DESALVO, THE BOSTON STRANGLER

and to acquire even more media attention, as serial killers tend to crave notoriety. Although geographical profiling would not be readily used until the 1970's and psychological profiling was still in its infancy, had DeSalvo become a person of 'interest' in the investigation would a criminal record check have potentially flagged him as a suspect?

Albert DeSalvo had several convictions for theft, and as we know from more recent medical studies on the psychopathic condition, kleptomania forms a part of their psychosis as it is risk-taking behaviour that would stimulate somebody with a psychopathic personality, and again, the theft convictions and assaults were committed before he escalated into rape and sexual assault as, with all sexual psychopaths, there is a constant need for 'stimulation' and a normal life would not adhere to their psychopathy. There are extreme dangers of labelling somebody as a 'sexual offender' simply because they suffer with kleptomania, however, in the case of DeSalvo, if he was flagged as a suspect, his criminal records check alongside his employment checks should have been assessed against each other and this would have showed that he had a lack of remorse for the rules of a moral society, and offenders like this should be noted as a person of 'interest' until the investigation reaches its conclusion.

Albert DeSalvo was arrested in January 1955 when he was charged with the molestation of a nine-year-old girl. When the likes of DeSalvo are arrested for any form of a sexual offence, an extensive check on their criminal history should be thoroughly conducted, as it seems to be a reoccurring theme with serial murderers. If we fast forward to London, England, and the case of the British serial killer Robert Napper, he had been sexually assaulted as a boy. Napper bullied other children in his neighbourhood (as did DeSalvo). Napper was accused of committing a rape and the police made an error and let him go. Napper had convictions as a youth for theft. I believe that, to an untrained investigator, there would be no consideration to link such acts together. However, these types of perpetrators appear to have a high veracity for serious criminal acts and therefore they should be given more consideration in terms of longer-term assessed treatments, especially in areas where a series of crimes appear to be occurring with a high level of frequency. In view of my opinion, I believe that a criminal record check on DeSalvo did suggest the possibility of the commission of such offences because of his psychopathic personality and persistent need for stimulation and there have been cases where rape progresses to murder.

PEN PROFILES OF THE OFFENDERS

Pen Profile

I, Samuel Hodgins, can confirm that I have researched the case of the Boston Strangler and the crimes committed by the serial killer Albert DeSalvo (Italian/American, male). Albert DeSalvo committed his crimes (that are known of) between the ages of 24 (1955) up until his arrest on the 27th of October 1964, the crimes appear to escalate from obtaining sex under false pretences, to rape, to brutal murder, which is not uncommon amongst a serious sexual sadist offender.

As DeSalvo (and nobody else to date) has ever stood trial for the crimes committed by the Boston Strangler, I am therefore not trying to offer a psychological profile of an *unsub*, I am therefore in effect trying to offer a psychological post-mortem of the offender in question, Albert DeSalvo, whom I believe to be the Boston Strangler, and nobody else to be an accomplice to the crimes. I will state my reasons in the conclusion at the end of the offender profile. The pen profile of the offender in question is based upon the information contained within the above profile information, and I will try to explain the motivations of Albert DeSalvo to try to explain why he committed heinous crimes and left the women of Boston living in a state of fear up until his arrest in October 1964.

1. The criminal acts committed by Albert DeSalvo were all of a serial nature, e.g., the acts of theft, sexual assaults, the 'Measuring Man', the case of the 'Green Man' right up until the crimes of the 'Boston Strangler'.

    Each respective case is of a similar nature and in each of the first two cases, we know the offender gained access to the victims apartments under false pretences, and I also believe that the 'Boston Strangler' also gained access to his victims in this way and this also provided him with the opportunity to act out his perverse sexual fantasies and murder his victims after stalking them for several days, during which he was making sure he would be safe to commit the crimes, and it was a build-up of arousal within him from his fantasies that would be consuming his thoughts all day.

    Albert DeSalvo, I believe, was all three of the criminals mentioned above and was a cunning and calculated serial killer. Albert DeSalvo shows many of the classic symptoms of a serial killer in the sense that he came from an unstable background with at least one abusive parent. He committed acts of animal cruelty. He was highly sexualised and became sexually active at a young age (aged ten, he became a 'rent boy'). He did not develop socially and would frequently fight with other children. He was sent to a reform school twice for violence and grand theft auto. The reform school did not turn his life around (psychopaths do not adhere to treatment). He had a conviction for sexual assault at the age of 24, just before the 'Measuring Man' appeared, and when his wife, who I believe to be the only woman he loved, did not want to have sexual intercourse with him as she bore her a disabled child, this became his alter-ego and his modus operandi for obtaining victims under false pretences.

The other striking factor is that DeSalvo admitted to 300 rapes in a four-state area, and many believe this to be an exaggeration and it may well be. However, the first victims of the strangler occurred in 1962, when DeSalvo would have been 31, and this fits in with the theory put forth by Symanius (1998) that the average age of a serial killer is 28.5 years. This theory would tie in with DeSalvo, as he was only 2.5 years older than the average age when a serial killer commits his first murder, and we see an escalation in his crimes. Albert DeSalvo may well have committed more murders that have not been connected to the case as he had an abnormally high sex drive even in the company of his wife, who he demanded intercourse from five times a day, which provides a psychological basis for his primitive obsession with sexual intercourse.

2. The mean average of the age of the victims is 53.1 years of age (combined age of 691 years divided by number of victims 13). As the age range of the victims vary considerably with the youngest victim, Mary Sullivan being aged just 19, and the oldest being Mary Mullen, aged 79 gives us an age gap of 60 years between the youngest and oldest victim. This shows that if the access and opportunity would arise, DeSalvo's sexual psychopathy would be in overdrive, and he posed a pertinent risk to any woman whom this predator set his sights upon.

In view of this situation, I believe that the women who lived or resided in the Boston area during this period where exposed to a high level of risk as DeSalvo was a psychopathic sexual sadist, who suffered from misogynistic rage, which was evident by the manner in which DeSalvo humiliated some of his victims by posing their nude corpses and leaving several victims with brutal and excessive slashing/stabbing, laying testament to my theory that he inhibited misogynistic rage within his psychosis. DeSalvo was a *psychopathic sexual sadist* as he objectified women for his own sexual gratification, and age, race, socio-economic group et al. did not matter to him one iota as the obsession for power and control were his primary psychological motivations.

3. If Albert DeSalvo had never been caught, then due to his abnormal sex drive, today, journalists, police forces, amateur sleuths, crime writers etc. would be writing about an unknown perpetrator in the same breath as the *Zodiac Killer*, who is believed to have killed more than 37 victims. Although it is a common misconception that serial killers cannot stop killing, there are some who do, according to the FBI. Denis Rader murdered ten victims between 1974–1991 and then he did not kill another victim prior to his capture in 2005 (Morton, 2005). DeSalvo, unlike Rader, the latter of whom was still sexually active at home, would have gone on to kill many more to serve his sexual desires and fantasies and therefore DeSalvo had the potential to be the worst serial killer of all time.

4. Albert DeSalvo became a serial killer due to being nurtured in not one, but two awful environments. Albert DeSalvo saw horrific acts of abuse, usually against him or his mother. The drunkard father would force himself upon his wife in front of the children and would also use extreme acts of violence, and in one incident bent Mrs DeSalvo's fingers back so far they broke. The father would also bring home sex workers and force the children to watch. This is crucial in his sexual development, as DeSalvo began to fuse sex and violence together within his psyche and this would eventually lead to him acting upon his inner urges. This is crucial to the development of Albert DeSalvo as he was witness to these acts. We know that he became a violent and wayward child in his neighbourhood and would often commit crimes that would lead him onto the path to reform school on several occasions, which did not work (see point number 5 for further details), and he became highly sexualised from a young age and was active in prostitution at the age of ten.

The formative years are crucial in the development of any child and Albert DeSalvo became as violent, misogynistic, and sexually driven as his father. This is what psychologists call 'imprinting'; the dictionary refers to imprinting as *'rapid learning that occurs during a brief receptive period, typically soon after birth or hatching, and establishes a long-lasting behavioural response to a specific individual or object attachment to a parent/parents, offspring or site.'* In terms of 'imprinting', Albert DeSalvo became a misogynistic monster as he saw his father commit such acts and abuse, sex, power and a feeling of inadequacy became a part of his psychosis, and he would later come to view women as objects for his sexual gratification. It is also important to remember that Albert DeSalvo was at the forefront of his father's rage in comparison with the other children, and it may go some way to explain why his siblings went onto lead normal lives in comparison to him.

a. DeSalvo's mother also contributed to her son's psychosis, although unwittingly. When Frank DeSalvo finally left his family in 1939, Charlotte DeSalvo met a man named Paul Kinosian who was just as brutal as Frank, who would often vent his violent temper upon Albert and his other stepchildren. I am therefore led to believe that Albert DeSalvo developed an Oedipal complex in which he loved his mother dearly and he hated the two father figures in his young and formative years. I am led to believe that DeSalvo had an Oedipal complex due to the phallic objects used upon his victims, which was brought about by his belief that his mother (who he dearly loved) did not protect him from these brutal men whilst he was young, and therefore sex, violence, love, hate, anger, lust, possession, desire, power and control all became a kaleidoscope of confusion in the formation of his psychosis.

b. It has been recorded that Albert DeSalvo bore the brunt of the frustrations of his father figures in comparison to his siblings and this is not uncommon with serial killers, for example, Jerry Brudos mother had three boys already and had wanted a girl and dressed him up as a girl and belittled him for it (Ramsland, 2006). Edmund Kemper's mother got it into her head that her son would rape his own sister if he had the chance, despite no evidence of this, so she locked him up every night in the windowless basement, which terrified him and instilled a hatred for his mother that festered inside him for years (Roland 2007). Unlike the two mentioned serial killers, Charlotte DeSalvo dearly loved young Albert, however, due to Albert's underlying psychological problems he would have blamed his mother for his troubles, as Brain (2009) cites Bowlby (1953), *'Mother Love in infancy and childhood is as important for mental health as vitamins and proteins are for physical health.'* DeSalvo became completely confused between love and hate and the elements that constitute each respective human nature.

5. Albert DeSalvo was formed into a sexual psychopath and was not born as one, due to my theories outlined above. The early childhood experiences of Albert DeSalvo brought about frustration from his father's actions and his general impoverishment which led to him becoming aggressive to other children as outward act of 'transference' and later this absence of power in early life and sexual inadequacies was transferred onto his female victims. Doherty (2005) refers to the psychopathic personality in the form of, *'Since the victim is invariably a stranger there can be no suggestion of the victim being the external cause of the attack. It may well be that the psychopath, because of early life experiences, has internal frustrations that provide a further basis for his behaviour.'* As Albert DeSalvo did not respond to the reform school and neither did Edmund Kemper, this is again a classic symptom of a psychopathic personality not being able to respond to psychiatric treatment. Johnson (2007) in his report on physical abusers and sexual offenders (2007) cites Hare (1993), *'Psychopaths do not recognise that they have a problem (and) are not likely to benefit from treatment programmes because the brains of psychopaths are wired differently, they do not respond to emotional words or cues. In short psychopaths simply become better at offending with treatment interventions.'* This appears to be the case with DeSalvo as he became more deviant and more cunning as his crimes escalated.
6. Although it has been established that the crimes committed by Albert DeSalvo were of a serial nature, I believe that his criminal acts intertwine between the *hedonistic, anger-retaliatory and power/control-orientated type serial killer*, as outlined by Holmes and De Burger (1989) cited by Williams (2005), and I also believe that he may have stalked some of his victims and he would be categorised as a *predatory stalker* by Ainsworth (2001). I also believe that DeSalvo was a *sexual sadist* and *'signature' serial killer*, and therefore the combination of these typologies combined with DeSalvo's psychopathic personality make him one of the most lethal predators from the annals of North American criminal history.
    a. Holmes and De Burger (1989) define a *power/control-orientated type serial killer* as 'these criminal acts out of a desire to show absolute power over another human by taking ultimate control over life and death. To prove control, he may commit sexual acts, but the sex acts as a form of power over the victim. The victim will usually be a stranger who has specific characteristics, the crime will be organised and

planned. The killing is often of a highly sadistic nature.' Albert DeSalvo needed to be in control, and this is evident in the places where each of his victims was murdered, which all occurred within their apartments. This is to provide him with total control over the victim as he is unlikely to be disturbed. The act of rape was to reassert the power that he never had during adolescence and to satisfy his perverse sexual fantasies. Each victim was a stranger to DeSalvo, and I do believe that in the most part, the murders were planned for at least a few days prior to each attack (other than the Helen Blake murder, which was committed a few hours after the Nina Nicholls murder). The killings were of a highly sadistic nature, and often several of the victims suffered lacerations to both the anal and vaginal area.

b. I believe that Albert DeSalvo stalked the victims prior to the actual murder(s) because if he knew the women had a partner and/or were visited regularly, then there is a higher risk in the committing the murders as he may have been caught. DeSalvo fantasised about committing the 'perfect murder' and this ideology and with his sexual fantasies, combined with his modus operandi were all part of the 'game' that he was playing, and it would have almost given him a sense of hedonistic power over these women.

The stalking was part of the 'game', which became intertwined with his sexual fantasies, and he did not want this cycle to be broken or disrupted at any time, for example, during the attempted murder of Gertude Gruen, he told her (when she had his back to him) '*You are pretty enough to be a model*,' and then he strangled her. However, she began fighting back, biting his arm, and sinking her teeth into his flesh and she screamed, and the offender ran off. Instead of brutally murdering her he ran away, because his ideological fantasy of murder, e.g., a submissive victim, did not come to fruition as he was not planning on retaliation from the victim, because fantasy is sometimes better than reality; in the realms fantasy a person is in complete control, there are external factors and stimuli that can change the dynamics of any given situation and a person is not in control.

c. DeSalvo was a *sexual sadist/rapist serial killer*. Albert DeSalvo can uniquely be classified into all four of the FBI sub-definitions of their rapist typologies as outlined by Owen (2004); power-reassurance, anger-retaliation, power-assertive and anger-excitation (sadistic) rapists. Owen (2004) states; *'The power-reassurance rapist, is the least violent of the four types.'* I believe that DeSalvo fits into this category because he needed to reassert his inadequate male dominance over the victim, as the murders (known) began to occur when his wife rejected his sexual advances, and once again a woman whom he loved in his life was rejecting him. Owen (2004) also states about the *power-reassurance rapist*: *'Providing the location is secure enough to avoid being discovered by a passer-by, he will spend a considerable amount of time with the victim, over and above to complete the rape.'* Unfortunately, with a *sexual sadist psychopath* such as DeSalvo, rape was not the only mitigating factor in his psychological motivations.

d. Owen (2004) explains that for the *power-assertive rapist 'the reason for the attack can be due to the belief that a man has a fundamental right to attack women to take the pleasure they seek, though in these cases the rape itself involves aggression as well as sexual release'*. I believe that DeSalvo fits into this category due to his early childhood experiences and the fact that he witnessed his father's deranged treatment of women in the sense that Frank DeSalvo brutalised his mother, as did his stepfather, Paul Kinosian, and he believed that women are just objects to be used for sex and reproduction. DeSalvo to a degree may have viewed his wife from his own patriarchal view that she was there to serve his sexual desires, as evidenced by the overzealous sexual demands that he forced upon her and this became imprinted within his psyche from an early age and to DeSalvo, this abhorrent treatment of women was simply 'normal' in his psyche.

e. Owen (2004) defines the *anger-retaliation rapist* as *'driven by the uncontrollable anger against dominating women in his life ...'* I believe that as Albert DeSalvo developed an Oedipal complex and he also hated his mother but loved her at the same time, and she brought him up in the world under two violent men, he felt he never had any control over women and with his wife's rejection this was another blow for him, and his ego and sense of self-worth were completely shattered. Therefore, he sought to destroy the hated object of his frustration, which was women. I believe this theory to be evident in the excessive stabbing and mutilation of several of his victims. DeSalvo also targeted different races and ages as to him women were all women, or mere objects for his twisted pleasures.

f. Owen (2004) explains that for the *anger-excitation rapist 'the sexual element of rape is merely a means to the ultimate end of inflicting physical and psychological damage upon the victims. In many cases, the attitudes and behaviour patterns which result in a compulsion to deliver these terrible attacks originate in childhood, usually with a combination of single-parent upbringing and physical – and often sexual abuse. However, the degree of control the anger-excitation rapist wants to exert over his helpless victims is reflected in his own personal and criminal life.'* In the case of DeSalvo the sexual imprinting that developed in his formative years and the sexual abuse he suffered due to his father renting him out for money is shown in his crimes in the essence that he tied his victims for control (more than likely after rendering them semi-conscious). He appeared to slash or stab the victims, not just on the body but also the anal and vaginal areas, which is another sign of his anger-excitement as he could have derived multiple orgasms from such an act, as we know that semen was found at several of the crime scenes, and it is not uncommon when dealing with serial killers, e.g. Peter Kurten, who claimed that he could generate multiple orgasms whilst excessively stabbing a sheep (which later transferred to people), as the sight of blood was his 'ultimate pleasure'. DeSalvo gained sexual excitement from witnessing the pain and suffering of another human being.

g. Albert DeSalvo is also classed as a 'signature killer' in the sense that he posed several of the victims, for example, the murder of Ida Irga in which the killer had spread her legs approximately four to five feet from heel to heel, and her feet were propped up on individual chairs and a standard bed pillow, with the cover placed under her buttocks. The 'signature' of the bow and the posing of the bodies is for the killer to reassert the power and dominance he held over the victim, police, and society, as people will know that it is he who has committed the crime, and he can leave people living in fear of where and when he will strike next. Albert DeSalvo was like many other serial killers, who are wholly inadequate human beings, and this may be the only form of power they can acquire throughout their lives.

7. I believe on the majority side of the argument, Albert DeSalvo could be classed as an 'organised' serial killer, although each crime scene appeared to be left in a chaotic state and even DNA evidence was left at the crime scene. It must be remembered that this was an era before the advancement of crime scene investigation (CSI) and before advancements in forensic science techniques. Albert DeSalvo would acquire the trust of his victims by pretending to be a figure of authority to make the victims lower their guard. He ensured the women lived alone, however, the actual murders show a degree of disorganisation in the sense that he may well have used his bare hands (as with the attempted murder of Gertude Gruen), he left the scene in a chaotic state, and he committed the murder of Joann Graff after speaking to her neighbour, who would provide a description of him to the police. I believe that overall, though, DeSalvo was a predominately organised killer but he could also be classed as a 'mixed killer'. However, a crossover of both and 'organised' and 'disorganised' serial killer is highly unlikely in any respective case, and in DeSalvo's case, from early crime scene reports and witness reports, he started off 'disorganised' and the more murders he committed the more 'organised' he became throughout the spate of murders, and this is where there are grey lines between the classifications.
    a. The crimes committed by Albert DeSalvo were mostly of an organised nature in the sense that I believe that he went out solely to obtain a victim for his own 'pleasure', and it was not just 'opportunity' as there appears to be a degree of planning as he may have stalked some of his victims prior to their rape and murders. In the sense that he was an organised serial killer was the way he firstly gained access to his victims, e.g., posing as a figure of authority, the 'Measuring Man' or 'Green Man', thus gaining access to the women whom he intended to rape and kill. It wouldn't be surprising to find that he posed as a police officer because despite the crimes being given media attention, lone women would have been more wary of who they would let into their homes. However, his crimes continued unabated, and this modus operandi is a real possibility in the case of the Boston Strangler. It has been established that a decisive factor for a serial killer when selecting a victim is the 'access and opportunity', and the deception which formed a part of his modus operandi helped him achieve this. I also believe that the notoriety he was

ALBERT DESALVO, THE BOSTON STRANGLER

gaining from the media and the narcissistic feeling of 'achievement' of inducing a paralysis of fear upon a city was giving him an almost God-like sense of power, as he would have followed his crimes in the media, which is a common factor with an organised serial killer as they see it as taunting society, and it becomes almost like a 'catch me if you can' scenario. However, the more grandiose and the narcissistic this thought process manifests itself, the more likely they are too be captured. DeSalvo took trophies from his victims to relive the memory of each crime he committed, which is another classic sign of organised serial killers.

b. Albert DeSalvo did not entirely show signs of organisation, e.g. he left evidence at the scene including cigarette butts, although he did not smoke (I will explain my hypothesis on this in my conclusion), he showed signs of excessive overkill (this could, however, not only be to heighten his sexual 'pleasure' but as a means to an end to scare the tertiary victim, which is general society), he did not appear to bring a 'murder kit' to the scene and may have used his bare hands or an item that came to hand, such as cables or pantyhose. Although DeSalvo may be classed as a 'mixed offender' I believe that overall, he was organised, or at least progressed to an organised offender, which made him much more dangerous. A final point on his disorganisation is the fact he left DNA at every scene and made no attempts to clean up; in 2013, his DNA was linked to his youngest victim, Mary Sullivan (19), as his semen was retained and his remains were exhumed, and this process solved a 49-year-old cold case. It does make one wonder whether if DNA evidence had been widely available at the start of his series of murders, would DeSalvo been apprehended much quicker? Tragically we will never know, and we can only assume, and assumption will not bring back the dead and neither will it undo DeSalvo's vile and wicked crimes.

In further reference to the previous two points, if more research had been conducted on serial offending and serial murder, and had the following investigative tools been available – geographical profiling, offender profiling, criminalistics (CSI) and smallest space analysis (SSA) – then I believe that DeSalvo would have been apprehended much more quickly. I state the belief to my hypothesis in the fact that DeSalvo lived local to all the crimes and a map of where the crimes were committed could have shown some areas of 'inactivity' where the perpetrator may not have offended or at least was least likely to offend (geographical profiling). If offender profiling was more prevalent, then more psychologists could have cross referenced with Dr James Brussel, who believed that there were two offenders, however, in the modern day this seems unlikely to have two offenders with the same modus operandi and the same warped sexual psychological beliefs working in tandem at any one given time, and the signature of the knotted bow was always the same. With all this information available a profile could have been generated on who was likely to offend and why he would be committed to such acts.

As DeSalvo had previous criminal convictions, his name may well have appeared on the 'person(s) of interest', and if he lived in an area of low activity or 'inactivity', he most would have been a subject of interest to the investigation. Crime scene analysis was not given as much due care in the USA and Britain at the time of the murders, and therefore vital evidence could have been unwittingly destroyed by police, therefore allowing the offender to have a greater chance of remaining anonymous. Yet the advancement in forensic science is so far advanced in the modern age, for example, the British serial killer, Colin Pitchfork, who killed two girls in Narborough, left a small trace of semen on one of his victims and forensic scientists linked this specimen to a person with type A blood and an enzyme profile that matched only 10% of men (Owen 2004). Pitchfork was the first criminal convicted in Britain via forensic science.

In terms of smallest space analysis (SSA), in the cases of the 'Green Man' and the 'Measuring Man' if we had taken the relationship between the variables and linked them to together to establish the common variables and how common they were in each crime e.g., aggressive use of language, threats, apologies etc. The use of language by a perpetrator in an investigation can be critical in the sense that a perpetrator may use a certain phrase that somebody recognises, for example. If this was the case, combined with the other stipulated investigative tools, the suspect pool could have been narrowed down by use of identity parades etc. to help the police focus their resources on a prime suspect or suspects as in the use of language, we all have unique phrases and speech and the smallest space analysis (SSA) technique could have been a useful tool in

8. In further reference to the above stipulated hypothesis, I believe that the above coupled with an extensive criminal record check of Albert DeSalvo would have made him become an interest to the police. Albert DeSalvo possessed a criminal record for a sexual assault against a nine-year-old girl and he had been to reform school as a youth on several occasions. As we know from later studies on serial killers, many of them have an extensive criminal record, e.g., Jeffrey Dahmer was arrested in 1982 for indecent exposure to two young boys, and again in 1986 for masturbating in front of two young boys (Golgowski, 2013). Serial killers with a high sexual drive usually commit prior criminal acts of a sexual nature and Dahmer and DeSalvo are not the only two; others such as Brudos, Gacy et al. have prior convictions for sexual offences on their rap sheet before their final incarceration or execution.

   Albert DeSalvo also shows another common trait with serial killers: they do not obey rules set out by society or a governing authority, e.g., the army, the police, the courts etc. In DeSalvo's case he dropped out of reform school twice, Dahmer dropped out of the army, as did John Wayne Gacy. Serial killers and psychopaths in general struggle to conform to rules set by others as they are psychopathic and narcissistic; they see themselves above law and order. I therefore believe that had an extensive criminal record check on DeSalvo been conducted and more literature was written about serial killers and their victim typology at the time of the murders, then DeSalvo may have become a prime suspect earlier.

9. After reviewing the case of the Boston Strangler in great depth, I believe that Albert DeSalvo was indeed the Boston Strangler and I have arrived at this conclusion firstly due to a thorough and in-depth analysis of his personality type. DeSalvo firstly shows the classic symptoms associated with serial killers and serial rapists. Albert De Salvo had prior convictions for sexual assault and was posted to Germany during his five years of service and there is a possibility that sexual assaults may have happened in Germany as well as the USA, as serial killers/rapists have no boundaries and will kill when opportunity and access to a victim arises; for example, Jack Unterweger, killed sex workers in four different countries due to the nature of his employment as a journalist. Albert DeSalvo was highly sexualised and when his wife refused intercourse

with him the Measuring Man appeared. After the Measuring Man appeared, the strangler appeared. This is not uncommon in serial murder, and a psychopathic personality as DeSalvo may have firstly become more confident that he was getting away with the rapes, he would have needed to heighten his neurotic and psychopathic personality and at the same time turn his perverse fantasies into reality for him to achieve sexual gratification.

On March 17th, 1961, Cambridge police arrested DeSalvo as he was trying to break into the house of a potential victim and he confessed to being the 'Measuring Man', and no further rapes occurred during his 11 months of imprisonment. The first Boston Strangler murder occurred two months after his release. During the murder of Sophie Clark, a witness described the 'Green Man' as having honey-coloured hair, as I believe DeSalvo to have been a predominately organised serial killer, this could have been a part of his disguise to make him harder to identify, as he also lived in the surrounding areas and needed to cover his tracks. There were many cigarette butts left at the crime scenes, although DeSalvo did not smoke and neither did all his victims, and the cigarette butts did not match his DNA when tested. However, this could have been another decoy to throw investigators off his scent; as serial killers are becoming more forensically aware, they are using anything to throw off detectives, for example, the Green River serial killer, Gary Ridgeway, would leave chewing gums and cigarette butts amongst other general waste items at the crime scenes to confuse the police.

Upon the last rape of a woman in her apartment, the offender left and apologised for his actions, and upon his arrest was identified by his victim. Upon his arrest, his own wife was not surprised and told him to tell the police everything as she knew that her husband was hyper-sexualised, and due to his behaviour, she may have harboured suspicions that he was the mysterious Boston Strangler. Although the last crime does not fit in with his modus operandi, e.g., he acquired entry without speaking to the victim first and he did not kill her, it is a popular myth that serial killers cannot stop killing, and they do not necessarily kill every victim that they encounter; for example, Dennis Nilsen allowed one of his victims, Carl Stotter, to live. Fred West and Rose West allowed Caroline Roberts to live after keeping her captive for several days and subjecting her to psychological and sexual torture, and this did not fit their previous profile. Yet it must be remembered that offender profiling is only a tool to be used to assist an investigation and may not always be accurate. Serial killers may allow victims to live for one of two reasons, with the first being that they may feel remorse for that short period of time, the second being they like playing 'God' and they can choose who lives and who dies. Only DeSalvo would have known why he did not proceed to kill his last victim. Thankfully her life was spared, and a city had finally apprehended its most notorious monster that had once existed amongst its citizens lurking in the shadows amongst them.

John George Haigh, the Acid Bath Murderer

John George Haigh was born in Lincolnshire, England in 1909, and he would eventually go onto commit some of the most heinous and gruesome crimes known in British criminal history by killing at least five people and disposing of their remains in an acid bucket. John George Haigh's crimes would be classed under the definition of 'serial murder', as Haigh's known murders (he confessed to nine as opposed to the six he was convicted for) were committed during a five-year period between 1944–1949. This also fits in with the FBI's definition of what constitutes the classification of serial murder: *'The unlawful killing of two or more victims by the same offender(s) in separate events with a cooling-off period in between each murder,'* although Haigh fitted the definition of a serial killer, however, we need to firstly assess his modus operandi and work backwards to establish a motivation for his crimes and criminal acts.

Haigh, on the surface did not appear to be a monster and this formed a part of his modus operandi and would ultimately allow him to acquire the trust of his victims. Haigh was always smartly dressed, and he was a very charming person and outwardly he oozed sincerity and a 'caring' demeanour. Haigh, during 1940s Britain, cloaked himself as the perfect British 'gentleman', and he used the virtues of British sincerity to aid him in his killings by enticing, swindling, and murdering members of the middle classes.

Haigh is the type of person M.D. Cleckley wrote about in his 1941 book, *"The Mask of Sanity"*. Haigh was manipulating his victims trusting nature by acquiring their trust to eventually kill them and seize their assets, including their estates. For example, in his first murder in 1944 of three members of the McSwann family, he made £8,000 (around £357,095 in today's money) from selling their possessions and property and managed to gamble it all away within three years, and therefore a part of the reason to commit these crimes was greed. The fact that Haigh gambled this money away shows his psychopathic and impulsive personality almost immediately, as he could have acquired the money and retired from killing immediately. However, psychopaths need constant stimulation and Haigh was a narcissist who believed he was incredibly intelligent, points of which I will refer to later.

Haigh had already committed acts of fraud and I would define him as a 'psychopathic personality', and the acts of fraud were used to not just make money but to stimulate his psychosis, and his narcissistic personality disorder (NPD – DSM-IV) that he was 'smarter' than everybody else. It is known from research that psychopath exhibit less fear of punishment, and that they are constantly in search of stimulation to excite their listless nervous system (Roland 2007). Haigh's modus operandi of drinking the blood of his victims may very well have sexual undertones as it was him 'owning' and 'controlling' the victim forever, as he saw the victim as being a part of him and his for eternity. Although even in serial murder this occurrence is extremely rare, there have been several serial killers who have undertook to this perverse 'pleasure', for example, Peter Kurten, who used to get excited and aroused by the site of blood and claimed to investigators that he could have multiple orgasms upon seeing blood and the crime scenes need to be evaluated to establish if there are further psychological motivations for the commission of his crimes.

Each crime scene was almost a personification of Hague's narcissistic personality and mental state in the sense that he had them alone in his 'workshop', which was just a rented basement, where he would be in complete control of them, as this was his base of operation and a place where he would have ultimately felt powerful.

The victims were either bludgeoned to death or shot, which represents a less intimate approach to murder as, say, a serial killer who strangles his victims, as Safarik (2010) states, *'Serial killers who strangle want to look into the eyes of the victim, that's really the ultimate control and power they can have over somebody, they are playing God. That power and control can also lend itself to sexual stimulation.'* Even the modus operandi shows us that the way Haigh befriended each victim and then ultimately disposed of them quickly and brutally shows the workings of a psychopathic personality, as he had intended to kill them all along.

Haigh drank the blood of all his victims and therefore could have suffered from Renfield Syndrome, which is overwhelming compulsion to drink blood. However, this could have been a deliberate ploy if he was caught, which will be outlined in greater deal throughout the course of the profile.

PEN PROFILES OF THE OFFENDERS

Each victim was trussed into a barrel containing acid to remove the evidence, as Haigh had misunderstood the law of 'Corpus Delicti' as he thought if no body was found then prosecution could be sought. Once again, I will refer to this issue further on in this profile of Haigh, however, before discussing Haigh's lack of understanding on the concept of English law, we need to assess his victim typology to attempt to establish whether there is a psychological motivation for killing them and whether it was solely down to Haigh killing them for 'greed', as this is an important exercise to undertake as the victims are always the key psychological facet in the fantasies and psychological motivations with serial killers.

The victims ranged from a variety of ages, with the known youngest victim being William McSwann his first victim, with the oldest being Henrietta Roberts Durand-Deacon (last victim). Serial killers usually kill victims based on several factors, such as to serve a fantasy, access, and opportunity to a potential victim. In the case of John Haigh, I believe that the killings did serve a psychological purpose in the essence that, like many serial killers, he derived a feeling of supreme power, and he was also monetarily gaining from the death of his victims, for example he forged the power of attorney for the McSwann's estate and benefited in the excess of £6,000 (£267,821 today).

Serial killers usually target a certain demographic of society, for example, Jeffrey Dahmer targeted young Black men whereas John Reginald Christie targeted women, including his own wife. Haigh targeted the middle class of British society, who to him were easy targets, possibly because there was some naivety on their part and Hague knew after the war many middle-class people would have been desperately trying to rebuild their lost fortunes, and Haigh exploited this in deadly fashion. Haigh, in this respect, is no different to a serial killer such as the Green River Killer or Jack the Ripper, who targeted sex workers who are classed at the bottom rung of the societal ladder. However, both demographics were trying to make money to live and survive, and both groups were ruthlessly dispatched for the basic human need of trying to simply survive and get by. Haigh lacked common decency and the moral values that his victims held dear to them, and therefore we need to delve further into the psyche of Haigh to establish more of his psychological motivations.

Haigh was evaluated as suffering from a 'paranoid constitution' which was the same mental disease that Adolf Hitler suffered from, and unfortunately both men suffered from delusional beliefs believing that certain people were against them, and each respective case would result in devastating circumstances. Hague had an acute sense of omnipotence and believed that he was above the law. He was in effect an 'egocentric paranoiac' who, although being more than aware that killing people was against the law, claimed that he believed it was him 'fulfilling his destiny'.

Haigh, like many other serial killers, had developed a narcissistic personality, and this was evidenced in the following quotation from Lane (1992); *'Haigh was labouring under the not uncommon misconception that the legal term "Corpus Delicti" which he had come across whilst scouring the prison library for law books when serving one of his many prison sentences, was referring to an actual corpse. In fact, the term refers to the body of the crime itself; that is the essence of the crime has to be established by the crown to bring a successful prosecution.'* Haigh had allowed his own narcissistic personality to allow himself to hold the British legal system with contempt and this attitude would later result in his downfall and execution. Haigh deluded himself so much that he thought he had found the perfect way to dispose of his victims, when in fact it was only necessary for the crown to prove that person had been killed and that the death had occurred because of unlawful violence against that person. Along with his paranoid constitution, Haigh more than likely suffered from a schizoid personality disorder (SPD) in the sense that even his interpretation of the corpus delicti law was another elaborate fantasy where he had 'outwitted' the law, just as he had 'outwitted' his victims. Sufferers of SPD tend to create elaborate fantasies as a way of coping and detaching themselves from precarious situations and life in general, and Haigh may well have suffered from this condition, and it does warrant further investigation as SPD was not a common mental illness at the time of his murders.

In further reference to the above paragraph, I also believe that Haigh's narcissistic personality is evident in some of the murders and the events after, e.g. his final murder of Mrs Durand-Deacon, where he went to Chelsea police station in order to attempt to convince the police that he was a concerned 'friend', when in reality he was desperately attempting to mislead an investigation of a missing person, although he was not under any suspicion at the time and this backfired terribly as the police began conducting background checks on Haigh and found he had an extensive criminal record of fraud. Therefore, he became a 'person of interest', and the police obtained a warrant for his premises and found a receipt for a Persian lamb coat, a coat which had previously belonged to Mrs Durand-Deacon.

PEN PROFILES OF THE OFFENDERS

During their search, the police also food ration books belonging to Mr and Mrs McSwann which helped lead to his ultimate arrest and would be used as evidence against him in a court of law. Similar to his first murder, Haigh and his narcissistic personality could not stop while he was ahead, and I also believe that when he initially visited the police, like many psychopathic serial killers, he wanted to initiate a game with them as he believed that he was 'superior' to them, and he knew something that they didn't and was trying to act 'concerned', and again this is the psychopath trying to mislead the police. This act also serves another purpose, serial killers are obsessed with law enforcement and try to befriend the police, and they do this by frequenting the places they visit to try to acquire information on the investigation and its procedures. A notable instance of this comes from America in the case of David Meirhofer, who was killing young children, both male and female, and a woman. Meirhofer took the 7-year-old Susan Jaeger from a camp site she was visiting with her family. Meirhofer decided to befriend the FBI agents in the local bars, and they became suspicious of him. Unbeknown to Meirhofer, the police and FBI were trialling psychological profiling for the first time, and they realised he fitted the profile extremely accurately, and when the FBI tracked him down after a phone call a year later to Mrs Jaeger, the FBI arrested him and upon interrogation he admitted everything to them, and he would ultimately commit suicide herewith after.

Haigh's motives for the offences were predominately financial as he targeted middle-class members of society who had wealth that he could unlawfully obtain for his own gain, for example, when he sold the property portfolio that belonged to Mr and Mrs Henderson, he acquired the sum of £8,000 (around £357,095 today). Haigh claimed many nefarious activities and nobody is completely certain to this day if Haigh actually drank the blood of his victims, which he claimed were brought on by the terrible nightmares which dated back to his overzealous religious upbringing, which could have firstly been used as a ploy to convince the courts that he was mentally insane and therefore not responsible for his actions; secondly, he would have been in control over his own fate and he could have avoided execution; and thirdly to 'mock' society and keep him in the news, as all sects of the British media wanted the story (the *Daily Mirror* got the exclusive from Haigh just prior to his execution in August 1949).

Although Haigh, during committal proceeding, was found by EG Robey and 33 expert witnesses to be mentally culpable and murdering for monetary gain, it should not be ruled out entirely that he did not drink the blood of his victims as the drinking of a victim's blood, if such a compulsion is genuine, will be part of a deeper sexual deviation related to the act of violence itself, although this was dismissed as Haigh appeared to have little interest in sex and gave no indication that he suffered from any mental disorders. The previously stipulated conclusion was written in 1948, almost three decades before the FBI began to study the phenomena of serial murder in greater depths. The drinking of the blood may have acted as the ultimate possession/retention of the victims, as evidenced by the American serial killer Jeffrey Dahmer, who admitted to the FBI agent Robert Ressler in 1994, 'I ate them in an effort to possess them more completely and therefore they would be a part of me forever more.' (Cited by Cawthorne, 2000.) I believe that Haigh drank the blood because of his own perverse fantasises of 'power' and 'control' and due to his lack of understanding of criminal law; if caught, he would simply claim 'insanity' and be sent to a mental institution as opposed to receiving the death penalty in a prison. Due to this perverse behaviour, anybody who was alone with Haigh in his basement, whether they were wealthy or poor, would have been at an extreme level of danger and risk.

As the victims would have been alone with Haigh in a basement with only one access and exit root, they would have been at an extreme risk of danger as Haigh was in control, and as many victims were bludgeoned and/or shot from behind this is again Haigh exercising his 'God complex' as he was deciding if these people lived or died. If Haigh was a psychopath, then he would have shown a lack of empathy for others when his 'mask of sanity' slipped, and he also would have had very shallow emotions, which is a common occurrence with psychopaths. Sometimes, albeit extremely rarely, serial killers and their victims can converse, and sometimes the serial killer can see that their actions are wrong and spare the victim. Haigh did not wish to give them a chance as he needed the money for his own survival, as he was spend-thrift and he knew if the victim was spared, he would be exposed as the conman, and therefore he simply saw his victims as 'dispensable', and this shows how empty and shallow he was as a human being. Haigh's insatiable greed and perverse fantasies meant he would undertake great risks whilst murdering his victims.

Haigh killed all his known victims in his grisly 'workshop', which was his base of operations. In terms of the actual act of murder itself, this was very low risk on his part as the chances of him getting caught were virtually non-existent, as he had already acquired the trust of the victims by befriending them prior to their murder, where the risk for him would have been if the victim had told a relative or friend where they were going.

In terms of the risk he took in victim selection, Haigh took a high risk in his chosen victim typology. Serial killers who target sex workers, for example Peter Sutcliffe, Gary Ridgeway, choose this group as they are outcasts of society and are the most vulnerable people because they are easily accessible, and search for the one they find most appealing to pursue a particular fantasy (JA Fox, 2011). Sex workers, once they have dropped out of society, are almost expected to die of alcohol or drug abuse, or their pimps killing them, and as they drop off the societal radar they are tragically forgotten. Haigh's victims, on the other hand, would have been known and had enough family and friends that cared about them and would certainly have not forgotten about them in a hurry.

Haigh's victims were middle-class professional people who had the wealth and social status that he desired but could never achieve and as mentioned, I feel that Haigh possibly suffering from a schizoid personality disorder and was creating a fantasy world, which is common with SPD sufferers. Yet in his fantasy world, he was a respectable gentleman. However, the reality was that he was loathed by many people who had the misfortune of meeting him. The only similarity between the victims of those of Sutcliffe and Haigh is that each victim voluntarily went with their killer, albeit in extremely differing circumstances. Haigh took a high risk in the sense that before killing Mr and Mrs McSwann, he convinced them that their son had run away to Scotland to avoid conscription to the army (Haigh had already disposed of William McSwann). Haigh wrote letters to Rose Henderson's brother and managed to convince him that the Hendersons had moved to South Africa on the grounds that Dr Henderson had carried out an illegal abortion. Ironically, Haigh's risk-taking behaviour, combined with his narcissistic personality, was his undoing, as the police did not believe his façade in the case of Mrs Durand-Deacon being missing. As it was believed that Haigh suffered from a 'paranoid constitution', he would have believed that he was untouchable and above all others, including the law, but he was equal under the eyes of the law as the same as any other British citizen. I believe that by assessing the sequence of acts and behaviour by Haigh before, during and after the crime will provide us with more psychological information in better understanding his motivations for the commission of some of the most truly appalling crimes we will ever have to read about.

JOHN GEORGE HAIGH, THE ACID BATH MURDERER

The sequence of acts before the killings would be for Haigh to befriend his unsuspecting victim(s). Haigh, who was well mannered, well-spoken, and well dressed, with an admirable level of intelligence, Haigh would not have had much difficulty in being trusted by the middle classes, whom he was misleading from the start. Haigh's acts after the killings would be firstly, according to his own statement, to drink the blood of each victim before submerging the body in an acid bath to destroy all evidence (although there were still traces, which helped lead to a conviction). Haigh, after each murder, would carry on as normal, deciding on who would be his next victim, and he would mislead some of the victims' relatives in the process. Haigh would fit into the definition of a psychopath as outlined by Mitchell and Blair (1999); *'The underlying problem in the psychopathic personality is a lack of empathy with others.'*

The actual act of murder took seconds, as he shot some of his victims with a gun, others he clubbed to death with a blunt instrument, which took a bit longer and is actually more personal, as you have to be closer to the victim to perpetrate such an act, and on occasion it may have suited his cognitive process as, with all serial killers, the urge to kill would have been borne out of a growing fantasy for several weeks.

The actual act of dissolving the bodies was an attempt to destroy all evidence and could take up to 24 hours. And not all his victims' bodies did dissolve, for example, in the murder of Mr Henderson, the foot was left intact, and Haigh just threw the foot in the corner of a yard. The fact that most of the bodies did not dissolve completely helped lead to Haigh's conviction, e.g., the Home Office pathologist, Keith Simpson, found small bones and dentures at the scene. In terms of the acts preceding murder this could take months due to Haigh being an 'organised serial killer' (I will expand on this statement during the profile) during which time he was planning his cold and calculating crimes and fraudulent ways to obtain the victim's assets and the basement at 79 Gloucester Road became central to his modus operandi.

The crimes were committed in Haigh's 'workshop', which was a rented basement space at 79 Gloucester Road and was used as a grim death trap to lure his unsuspecting victim(s). The 'workshop' is central to Haigh's psychosis, and as we know from research those serial killers acquire stimulation of the feeling of being in control, there was no way the victims could escape as there was only one entry and in turn only one exit, this would have provided Haigh with an almost God-like power as he could choose if the person lived or died. The 'workshop' was his base of operation and the more organised serial killers usually do operate from a base; for example, Dennis Nilsen used his flat to lure his victims as this is the place, they are familiar with and feel most safe. The problem is that serial killers, once in their lair, know they are in control and anybody in that lair is a potential victim, and it becomes the human equivalent to swimming with sharks as neither have the empathetic understanding of the pain they inflict on others: they both commit primitive acts because their brains are cognitively wired to do so, the difference being a shark is doing it for survival, a serial killer is doing it for pleasure in sense of sexual or monetary gratification.

The bodies of Haigh's victims were moved over to the acid bath from the place in the workshop in which they originally fell. Haigh, I believe, did this to as a misguided attempt to destroy any trace of the victims ever being in the confines of Haigh's workshop. As Haigh had the victim in what I would define as his 'comfort' zone and he knew nobody was going to find him, it served no psychological purpose to him to move them elsewhere, because in the confines of his mind he had deluded himself into believing that he had committed the 'perfect' murder, and this would have gratified him psychologically as he had a narcissistic personality; he would have felt excited that he had 'outwitted' his victims and nobody else would have been none the wiser of his appalling acts and I believe that simply dumping their remains on his property was another psychological motivator for him being able to retain a psychological sense of 'power' over the victims, and as the murder site and the body discovery site were the same due to his narcissism, it helped the police link the series of murders together based on their gruesome findings.

The murder sites and the discovery sites were the same, as the police found evidence inside and outside the workshop which included the following:

1. *Twenty-eight pounds of human body fat.*
2. *Three faceted gallstones.*
3. *Part of a left foot that was not quite eroded.*
4. *Eighteen fragments of human bone.*
5. *Intact upper and lower dentures.*
6. *The handle of a red plastic bag.*
7. *A lipstick container of one of the victims.*

JOHN GEORGE HAIGH, THE ACID BATH MURDERER

Despite Haigh and his narcissistic delusions that he was committing the 'perfect' murders, he was completely ignorant to the way the police acquired evidence and conducted investigations, and this will later become evident when we analyse his knowledge of the corpus delicti law; a complete narcissistic delusion and lack of comprehension on the understanding of the law would ultimately help sentence him to the gallows.

I believe that the serial killer in question, John George Haigh, would be defined as an organised serial killer as his criminal characteristics fit the patterns of an organised serial killer. The characteristics that define John George Haigh in this category are as follows:

- *Haigh had a reasonable level of intelligence.*
- *Haigh was socially adequate on the outset and those whom he acquainted found him charming, and again this is common with the psychopathic personality, and Haigh also suffered from a narcissistic personality disorder (NPD), which allowed him to manipulate some individuals that he met.*
- *Haigh had an education, which is a regular occurrence with a vast majority of organised serial killers, e.g., Ted Bundy had a degree in psychology, Stephen Griffiths, aka 'The Crossbow Cannibal' was a Doctor of Philosophy (PhD) student at Bradford University studying homicide. It appears the more educated a serial killer is, the better their organisational skills are, and this is a common occurrence.*
- *Haigh had good hygiene and was always immaculately dressed, and this formed a part in his modus operandi in the sense that had he been scruffy the middle-class victims he was choosing would never have welcomed him into their world, particularly during 1940s Britain, when there were class boundaries and there was little contact between the middle and working classes due to socio-economic status. Some disorganised serial killers such as William Heirens (whom also had an unusually high level of IQ for a disorganised offender) can be well dressed, but many others, such as Richard Trenton Chase, are not due to their mental imbalance, and the mental chaos that they suffer from usually exhibits itself in their crimes in terms of a chaotic crime scene and the amount of evidence that they leave. Disorganised serial killers tend to leave messages for the police, for example, in the case of Heirens, he scrawled messages in lipstick, and once the police have a suspect they can check the use of language and linguistics to help them acquire a*

successful prosecution; a more organised serial killer will go to greater lengths to keep the police off their trail by hiding their crimes and the victims as much as possible, as they have a much more balanced psyche and are in much more control during the course of their crimes.

- *Haigh is diurnal (daytime habits) in the sense that he leads a normal life by day, and nothing would appear untoward those who know him during normal daily business.*
- *Haigh used his own murder kit and had weapons prepared to kill his victims upon entry into his workshop. Killers who usually use weapons that form part of the scenic makeup are disorganised, e.g., Cayetano Santos Godino, who used weapons such as rocks and even a horse's water trough to kill his victims as he was acting on his impulsiveness, whereas Haigh had premeditated all his five known murders as the planning, fantasies and act of murder intertwined with his NPD.*
- *Haigh used a base of operation to commit his crimes, and therefore he was sedentary and chose the basement of 79 Gloucester Road. Although Haigh was sedentary in the sense that he operated his killings from one base, some organised serial killers can be nomadic, e.g., Ted Bundy travelled around different states and universities as he was aware of the FBI investigative analysis tool, geographical profiling. Johan 'Jack' Unterweger killed in four different countries because of his job as a journalist.*

Although it is a difficult debate to say exactly what constitutes an organised and disorganised serial killer, the disorganised killers usually kill in one area and do not select a victim based on their 'typology', e.g. central to the serial killers desire, for example Ted Bundy killed middle-class educated girls as this social status was his aspiration throughout his whole life, which he could never acquire as he was diagnosed as suffering from bipolar disorder, and later multiple personality disorder (MPD), intertwined with his psychopathic personality; he would not have been able to achieve the long-term concentration levels to achieve his desired societal status as his mind was too fragmented. This is evident as he dropped out of several courses in each university. Bundy could only achieve a degree of middle-class idealism and sophistication through another common psychopathic trait of mimicking those around him.

Herbert Mullin would be an example of a disorganised serial killer in the sense that he struck anywhere at random, and the victims would range between the sexes and were from different age groups; the victims came from a variety of societal and economic backgrounds, for example from a vagrant to a priest, and each scene was left in a chaotic state. Haigh on the other hand selected his victims based on the typology which was central to his monetary desires and aims and went to great lengths to try to dispose of the evidence.

- *Haigh dismembered the body and placed each corpse in an acid bath to destroy the evidence as he misconceived the legal term corpus delicti and thought that, without a body, no conviction could be sought by the crown against him and in essence believed that he was committing the 'perfect murder'. This shows that Haigh had premeditated his murders prior to conducting them, and although he may have misunderstood the law, it shows that Haigh was always calculating and planning his next move or strategy once in custody to 'outwit' the legal system.*

- *Haigh went to great lengths to convince the family and friends of his victims that they had run off after committing a misdemeanour, for example, Haigh told William McSwann's parents that their son had ran away to Scotland to avoid conscription into the forces to avoid fighting and dying in war, and even sent postcards to the parents from Scotland pretending to be their son. The reality was that William was dead and Haigh trussed his body by the ankles into a barrel full of acid. Haigh was doing this not only to avoid suspicion, but it was also all a part of his psychopathic and cruel and twisted game, as I fundamentally believe that he was enjoying watching the McSwann's struggle with worry about their son, only to provide them with a false hope that their son was alive and well and would return. Haigh was already manipulating them into trusting them entirely, as they would give money to him and he knew that he could eventually murder them and seize their assets, which he ultimately enacted upon.*

- *Haigh, when the opportunity arose, wanted to 'help' the police in their investigations when Mrs Durand-Deacon went missing. Although not all organised serial killers act in such a manner, the American serial killer David Meirhofer killed four children over the course of seven years and was interested to talk to the police to see how the investigation was proceeding. However, not all organised serial killers interfere in police affairs. Ted Bundy, until his eventual incarceration, did not speak to police officers about the missing girls, and neither did Ian Brady and Myra Hindley speak to the police about the missing children in the*

> north of England, as they probably believed that the finger of suspicion would be firmly pointing towards them.
> - Each crime was controlled, pre-planned and calculated in the sense that he would manage to get the victims to his basement where he would kill them, and nobody knew they were there and therefore there was little chance of being caught or disturbed during the process of murder and the wanton destruction of evidence.

Haigh does show elements in his character and modus operandi that could easily be attributed to a disorganised serial killer in the sense that he lived by his victims and kept revisiting the crime scene, however, the latter is through necessity. Haigh contacted the victim's families, believed to be him 'playing games' with them. However, with Haigh this was done as a means to an end to make them believe that their loved ones were still alive and thus to keep suspicion from falling upon Haigh, as mentioned most notably in the case of the McSwanns. Haigh killed all the victims at one site, again this was done as a means to an end and to dispose of the person and thus the evidence of the murder. Haigh claimed to have drunk the blood of his victims. Whether this was true or not, the psychiatrists who evaluated Haigh after his arrest stated, *'Such a compulsion, if genuine, is part of a sexual deviation and related to the act of violence itself... Haigh, however, appeared to have no interest in sex and gave no indication that he suffered from the disorder.'*

It is widely believed that Haigh concocted the stories of his recurring nightmares about a forest of crucifixes that turned into trees that dripped with blood, where a man collected the blood in a cup and ordered him to drink it. Haigh was believed to have concocted this story and the act of blood-drinking to show an 'imbalance' within his mental state in the event of him being caught and therefore, if found legally insane, he would have avoided the death penalty. Haigh was known to be a compulsive liar, prone to say anything to extricate himself from a compromising position. The story of the 'forest' was more than likely to be Haigh trying to 'outwit' the psychologists and retain a form of 'power'. However, the psychologists did not believe the story and it became more evident that Haigh suffered from a NPD and that he committed the crimes with full premeditation for what was believed to be purely monetary purposes. However, the more we delve into Haigh's personality, we begin to see that this is not necessarily the only motivational factor in his crimes.

Alison et al. (2002) argue that psychological profiling should be treated

JOHN GEORGE HAIGH, THE ACID BATH MURDERER

with great caution in investigations and should be excluded entirely from consideration in court. The FBI also admits that profiling is not a perfect tool and the information gleaned from it can vary from one profile to another, despite being the architects of this investigation tool. Based on the two previously stipulated hypotheses, I believe that Haigh was overall an organised serial killer, however, he is not the first organised serial killer to show traits of a disorganisation; for example, it is believed that disorganised serial killers return to the crime scene to relive the memories. Ted Bundy used to return to the corpses that he had left on the Colorado Mountains to add a continuum to his warped psychosis and perversion of the fantasy of power where he would apply make up on the deceased before committing acts of necrophilia. In the process of my studies on serial killers, I believe that Ted Bundy is the most common example of the definition of an organised serial killer. The same would apply to Brady and Hindley, both of whom would return to the Yorkshire Moors and have picnics on the sites where they buried their victims and sit on their actual burial sites. This, I believe, was their warped way of the retention of power over their victims. Jeffrey Dahmer showed symptoms of both organised and disorganised serial murder in the sense that he worked from one base of operation but did not dispose of the corpses and killed outside his racial group (Dahmer was white and killed mainly young Black men) (Dvorsky, 2012) which is that could easily have aroused suspicion as he was a minority white man who resided in a predominately black community.

Haigh was an organised serial killer and did nothing to alter the crime scene to mislead the police or frighten the public etc., simply because the crime scene, in Hague's delusional beliefs, were 'non-existent', as he thought that if the police could not find a body, then no conviction could be sought against him. Hague did not stage the crime scene in terms of tampering with evidence and deliberately leaving forensic clues for the police to find to mislead them. Although Haigh is the personification of an organised serial killer, the advanced studies of serial murder was non-existent in the 1940s (although it has always existed), which led Hague to underestimate the police. Had there more been more information available on serial killers, Haigh may have read up in detail on forensic science and police investigative procedures, as he would have wanted to first and foremost get away with the crimes, and secondly, he would have seen it as a 'game' and a 'challenge' with the police if he was caught.

Organised serial killers in modern times, for example the Italian serial killer Danilo Restivo, who murdered two women in England and Italy, had a perverse obsession with cutting hair from women he never knew. Restivo killed Elisa Claps in Italy and Heather Barnett in Bournemouth, England. Restivo left a variety of strands of hair in Heather Barnett's right hand, and as there was hardly any other forensic evidence, this led the police to believe that with such a convincing piece of evidence the smart money was on a swift and brutally efficient manhunt and conviction (Litchfield, 2011). The police also initially believed that it may have been another woman that killed Heather Barnett. However, this shows how reliant modern-day law enforcement is on forensic science and how easy it is to exploit by an organised offender. Haigh would not have tried to mislead the police, he would, however, have gone to excessive lengths to cover his crimes by increasing his knowledge of forensic science had it been available at the time of his murders.

It is known that if a homicide is not solved within the first 48 hours, then the chances of solving the crime diminish rather significantly. The expansion in the media and TV programmes, e.g., CSI, the FBI Files, and the internet have made the modern-day serial killer more forensically aware and harder to apprehend. However, Haigh did not want to mislead the police as he thought he was forensically aware enough to commit the 'perfect' murder and he would go to great lengths to mislead the families into thinking their loved ones were still alive as opposed to misleading the police. When Haigh eventually did try to mislead the investigation of the missing Mrs Durand-Deacon, it led to his downfall as the police became suspicious of his manner and therefore conducted an extensive criminal record check and found that he had previous convictions for fraud, and the police obtained a warrant to search his premises of 'business', which was indeed littered with forensic evidence that he never thought to dispose of correctly.

Although we are aware that Haigh was trying to mislead the police and he suffered with a narcissistic personality disorder (NPD), which brought about his own delusional beliefs and ultimately his arrest and execution, we need to conduct further analysis against the victims to establish whether there are more psychological motivations aside monetary gain as to why Haigh killed his victims, and to enquire whether any patterns emerge during his series of murders.

Haigh would bludgeon three of his victims and shoot the other two victims. Haigh bludgeoned the victims from behind with a blunt instrument or shot them from behind. The actual cause of death implies that Haigh did not personalise his victim(s), which is usually common with organised serial killers such as Ted Bundy and Dennis Rader as they enjoy the 'emotional intensity' of the act of killing and they also derive sexual gratification from the act, as murder provides them with an excess feeling of power and is also an act of transference for their inner rages being used against a helpless being and they are 'God' in that instance.

It is usually disorganised serial killers such as Richard Trenton Chase and Herbert Mullin (the latter claimed he had to kill to prevent an 'inevitable' earthquake in the USA) who strike without the victim being aware of what is happening until rendered incapable of fighting back (Owen D. 2004). Organised serial killers are known to bind their victims before killing them, and this was a common modus operandi used by Ted Bundy, Richard Ramirez et al. Haigh wanted the victims killed and disposed of quickly for him to attain their financial wealth, for Haigh the actual way he murdered his victims does not appear to show sexual connotations. However, as Haigh was manipulative and deviant and the bodies were not found in their whole format, and thus forensic evidence was destroyed, Haigh may have committed the vile act of necrophilia upon his victims. After all, he claimed to drink their blood, which is similar the psychological gratification a cannibalistic serial killer would have in the sense that it is possession over the victim forever as they become a part of them, or at least this is the perverse belief of the serial killer. I do not think that sexual desires behind the acid bath murders should be ruled out in its entirety, as Haigh may have committed acts of necrophilia as opposed to killing for solely monetary gain, and as Haigh was executed and never interrogated further, we will never be entirely sure and can only theorise on his acts of necrophilia.

The location of the wounds on the McSwann family were multiple in the sense that he viciously bludgeoned the three members of the family to death from behind and shot the Henderson couple in the head and Mrs Durand-Deacon in the neck from behind. The location of wounds implies that he did not have any personal feelings or compassion for his victims as Haigh was what I would to deem to be a psychopathic personality, he saw these people as objects that were in his way of achieving his 'goals' and he did not recognise them as human beings. As Haigh disposed of each corpse in an acid bath we do not know if Haigh committed any further frenzied attacks by inflicting further multiple incisions on any of the victims, we can only go by what Haigh told the investigating team at the time of his arrest and conviction. Haigh, like all serial killers, told the investigators what he wanted to tell them as they feel that by retaining information, they still have a semblance of 'control'. However, as Haigh still believed that he had a chance of being exonerated by trying to 'outwit' the police and legal system, the gravity of the situation did not seem to faze him, and the serial killers' obsession and control cost him his life.

Haigh did not leave the body to be found and he did not leave a chaotic crime scene as he attempted to obliterate all evidence that a crime had taken place, although the police did find forensic evidence as Haigh's narcissist personality did not conceive the possibility that some traces of evidence could remain intact even when the body is not its original entirety. Haigh did not want others to find the bodies of his victims, unlike other organised serial killers who follow their crimes in the news when the body is found or a search is taking place, e.g., David Meirhofer (USA) and the Suffolk Strangler, Steven Wright. The latter left bodies in the open for people to find, and the Ipswich murders took place between 30 October 2006 and 10 December 2006, over the course of 41 days all 5 victims were found. As we saw with the Boston Strangler, Albert DeSalvo, he posed bodies and used a ligature as this became his 'signature' and he wanted the police to be certain that he was behind each killing so they would give the media the information and the focus would be upon him, and yet nobody knew who he was, where he was and were he would strike next. Haigh was not by the very definition a 'signature killer' as the 'signature' did not form a part of his modus operandi.

Haigh is a very complex serial killer because although he was not a 'signature' killer, he was a narcissist and a conman who seemed to progress from a crime such as fraud by deception straight to murder, which does not fit any patterns with serial killers, and neither does it make any logical sense. Haigh began to murder (what we are aware of) at 35 years of age when he killed his friend, William McSwann, in 1944. Haigh's last murder was that of Mrs Durand-Deacon in 1949. Haigh was middle-aged at the time, and it is highly unlikely that a serial killer begins killing at this age without committing some previous crimes or forms of cruelty against living beings and creatures. I do therefore believe that Haigh may well have committed more crimes prior to the murder of William McSwann. From extensive studies of serial killers, a common psychological warning sign that there is a growing abnormal personality shaping occurs during adolescence when they begin to torture animals, as Scott (2012) quotes Robert Ressler (1988), *"torturing animals is a disturbing red flag. Animals are often seen as "practice" for the later act of killing humans. Ed Kemper buried his family cat alive, dug it up and later cut of its head. Jeffrey Dahmer would cut of dog's heads and place them behind his house and dissolve the bodies in his grotesque experiments"*. Although Haigh never admitted to any acts involved in the MacDonald Triad, including animal cruelty, he may well have committed more crimes, as serial killers do not just begin killing during middle-age life as they would need to satisfy their psychological needs throughout their life up until the point of the initial known murder. Every human being will have psychological needs to fulfil, for example, for a businessperson it may be the acquisition of a business contract, a normal person may want to beat a time in their daily gym routine, as these are areas that can psychologically stimulate mental wellbeing in our day-to-day routines and serial killers are no different in this respect.

Haigh already had a criminal background for fraud and deception, and he existed amongst us as all psychopathic personalities do, without the restraints of conscience and he may well have killed other people to obtain their assets, Haigh may well have committed other crimes similar to the ones he did commit and linkage analysis would be able to provide further information if cold case investigative teams looked into them based on his modus operandi, and this procedure would more than likely solve cold cases. However, whether it would still be in the realms of public interest nearly one hundred years later is debatable. I do believe that in order to seek justice for the victims and with modern technology, if Haigh is suspected of additional crimes, then it is worth further investigation because the modern tool and linkage analysis helped provide a further conviction against the serial killer Robert Black in the murder of Jennifer Cardy, as this murder fitted Black's modus operandi and Cardy was Black's first victim and he wasn't convicted of the murder until 2011 when the Crown Prosecution Service imposed a further 25-year sentence onto his existing tariff for the rape and murder of Jennifer Cardy. Linkage analysis has linked Robert Black to at least another fourteen victims in the UK and Europe and the odds of having two serial killers operating on the same psychological basis, the same victim typology and in the same geographic areas is extremely unlikely and therefore Robert Black must be the guilty party and this is why I believe that John George Haigh should be investigated further using linkage analysis because there is too much of a gap in his life were there are no 'offences' and then a sudden series of murder over the course of six years, which would appear that he has had a 'sudden change' in character. However, a serial killer does not suddenly go through a metamorphic transformation, I fully believe that Haigh is guilty of many more crimes than he was convicted for and even when we review his previous married life, he exhibits deception throughout and therefore this shows that Haigh was a deviant and psychopathic creature, and there is an extremely good chance that he was committing acts of murder during this period of his life.

Haigh was originally married on the 6 July 1934, to a 21-year-old woman named Beatrice Hammer. The marriage lasted four months. Even in his marital life (a term that can be applied very loosely) Haigh shows his psychopathic tendencies, because whilst he was incarcerated, Beatrice gave birth to a baby daughter, whom she immediately gave up for adoption as she could not cope, and Haigh did not seem very bothered by this fact. Haigh saw Beatrice once more, briefly, to lie to her by telling her that they were never officially wed because he already had a wife at the time. He then completely ignored her as though they were never married. This was the event in his life that Haigh's family decided to ostracise him for, as they were a very conservative Christian family and when they found out about Haigh's behaviours and fidelity, they decided enough was enough. A normal rational human being, if ostracised from their family, would find it a traumatic experience and soul-destroying. However, I believe that Haigh saw it a 'liberating' due to his psychopathic personality. He saw it as an opportunity as the chains had finally been cut and he was 'free' to act as he pleased and there were no longer any rules to abide by and in his ostracization he saw nothing but 'opportunity' to satisfy himself as he saw fit, unfortunately for others it would result in the end of their life.

It is known that psychopaths suffer from incurable personality disorders and cannot form long-term meaningful relationships, and those who form a relationship with them are building a relationship on sand. Moscovici, (2010) cites Babiak and Hare (2007); *'The psychopathic bond follows certain predictable stages: idealize, devalue and discard. The psychopath may discard you after years, months or even a few hours dependent upon his/her needs. If the psychopath wants the semblance of respectability – a screen behind which he can hide his perverse nature and appear harmless and normal – he may establish a long-term partnership with you and even marry you.'* Haigh committed all the stages as outlined by Babiak and Hare during his short marriage to Beatrice Hammer and she was merely another vessel in his societal class fantasy as he wanted to be seen and deluded himself to perceive himself as a respectable middle-class person and this is yet another example of his grandiose and delusional beliefs that manifested themselves within his psychosis. Haigh more than likely married Beatrice to appear respectable as this was also an era when sex and living with a partner outside of marriage was frowned upon in society.

After Haigh was released from prison, he prepared to carry on his heinous plans. In the interim prior to his murders (known) he stayed with the Stephen family, where he began a close friendship with one of the daughters, Barbara, who despite the 20-year age gap believed that she would eventually become the next 'Mrs Haigh'. This is another relationship in which Haigh shows his narcissist and psychopathic tendencies, as he was more than likely manipulating Barbara to harbour this fantasy, as psychopaths are charming, glib and superficial, and like all psychopaths, Haigh probably claimed to share her interests and desires as he was more than likely grooming her for his own warped fantasies and there may have been some acts of sexual intercourse as this would have been Haigh's way of ensuring she stayed under his control. Hare and Babiak state the following: *'The psychological bond capitalize on your inner personality, holding out the promise of greater depth and possibly intimacy, and offering a relationship that is special, unique, equal-forever.'* It is not quite clear why Haigh never married Barbara. However, we can assume that she was another pawn, and he was possibly planning to murder the Stephen family, it can never be known as to why he allowed them to live and did not carry out their murders as it appears, based on his latter victims, they were his victim typology, and he befriended all the victims before killing them and they all fit into the class barrier of the people he would ultimately later kill. Haigh's deceptive personality was not just constricted to his home life or his victims, this behaviour was evident throughout his legitimate working life as well, and when profiling serial killers, I believe that it is imperative to review their employment history as there will be clues to their psychology from their past behaviour as human beings, like all social animals, cannot suddenly change their behaviours without a form of psychological conditioning and in the case of John George Haigh, this appears to be all too evident.

Haigh's first known job was as an apprentice at a firm of motor engineers, which allowed him to indulge in his passion for cars. Whilst Haigh was in love with cars, he was also obsessed with cleanliness, possibly a legacy of his puritanical upbringing, and he detested being soiled by the oil and grime associated with working on engines. As Haigh suffered from an NPD, I believe that as he wanted to be 'respectable' and in a higher echelon of class barrier, then he would have seen the job of a mechanic as 'below' his perceptions of himself and his societal class stratosphere. Although I am theorising, if we look at his next job, it intertwines more with the association we would perceive with the middle classes and Haigh was begging to enact out his delusional fantasies.

Haigh then gained employment as an insurance clerk before moving on to work as an advertising copywriter, in which he was duly sacked from his employment after being suspected of stealing petty cash, and he also learned about the world of finance and how to embellish the truth. Haigh by now was committing theft, and the element of fraud was beginning to manifest itself in his warped psyche and I do believe that he was planning already on how to con people out of their money and assets, and if murder formed part of this fantasy, quite simply, then so be it.

Haigh set up a legitimate dry-cleaning business during the era of the 'Great Depression' and dry cleaning was one of the first luxuries to be cut back by the hard-pressed middle classes, and when his partner was killed in a motorcycle accident and the business ultimately collapsed. The fact that the business collapsed, and Haigh could not run a legitimate business on his own, shows that his misconceptions and delusions of his intelligence were nothing but grandiose delusions and this does become evident throughout his trial, which we will refer to later. Haigh then took a job as a chauffeur for his first victim, William McSwann, which would tragically be William McSwann's innocent and yet fatal mistake, because the relevant background checks were not conducted on Haigh. Had they been, then nobody would hire Haigh due to his questionable character and his previous misdemeanours.

The types of employment Haigh chose is central to his hedonistic and narcissistic personality in the sense that the manual work was 'below' him and he should be working in middle-class employment and Haigh would have believed this possibly due to earlier in life when he had won a scholarship to the Queen Elizabeth Grammar School in Wakefield. Haigh, however, was not actually up to the high standards set at the time in the middle-class professions and failed in every role he acquired, and he had no alternative but to resort to fraudulent crimes to achieve his middle-class wealth aspirations. It is believed that serial killers tend to be insecure, and irrationally scared of rejection or humiliation (Blake, 2007). Although the statement by Blake is referring more to the sexual-orientated serial killer, we can see that the serial killer Ted Bundy suffered from this irrational fear, and his victim typology was chosen as he was killing the very thing he aspired to.

JOHN GEORGE HAIGH, THE ACID BATH MURDERER

Haigh also aspired to be accepted by the middle classes, the only difference being Haigh is what Lane and Greg (1990) refer to as a 'gain killer' and Ted Bundy would be classed as a hybrid of the following types of a serial killer; *hedonistic* (Haigh would also fit into this category), *lust, thrill, power-reassurance, power-anger-retaliatory*. I will expand further on this statement in relation to Haigh during this profile as Haigh had a very deranged and duplicitous personality that made him an extremely dangerous offender.

Haigh was a psychopathic personality who had no compassion for others and killed as a means to an end to fulfil his own psychological and material needs without any remorse. Haigh was a *hedonistic narcissist* who believed that he was smarter than anybody else, and that he could kill for financial gain, and he would never be caught and therefore could never be tried for murder, which manifested within his delusional beliefs with devastating consequence, ultimately, for himself. Haigh suffered from a narcissistic personality disorder and Haigh showed all the symptoms associated with this illness in the sense that he had a grandiose sense of self-importance, a preoccupation with unlimited success, an overriding belief that he was 'special' or 'unique'. His crimes show that he was exploitative of others, he lacked empathy and was indifferent to the pain and distress of others, he was arrogant even during his trial, he was jealous of others, in this sense the middle-class people he killed, and all these traits became more transparent once the police had him in custody and began to question him about his crimes.

Haigh told the police in a statement that he had in fact committed eight murders that involved the disposal of all the victims in his acid bath, and not the five he was originally arrested and convicted for. As previously mentioned, Haigh's first known murder was committed when he was 35 years old, and this is a very late age for somebody to become a serial killer. Although serial killers do lie once in custody, as they enjoy the attention and enjoy playing games with the media, police, and society, I do believe that Haigh did kill more victims than the five he was convicted for. He may have even killed random innocent people in an impersonal way e.g., shooting for example, to achieve the feeling of 'power', and he may have used these victims as 'practice' with his later crimes being more pre-planned with the aim of 'perfecting' the murder, and in this instance of a serial killer claiming to have killed more victims, I believe that the claim should have been taken more seriously by the police.

Haigh had misconstrued the corpus delicti law, and he thought that because the police could not find any bodies no convictions could be sought against him, however, he was wrong. He told the police that he had drank the blood of some of his victims through a straw and he did this when he had suffered from his so-called nightmares which may have been a ploy to be convicted to Broadmoor Hospital and thus avoid the death penalty. Haigh may well have concocted the stories in relation to his nefarious blood-drinking activities to be committed to a mental hospital as he asked Inspector Webb: *'What are my chances of being released from Broadmoor?'* In this case, I do believe that Haigh did indeed drink the blood of his victims as it was about 'possession' initially and sexually gratified his warped sexual desires, afterwards, he used his previous behaviour as a last-ditch attempt to avoid the death penalty and a meeting with the notorious executioner, Albert Pierpont.

The police were very quick to become suspicious of Haigh when he walked into the police station during the disappearance of Mrs Durand-Deacon, and a simple check on Haigh's previous criminal records would have provided the police officers with an insight into his devious, deviant, and duplicitous nature as a criminal record check on the extensive criminal history of John George Haigh would have gleaned the following information:

- *October 1934 – Convicted of fraud and imprisoned.*
- *1936 – Imprisoned for fraud for setting up a false solicitor's office, spends 15 months in jail.*
- *1937 – Spends a further 21 months in jail for theft.*

Although Haigh was a serial offender in terms of fraudulent behaviour to obtain money and land under false pretences, the crimes of serial murder and fraud are paradoxical to each other as fraud is committed for purely monetary acquisition, whereas serial murder is committed to aid a fractured and destructive psychopathic personality. Haigh was committing both crimes to show how clever he was and to convince himself that he was powerful, these two mitigating factors were internal manifestations of his narcissistic personality disorder.

Frank Abagnale Jr, a conman in the USA, cashed embezzled cheques by acting under many pseudonyms to obtain money and acquire a pilot's license, yet Mr Abagnale did not kill anybody as the personality type of Frank Abagnale Jr and John George Haigh differ on an extreme basis. The police became suspicious of Haigh due to his extensive criminal record when Mrs Durand-Deacon went missing. The police were not ready, and neither were they trained well enough and prepared for the crimes that Haigh was to confess to, as this was the 1940s and nobody had heard of the term 'serial killer'. Haigh's criminal record would make one assume that he is a serial fraudster as opposed to a serial killer. Unfortunately, Haigh was both as the police would be horrified to find out when he explained his lurid tales of murder and blood-drinking.

Pen Profile

I, Samuel Hodgins, can confirm that I have researched the case and the crimes committed by the serial killer, John George Haigh, who is also known as the 'Acid Bath Murderer' (Caucasian male). Haigh committed his murders (that are known of) between the ages of 35 and 40 before his ultimate incarceration and execution by hanging at Wandsworth Prison, England, on 10 August 1949. I am therefore unable to offer a psychological profile of an unsub. I am therefore in effect trying to offer a psychological post-mortem of the offender in question based upon the information contained within the above offender profile to attempt to try to establish a motive for the criminal acts committed by John George Haigh.

1. The criminal acts that were committed by John George Haigh were of a serial nature. Haigh began his killing career on the 9 September 1944, when he murdered his loyal friend and employer William McSwann, and Haigh would continue to murder on at least four more occasions (he confessed to eight murders) and he committed his last murder on Sunday 20 February 1949, when he murdered Mrs Durand-Deacon. As Haigh killed over a period of five years, he averaged a victim once every year (although in two cases he killed two people in one day and/or at once) and he would therefore fit the definition of a serial killer as outlined by Lane and Gregg (1992): *'Killings are repetitive (serial) occurring with such greater or less frequency, often escalating over a period of time, sometimes years; and will continue until the killer is taken into custody, dies and/or is himself killed.'*
2. Although Haigh does fit into the standard FBI definition of serial murder, I have used the definition outlined by Lane and Gregg (1992) as

Haigh's murders were repetitive in every sense of the word from his *modus operandi* of acquiring the trust of his victims, to the way he convinced them to accompany him to his 'workshop', where he would either shoot or bludgeon the victim(s) from behind. He would then proceed to dispose of the corpse in his acid bath. He would then set about acquiring their assets and go to great lengths to convince family members that their loved ones were still alive.

Haigh, unlike other serial killers, seemed to kill at a less frequent pace. For example, Randolph 'Randy' Steven Kraft killed an estimated 67 victims (convicted for 16) over 11 years between 1972–1983, and thus averaging 5.5 victims a year. William Bonin, 'the Freeway Killer', killed 49 young boys between 1978–1981 (Newton, 2012), thus averaging 16.3 victims per year. Haigh, unlike Bonin and Kraft, did have differing motivations. Whereas Haigh was a 'for profit' killer, the two other examples where sexual sadist psychopaths and the victims of Haigh needed to be in the middle-class society bracket for him to achieve his aims. Bonin and Kraft targeted sex workers and runaways and these victims are much easier to acquire than the middle classes as people care about the latter whereas the formers have dropped out of society. There is another possibility as to why Haigh did not kill as many people, the fact that he had several stints in prison, and this fits into the hypothesis as outlined by Gregg and Lane (1992). It is extremely unlikely that a serial killer begins their murderous career during middle age.

3. Haigh, from as far as we are aware does not show the classic symptoms associated with serial killers in the terms of the 'triad of evil', as we do not know if he suffered from enuresis (consistent bedwetting after the age of ten), he never stated and there is no evidence to suggest that he committed acts of arson or committed acts of zoo-sadism. Although there is no evidence to suggest that Haigh partook in the latter two crimes or suffered from enuresis, when dealing with serial killers it should never be ruled out as they usually only tell you what they want to, and again this is a form of the retention of power by withholding details of crimes and information about their life.

Haigh, I believe, had a psychopathic personality, and I therefore classify him as a psychopath, he may have committed these acts associated with 'Triad of Evil' at an earlier stage in his life and more than likely during adolescence, the problem was nobody realised it at the time and Haigh would not have been able to discuss his psychological problems with his puritanical parents. Haigh sold his story to the *Daily Mirror*, and he never spoke of these acts, and neither to my knowledge was he questioned (this was before the study of serial murder was common practice). However, I doubt that Haigh would have admitted to such acts/problems as he liked to see himself on a higher plane, and as a respectable and fully functioning member of society, therefore he would not have admitted to these acts as this would have brought his 'social standing' down with the public. Due to his narcissistic personality disorder, his own mental suffering and cognitive dissonance, he could not comprehend that the public reviled him and his criminal acts. Although Haigh was not born into a socio-economic middle-class background, he aspired to attain this level in the social stratosphere, which was evidenced in his desire to be employed in middle-class professions and associate with this class of people. As Haigh associated with the middle classes, he was in essence living out his fantasy, and as Haigh was a psychopath it is known that people with a psychopathic personality have no real emotions, they develop their own personality throughout life by mimicking others around them (Montaldo cites Cleckley, 1941). Haigh, I believe, until the bitter end tried to maintain as what he saw as a level of respectability and Haigh would never admit to any such acts that might damage his respectability.

4. Outwardly, Haigh may not have shown common traits that we can attribute to serial killers. However, due to the enhanced research by modern law enforcement agencies and academics, we do know that like most other serial killers, Haigh was reared in a dysfunctional environment, which is a factor that tends to be the base for the future of a serial killers warped future behaviours. Haigh's parents, John, and Emily Haigh were both fanatical religious puritans and forbade their son from indulging in sport or any form of light entertainment, as they believed it was dirty and impure. John Haigh Senior erected a ten-foot-high fence around the house to keep out prying eyes and any form of social contact. Haigh is not the only serial killer to have suffered from overbearing puritanical parent/parents; Denis Nilsen had a drunkard father and a puritanical mother. Nilsen's troubles began when he was seven years of age, when he was taken by his mother to see the corpse of his grandfather, to whom he had formed a deep attachment due to a lack of empathy and love he never received from his father. From the experience of seeing his grandfather's dead body, Nilsen

developed a necrophiliac obsession with dead male corpses (Wilson and Seaman, 2007). Ed Gein was another serial killer whose mother, Augusta Gein, enforced her puritanical beliefs upon her sons. Ed Gein was once caught masturbating by his mother and was severely punished by having scalding hot water chucked at him. In the case of Gein, Lane and Gregg (1992) state, *'early teachings of an obsessive mother that sex was a sinful thing, serving only to make that sin a profound misery that Ed would later explore so gruesomely. It is no surprise that Gein's study of the human anatomy was heavily supplemented by pulp horror and pornography magazines. It was a world of fantasy that would erupt into necrophilia, cannibalism, and murder.'* Haigh's motives may not have been predominately sexual (I will refer more to this later in the profile), however, as Haigh had no contact with the outside world and no friends other than a neighbour's dog, which he cared for, Haigh may well have concocted his fantasy world where he could escape from the misery of his normal life as a form of a coping mechanism. I do believe that there was an element of sexual psychosis that became intertwined within the murders committed by Haigh, which I will refer to shortly.

5. Ironically, often serial killers who have had to endure and suffer at the hands of a fanatical parent (the mother is usually the main protagonist) go on to break many of the ten commandments, with most notable one being commandment number 6, *'Thou shall not murder'*. Serial killers such as Ed Gein would have learned their *operant conditioning principles* via the psychological principle of *negative reinforcement*, e.g., in the case of Gein, normal sexual desires and experimentation, e.g., masturbation, are scientifically linked with the natural hormonal development associated with adolescence. Gein would have almost associated sex as a forbidden fruit as his mother was his 'world' and she decided that it was 'wrong' and against God and therefore punished him severely, and sex and violence became intertwined within his psyche. As he was not allowed to interact with anybody else in his community, let alone girls, as his mother seen them all as sinners', Gein, during his entire life, suffered from the Oedipal complex. Because of his mother's puritanical and obsessive doctrines, Gein was never allowed to develop correctly psychological, socially, and sexually and this developed him into a becoming a serial killer, and the love and hatred he bore for his mother would eventually be unleashed upon Plainfield, Wisconsin.

I believe that due to his warped upbringing, Gein developed

unnatural sexual feelings for his mother and the two known victims he killed resembled his mother, which I believe was a manifestation of his combined love and hatred of his overbearing mother; it was in Gein's psychosis an act of 'transference' where he was exhibiting his inner rage outwardly against two innocent people. In terms of Haigh, his father used to tell him that he had acquired a scar on his forehead by being 'branded' by the devil for sins he committed when he was young. Haigh became terrified that he would one day be 'branded' and get the same mark. However, when Haigh did not get the mark, he became cynical of religion and its controlling doctrines. By adolescence, Haigh had already developed into a psychopath and 'rules' don't apply to psychopaths, and he more than likely resented his parents and their myopic religious view of the world, a world which was not for him in this sense. This would have been a central element in Haigh's criminal activities as for the first time he would have realised that there was no authority over him and would have felt empowered to do as he pleases, and due to his psychopathic personality this was a dangerous concept, as once all authority and boundaries, and even the fear of an existential being were removed, Haigh saw it as he had nothing to lose and everything to gain.

6. I believe that John George Haigh had a psychopathic personality, as Haigh shows many of the psychopathic personality traits as outlined by Cleckley (1941). Cleckley states; *'Psychopaths have superficial charms and average intelligence.'* Haigh used his charms to manipulate and con the middle classes by oozing sincerity and a veneer of being more educated than he was, which was all part of his game based on his psychopathy. Cleckley states, *'Psychopaths show signs of absence of delusions and other signs of irrational thinking.'* Haigh showed his delusional behaviour by setting up a business aimed at the middle-class section of society when the Great Depression was peaking. He showed a lot of irrational thinking when he committed fraud, and this led to numerous arrests, which helped the police investigate him and realise that he was not the concerned 'friend' that the claimed to be after he had committed his final murder of Mrs Durand-Deacon.

7. Cleckley (1941) states; *'Psychopaths show an absence of nervousness or neurotic manifestations.'* When Haigh was arrested for the murder of Mrs Durand-Deacon, he made the following statement to the police; *'If I told you the truth you would not believe it, it is too fantastic for belief. Mrs. Durand-Deacon no longer exists. She has disappeared completely, and no*

trace of her can ever be found. I have destroyed her with acid. You will find the sludge that remains at Leopold Road. Every trace has gone. How can you prove murder if there is no body?' Haigh in this statement shows his neurotic and narcissistic personality as he believed that he had committed the 'perfect murder' as he had misunderstood the *Corpus Delicti* principle of English law, and he believed that he was going to be commited to a mental institution instead of facing the death penalty. Psychopaths also enjoy high-risk taking endeavours and behaviours and this is evident in this statement that Haigh wanted to play a game with the police, and he wholly underestimated the grave predicament he had entered.

    a. Cleckley (1941) states; *'Psychopaths show a lack of remorse or shame'*. This is evident with Haigh throughout his crimes, his arrest and up until his execution, as he showed no remorse and could not wait to relive the murders with the police, the psychiatrists and above all the media who would serialise his story in the national newspapers and this brings me on to Cleckley's next point about psychopaths; *'Psychopaths have a pathological egocentricity and incapacity to love,'* Haigh throughout showed his egocentricity as believed that he would be able to manipulate and convince all educated people that he was insane and not a cold and calculated killer (I will expand on this later in the profile). He showed his incapacity for loyalty in the way he murdered his best friend, William McSwann, and his incapacity for love by marrying Beatrice Hammer and then dumping her after four months and telling her that they were never wed due to him already being married and he was therefore a polygamist. Haigh shows his egocentrically motivated personality by adhering to the request from London's Madam Tussauds to fit a death mask, which he duly obliged and even offered his own suit for the model, in which he has now been immortalised for all future generations to gaze upon. To Haigh, and his narcissism, he would undoubtedly have seen this request as having himself a place in history alongside other great Britons, e.g., Sir Winston Churchill, Queen Boudica, Lord Nelson et al. and he would have derived an intense feeling of pride at the time of this request.

8. Professor David Wilson, the UK's leading expert on serial killers in his book, *A History of British Serial Killing: The Shocking Account of Jack the*

JOHN GEORGE HAIGH, THE ACID BATH MURDERER

Ripper, Harold Shipman and Beyond, states; *'Victims of British Serial Killers have belonged to marginalised groups in our culture: the elderly, gay men, prostitutes, babies and infants, and young adults trying to find their feet in life away from the comfort of their home.' (Wilson, 2009)* Wilson is basically saying serial killers target the most vulnerable and accessible people in society, as these groups represent an opportunity for serial killers to commit their crimes against. Haigh, however, in terms of serial killing makes him unique as his victim typology targeted people not on the peripheries of society; they were functioning normally in society, and this is what makes Haigh one of Britain's most notorious serial killers.

a. Haigh, unlike his other British serial killer counterparts and their choice of victims, for example Peter Sutcliffe murdered sex workers, Harold Shipman murdered the elderly, Beverley Allitt murdered infants, Colin Ireland murdered gay men, Hindley and Brady murdered young children and a teenager, Haigh chose to kill victims from the middle-class stratosphere of society and I believe that Haigh committed these acts for a number of reasons; *(i) He killed for monetary gain, (ii) I believe he killed them as he aspired to be like them and become them, however, he actually hated them as he would never truly be in this bracket of society as he was not born into money and every attempt he did to make money, either fraudulently or legally, failed.* I believe that is why his psychopathic personality mimicked their behaviour, as people who were acquainted with Haigh found him to ooze charm and sincerity. Haigh was always looking inwards as opposed to outwards, as Haigh loathed himself and this escalated from his constant failures to succeed in general employment and his failed business ventures, and his narcissistic personality would have been fighting against his psyche, causing, and exacerbating further rage that began to manifest itself further within his psychosis.

British serial killers tend to kill victims that people still care about within society and are not in what society always deems as the 'outgroups'. However, if we look at the victim typology of American serial killers, many of them kill victims predominately from societies 'out-groups', for example, Gary Heidnik killed sex workers, as did Gary Ridgeway, Randy Kraft and William Bonin killed teenage runaway boys, many of whom had a troubled home life as examples.

Although there are American serial killers that kill victims from societies 'in-groups', where people will care that they are not coming home, for example Dr Donald Harvey, like his British counterpart, Harold Shipman, killed many elderly patients and claimed they were 'mercy' killings, Ted Bundy killed attractive middle-class educated young women at several state universities. I believe that Haigh, like Bundy, had always wanted to be in the middle-class stratosphere of society and it was never quite attainable for either and due to their psychopathic personalities and the feelings of inadequacies brought out a homicidal rage within both warped personalities, although their modus operandi and victim typology differ, I believe that this is where Bundy and Haigh do share a common psychological trait during their murders.

9. The reason I believe that American serial killers choose more victims on the peripheries of society is firstly because of the size of each respective country, the UK is only 243,610 km² whereas the USA is 9,826,675. So, in essence, the USA is vastly greater and the result of this is inevitably a larger population and, therefore, due to the land mass and density, this offers a serial killer more access and opportunity to kill and remain undetected compared to Britain. The serial killer who operates in the USA can commute from one state to another and have a larger geographical profile, and therefore can be much harder to apprehend, particularly if the law enforcement agencies in any respective state do not cooperate with each other correctly. American serial killers' victims can run into the hundreds because of the size and density of the country. For example, Gary Ridgeway admitted to over one hundred victims, as did Ted Bundy. In Britain the only killer to exceed the 'one hundred victims mark' was Harold Shipman with 215 known victims (he may have committed many more). The next British serial killer in the list with the highest number of victims is Dennis Nilsen, with fifteen known victims. America's political and social landscape in comparison with Britain's is extremely different. America is the epitaph of Capitalism and has been despite changes between conservatism and democratic socialism, in the sense that *if you are poor, you are poor*, as the 'American Dream' is the beacon of aspiration all citizens should aspire to achieving, and therefore this means that there are many citizens that have greater propensity to drop out of mainstream society. Britain's political landscape is different as ideology shifts every so often between Labour

(Socialist) and Conservative (Capitalist), and therefore each party has had to reach central ground over the ensuing decades as opposed to remaining loyal to the extremities of one political social ideology, and therefore the more vulnerable in society are cared for, giving less access and opportunity for a serial killer to commit crimes against marginalised groups.

10. John George Haigh was tried, convicted, and sentenced for five murders and he was hanged at Wandsworth Prison for his heinous crimes. Haigh's first known murder was the murder of his friend, William McSwann, on the 9 September 1944, when Haigh would have been 35 years of age. I am therefore working on the assumption that Haigh has committed more than the five murders than he was convicted for, as serial killers do not suddenly start killing during middle age, as the life expectancy in Britain in the 1940s for a man born in the early 1900s was 47 years of age (Lambert, 2012). Haigh even admitted to at least eight murders that may not have been investigated correctly at the time, and as previously mentioned, I believe that Haigh did commit more murders and the modern investigative tool of linkage analysis should be deployed against these cold cases to hopefully solve them once and for all and provide peace to the victims. The other issue with Haigh's low count of victims is partially to do with the fact that he was in prison sporadically over the ensuing years up until his final arrest for murder. As too much time has passed it may well not be in the public interest to investigate as to whether John George Haigh did commit any more murders. However, using modern investigative psychology and other arsenals in the analysis of serial murder may reveal that Haigh could be linked to several cold cases, and there may be more clues to his modus operandi and serial killers such as Haigh are rarely discussed, as the media, public and society are more transfixed with more household names such as Fred West, Ted Bundy, Peter Sutcliffe et al. In short, we are transfixed on 'sex killers', as this is our deepest primitive instinct and is a taboo subject, whereas we need to give more study to the 'monetary killer', as they may be operating under the radar and the public could be at greater peril because of this lack of study on these types of monsters that exist amongst us and yet little or hardly anything is written about them.

11. Haigh, I have stated on several occasions throughout the profile, suffered from a myriad of psychological problems in the sense he was a narcissistic, psychopathic, and arrogant personality who believed that

he would be able to commit 'the perfect murder' by removing the body by dissolving the corpses in acid to leave no evidence, yet he was gravely mistaken.

Haigh also showed his narcissist tendencies by concocting a story about the reoccurring nightmares in which a forest would turn into crucifixes which would proceed to drip with blood, and a dark figure who would come and collect the blood in a cup and offer it to Haigh to drink. Haigh claimed to have drunk the blood from his victims and there is speculation as to whether he did or whether it was a ploy used to try to convince everybody he was criminally insane as opposed to a coldblooded and premeditated calculating killer. Haigh is not the first serial killer to claim that he 'suffered' from bad dreams that made him commit his heinous criminal acts. The Indonesian serial killer, Ahmad Suradji, claimed to have had a dream in 1988 in which his father's ghost told him to kill 70 women and drink their saliva, so that he could become a mystic healer, whereas Haigh drank the blood of his victims. Haigh was not suffering from mental illness and knew he was committing crimes, and organised serial killers do not usually have a mental impairment (I will explain this in more detail during the profile). The drinking of the saliva for Suradji and the blood-drinking for Haigh, I believe, was a form of the retention of possession over his victims. As mentioned in this profile, the American serial killer Jeffrey Dahmer admitted to the FBI agent Robert Ressler in 1994, *'I ate them in an effort to possess them more completely and therefore they would be a part of me forever more'* (cited by Cawthorne, 2000). Forensic psychology was not as mainstream back in the 1940s as it is today and we are aware from studies that serial killers take and retain 'trophies' from their victims, e.g., Jeffrey Dahmer, who kept photographs and body parts, and Jerry Brudos, who would keep the shoes of his victims and masturbate whilst wearing them or looking at them, for example. The trophies are taken by serial killers as a reminder and therefore as a way of reliving the crimes, but also as the ultimate way of retention of power over that person, as the serial killer chose when that person died. Haigh did this in the most extreme way by drinking the blood of his victims.

Haigh showed his psychopathic tendencies when he indulged with intimate relationships with the opposite sex. Haigh mislead several women and then discarded them after they had served a purpose to him. It is known from more modern-day research that psychopaths cannot form lasting and meaningful relationships, as we see from more modern-day serial killers such as Ted Bundy, who had a girlfriend by the name of Stephanie Brooks whom he was originally due to marry until she broke the engagement off in 1967 due to his immaturity and lack of direction in life. Bundy deliberately reacquainted himself with her back in California 1973, and she could not believe the transformation in him, and Bundy mentioned marriage more than once. When Stephanie Brooks agreed to his marriage proposal, Bundy suddenly became cold and despondent. His plan of revenge had worked. He rejected her as she had once rejected him (Bell 2009). Jerry Brudos married a young and impressionable girl (who would later become his wife) and he would make her walk around the home naked apart from wearing a pair of stilettos, she was told to avoid his workshop and the attic and obeyed his every command (Ramsland, 2013). For psychopathic serial killers like Haigh et al. a key aspect that is central to their psychopathic personalities is the retention of power over a person, and therefore I believe Haigh had a psychopathic personality disorder as he exhibited all the necessary psychological characteristics that we have associated with this disorder.

12. I believe that Haigh became a serial killer in part due to his overbearing and zealously religious parents, although there may have been other events in Haigh's life that would have played a part in his development, and thus the crimes he committed in later life. As Haigh had no brothers and sisters and he was not allowed to socialise with other children, as they were 'sinners', or partake in sports because it was 'dirty' (his mother was obsessed with cleanliness), I believe that Haigh, being reared in an oppressive and regimental environment, was not allowed to develop into a normal member of society due to a lack of socialisation skills and natural development from partaking in normal social practices that many people take for granted. Due to a lack of socialisation practices, Haigh had no alternative other than to develop his own fantasy to act as a coping mechanism to escape his overbearing reality, and this could be evident of the images contained within dreams which he stated made him kill. These dreams may have been a figment of his imagination initially, after all we all fantasise as it acts as a form of escapism from our daily realities, and we would go insane without this mental mechanism. In Haigh's case, I believe that these 'dreams' were fantasies whilst he was awake, and they became more lucid over a period where fantasy and

reality became intertwined and there became no difference between the two concepts within his psyche.
13. I believe that Haigh, in part, became a serial killer due to his overzealous parents, who did not allow him to develop within the normal psychological stages of development, as previously established. The parents were not the only singular factors in Haigh's development of a serial killer, there were other factors that contributed to his development enroute to developing into a serial killer. However, as his trial and execution from the date of his apprehension was just over six months there was not enough time to forensically study Haigh in more depth as this was not common policing practice at the time, and it is another argument for keeping these people alive as long as possible in the event that we need to study them forensically to hopefully find the best methodology to prevent somebody else becoming a serial killer, thus preventing somebody else becoming their victim.

    Haigh, like many other serial killers, either have a patriarch or matriarch (or sometimes both) that controls them whilst young, for example, Albert DeSalvo (the Boston Strangler) and Peter Kurten (the Vampire of Dusseldorf) were terrified of their abusive drunkard fathers, Aileen Wuornos's grandfather would sexually abuse her, Gary Ridgeway's mother was domineering, as was Edmund Kemper's. The common denominator in the cases of the mentioned serial killers, and John George Haigh, is that once they are free from the 'shackles' of their domineering parents, they commit more than just petty crimes, as there is nobody there to 'control' them anymore and murder is the ultimate power and supreme control another human being can have over another, and this is epitomised by the French biologist, Jean Rostand (1934); *'Kill one man and you are a murder. Kill millions of men, and you are a conqueror. Kill them all and you are a God.'* Murder for a serial killer becomes an addiction as bad as any drug addiction and they need to exacerbate and refine each murder to achieve the 'high' that they feel from committing these acts.
14. Although I have established previously the John Haigh's murders and other criminal acts were of a serial nature, I believe that his criminal acts intertwine with four different types of serial murder as outlined by Lane and Gregg (1992). I will outline the following points for numbers 15–18 in the order for what I believe to be Haigh's motivations in committing murder with an explanation next to each sub-section of the profile.

JOHN GEORGE HAIGH, THE ACID BATH MURDERER

15. I believe that Haigh was what Lane and Gregg (1992) refer to as a *'comfort-orientated killer'*. Gain killers exhibit the comparatively rare motive among serial killers of personal, usually financial acquisition. For this type of murderer, the act of murder is usually incidental, often irksome in the pursuit of some other goal, and usually it is a family member (Lane and Gregg, 1992). Haigh killed for monetary gain, or 'reward'. As we saw with the murder of William McSwann, Haigh pretended to the parents that their son, William, was hiding in Scotland to avoid conscription to the army during World War Two. When William never returned home after the war, the parents became suspicious and Haigh murdered them and forged the deed to their estate, which netted him £8,000, which he lived off for the next three years. Lane and Gregg (1992) also state; *'A sociopathic outlook which has reduced humankind to "objecthood" is a prerequisite even for this type of killer, but an outward respectability and believability that will deflect suspicion from a theoretically obvious suspect is essential.'* This, by Lane and Gregg, fits John George Haig perfectly as to the world he presented himself as what he wished to be seen as and not the monster behind the suit that he truly was, and this psychopathic chameleon-like behaviour allowed him to commit and get away with murder for a long period of time.

16. Gregg and Lane (1992) define a *power-seeking serial killer* as the following: *'A common complication among personalities showing low self-esteem is the desire to have control over the life and death of others to such a degree that it serves as an intrinsic motive to murder.'* Although Haigh did not show the classic signs of using power over his victims, such as tying them up and using physical and psychological abuse, I believe that the base where killed his victims was central to his psychopathic personality, as once in his 'workshop' there was only one entry and exit and this base was not only chosen as a means to an end, it would have gave Haigh's narcissistic personality a sense of the power he never had before as he was actually an inadequate person in the sense that his businesses failed whilst the middle-class victims he chose all had achieved success and a form of authority that Haigh never had, and his murder was not also monetary, it became an act of the transference of the inner turmoil and rage that existed within his psyche.

17. Gregg and Lane (1992) define a *hedonistic serial killer as the following*: *'In its broadest sense, "pleasure" is the reward for murder.'* I believe that

Haigh enjoyed the feeling of power that accompanied the actual material acquisition from his murders. I also believe that when Haigh was convincing people that the victim was still 'alive', due to Haigh's psychopathic personality, normal mundane activities would not have stimulated him, yet fraudulent behaviours, both financially and misleading the families, would have given him a hedonistic sense of power and stimulated his narcissistic personality in making his ego believe that he was 'smarter' than anybody else, as he was committing murder and nobody was suspecting anything untoward, until the police who were trained with dealing with criminals suspected Haigh of committing fraud and possibly worse. Haigh was a *hedonist* and he believed that he was outwitting the police.

18. Haigh may also fall into the *'lust killer'* category. I state this reason because if the story of blood-drinking is to be believed, as he stated suffered this reoccurring nightmare from ten years old, this may have been an underlying fantasy and a sign of the formation of a deranged personality, and he may possibly have been fantasising murder from a young age, which is common with many serial killers and not just *lust killers*. Gregg and Lane (1992) believe that the next stage in the development of a *'lust killer'* is the *'hunt'* stage, and Haigh may have waited to find the right victim(s) before deciding to murder them, for example he stayed with the Stephen family but left abruptly, possibly because they were a large family compared to the victims he later killed, and therefore suspicion may have fell upon him, although it has never been clear as to why he allowed the Stephen family to live and we will never be quite certain. The next stage in the process of the *'lust killer'* is the *'kill'*, as Gregg and Lane (1992) state *'The degree of overkill is extreme – torture, mutilation and knives, necrophilia, dismemberment, even blood-drinking and cannibalism are characteristics.'* Haigh committed acts of dismemberment, overkill, and blood-drinking. The final phase in the process for a *'lust killer'* is the *'post-kill phase'* (Gregg and Lane, 1992). This phase compromises of *'the passing of the experience of killing results in a feeling of emptiness and depression, often aggravated by a realization that the primary 'defect' in the psyche (the restrictive childhood, rejection by female peers etc.) has not been repaired by the act of killing, and the killer will be obliged to more lives in the search of temporary relief.'* Haigh even admitted after the murder of William McSwann that he had felt guilty, but the sudden urge for blood had been

so bad he had given in to his compulsions and Haigh once again fits this definition.

19. I believe that Haigh was what we can refer to as an organised serial killer, in the vast degree of the term. The reasons that I believe Haigh was an organised serial killer is firstly because he killed the victim(s) when the opportunity arose, and he would bide his time and commit the act, when he thought the time was right as opposed to acting on impulse. Serial killers usually kill when they have access and opportunity to victims. With Haigh, however, he would befriend the victims for months before killing them, possibly to avoid any suspicion from falling upon him and strike when he felt necessary. I also believe that the befriending stage was his way of manipulating them, and a part of his game as he was manipulating his eventual prey. Haigh's modus operandi differs from a disorganised serial killer such as Peter Kurten and Richard Trenton Chase, who killed at random and across a variety of victim typology e.g., old, young, male and female; Haigh killed the middle class to an end for his own personal gains. Haigh always had his own 'murder-kit' with him and even pre-planned how to dispose of the evidence, which shows a degree in his level of planning and calculation before acting, whereas disorganised killers are usually more impulsive, and they usually turn over a higher victim count in a short space of time before being apprehended.

20. As previously stated in the profile, I have outlined the reasons as to why I believe that Haigh was predominately an organised serial killer. However, he does show some signs of being disorganised, to which I believe there are two contributing factors for this characterisation and classification. Haigh believed that by destroying the bodies of his victim(s), in essence he was exonerating himself from being associated with the crimes. However, as previously mentioned, Haigh had misconstrued the corpus delicti law, and although his planning shows organisation it is almost paradoxical, but at the same time he also shows disorganisation in not understanding the relevant statute to its full meaning. Haigh did not, unsurprisingly, have a sound knowledge of forensic science in the sense that he did not realise that dentures are acyclic and are therefore they are unusually resistant to the corrosive actions of acid. Haigh may have thought he had committed the 'perfect murder'. However, due to the narcissistic personality types associated with serial killers, they always believe that each murder is perfect. There

is no such thing as the 'perfect murder', even in the case of modern serial killers such as Danilo Restivo, for example, who naively attempted to clean any trace of forensic evidence after the murder of Heather Barnett and had bus tickets to use in his defence of where he was, but computer records in the local job centre showed he had not logged in until Heather Barnett had been murdered. Haigh's narcissistic personality believed that he was smarter than anybody else and this may be in part why he did not dispose of all evidence including receipts from pawn brokers that he sold to after the murder of his victims.
21. If modern-day advanced police work had been available to the police, forensic psychologists et al., including the amount of text written on the subject of serial murder and serial killings, along with the following investigative techniques geographical profiling, criminal profiling and investigative and criminal psychology, I still do not believe that Haigh would have been apprehended any quicker than he was, as the police were not aware initially that the victims were going missing, and this was in part due to Haigh's deviance as he was an almost maleficent entity. Haigh went to great lengths to cover his tracks, and he would dispose of anybody who suspected him of foul play and this was evident when he attempted to mislead the parents of William McSwann, who were becoming suspicious, before murdering them. Haigh convinced Rose Henderson's brother that the Henderson couple had emigrated to South Africa due to a 'botched' abortion, so nobody reported anything untoward to the police and therefore no leads meant no theory could be deduced about the whereabouts of the missing persons, and therefore there was no information to base a psychological profile on an unknown offender. The investigative tools mentioned can only come into use when there is something to work from, and in the case of Haigh there was nothing for police to use in terms of deduction to provide any theory, and again this shows Haigh's deviant cold and calculating manner.
22. There was no brilliant deduction by the police that resulted in the apprehension of the serial killer John George Haigh, just good old-fashioned standard police work and luck that Haigh came into the police station to speak with detectives searching for Mrs Durand-Deacon. Haigh was found to have an extensive criminal record, including spending four years in prison for fraud. The police officers he spoke to did not like his demeanour, and therefore they obtained a warrant to search his premises, in which they would find all the

JOHN GEORGE HAIGH, THE ACID BATH MURDERER

necessary evidence which led to Haigh being convicted as a killer. Haigh, again in the instance of speaking to the police, shows his narcissistic personality in the sense that he thought he could fool professional law enforcement officers as he had done with the general members of the public. Haigh has also showed another classic trait of an organised serial killer in the sense that they like to speak to the police about the investigation and like to offer any 'assistance' they can, and therefore at the same time try to fool the police and be updated on the progress of such an investigation. Although this was not a common known trait of the psychopathic murderer at the time, the police are trained in this area in modern-day practices of forensic psychology, and I believe if Haigh had been aware that people in his position seek to mislead the police by pretending to be 'concerned', as he was an organised serial killer, I believe today he would have steered clear of the police as much as possible to stave off any potential suspicion and unwanted attention, as he would have been aware that this could lead to his arrest and conviction.

23. To conclude the profile of the Acid Bath Murderer, John George Haigh, having reviewed all the psychological states and his personality, I believe him not to be insane under the law of diminished responsibility under the Homicide Act 1957, although I do agree with the psychiatric evaluations that stated he suffered from a 'paranoid constitution', as I believe that this was formed in his early years from his parents making him excessively nervous of the outside 'evil' world, and to elaborate on this point further, a sufferer with a paranoid constitution does tend to exhibit a narcissistic personality within their psychosis, and I believe this personality type to be the foundation of John George Haigh's psyche. Another trait is bearing grudges against others, and in terms of his victimology type, e.g., the middle class, Haigh bore an illogical envy and suspicion of these people, despite aspiring to be them, which undoubtedly would have led to a deeper and fragmented quagmire that was already fermenting and existing within his psychosis before his spate of serial murders.

I believe that Haigh was fully in control and aware of his criminal actions, and this was shown in his planning and predisposition to murder. I believe the act of the blood-drinking was committed by Haigh to serve two purposes brought about by his personality. Haigh drank the blood as a form of trophy-taking, and at the same time as this acted as a form of 'power and possession' over the victims. I feel that he believed if caught he would use this deviant act as a defence to show he was 'mad', and thirdly it would have repulsed society, and serial killers enjoy holding power, and it is not just over the victims, this can be the family, the friends and society. Haigh again shows his narcissistic tendencies in this heinous act in that he thought he would be classed as 'mad' and sent to Broadmoor Hospital, upon which he could be released and spared the death sentence. Haigh misinterpreted and exhibited a complete lack of understanding of any of the laws associated with mental health, and instead of being classified as mentally insane he was executed on August 6th, 1949, by being hanged at Wandsworth Prison. Haigh was one of Britain's most notorious serial killers and yet he is rarely mentioned, yet at the same time he is an interesting study; did he kill for monetary purposes or psychological purposes, or a combination of both? As the media and public become more obsessed with sex killers, as it taps into our very own primitive behaviours, John Haigh is an interesting criminological study.

Dennis Nilsen

Dennis 'Des' Nilsen was born on the 23rd November 1945 in Aberdeenshire, Scotland and would become one of the most reviled serial killers in British criminal history. Denis Nilsen, from his own confessions to the police, confirmed that he killed twelve victims between the years of 1978 and 1982, thus averaging three victims per year or one every four months. As there was a 'cooling-off period' between each murder, Nilsen would fit into the classification of a serial killer based upon the FBI's definition: *'The unlawful killing of two or more victims by the same offender(s) in separate events.'* Dennis Nilsen had told police that he had killed fifteen victims; three of them would remain unknown, and without any physical evidence, the claims by Nilsen cannot be corroborated. Nilsen may have killed before, because he would have been thirty-three-years of age in 1978, which was his first known murder, and this is a late age for somebody to begin the act of serial murder if they have not previously killed. I therefore do believe that Nilsen has killed the other three victims and he knew who they were. However, as much as he enjoyed cooperating with the police, he also liked to hold back so much information to keep the focus on him, and in his mind, he was outwitting the police and exercising power over them and retaining power over the three unknown victims. To understand the psychological motivations as to why Dennis Nilsen killed his victims, we need to firstly assess his modus operandi and work backwards to establish a motivation for his crimes and criminal acts.

Denis Nilsen's act of criminality was the unlawful murder of another person(s). Denis Nilsen's modus operandi was not dissimilar from that of his fellow British serial killer, Colin Ireland, aka 'The Gay Slayer' and his American counterpart, Jeffrey Dahmer, in the way he would meet victims in the local gay bars and befriend hem and buy them drinks before enticing them back to his home under the pretence of a sexual encounter, food and more alcohol, or a combination of all three.

Once they had entered his flat, this is where Nilsen would have felt completely empowered and a grandiose sense of control would have engulfed his psyche, as he knew that nobody would disturb him and he was alone with him and the victim, the victim usually being incapacitated by alcohol or drugs. Nilsen's modus operandi was to get the victim drunk before strangling and drowning them to ensure that they were deceased, upon which Nilsen would retain the victim for his own 'pleasure' and 'company'. Greig (2009) cites Brian Masters (1985) when he stated that Nilsen claimed to have killed his victims *'so they would not leave him.'* Nilsen would wash and bathe the bodies of his victims, caress them, and he would even speak to them about his day at work, which I believe would have acted as a sexual stimulant for somebody with a depraved psychosis such as Nilsen, due to two previous well-documented encounters with the men he loved in his life. Nilsen, according to Cawthorne (2007) stated the following: *'To him (Nilsen), their seduction and murder were sad, mechanical processes, but once they were dead, they really turned him on as just touching a corpse would give him an erection.'* Nilsen's former partner, David Gallichan, was in a relationship with Nilsen for two years between 1975 and 1977, however, temperamental differences drove them apart and Gallichan ended the relationship, which devastated Nilsen. Gallichan's exit from Nilsen's life would undoubtedly have felt like a déjà vu moment for him, mentally destroying him further in the process.

At the age of six, Nilsen was invited to view his grandfather's corpse (the grandfather whom he adored), and thus got his first sight of a corpse. From that moment on sex and death became fused together in his mind (Cawthorne 2007). Nilsen committed his first murder after David Gallichan left him as he killed Stephen Dean Holmes, as he *'could not bear to see him leave.'* Nilsen, I believe, committed his murders in part as he became afraid that all the men in his life would leave him lonely as he was before, due to severe imbalances within his personality and general psychosis, as he suffered from a paranoid personality disorder, brought on by his father's abandonment and his grandfather's death. I believe that, in his psyche, he believed that men all wanted to 'leave' him, and it was men that he desired in terms of sexual intimacy and a desire to form an everlasting relationship. This confusion between the differing concepts of 'love' and 'death' would become all too evident in the specifics of the crime scenes later in Nilsen's life.

The crime scenes for Denis Nilsen were situated at two different locations: *Melrose Avenue, London* and *23 Cranley Gardens, London*. These two crime scenes, and Denis Nilsen's impulsiveness meant that he left a lot of forensic evidence such as blood splatter patterns at each scene and bone debris from the bonfire of the victims at Melrose Avenue, all of which corroborated with his confession and helped aid his conviction in court. At Cranley Gardens, Nilsen tried to flush the remains of his final victim, Steven Sinclair, down the drain as he was in an attic flat. An employee of Dyno-Rod drains repairs realised that the remains he found were suspicious and duly called the police to come and investigate, upon which Chief Inspector Peter Jay took the flesh and bones to Charing Cross hospital where pathologist David Bowen, professor of forensic medicine at the University of London, confirmed that the remains were indeed human and had come from a man's neck. The impulsive behaviour exhibited by Nilsen became his downfall, as it was easy for the police to establish where the remains had come from within the premises as there was only Nilsen and one other tenant within the property at the time. Nilsen did probably believe that he had got rid of all the evidence and would never be caught. However, he did not understand how drainage systems functioned and this would ultimately become his downfall.

In order to understand the criminal and psychological motivations further, we need to provide an analysis of his victim typology as there have been too many commentators and media-driven 'experts' that incorrectly blame David Gallichan for the serial murders committed by Nilsen, as much in the same way as these 'experts' provide their opinions that Stephanie Brooks ending her relationship with Ted Bundy was the catalyst for his murders; this is not true at all because serial killers develop perverse sexual fantasies over the course of their lives based on a victim typology and this ferments and manifests itself within their psyche, before they can no longer control their inner stresses and turmoil any longer and act upon their psychologically primitive impulses, and therefore we need to provide an analysis of the victims of Dennis Nilsen as these poor souls would have been the end of years of fantasies in order for Nilsen to be able to commit his crimes.

The victims of Nilsen were all young men, and contrary to what has now become a popular myth associated with the Muswell Hill murder, not all the victims were homosexual, as they came from various backgrounds including straight, working professionals and of course homeless people and drug addicts, people who have fallen out of society and can become easy targets for serial killers. Nilsen played and preyed on their destitution and desperation by offering food, shelter, alcohol, and drugs.

Nilsen did not come across as anything other than another mild-mannered person that anybody could meet in a pub, or at work for example. Even the police officers were astounded by his very gentle manner. The youngest victim, Stephen Dean Holmes, was aged eighteen and the oldest victim, Billy Sutherland, was twenty-seven-years of age at the time of death. If we include all the murdered and attempted murder victims, the average age range of the victims in the case of Nilsen was twenty years and three months (two attempted murder victims have not had their ages disclosed). The victims were all victims of opportunity for Nilsen, as many of them he had never met before, and there is no evidence on the contrary to suggest that he had previously stalked any of them. Nilsen even killed Billy Sutherland because he had, according to Nilsen, pestered Nilsen for sex, which had 'annoyed him'. Nilsen killed the victims because many of them were either runaways or away from home in a big city. For example, Kenneth Ockendon was visiting London from Canada for Christmas, and therefore many of them had accepted Nilsen's 'offer' of a place to stay and to acquire a hot meal. Nilsen may have killed the victims because he may have hated the fact that he was himself homosexual, which I believe is evident specifically in the murder of Billy Sutherland.

Nilsen, like many serial killers that have been studied, had an innate desire for power and this was evident with one of his jobs after leaving the army as he became a police officer, and I believe he left the police force after a year due to the prevalent homophobic and macho atmosphere, as Nilsen hated the fact that he was a homosexual, as he stated to his biographer, Brian Masters, in 1985; *'I was killing myself only but it was always the bystander who died.'* Britain's leading criminologist, Professor David Wilson, believes that gay men are one of the groups that are targeted by serial killers in Britain due to antipathy towards homosexuals, as Wilson (2009) quotes Fone (2000) when he states, *'Antipathy towards (homosexuals) – and condemnation, loathing, fear, and proscription of homosexual behaviour – perhaps the last acceptable prejudice in British society'.* David Wilson (2010) has stated the following: *'Serial killers look for access and opportunity (to kill victims) first and the motivation should be the last worry.'* Wilson (2009), when he talks about Colin Ireland, stated the following: *'Perhaps editors (of newspapers) simply felt that they could not print details of the S&M scene in their "family newspapers", so they gave the case scant attention.'* The same could also be said for Nilsen when we analyse the social mechanics of the era and the fact that many of his victims were last seen in London's gay hangouts. Unfortunately in the 1970s homophobia was rife in Britain, which would have given Nilsen the access and ultimately the opportunity to kill his victims, and the motivation may have come second with Nilsen as the overriding paranoia that he would be 'left alone' could have become the overriding psychological factor once they were in his flat, which led to the commission of murder and we need to psychologically further assess the psychological characteristics of Dennis Nilsen.

Nilsen does not show all the classic signs that we have come to associate serial killers with over the years through a plethora of research, other than that his mother was overbearing and that his father was an abusive alcoholic. Nilsen did not show any of the symptoms associated with the 'MacDonald Triad' in the sense that he did not wet the bed consistently after the age of ten, he did not seem to have a pyromania problem and he did not torture animals, and when he killed it was not in a sexual frenzy, but whilst his victims slept (Greig 2009). Although, according to Greig, Nilsen may not have exhibited the conventional signs of a future killer. However, I believe that Nilsen did gain a sexual stimulation from strangling his victims as Kocsis (2007) cites Brittain, Gratzer and Bradford; *'the offender(s) is able to exert greater control and power over the victim by strangulation'*, and the fact that Nilsen wanted to 'possess' them due to his own innate fear and paranoia of loneliness. I believe that whilst he was committing the act of strangulation, Nilsen would have climaxed, possibly multiple times, as sex, death and power were far to intertwined within his psyche during the build-up preceding the murder and the murder itself. Nilsen shares many of his psychological traits and modus operandi with the American serial killer Jeffrey Dahmer, for example, the victims of each killer were all young men and were for the most part homosexual, with the only differences being that one killed only white men (Nilsen), the other (Dahmer) killed predominately Black men. Nilsen and Dahmer strangled their victims to gain control and 'power' over their victims (Dahmer did hit one with a dumbbell to acquire dominance over his victim). Nilsen and Dahmer had held conversations with the victims, bathed and caressed the victims after they became deceased, and both had lonely childhoods, which can explain this warped behaviour of an overriding desire for sex and 'company'. Nilsen and Dahmer exhibited extreme signs of violence after the consumption of alcohol. This is when all their victims were murdered, as it more than likely destroyed any small number of inhibitions they may have held whilst sober. Both cooked parts of the victims. Dahmer even admitted that it was a *'way of the victim being a part of him forever'*, in other words eating the victim became about possession and is a substitute of 'trophy-taking', which is a common trait of serial killers, because when we look at the cases associated with Nilsen, Haigh and Dahmer, they all ate or drank the blood of their victims, yet there is no evidence of them retaining possessions from the their victims as the act of cannibalism may have stimulated their psychosis more than retaining a watch, or an item of clothing, for example, as cannibalism is the ultimate act of 'possession' for a serial killer. Nilsen claimed he never practised cannibalism; however, this is debatable, as this would have stimulated his sexual psychosis and he admitted to boiling parts of the corpses, and the fact that he kept them for days after their death, they would have become almost his 'toys' and were at his 'leisure', however, it still needs to be established what the primary motive was for his criminal offences.

I believe that the primary motive behind Nilsen's crimes consisted of a sexual nature, as he admitted to masturbating over the corpses once they were dead, and according to Greig (2009), his live-in partner, David Gallichan, and Nilsen shared all bills and domestic duties etc., but apparently did not have sexual interactions. If this is true then it could show that Nilsen could possibly only be sexually stimulated once the victim was dead and became his 'possession', as he also previously had another partner in the army, who he claimed to have never had sexual relations with Nilsen. However, in a disturbing sexual incident on one occasion he made his partner cover himself in white talcum powder and put on blue lipstick to 'play dead', upon which Nilsen took photos, which he masturbated over on several occasions, and therefore this is evidence that Nilsen was harbouring perverse fantasies involving dead men, and I believe that this may have been his first instance of crossing the psychological boundaries in regards to what is deemed as both socially and sexually acceptable. Nilsen, based on his previous relationships, was indeed homosexual, and he was probably ashamed of his sexuality, and this would have caused turmoil within his psyche. Nilsen admitted that seeing his grandad dead in a coffin gave him an erection, and as this was Nilsen's first sexual experience, I believe that Nilsen could be classed as a *'demisexual'* as he could not appear to form or experience a sexual attraction with another man as he could not form a strong emotional connection with them. The opposite is true with a dead man; Nilsen could form a 'strong' emotional and sexual relationship with the dead, and this became the overriding psychological motivation for the commission of his crimes.

Once the victims were alone in the home of Nilsen, they would have experienced a great degree of risk as they would have been alone, and Nilsen could turn from a gentle, normal human being to a monster almost like a light being switched on and off. Nilsen killed Billy Sutherland (27) because he had simply 'annoyed him'. Nilsen became angry with Kenneth Ockendon because he decided to listen to the music set and not pay attention to him, which shows how dangerous a character Nilsen really was, and I feel that these two murders are significant when trying to understand Nilsen's criminal motivations as the murder of Billy Sutherland was Nilsen fighting his own innate sexual desires and, as he admitted to Brian Masters, he was in effect 'killing himself'. The murder of Kenneth Ockendon occurred because, in Nilsen's overbearing paranoia, Ockendon had been deemed within his psyche to have 'rejected' him as everybody else had done throughout his life, despite the fact he had only known Ockendon for several hours. This shows how dangerous it was to enter Nilsen's domain on your own, and the risk was incredible. Nilsen admitted that he did not kill everybody that entered his home, and I believe it is solely because those that left the flat alive never triggered his paranoia by their actions, possibly albeit unwittingly. However, those like Sutherland and Ockendon enacted small everyday human traits or endeavours that we are all capable of enacting, and therefore Nilsen became 'triggered' by their actions or behaviours and decided that they should die as a result, which is a truly harrowing and frightening concept. Nilsen, although impulsive, was taking risks in killing his victims, and I will expand on this statement as to why I believe that this would have been the case.

It could be argued, due to an existing social prejudice at the time, Nilsen did take some considerable risk in killing the victims, because if the police realised that many of the missing people were all last seen in the gay quarter of London, this may have aided the investigation as somebody may have reported seeing Nilsen as the last person with the victim. As Nilsen was moving the body of one of his victims late one night, he disturbed a neighbour who could have easily looked out the window and witnessed Nilsen's strange behaviour, which would have undoubtedly aroused suspicion. Nilsen also lit bonfires for unknown reasons, and he would place old tyres to mask the smell of burning flesh. Unbelievably, none of his neighbours questioned what he was doing and the reasons as to why he was lighting bonfires in their shared back garden. The actual murder of the victim became a risk to Nilsen in placing himself in harm's way, for example, during the murder of John Howlett, who Nilsen dubbed 'John the

Guardsman', who he severely strangled with brute force as he feared being overpowered by Howlett. The reason Nilsen took more risks in the murder of his victims is because he was a disorganised and impulsive killer, and the murders happened based solely on opportunity as opposed to pre-planning, and Nilsen, as mentioned became triggered in his psyche with his overwhelming paranoia of loneliness and these intertwined feelings became all too evident before, during and after the commission of his crimes.

Nilsen would visit the pubs situated in the London's gay quarter and entice victims back to his flat with the promise of a combination of sex, booze, and food. Nilsen claimed that many of the victims were asleep or in a comatose state before he strangled them with items that were available at the time, for example, Nilsen strangled his first victim Stephen Dean Holmes with a necktie, and for the murder of Kenneth Ockendon he used the cord of the stereo headphones that Ockendon was listening to at the time. During the murder of John Howlett, Nilsen used length of loose upholstery from a chair and strangled Howlett.

After the victims were dead, Nilsen would bathe and caress their bodies, and he would even hold 'conversations' with their corpses upon his return from work, and Nilsen even admitted that he committed sexual acts upon some of the corpses. For example, he used to masturbate over the corpse of Martyn Duffey, until the corpse became to putrefied that he was left with no choice other than to dispose of it. I believe that for several days, whilst Nilsen had the corpse residing in his flat, he entered a conscious state of 'euphoria' as he finally had a submissive partner that would never be able to leave him. Unfortunately for Nilsen, this newfound 'partner' would eventually rot and decay until putrefaction was completed, and Nilsen had no alternative but to begin dissecting the corpse. I believe this process was emotionally draining for Nilsen, not because of the act of dissecting the corpse, more so to do with the fact that he would be 'alone' yet again, and the innate and inhibited feelings of inadequacy that he harboured resurfaced yet again and the urge to kill during these periods would intensify until it became unbearable for him.

Nilsen also admitted to the police instantaneously upon his arrest and questioning to dissecting and boiling some of the remains of the victims, and this is where Nilsen may have possibly committed acts of cannibalism to act as the final power over the victim before he had to dispose of the body due to putrefaction. Nilsen, however, at the time of his arrest, had one victim in his wardrobe as he had not yet managed to dispose of the corpse and Nilsen retained them as long as possible due to his psychological innate fear of 'loneliness', and when we review the murders again from the start, his murders were very emotive to him from the start to the finish, i.e. when he had no alternative other than to dispose of the body.

Strangulation is defined as a form of asphyxia (lack of oxygen) characterised by closure of the blood vessels and air passages of the neck because of external pressure. The three forms of strangulation are hanging, ligature and manual. Almost all attempted or actual homicides by strangulation involve either ligature or manual strangulation (Strack and McClane 1998). Based upon this definition, Nilsen fitted into the same pattern as many other serial killers who kill using this method, for example, Kenneth Erskine, aka 'the Stockwell Strangler', killed using both ligature and manual strangulation. According to Strack and McClane (1998), to completely close the trachea around 33lbs of pressure is required, and brain death will occur in four to five minutes if strangulation persists. Although the likes of Nilsen and Erskine would not understand the medical science, and neither would they care for it when killing a victim, it was done as a means to an end for them to achieve their cruel psychological aims and enact a fermented warped fantasy on a weaker victim. For Nilsen and Erskine, the act of strangulation becomes personal and emotional, and would more than likely have heightened the thrill of killing and provide them with a highly orgasmic sexual experience, and this became a part of the addiction of murder in itself and to achieve this high they needed to repeat the act over time, as much as an alcoholic needs to drink to persistently achieve that 'high', the emotional act of strangulation for interpersonal killers such as Nilsen and Erskine was needed for every act of murder that they committed. The overriding difference in the murders between Erskine and Nilsen is where each respective murder was committed, as Nilsen used his own residences because he would have felt 'empowered' and he could relive the fantasy again and again and he needed to retain the body for his own sexual pleasures afterwards, whereas Erskine killed the victim at the site and ejaculated whilst committing his crimes and then left. The type of behaviour exhibited by Erskine would not have psychologically stimulated Nilsen, and therefore he would not kill in this manner.

The crimes were committed wherever Nilsen was residing at the time. However, the murders only took place at two known locations, both of which were in London, Melrose Avenue and Cranley Gardens. The victim typology chosen by Nilsen was no coincidence, as Nilsen would not have been likely to overpower a potential male victim in the street, as he was not very physically commanding for a man. He would not have felt empowered or any sense of control as there were to many external variables that could have stopped him committing his crime, and the act of murder was only a part of the fantasy, as the cruel act of murder became a means to an end in him acquiring a submissive and passive partner. I do not believe that Nilsen went out solely with the act of killing the victims that he did. However, I do believe that enticing the victims back to his home does show a degree of planning and premeditation. From my research into him, I believe that predominantly Nilsen would fall into the *disorganised* classification of serial murders as he acted on impulse, which is evident by the types of weapons he used to kill his victims as they were just there; there was no murder kit ready for him to use upon their entrapment in his home. I will expand more on Nilsen's flight between the *organised* and the *disorganised* classification of serial murder later in the profile. Although serial killers can be either nomadic, commuting and/or marauding, this does not mean that they will not hunt elsewhere. However, many have a nomadic base where they feel psychologically empowered and in complete control, for example Brady and Hindley had the Yorkshire Moors and Gary Heidnik used his soundproofed basement, whilst David Parker Ray had his 'toybox', which was a caravan transformed into a torture chamber. Dennis Nilsen had his flat, which became central to his modus operandi and provided him with the access and opportunity for him to commit his crimes.

The first victim, Stephen Dean Holmes, was killed at Melrose Avenue, London, and was originally buried under the floorboards before being taken out and burned on a bonfire within the back garden. Interestingly, Stephen Holmes was the only victim that Nilsen did not dissect, and this could be because Nilsen was not used to committing murder and he possibly perceived the act as 'below' him initially. However, Nilsen soon began to realise that wrapping up a dead boy in carpet and trying to burn it whole takes longer than one could imagine, and Nilsen would have to dissect all future victims as it limited the risk of him getting caught. Nilsen kept all the other victims at Melrose Avenue, under the floorboards. I believe that there is a strong psychological reasoning for this behaviour exhibited by Nilsen in the sense that the first murder had not satisfied his initial fantasy, and this did stimulate him sexually as he never achieved the fantasy of sexual fulfilment and power that he was craving, as he more than likely fantasised that committing murder would help him attain psychological solace. The act of murder rarely provided a serial killer with the psychological solace that they crave because the act of murder is an extremely emotionally stressful, and therefore he would keep the bodies under his floorboards, and this would act as a form of 'possession' over the victims even after death.

Once Nilsen moved to Cranley Gardens, London, this is where he began dismembering the bodies and even boiling them, whilst he would discard some of the body parts down the drainage system, and therefore I believe that Nilsen did practice in the perversion of cannibalism as he could possess the victim by eating them (Jeffrey Dahmer also admitted to committing acts of cannibalism), and not having the risk of corpses rotting under the floorboards and beginning to decompose could have resulted in Nilsen being apprehended earlier than he was. In nature, we see that many insects and mammals, from slugs to spiders, practice what is known as 'sexual cannibalism', as this is their natural practice of consuming their sexual partner usually during or after the act of copulation. I believe that Nilsen practised this form of cannibalism upon the death of his perceived 'partner', and the bodies were not moved and/or initially destroyed as this would have entailed him destroying his own fantasy that the murder allowed him to pursue which psychologically gratified his psychosis and psychological cravings for a short period of time, and therefore we need to further assess the murder sites and discovery sites and how they intertwine with Nilsen's psyche.

The murder and discovery sites were the same, as the police found the remains of the victims in both properties that had previously been inhabited by Nilsen. As mentioned in the previous point, the moving of the bodies to another 'dump site' did not serve Nilsen's psychological needs and therefore he retained the victims within his property, and the common misconception with Nilsen is that many people who review his case believe that he was an 'organised' serial killer simply on the basis that he lured victims into his home without assessing his psychology in any real depth. I feel that Nilsen was a disorganised serial killer as opposed to being an organised serial killer, and I have outlined this in greater detail in the next points, and the greater details will be outlined below.

I believe that, from assessing everything, Dennis Nilsen was a predominately disorganised serial killer due to the following key factors:

- *He killed on impulse, and he usually waited until they (the victims) were asleep before he would kill them with a weapon that came to hand, e.g., the headphone cords, the necktie. Even though the murders*

were committed in his home, and he could have had his 'murder kit' ready for the victim's arrival, or he could have even drugged their drink, he never did, which was down to his impulsive and psychotic behaviour, which was exhibited outwardly upon the victims for his own irrational fears of paranoia and a fear of monophobia.
- Nilsen was socially inadequate and had no close friends at all, which is common with many disorganised serial killers as they struggle to form normal relationships, unlike their more organised counterparts. The lack of social skills with Nilsen would have formed from his dysfunctional upbringing, hence his first exciting sexual experience was seeing the dead corpse of his grandfather.
- He lived alone for much of his adult life, and he only had one live-in partner, who left him because of his violent temper. Nilsen's former partner, David Gallichan, claims to have found 'Des' too hard to live with as he had an extremely volatile personality. I believe that Dennis Nilsen, was a 'demisexual', which is when a person can only feel attracted to someone once an emotional bond is formed between the two. Although Nilsen would almost certainly have engaged in sexual intercourse with David Gallichan, I believe from profiling Nilsen that these acts would have been very sporadic and infrequent. I believe that Nilsen was a compulsive masturbator and Gallichan may have been submissive in this respect and obeyed Des's whims and strange desires. The act of compulsive masturbating is more common with disorganised serial killers, and I do not believe that David Gallichan could understand what Nilsen's psyche was really like with its dark manifestations which, on occasion, Nilsen would exhibit outwardly. However, I believe that because Gallichan was a submissive partner, Nilsen allowed him to live and possibly developed intimate feelings as he was finally not alone, and this provided Nilsen with both a consistent stream of psychological comfort and dissipated his feelings of inadequacies. However, I don't believe that the monophonic feelings ever left Nilsen's psyche and these feelings would exhibit themselves later in Nilsen's life in the most tragic circumstances for his victims.
- Nilsen, unlike most disorganised serial killers (who usually live or work near to the crime scene), resided in the scenes of the crime.
- Nilsen had nocturnal habits and all his victims were killed in the early hours of the morning, whereas organised serial killers usually kill in

both the day and night-time, dependent on the location and the opportunity available to them.
- Nilsen lived alone and he even claimed that sometimes he was confused and frightened both during and after the murders, and again this shows that he acted impulsively, and these impulsive acts shows his disorganisation. It also shows that Nilsen possibly never brought a victim back to his home with the initial intention of killing them.
- Nilsen tried to curb his murderous habits by moving residence and yet he still could not as his impulsive behaviour would not allow him to stop.
- He killed in one place, and he would consider the murder as completed.
- He did not have any idea of forensics and did not leave a 'dump site', as he tried to burn the bodies and police found fragments at each crime scene.
- He responded best to a counselling interview with the author Brian Masters, to whom he admitted everything regarding his early life experiences, the feelings of being a homosexual and his feelings during the crimes, as he had never tried self-help programmes before, and these feelings manifested themselves in his psyche with lethal consequences.

The crimes were not staged to mislead the police as Nilsen did not comprehend ever being captured as he thought that by burning, burying, and flushing the remains of the victims down the drains he would never be caught as there were no bodies, and the police had not even questioned him about the missing people as he was not on their radar, and nobody suspected a serial killer was on the loose. As Nilsen was an impulsive killer and disorganised, these acts of miscalculation resulted in his own downfall and this area of his psyche needs to be assessed further in terms of his motivations by the cause of death to victims. Are there any psychological clues to the wounds left on the victims that may give us further insights into Nilsen's psychology? What were his final acts with the dead bodies that may provide further psychological clues as to the confusion in his psyche?

As Nilsen strangled all his victims, I believe that the following definition by Greig (2009) will help provide a unique insight into his motivation: *'Strangling is perhaps the most common and certainly the most intimate mode of murder, allowing the killer to literally squeeze the life out of the victim. Its intimacy has a particular appeal for the sexually motivated murderer, who often strangles victims to death whilst raping them.'* Nilsen strived for intimacy with these men, some of whom were not even homosexual, and Nilsen would have realised this. However, we are aware that Nilsen did not want them to leave, and the feelings of monophobia fermented and became ingrained in his psyche over the years due to the experience of his father leaving him, his grandfather dying and David Gallichan leaving him during adolescence, and therefore Nilsen did not want any more men he 'loved' or perceived that he loved to leave him all alone yet again.

Nilsen, unlike most normal sexually healthy men, could not acquire an erection and as previously mentioned due to Nilsen's fear of monophobia, I believe that he could not form loving and meaningful relationships. The act of strangulation became his only way of achieving an erection and subsiding the monophobia that manifested itself within his psyche. This is evident in the murder of Kenneth Ockendon, and Nilsen admitted the following: *'We got along very well, and the more I enjoyed his company, the more apprehensive I felt about him flying home the next day.'* Nilsen also stated after he had killed and had sex with the corpse of Ockendon; *'I thought that his body and skin were very beautiful, and I would dress him in something fresh and put him to bed and tell him goodnight.'* Nilsen may not have necessarily initially wanted to murder the young men he encountered. However, the only way he could become intimate with another person was to kill them and therefore he would be in complete control, and in a perverse way he may have believed within his warped psyche that he had found 'love'. Nilsen, as we are aware, became fascinated seeing his grandfather's corpse when he was a boy and he also claimed that at the age of eight he nearly drowned and was revived by an older boy, who exhibited a sexual interest in him (Cowing 2009). Again, this is another instance in his formative years whereby both sex and death become fused together and intertwined within his psychosis. The latter instance with the boy saving him from drowning may be a complete fantasy that Nilsen has created in his mind to quite possibly to sexually stimulate him, as serial killers create an elaborate fantasy world to cope to psychologically reason with their warped own behaviours. Nilsen was associating love, sex, and death as the same entity within his psyche throughout his formative years.

I believe that Nilsen strangled them so he could keep the body intact as, if he would have bludgeoned them, there would be blood splatter and to a degree this would have destroyed Nilsen's elaborate fantasy of a 'partner', and strangulation, once linked with serial killing, can also act as an intense moment of sexual gratification. As Nilsen's psyche and fantasies had intertwined sex and death into the same concept, I believe that Nilsen would have been in a state of heightened sexual excitement during the act of strangulation of another man and therefore I believe it is unequivocal that during these acts that he would have orgasmed on multiple occasions.

The bodies were not positioned in any way and Nilsen would keep them and dress them, talk to them and try to have sexual intercourse with them before they putrefied, and he had to dispose of the body. The motivation for this behaviour is Nilsen trying to possess the victim and to have a form of a 'relationship' with the deceased, and Nilsen didn't start killing until a late age from his own testaments to the police, and therefore I believe that Nilsen did indeed kill more victims due to the social climate and homophobia at the time, and he knew this and chose to retain it as it provided him with a grandiose sense of 'power' over the victims and the police, and I will expand on this statement in due course.

When Nilsen began his series of murders, he would have been 33, which is unusually late for a serial killer to begin their series of murders, and he committed his last known murder at the age of 37. Nilsen was only convicted for six counts of murder and there have been other unidentified victims, who Nilsen claimed to have 'forgotten' the identities of. I believe that Nilsen killed prior to the victims we know of in London. As Nilsen served in the army he may well have killed whilst in service as this would have gave him the perfect excuse to do so and could have been an 'experiment' in the act of killing for him, as not all serial killers kill animals as children, and Nilsen was one who did not and therefore his developmental stage in the process of serial killing quite possibly developed later than that of other serial killers. I also believe that Nilsen, due to his intellect, knew the names of the three unidentified victims. However, this was his last semblance of power and control over the police, society, the victims, and their families that he could hold. Unfortunately, as Nilsen died in 2018, we will never identify the victims and they will remain 'John Doe', as Nilsen took this information to the grave with him. I have no doubt that Nilsen knew the names of these victims as he would have treated them as 'partners' because he could not form healthy, loving and normal relationships with the living, and when he did, they became destructive because of his explosive personality and temperament.

Nilsen only ever had one live-in partner and was not married at the time of his arrest, and there is no record of him being married to anybody previously. As mentioned, as Nilsen was demisexual, and due to his paranoid personality, I do not believe that he could form the normal relationship bonds to live with another person for a long period of time, and his strange and erratic behaviour, coupled with his temper, would have frightened normal people into realising that he had an imbalanced psyche. Although gay marriage was not legal in the United Kingdom at the time, gay people still lived together and had relationships like any other couples. Nilsen's relationships, on the contrary, could not last because of his destructive mental state and violent temper, however, when further assessing Nilsen and looking for psychological clues throughout his employment history, it is quite an exemplary record for a serial killer as there are usually dismissals, however, Nilsen from the outset appears to have been a fine and varied civil servant, however, upon reviewing this in some depth, there are several psychological factors to suggest there is much more to his psychology and employment history as opposed to simply wanting to serve the public.

Nilsen's employment record is varied, as his first job was serving as a cook with the Royal Fusiliers from 1961 until 1972, where he learned dismembering skills and realised that he was a homosexual because of having a brief relationship with a young Arab boy. Nilsen, in 1972, joined the Metropolitan Police where he discovered a macabre fascination for morgue visits and autopsied bodies. When he left the police, he joined the civil service as a jobcentre worker originally, where he became the branch secretary of the civil service union, developing increasingly radical left-wing political views (Cawthorne 1998). If we look at Nilsen's employment history, they all, to a degree, have a sense of authority and power, and this includes his political activism. This reverts to a common psychological trait with serial killers that they are obsessed with power and the pursuit of power, which they will ultimately enact and transfer upon a hapless victim. The common denominator with Nilsen's employment history is that all his jobs were associated with positions of power and responsibility, and this is not uncommon with serial killers. For example, Gerard John Schaefer was a police officer and Colonel David Russell Williams served in the Canadian Forces whilst at the same time committing rape and murder.

The psychological beliefs of Nilsen stemmed from his formative years when the male role models in his life abandoned him and/or died. The main adult influences in his life were his dad, who was a violent alcoholic, and his grandfather, whom he adored and looked up to whilst just a boy, and the latter would bear the biggest influence on his life and later his warped sexual fantasies and murderous desires. The feeling of rejection, love, innate sexual desires, and anger became fused together, and because of these issues not being aligned within his psyche in terms of normal relationships and developmental psychology, this led to an extremely fractured psychosis. Nilsen could never form a close relationship with anybody during his school life, early adolescence, throughout his chosen career paths or general adult life. Nilsen did not see the boys and men that he killed as people; he saw them as objects there to be kept for his own desire, and in a perverse way and in his own psyche he believed that he was showing the corpse 'love' and 'affection' by trying to do every day mundane activities that a couple in a normal adult relationship would do, e.g., talking, watching television, and of course engaging in sexual intercourse. Nilsen could not attain this normally like most people. The fear of loneliness and rejection consumed and overpowered his psychosis to help him perpetrate the criminal acts that he committed. As mentioned, I believe that Nilsen was a demisexual, and this was a base for his psychological traits, sexual desires, and relationship problems. Nilsen could not form emotional bonds with the living, and he developed an early fascination with sex and death and Nilsen formed an emotional bond with the dead as opposed to the living, and this in a sense became his own warped sexual identity, as Nilsen quoted to his biographer, Brian Masters, in 1985; *'Emotions are the most toxic substances known to man and anonymous sex only deepens one's sense of loneliness and solves nothing.'* This quote is significant and interesting as it shows that Nilsen does not possess the normal human emotions to form bonds and relationships, and we also gain an insight into his motivations for the murders, as the thought of a one-nightstands repulsed him and made him afraid, as the loneliness would return once they had left the next day. All this would be explained by Nilsen to the police upon his arrest, and Nilsen talked without much prompt from the police.

Nilsen was questioned by Chief Inspector Jay at his flat in Cranley Gardens, and at first Nilsen pretended to not know anything about the body parts found in the drains. Nilsen within a matter of moments after the initial denial calmly admitted to the police that he killed fifteen men and young boys, and that on occasion Nilsen could not recall how he killed some of them. Nilsen was very cooperative with the police, and although the media have construed this as a desire to 'help' the investigation, it should also be considered that Nilsen knew the media were going to take an interest in his crimes due to the severity and repulsiveness of their nature. Nilsen asked the police on several occasions about the media interest in him and this shows that Nilsen was enjoying the notoriety that was surrounding him. The intense media interest in his crimes would help him develop a sense of grandiosity within his psyche that he had probably never felt before in his entire life. Nilsen admitted to the police about conducting in intercrural sex whereby he would place his penis between the legs of the dead victims and would thrust until ejaculation. This was a practice that had its origins in Ancient Greece as they perceived homosexual anal sex as demeaning to the receiving partner. As Dennis Nilsen was a homosexual, I believe that he despised his sexuality and he hated himself for it, as he once told Masters; *'When I was killing them, I was in effect killing myself,'* therefore, Nilsen, in his warped cognitive processes, used his own cognitive dissonance to convince himself that the act was more 'moral' than committing anal sex on the corpse of the victim, when in fact neither act is humane and degrade the victim even more after death in a sickening and grotesquely perverse act.

A final indicator with Dennis Nilsen, as with all serial killers and serial offenders, should be to assess their criminal records to check whether there are any prior crimes that tie in with their later crimes, e.g. a history of sexual assault can show us why a serial killer may progress from rape to murder as they don't want to get caught possibly, or the act of murder is the urge that they have been fighting against in their psyche, until the tension becomes unbearable and any moral boundaries they have against committing this act simply collapse.

Denis Nilsen had no prior convictions for any minor offences let alone any serious offences, and therefore had Nilsen became a suspect, a criminal records check could have misled the police to focus their investigation elsewhere if there were bodies appearing all over London of missing young men, as Nilsen had an exemplary employment record as well. Nilsen's behaviour and employment record are yet again another prime example of a serial killer appearing to be 'normal' and living amongst us as one of us, and this is a truly alarming aspect as we now know the crimes Nilsen was committing once he closed the door of his flat.

Pen Profile

I, Samuel Hodgins, can unequivocally confirm that I have researched the case of the 'Muswell Hill Murderer', Denis Nilsen (white Caucasian male). Denis Nilsen committed his crimes (that the authorities are aware of) between the ages of 33, when he allegedly killed his first victim, until he committed his last murder before his arrest in 1982 when he would have been aged 38. Nilsen claims that he committed his first crime at the age of 33, however, the police believe this to be a lie and that Nilsen has committed many more crimes against vulnerable homeless people and the gay community at the time when Britain was prejudiced against these so-called societal 'subgroups'.

According to McCready (2002), the average age based upon studies that a serial killer starts their series of killings is between the ages of 25 to 34. If we look at the case of Nilsen he killed five weeks after his thirty-third birthday and Nilsen may well have killed many more prior to the 'initial' murder, as the first victim, Stephen Dean Holmes, whom Nilsen killed in 1978, was an unknown victim to the police until Nilsen sent a letter to the London Evening Standard Newspaper confessing to the murder in 2006, which was twenty-eight-years later, and this is one of the reason why I believe that Nilsen had many more victims, and he also knew the names of the unidentified victims the police found at his property. This is a classic act of a serial killer, whereby they retain information and feed the information when they see fit as they are retaining a semblance of power and control and Nilsen knew that he would remain in jail for life after the parole board rejected his chances of ever attaining freedom into society ever again. Nilsen used this information as a taunt at the police, the government, the victim, and wider society as he is aware that the police know he knew much more information in relation to the victims that he was withholding.

In the same letter, Nilsen also promised to help police identify the rest of his victims, although Scotland Yard has ruled out ever knowing definitively the names of the other men he murdered, according to the Daily Mail newspaper article published in 2006. Nilsen in his letter is admitting to more victims and based on this premise Nilsen may well have killed before the age of 33. As Nilsen had already been convicted, and a whole life tariff sentence has been imposed by successive home secretaries, I am not trying to offer a criminal profile of an *UNSUB*, I am in effect trying to offer a psychological post-mortem of the offender in question, Denis Nilsen, in the hope that I may be able to provide a motive for the crimes that he committed in North London between 1978 and 1982. In relation to the unknown victims, sadly we will never be able to establish who they were or their stories of how they ended up falling prey to the monster that Dennis Nilsen was, as Nilsen died of retroperitoneal haemorrhage on the 10 May 2018.

PEN PROFILES OF THE OFFENDERS

1. The criminal acts committed by the offender, Denis Nilsen, were of a serial nature ranging from assault to murder and in extreme circumstances acts of necrophilia. The cases that involve Denis Nilsen are all similar from the start to the end of each murder and beyond within his modus operandi, which remained consistent throughout his series of murders. Nilsen would meet homeless men, gay men and straight, and he would drink with them in the London gay quarter public houses (this is where he gained the access to the victim). Nilsen would endeavour to entice them back to his flat with the lure of food, alcohol/drugs, sex, or a combination of all three (this would have granted him the access and opportunity that a serial killer need to kill his victims), once inside the flat, the victims being alone with Nilsen would have unwittingly placed themselves in grave jeopardy. Nilsen has admitted that he did not always kill everybody that entered his home, and some victims such as Carl Stotter and Andrew Ho have lived to tell us of their experience at the hands of Denis Nilsen, which have provided us with insights into the horror that was taking place inside 23 Cranley Gardens and his flat in Cricklewood, London.

   Nilsen acted on his impulses, which stemmed from his own innate fears of loneliness, and I believe that this was all down to how 'attached' he felt to the victim at the time (I will elaborate further on this during the profile). Nilsen does not show the common signs that are now commonly associated with serial killers in the sense that he does not show any symptoms of the MacDonald Triad, as he did not wet the bed past the age of ten, he did not torture animals and in fact he loved his dog, Beep, and he did not show any obsession with pyromania (fire starting). Nilsen, however, developed a perverse fascination with corpses from a very young age after witnessing the corpse of his grandfather, and he became fascinated with death and claimed it was one of the first memories of him acquiring an erection. The problem is this fascination firmly fermented itself into the confines of his psyche and became fused with the normal human feelings of love, fear, lust, desire, depression, emptiness and with devastating consequences. Nilsen unsurprisingly never admitted that he had a perverse attraction to the dead during his formative years and this would have dire consequences for him and those who would meet him during his later life.

2. Nilsen may not have shown the classic symptoms that we have come to associate with serial killers over the proceeding years, through a plethora

of research both in the United Kingdom and abroad. Nilsen does, however, show some of the signs associated with serial killers in the sense that firstly he had at least one abusive parent, in this case being his father, who was an overbearing religious zealot and a violent drunk. Nilsen's father was abusive both physically and mentally to his entire family. This early instance may have begun the confusion and fear within his psyche as his father was possibly providing mixed messages, one of which would have been about moral behaviours for example, *'Do to others as you would have them do to you'* (Luke Book 6: Chapter 31), and then he would see his father be a drunkard and abusive towards him and the family. This may have been the first instance of a warped sense of love that became imprinted within his psyche. Nilsen also despised the fact that his stepfather, grandmother, and mother would bestow attention on his older brother and younger sister, and I believe that was the beginning of Nilsen feeling isolated and unable to form relationship bonds with others. Nilsen's family claimed that a young Dennis would reject their advances to demonstrate any affection towards him after the death of his grandfather. Williams (2005) cites Bowlby (1953) when she is discussing the formation of the *super-ego* and theories of the causes of criminality; *'Bowlby found similar results when he focused on early maternal depravation as being the cause of criminality. His argument rested on two basic premises: first, that a close, unbroken, and loving relationship, with the mother (or permanent mother substitute) is essential to the mental health of the child, and secondly, that rejection by the mother or separation from her (or substitute) accounts for most of the more permanent cases of delinquency.'* As any psychologist would clarify, Bowlby believed that attachment behaviours are instinctive and will be activated by conditions that appear to threaten achievement of proximity, namely separation, insecurity, and fear. I believe that once the maternal father left a young Denis Nilsen, Nilsen turned to his grandfather as a substitute for both his mother and father, and I believe that he looked to his grandfather for the basics a child would need to survive and develop within the normal psychological acquisition: the psychological nourishment that two parents should be giving to their child to allow them to develop within the normal childhood and adolescence stages of development.

The death of his grandfather devastated Nilsen, and this is where all his emotions and developmental psyche became confused even further.

If we look at Denis Nilsen's employment history, we find that he served in both the British Armed Forces and the police as this would have provided him with a disciplined lifestyle that he never had before in his life and this is not uncommon with serial killers, for example, Donald Neilson, was a wayward teenager with a youth offending history and yet when he joined the army, he became a model soldier. The problem was that he tried to enforce this way of life on his wife and daughter upon his release, and he would take them on army exercises into the Yorkshire woods as he would have seen army discipline as the only form of 'order' in his life due to a complete lack of discipline in his later formative years and an overbearing disciplinary figure in the form of his father, both of which created a confused message and, almost certainly when his father left, there was no more real discipline for him to follow and he had nothing to fear anymore and he became a law unto himself. Nilsen began to develop his fantasies of a 'submissive' or dead partner whilst in the army, as he woke up on the floor of a German youth soldier completely naked after a drinking session (Nilsen claims he never had sex with the soldier), and Nilsen said he saw the German soldier sleeping and he looked at peace and was so beautiful. Nilsen used to drink excessively whilst in the army and he used to pretend to be asleep from the drink in the hope that one of his colleagues would molest him whilst 'unconscious', this again shows his inability to bond within the realms of a normal sexual context and his fantasies of a submissive or a dead partner were now beginning to permanently reside within his thought processes and these thoughts would be become all consuming.

3. Denis Nilsen is Britain's third most prolific serial killer with fifteen victims, behind Peter Dinsdale with 26 known victims and Harold Shipman with two-hundred-and-fifteen known victims. The average age of Nilsen's victims was twenty-years of age and three months old in comparison with Harold Shipman whose average victim age was 73 and nine months. The victims on Nilsen's radar were all young men, and although serial killers usually choose a typology of victim, e.g., either one sex, one ethnicity etc., Nilsen appeared to choose either runaways, tourists, or homosexual men and all the victims were white men, as Nilsen was a homosexual himself and therefore targeted men as they formed the sexual desires deep within his darkest fantasies.

Dinsdale was a bisexual, and he would be categorised as a *'thrill killer'*, whereas Shipman would be classed as a *'monetary kill for gain killer'* (due to a change in his modus operandi). I believe that due to the social prejudices of homosexuality prevalent in the United Kingdom at the time Nilsen was an active serial killer, this gave Nilsen more of an opportunity to commit his murders due to the prejudicial fear and loathing of the gay community at the time, and therefore this placed many young men at risk as homosexuality in this era was slowly becoming more mainstream, however, many in the gay community had to hide their sexuality for fears of prejudices against them and this allowed Nilsen the perfect chance to access victims and the opportunity to kill them, and I am therefore categorising Nilsen into the sub-category of serial murder as *lust killer*. Lane and Gregg (1992) outline this type of killer as; *'The largest sub-section of serial killers, for whom sexual gratification is the primary motivation and whose crimes most frequently exhibit a considerable element of sadism. Quite at variance with popular misconception of the lust killer (or any serial killer) as a wild-eyed-essentially opportunistic-psychotic, the procedure through which these killers go in planning and executing their crimes is one normally associated with highly organised personalities'*. To an extent is true, e.g. Ted Bundy is the classic example of an organised lust killer who was highly organised and methodological in his planning prior to the murders of his victims, whereas Nilsen was impulsive and opportunistic, and this is the problem with anybody studying or working with serial killers as their methods and madness do not fit a generic template, as their psyches and personalities are all different, and therefore profiling them should be based solely on the individual and not become too obsessed with the 'organised' or 'disorganised' typologies, as there are areas of both classification that every serial killer will exhibit. Lane and Gregg (1992) also place the lust killer into four different phases: *fantasy, the hunt, the kill phase and the post-kill phase*. I believe that Nilsen exhibits at least three of these phases and I will outline my hypothesis in the forthcoming points.

a. Lane and Gregg (1992) define the *'fantasy-phase'* as the following: *'The desire to kill is cultivated, often with the use of pornographic books and films. In this phase, the killer may act out the crime over and over in his head during a greater of lesser period of time-even years before, like a switch being thrown, phase two is entered and fantasy begins to establish itself as reality.'* Nilsen has admitted that he liked to sit in front of his mirror and pretend that he was dead whilst masturbating several times, and he even managed to convince a fellow colleague in the army to pretend to be dead, upon which Nilsen took photographs, which he masturbated over. Another alarming factor in Nilsen's obsession with his mirror was that he knew if he tilted the mirror one way, the head of the person looking into the mirror was cut off and Nilsen would excessively masturbate over these images. I believe that these were the early instances of Nilsen beginning the 'objectivization' process of turning people into 'objects' for his own warped sexual desires, and eventually these types of acts would not stimulate him fully within his psyche. As I have previously mentioned, I believe that Nilsen always suffered with a warped psychosis, however, he transitioned into a serial killer and exhibited their common psychological traits and behaviours in later life. These early acts were the *fantasy phase* for Nilsen, and phase two began to enter the reality stage when the young men were alone with him in his flat. However, this phase alone was not necessarily what drove Nilsen to kill, as the other phases needed to become intertwined for him to commit the crimes.

b. Lane and Gregg (1992) define the *'hunt-phase'* as *'during his search the killer has a very clear image of the 'right' victim; a specification such as Ted Bundy's women with straight hair parted in the middle. He may also favour certain locations, such as streets or woods, college campuses of shopping malls.'* As I have previously stated, I believe that Nilsen was an impulsive killer who even moved properties from Melrose Avenue, Cricklewood, to Cranley Gardens, Muswell Hill, in the vane hope that he would not kill people if he could not bury them under his floorboards. However, he was too impulsive to stop killing other human beings. Nilsen knew who his 'right' victim typology was and that is why he targeted the London gay quarter, as this is where he would gain access and ultimately the opportunity to kill and possess his chosen victim type. Nilsen may initially not have necessarily hunted them or wanted to kill them, but due to his own inadequate psychosis he became a serial killer.

c. Lane and Gregg (1992) define the *'kill-phase'* as, *'for the lust killer the kill is an intensely personal act-indeed it is his only motivation. Alone with his victim, the lust killer has the freedom to make real his fantasy. As one might expect, the lust killer favours 'personal' weapons such as hands and knives, and the degree of 'overkill' is extreme – torture, mutilation, necrophilia, dismemberment, even blood-drinking and cannibalism are characteristics.'* Nilsen may have used weapons that came to hand as he was impulsive and disorganised and therefore needed to subdue the victim as quickly as possible in order to achieve his fantasy of possessing that person and their corpse after death, and this became part of his fantasy of having a 'live-in partner' and I believe that Nilsen's father, grandfather and the one and only live-in partner, David Gallichan, were dearly loved and all of them in his psyche 'abandoned' him. We are aware that Nilsen performed necrophilia upon several of his victims and he would proceed to keep them under the floorboards for this particular purpose and for 'company'. The overkill that Nilsen used was excessive in the sense that when he could not keep the victim any longer due to putrefaction, he cut them up and boiled them and I believe that this was the stage when he practised cannibalism for him to permanently possess the victim and complete his perverse fantasy, and for a short while, I believe that he felt psychological content. However, it was a temporary feeling as the feeling of contentment would disappear very quickly and his need to acquire another victim for 'company' would begin to manifest itself once again in his psychosis. Nilsen never actually admitted to cannibalism as this is a social taboo that even many serial killers would not admit to, as it is one of the most repulsive acts for a human being to commit. For example, many humans can kill as we all have the primitive instinct contained within the hindbrain and the medulla and we can kill if we feel necessary, e.g., in warfare or in a fit of rage, however, not many humans could commit an act of cannibalism as the mere thought of enacting such an act makes us feel sick.

d. Lane and Gregg (1992) define the *'post-kill phase'* as, *'for most serial killers the passing of the experience of killing results in a feeling of emptiness and depression, often aggravated by a realisation that the primary 'defect' in their psyche (the restrictive childhood, rejection by female peers etc.) has not been repaired by the act of killing, and that the killer will be obliged to take more and more lives in search of temporary relief.'* Nilsen admitted that he sometimes blacked out after killing, which was possibly his way of coping with his abnormal acts as much as anything. Nilsen needed to keep killing and killing to retain his power and as a completely innate and selfish desire to not remain lonely. Nilsen may have killed when the feeling of helplessness overcame him, and his inadequate social skills did not help acquire a meaningful adult relationship in the way that normal consenting adults would do because of the myriad of sexual and psychological problems that engulfed his personality.

4. Due to the above statements, I believe that if Nilsen had never been caught, and had he been a more organised or forensically aware serial killer, I believe that he would have undoubtedly claimed more lives than the known fifteen victims he managed to murder. Nilsen killed because he needed to do so due to the defects in his psyche and the victims, many of whom were vagrants or runaways, were targeted by Nilsen, and the social prejudices that existed at the time in British society would have given Nilsen more access and opportunity to victims than he should have otherwise been warranted, as there was economic poverty at the time around London with thousands of rough sleepers that Nilsen was targeting by exploiting their desperation.

   a. Nilsen may well have killed before whilst he was employed within the army and he was stationed abroad, and he may have killed whilst on duty as he was travelling around different parts of the world, and this would have given him a greater geographical field for the access and opportunity of victims. Due to the age that Nilsen began killing, I believe that this was a very late age for a serial killing to supposedly begin their series of murders. Therefore, I believe there to be other victims that have never been identified due to the corpses being destroyed on one of Nilsen's bonfires. Nilsen's first known murder was committed when he was aged 35, which is unusually late for a serial killer to begin committing a series of sexually motivated murders. There are strong reasons to believe that Nilsen committed more murders, as he only admitted to the murder of his first victim, Stephen Dean Holmes, in 2006, which was 28 years after he was killed, and Nilsen may well know who the other victims are, but this could be his way of retaining a form of power as, in his letter to Tim Barlass, the Chief Executive of the London Evening Standard Newspaper, Nilsen states; '*My own autobiographies have been obstructed and banned by the Home Office...every inch of the way. A whole list of writers, journalists and independent academics (some from the US) have wished to visit me in prison, but all applications have been rejected by the (mostly) New Labour Administration ...under Straw, Blunkett, Clark and (now) Reid...as the Stalinist 'Red Flag' keeps flying, if not in their pasts, then presently in their mind when it comes to censorship.*' This may seem an innocuous comment from somebody with a political theory, however, when analysed in its full depth this is Nilsen's psyche or his 'super-ego' being detached from the moral reality of his crimes, and once again he was trying to assert his power over society, the police, the government and of course the victims. It must be remembered that whilst he was employed at the job centre, he developed radical left-wing views himself and he was even planning to stand as a union leader. Again, this is Nilsen's psychopathic personality that from the outset appears to be caring and altruistic, yet all the time it is his psychosis yearning for the power that evaded him throughout his life up until that point. Nilsen was also objecting and acting out in the only way he could for others holding power over him and admitting to a new victim all those years later keeps him in the public eye and therefore is another form of the 'redemption of power'. Nilsen also wanted his life story told which may possibly contain a theory on why serial killers kill somewhere within the text. This is not uncommon with serial killers. For example, Myra Hindley was writing a book that was never released; Ian Brady wrote a book entitled *The Gates of Janus* (2001) that has been studied in criminological studies religiously in the USA, and Ted Bundy helped write criminal profiles on the 'Green River Killer' for the FBI whilst incarcerated, all of which appeared to be highly accurate upon the arrest and conviction of Gary Ridgeway. The common denominator with all three mentioned serial killers is that they never, or have not as yet, told the authorities where the remaining victims are and the identities of who they are. For example, Ian Brady never told the authorities where Keith Bennett was buried, despite taking the police on several trips and excavations on the Moors. I believe that Brady during these trips was exercising his power by taking the police near to the burial site, but never providing them with the actual site, and as these types of 'games' psychologically satiate the serial killer with a form or a retention of power and control of what little they have over their meaningless lives, it also serves as a second victimisation process for the surviving victims' families as the serial killer, albeit by proxy, is exerting their warped version of power and control over the families of their victims. In Brady's case, he would have been more than aware that Keith Bennetts's mother, Winnie Johnson, was constantly in the media and even begged Brady to provide the information so she could give her son the correct burial he deserved.

    b. I believe that Nilsen saw the victims as mere objects who were there to fulfil his warped desires for power, love, control and company, the latter being the worst form of 'company' imaginable to the rational mind as the 'company' he was keeping was the victims whom he had just killed, and he was taking them from wherever he had him them upon returning from work. Nilsen would 'converse' with the corpses of his dead victims about his day at work and he would bathe the corpse before either using the legs of some victims to simulate the female genitalia, or he would masturbate over the body, as this became the 'normal relationship' in his mind that he had lusted and desired for all his life. Nilsen may well have hated the fact that he was a homosexual due to more than likely being told by his overbearing and brutal father that homosexual urges were wrong, and this would have been imprinted within Nilsen's psyche during his formative years. As Nilsen became aroused by seeing the corpse of his grandfather, this would have undoubtedly intertwined and became confused with the mixed messages from his father as Nilsen himself tried to repress his biological sexual urges, and this is why I believe that Nilsen did not have penetrative sex with the victims either alive or when they were dead; despite the crimes that he was committing he still saw the act of homosexual sex as 'immoral' and I believe that he hated them and thus hated himself. However, it must be remembered that not all the victims were homosexual, and this was also Nilsen's way of cognitively compartmentalising his actions. I believe that Nilsen committed masturbatory acts and may well have eaten parts of the victims to help sexually stimulate him rather than forcing himself to have sex, and again this would have meant that Nilsen felt in control, and he was more 'normal' for not having penetrative sex with the victim. In short, Nilsen was trying to convince himself that he was not homosexual, and this was one of the mitigating and motivational factors for him committing the murders.

5. I believe that Nilsen predominately was a disorganised serial killer, and

although he does show some elements of the mixed serial killer, there are far too few to elements to be able classify him into this sub-category. Although Nilsen was an impulsive serial killer, he knew that he could acquire a victim by hanging out in the London gay quarter and this does show an element of planning, however, Nilsen admitted that he did not want to kill them originally and it was only when he thought that they were going to leave him he felt a sense of dread and therefore he killed them so they would 'never leave him'. His acts of murder exhibit both his primitive and impulsive behaviours. The weapons of choice that Nilsen killed his victims with also shows that Nilsen was an impulsive killer, as he killed by using his work tie, the loose upholstery of a chair and the chord of some headphones when one victim was listening to music. The common denominator in the way Nilsen killed his victims show a high degree of impulse, as he killed them with what weapons came to hand and he did not have a 'murder kit' ready upon their arrival as he could have easily spiked their drinks to subdue them.

Nilsen actually had no real plan to dispose of the body, as he burned some of the victims in his back garden and used rubber car tyres to mask the smell of burning flesh, however, this is against environmental laws and Nilsen could have been stopped at any time as we know from Detective Superintendent, Peter Jay, who told Nilsen, *'We have found body parts in your drain'* to which Nilsen replied calmly, *'Good grief, how awful.'* (Lane and Gregg 1992) This shows that Nilsen could not lie under pressure, unlike a more organised offender such as Ted Bundy, who even had the temerity to defend himself in court in front of the public of the USA. As Nilsen was an impulsive serial killer, Nilsen had no plan of action. This is what led to his downfall as the employee from Dyno-Rod found the remains of one of his victims. The irony when talking about Nilsen as a disorganised offender is that he did not once feature on the police radar, and nobody connected that many young men who frequented the gay quarter were going missing on a regular basis. However, it must be remembered that social prejudices existed at the time and the study of serial murder was still in its relative infancy and, for the most part, Nilsen was targeting victims that had already dropped out of society and therefore nobody knew if they were alive or dead anyway at that point.

6. I believe the Nilsen kept many of the bodies in his home due to several reasons, with the first motivating factor behind his murders being his

fantasy of possessing another human being who would be completely subservient to him and would therefore never leave him and in effect always be 'his' to 'love' forever. The 'theme' of power is usually central to the innate motivations of a serial killer. The second motivating factor is that the corpse of each respective victim would have helped to fulfil his sexual fantasies that he could not attain with a living person as Nilsen had a paranoid personality disorder and it consumed his thought process that everybody would leave him. The way Nilsen disposed of some of the bodies again shows his impulsiveness and his categorisation into the 'disorganised serial killer' typology, as once the body began to decompose, in his psyche the victim had served their 'purpose'. Nilsen did not know how to dispose of them as he had acted solely on impulse alone and had not planned or thought of just how difficult it is disposing of a dead body. Nilsen, unlike John Wayne Gacy, may have not always initially wanted to kill the victim, until of course his impulsive and sexual fetishes became all controlling within his psyche. Nilsen has since admitted that sometimes after he killed the victim, he went into a trance and was extremely shocked and alarmed at what he had done. I believe that when Nilsen was burning the bodies, cutting them up etc., I believe that not only was he trying to destroy evidence, but he was also trying to almost exonerate himself from his warped behaviour in his mind as he always promised himself that he would never commit the act again. However, with a serial killer, killing becomes an addiction and killing becomes the means to the end. Gacy on the other hand only started dumping the boys in the Illinois River when the space in his home had expired, and I believe that this ruined the fantasy for Gacy more than it would have for Denis Nilsen, as Gacy liked the retention over the dead, despite the smell being unbearable in his house at the time as in Gacy's mind this was the ultimate fantasy: possessing and holding power of the victims forever. The previous statement is not implying that Nilsen did not enjoy the 'pleasure' of possession that he derived from murder, Nilsen did not actively always seek murder whereas Gacy planned his murders and enjoyed the psychological and mental torture that he inflicted on his victims.

7. In view of the previous points and throughout the general profile, I believe that although the study of serial murder was in its infancy at the time, had the following investigative tools been available at the time *geographical profiling, offender profiling, criminalistics (C.S.II) and*

smallest space analysis (SSA), Nilsen still would not have been caught. Although Nilsen was a 'disorganised serial killer', the fact that he targeted tourists and runaways allowed him to commit his crimes as these people had fallen out of society. Serial killers will usually target the most vulnerable individuals and groups within society as it helps them get away with their crimes for long periods of time as opposed to targeting people who others still care about. This is evident in the case of the Yorkshire Ripper, who had killed four sex workers, as the public ignored the story, however, as sex workers are what could be classed as society's 'out-group', many people did not care as much about them and initially perceive them as victims. The public perception of the Yorkshire Ripper murders did not change or alter until he murdered the student, Jane MacDonald. Professor David Wilson elaborates on this issue in his book entitled *A History of British Serial Killing*, when he states, '*The victims of British serial killers are almost always drawn from just five groups: the elderly, gay men, babies and infants, young people who have left home, and sex workers.*' (Wilson) Due to society's prejudices time and homosexuality being another 'out-group' within British society at the time many people may have been reluctant to report missing partners to the police for fear of the homophobic abuse that they would receive. It could even be argued and theorised that the political principles of 'Thatcherism' may have inadvertently helped Nilsen to continue to commit his crimes. Margaret Thatcher believed in 'new-right' policies as she felt that the state had become too involved in everything, and excessive state interference was limiting business and individuals from maximising profit-making potential to create more wealth for Great Britain during her era of government. Thatcher believed that individual spirit would make Britain great again and this is encompassed in her speech on society; '*They are casting their problems at society. And, you know, there is no such thing as society. There are individual men and women and there are families. And no government can do anything except through people, and people must look after themselves first. It is our duty to look after ourselves and then, also, to look after our neighbours.*' (Thatcher 1987 – cited in the Guardian Newspaper, 8 April 2013) Thatcher was criticising the 'top-down' approach principles of a socialist government, yet at a time of 'individualism' the strife and trouble that was facing the gay community in their desire to be seen as anybody else in Britain was widely ignored, and I believe that this aided Nilsen and would also later aid Colin Ireland to be able to commit their crimes against a marginalised 'out-group' of society, and the media also pedalled their prejudices at the time. Even in the case of Colin Ireland, the Sun newspaper labelled Ireland (whilst unknown) as the 'Gay Slayer', and yet had it been another group in society there would have rightly been widespread public outrage, which shows the barriers facing the gay community at the time, and I do believe society's discrimination at the time did unwittingly aid and abet the likes of Nilsen and Ireland to quite literally get away with murder and allow for a serial killer to be on the loose and exist amongst us.

a, Due to the issues mentioned in point number 7, I believe that had any of the investigative tools been widely available at the time for the police, Nilsen would not have appeared on the police radar because nobody reported anybody missing as there were no bodies appearing at 'dumpsites' that would have gained the media's interest. With forensic evidence only discovered upon the arrest of Denis Nilsen and his subsequent conviction, and with no real evidence, and with Nilsen commuting in and out of London's gay quarter, and with no other clues, geographical profiling would almost certainly been of no assistance to the police.

Another key factor in why Nilsen evaded arrest for so long was, I vehemently believe, due to the homophobia in Britain at the time, as if the young men going missing had been reported somebody may have recognised them and possibly provided a description of Nilsen to the police. Due to society's prejudices at the time this became a key factor in Nilsen not being arrested sooner and the gay community not being more vigilant that some of their own were going missing. The irony was that Nilsen is a highly disorganised serial killer in comparison to other British serial killers who could be classed as 'organised', such as Hindley and Brady who claimed five known victims. Fred and Rose West who claimed ten known victims and John Haigh claimed six known victims and yet Nilsen claimed more victims on an individual basis to those British serial killers mentioned solely due to the prejudice against the gay community at the time which makes the case even more tragic.

8. To sum up the profile of the serial killer Denis Nilsen, I believe that due to the early experiences that Nilsen endured, in the sense that his father abandoned his family when Nilsen was four and then the next male in

his life, his grandfather, died suddenly at the age of 51 when Nilsen was eight years old, he had an irrational fear of loneliness, along with the fact that also his mother was at times overbearing with her religious beliefs, so overbearing she was the one who insisted (he refused to begin with) that he view his grandfather's dead body in the open casket. The action taken by the mother that day may have provided confusion in the young boys' psychosis whereby he associated the following, *death, love, lust, power, and authority*, with death and they all became intertwined as a single entity within his psyche. Nilsen developed an innate fear of being alone and he also did not develop socially throughout adolescence often being bullied at school and not making many friends. Nilsen developed anxiety and fears from a very early age and as they were not treated, they had dire consequences for him and many others later in life. Due to the previous statement, I believe that Denis Nilsen developed a borderline personality disorder (BPD) and a paranoid personality disorder (PPD), as he was an emotionally unstable person who showed signs of impulsivity and instability of affects in his life such as interpersonal relationships, his own self-image and sense of self-worth. We know that his other symptoms included an intense fear of abandonment and an intense anger and irritability that others have difficulty understanding the reason for (this was evident by his live-in partner who stated that 'Des' could change his mood almost instantly). Nilsen exhibited all these signs, and the problem was that nobody could recognise it as Nilsen was extremely introverted and could not be open and discuss his problems with anybody due to suffering from a form of arrested development which later turned to tragedy for many young people who had their lives cut short by Nilsen. McBride (2011) cites Falk (2007) when she states, *'We are meant to be in relationships with other people, but, just as surely, we are meant to partake of aloneness. To deny this part of our existence is a little like trying to walk the earth on one foot instead of two.'* Unfortunately, Nilsen's psychosis never allowed the two to co-exist.

John Wayne Gacy

According to the Federal Bureau of Investigations records, John Wayne Gacy began his murderous career on New Year's Day 1972, with the murder of Timothy McCoy, who was only sixteen years old at the time of his murder, with his thirty-third and last known murder occurring on the 24 November 1978, with the murder of James Mazzara, aged just twenty-years-old. However, despite Mazzara being the last victim, the last body to be found was that of Robert Piest, aged just fifteen-years-old at the time of his murder, who went missing on the 11 November 1978. We can see from the three victims mentioned that they are young boys, and I will endeavour to provide further psychological analysis as to why I believe Gacy chose them as victims throughout the duration of this offender profile. As Gacy killed between a period of 82 months (five years and ten months) he was averaging a victim once every 0.4 months, and as there was a 'cooling-off period' between each murder Gacy is classed as a serial killer and fits into the following FBI definition of a serial killer: '*The unlawful killing of two or more victims by the same offender(s) in separate events.*' Gacy has since gone down in the annals of American criminal history for his crimes, and as we psychologically assess Gacy we can see why he has almost achieved a mythical bogeyman like status in the American conscious. Although Gacy may have gained a mythical bogeyman-like status within the American conscious, we still need to assess his modus operandi and work backwards to establish a motivation for his crimes and criminal acts.

Gacy's modus operandi had slight variations from other serial killers, where all the victims are usually strangers or they have fallen out of society, as we witnessed in the previous chapter with Dennis Nilsen. Gacy knew some of his victims and their families quite well, as some of the boys worked for him at his firm called 'Painting, Decorating and Maintenance (PDM) Contractors inc.', others he picked up off the street using the lure of money, alcohol and drugs, or a combination of the three, and again this is the same method of victim acquisition that Dennis Nilsen used to acquire the access and opportunities to his victims.

JOHN WAYNE GACY

Once inside the home of John Wayne Gacy, he would trick the victims by using the handcuff and key 'trick' whereby he would tell the boys he was going to show them a 'trick' that he uses at children's parties whilst acting as Pogo the Clown, whereby they would willingly proceed to lock themselves in the handcuffs with the only escape being the key that Gacy kept in his possession, and once they were locked in the handcuffs Gacy would choose whether they lived or died, which would have been a supreme sense of power and control for his psyche and provided him with a perverse sexual 'thrill'. Prior to his handcuff 'trick', Gacy would supply the boys with drink and drugs as this would lower their inhibitions and make them vulnerable and less weary of him and his intentions as there were rumours circulating around the neighbourhood of his sexual desires for young boys. For a serial killer like Gacy this would have heightened his feeling of supreme power as he had manipulated the victim to the full and this would have served his grandiose and narcissistic psyche and I believe this would have become highly sexualised as he was using the 'trick' and ultimately watching the panic and fear sweep the victim.

Gacy's motivations for his crimes were of a sexual nature, and solely about possession and control over another human being as he kept the bodies in his house when he could after their death, and therefore they were always with him and he managed to have the final act of power over the victims in their last moments in life, and he retained them in death (until his crawlspace became too full due 29 bodies being buried within its confines). Gacy may have brought harm to those boys because his father would verbally and physically abuse him when he was young, and therefore Gacy was transferring the abuse he suffered at the hands of his father to the victims in a way to make up for his own inadequacies as he and his father never had a relationship whilst alive and the act of killing also intertwined as an act of 'transference' of his innate rage upon to a hapless victim, which he once perceived himself to once be. However, he was now the one with the power and the one with the ultimate control over another person. Another part in Gacy's modus operandi that we are aware of comes from the testimony of one of his surviving victims, Robert Donnelly. Donnelly claimed that Gacy impersonated a police officer and he trusted him implicitly. This is not only an act to gain access to a potential victim, however. The act itself is important for the psychology of a serial killer, as this is also a way to feel important and be a 'somebody' or a figure of respect and authority within society, and Gacy is not the only serial killer to act in this manner as the

PEN PROFILES OF THE OFFENDERS

psyche of a serial killer and the main psychological tenant that dwells within them is the lust and acquisition of power. Ted Bundy disguised himself as 'Officer Rosalund' during his attempt to kidnap Carol Da Ronch, Bundy had applied to be a police officer on several occasions, and this may have formed a part of his fantasy whereby he knew he could acquire victims as a police officer, as the public generally trust law enforcement, and this could have been a way for Bundy to gain access and opportunity to his female victims. Gerard Schaefer became a police officer, and this became an easy way for him to gain access to his victims. In the United Kingdom we have had Harold Shipman who was a doctor in his profession. The common denominator with the serial killers mentioned, and in general, is that they thrive on an intense feeling of power and authority and many people in society will automatically become obedient to a figure of authority, and this allows the serial killer to mislead a person into believing that they are safe when they have just given the serial killer the access and opportunity to become their next victim, and evaluation of the crime scene at John Wayne Gacy's home just shows how this 'figure of authority' very quickly turned into a monster upon analysis of the crime scene.

The crime scene in question was John Wayne Gacy's home, *8213 West Summerdale Avenue, Norwood Park, Chicago, USA*, and the home became a personification of his psychological characteristics in the sense that within the confines of his own wall he became all 'powerful', and this is what helped him evade suspicion, detection and capture for so long as plenty of young boys were going missing in the area and there were no witnesses as to where the boys had gone. I believe that this would have undoubtedly helped nourish and develop Gacy's sense of narcissism as nobody knew were the boys were other than him, and he would have felt gratification from following reports in the media that only he knew at the time the fates that befell upon his victims, all the whilst the tertiary victim of the community were desperately trying to solve the disappearances of the young boys.

If the police had suspicions earlier, and if forensic science techniques were in common use, Gacy may have been captured earlier due to the murder of Timothy McCoy, who was stabbed with a butcher's knife. Had suspicion fallen on Gacy for McCoy's disappearance, or witnesses who knew that McCoy was last with Gacy, the use of luminal (blood stain detector) would have stopped Gacy in his tracks, and the fact that neighbours kept complaining of the smell coming from the crawlspace could have been Gacy's undoing earlier. I believe had these investigative tools had been in place Gacy would have at the very least run an extreme risk of being apprehended as Gacy was not forensically aware of the methods conducted within a police investigation. Gacy's need for the retention of power by keeping the victim would have also contributed in his downfall early on as it would later prove to be the case. Gacy did start eventually dumping the bodies of his last four victims in the *Des Plaines River*. However, I believe that Gacy hated having to use a 'dumpsite' as it killed the fantasy of the victim remaining as his forever and I believe that as the fantasy died the urge to kill within Gacy's psychosis would have been spiralling further and further into his own psychological quagmire, and therefore young boys in the area were at greater risk than when he had room under his crawlspace as his warped fantasies could not be maintained. As with all serial killers, the boys that John Wayne Gacy murdered were the end of a warped fantasy cycle, and therefore to understand Gacy's psyche better, we need to analyse the victims further.

John Wayne Gacy killed 33 young men between the years of 1972 and 1978 and yet even to this day, eight of those victims have never been identified and possibly never will, as Gacy was executed by lethal injection on May 19th, 1994. Gacy's methods of choosing a potential victim were very similar to Dennis Nilsen, who abducted young homeless boys as they dropped out of society and nobody seems to miss them, and this is exactly why the likes of Nilsen and Gacy target these vulnerable societal outgroups. The youngest known victim of Gacy was Michael Marino, aged just fourteen-years-old and the oldest known victim was James Mazzara, aged just twenty-one-years-old. The average age of the 25 known victims was only seventeen years old and this highlights his perverse obsession with young boys.

The victims of Gacy were not all runaways or homeless, and although some had been in trouble with the law, the majority had families who dearly loved and cared about them. This contrasts with another American serial killer, William Bonin, who killed young boys, many of whom were runaways, and Bonin dumped them on the freeways of America. Gacy's victims all had family who cared for them, for example, Michael Bonin was on his way to meet his stepfather when he disappeared and Robert Piest's mother became concerned when he never returned after meeting a 'contractor' about gaining potential employment. Gacy did not care if the victims had families or whether they were runaways or homeless, what mattered to Gacy was the psychological crisis and satiating the monster that lurked within him, and he was extremely selfish that anybody who was unlucky enough to be manipulated by him usually ended up being raped and murdered at his hands, and as mentioned, the victims are the end of a cycle of a warped fantasy for the offender and therefore we still need to delve deeper into the psychological characteristics of the offender to ascertain potentially why these victims were initially chosen by him in the first instance.

I believe that John Wayne Gacy harboured an extremely deviant and psychopathic personality and character as he manipulated and coerced his victims into believing that they would be safe with him whilst plying them with drugs and alcohol in order to lower their initial inhibitions, and yet his real plan was to torture, bind, sodomise and kill them, upon which he would proceed to bury them under his crawlspace in order for him to achieve his sexual fantasies and feelings of power and control and to provide him with 'ownership' of the victim forever.

Gacy was a psychopath in the sense that he could compartmentalise his deviant and sadistic actions and yet still lead a normal life, a life in which he was highly regarded in his community so much that the Democratic township committeeman for Norwood Park, Robert F. Matwick, was impressed by Gacy's sense of duty and dedication to the community that Matwick nominated Gacy to the street lighting commission. Matwick would not be the only person to be conned by Gacy, as he appeared to manipulate all who met him, including the top office in the world of politics. President James 'Jimmy' Carter's wife, Rosalynn, was so impressed by his act as Pogo the Clown at a local children's party that she had her photograph taken with Gacy and sent it back to him with her autograph. Gacy was not the first serial killer to become a respected member of their respective community. The fact that Gacy could manipulate senior politicians would undoubtedly have added to his grandiose psyche and he would have felt even more powerful and invincible, which would have made him become more hedonistic with each murder.

Gacy's psychology is not dissimilar to other serial killers who manipulate their community and acquire high positions of trust. However, with a serial killer, it is not about a sense of duty, the authority and feeling of control and power are their motivating factors for taking up positions of trust, and this occurs more frequently than we perceive it to be the case. Dennis Rader, aka the 'BTK killer', for example was a Lutheran congregation leader. Serial killers like Gacy and Rader act in this manner to keep up a pretence of 'normality' and to mislead those around them, Rader was a Lutheran congregation leader and on the Sunday after his arrest, his pastor, Michael Clark, told a congregation and the Wichita Eagle of his profound shock; *'Why us, God? It cannot be my son! It is not my father! I just do not believe it! This is where many of us are in these troubled times. How can it be?'* (Wichita Newspaper Article, 2007).

Gacy shows many of the common psychopathic characteristics as outlined by Hare (1941) as Gacy had *superficial charm and above average intelligence.* Gacy duped his neighbours the Grexa family into believing that he was the average hardworking American who had achieved the 'American Dream' through the fruits of his labour and sacrifice. The Grexas believed Gacy was the 'perfect' neighbour and yet all the time they held this perception of Gacy's character, they complained to him about the smell in his basement. They, like the rest of the neighbours, did not realise that young men had been buried under there, and why would they? If a neighbour dismissed a bad smell as a 'blocked drain' we would be inclined to believe them and we would continue about our own daily business. Gacy showed a *lack of remorse for his acts,* which is another common trait of psychopathy as outlined by Hare (1941) as Gacy did not seem to care for his crimes and even boasted to Robert Ressler that his victims *'deserved to die'* (Lynn-Scott, 2010). Gacy suffered from *poor judgement and failure to learn from experience* and again this is a common trait of the psychopathic personality as they do not change after any bad experiences and prison rehabilitation programmes with them are usually futile and fruitless endeavours. Gacy had previously served time in prison for committing the act of sodomy with a boy named Mark Miller, whom he later had beaten up by another boy. Thankfully Mark Miller did testify and Gacy was sentenced to ten years in prison, and he was released early for good behaviour. As mentioned, those who suffer with a psychopathic personality cannot respond to treatment. Gacy created his own façade, and because he was intelligent enough, he knew what the prison officials wanted to see in terms of behavioural standards, and this was another way for Gacy to impose his hedonistic belief that he was 'superior' in his intelligence over the authorities. Gacy was manipulating them the whole time and evidently from his latter crimes, we know that the prison rehabilitation programme had no effect on his warped personality and psychosis at all. Gacy was also a sadistic and sexual psychopath.

I believe that the primary motivation for Gacy's crimes can be attributed to a lust for power which became intertwined with a need to become sexually stimulated as he was a sexual sadist due to early events with his upbringing and fragmented relationship with his father, which I will expand upon later in the profile. Lynn Scott (2010) cites Meloy (1988), *'the psychopath is only capable of sadomasochistic relationships based on power, not attachment. Psychopaths identify with the aggressive role model, such as an abusive parent, and attack the weaker, more vulnerable self by projecting it onto others.* In reference to the last part, this is known psychologically as *'transference'*. The quote from Meloy (1988) can be attributed to Gacy very easily in the sense that his father was an aggressive and violent person towards his family and actively loathed their very existence, including a young John Wayne Gacy.

Gacy aspired to be like his father, despite how cruel and callous his father truly was, and Gacy always desired to win his affection, which Gacy could never acquire as his father saw Gacy as a 'queer' and a 'fairy', as Gacy's father believed that the young Gacy was 'feminine' and therefore deserved to be bullied by him for not being manly enough in his eyes. On the continuation of the issue of transference, all those young boys became vulnerable when alone with Gacy. Gacy was exhibiting his inner rage against them as he was exhibiting the behavioural standards that he had witnessed from his father, and this is referred to in the field of psychology as *imprinting*. Gacy was a sexual sadist and he enjoyed humiliating his victims and this was evident from his surviving victim, Robert Donnelly, whom Gacy committed several perverse sadistic acts against that included rape, urinating on him, whipping, making him watch homosexual adult movies and making him play Russian roulette using blank rounds. These acts would have sexually stimulated Gacy as he had acquired complete control both physically and mentally over the victim and they became completely dehumanised by him to become mere 'objects' for the purposes of his perverse pleasures.

According to Ainsworth (2001), rape can be more than an act to satisfy a sexual fantasy, it is a psychologically supreme act of power for the rapist and the act of ultimate degradation of the victim. In the crimes committed by Gacy, I believe that this was his way of exerting 'power' over the boys that he hated because he had unwanted sexual desires towards them, and his father had hated homosexuals and this was Gacy's way transferring his own sexual desires and inner rages outwardly and this is an act that occurs within a lot of homosexual serial killers whom the father belittles as they believe their son to exhibit homosexual tendencies at a young age. The British serial killer, Dennis Nilsen, was also a homosexual and Nilsen could never quite come to terms with the fact that he was homosexual, and Nilsen loathed himself for this, as did his domineering and patriarchal father, who would belittle him, and later Nilsen's brother would disown him as Nilsen fondled him whilst asleep. Nilsen analogised his self-hatred to the author Brian Masters in 1985 when he stated, *'I was killing myself only, but it was always the bystander who died.'* Gacy and Nilsen were very similar, and both needed their own homes to be used to commit their crimes, and therefore once a victim was in their home, they were at Gacy or Nilsen's mercy and anybody who fitted their victimology or warped fantasies was in grave and real and present danger.

As the victims were isolated from everybody else and were in the confines of Gacy's home, and Gacy knew there was no chance that he would be disturbed, upon his handcuff 'trick' the victims were bound firstly or intoxicated either by alcohol or chloroform, this would now render the victim unconscious and Gacy had complete control as even when they awoke, they would be in a daze and a state of confusion. The victims, being alone with a sexual sadist psychopath such as Gacy, were evidently at an extreme level of risk as Gacy had the power to decide as to whether they lived or died after they had served his warped purposes and sexual fantasies. If we go by the testimony of Robert Donnelly, we have been provided with a macabre and grotesque insight to the fate that more than likely befell Gacy's victims, whereas in the previous chapter, we looked into the crimes of Dennis Nilsen and whilst he was a more impulsive murderer, the victims suffered momentarily in comparison to Gacy, who kept them alive for longer periods to satisfy his depraved psyche and although there has never been any proof, I believe that a psychopath such as Gacy would have kept them alive for a number of days in some instances before the fantasy was beginning to wear off, upon which he would proceed to have the final act of 'power' over his victim and murder them, and then retain them under his floorboards. Although this act would have been Gacy's ultimate fantasy of 'possession', it was a very high-risk strategy for a serial killer to undertake, as once a body is found in the confines of their property, they will never be released from prison again. However, Gacy had a psychopathic personality disorder and even when choosing a victim, he always took high risks with them as many were not runaways or on the fringes of society; they had caring families and would almost certainly be missed once gone.

In some respects, Gacy took a high level of risk in the actual selection of his victims in the sense that several of the victims worked for Gacy at PDM Contractors Inc., for example, John Butkovich worked for Gacy and the night Butkovich disappeared, Butkovich went to Gacy's home to collect his pay, and a link or suspicion on this basis could have fell on Gacy quite easily in hindsight. Gacy took high risks in other areas too in the sense that he would pick up the boys from bus stops and somebody could have easily recognised him as he was well-known in the local community for his work in politics and running several businesses, he could have been recognised by somebody very early on in his crimes. Gacy also impersonated a police officer (which would have served as a grandiose experience of power that he never had before in his life) to abduct Robert Donnelly. The impersonation of a police officer in the UK and the USA can result in imprisonment, a fine and a permanent criminal record. Gacy, acting as a police officer if caught, could have brought suspicion upon himself particularly with his extensive criminal history and at a time when young boys were going missing could easily have made him a 'person of interest'. They exhibit an antisocial personality disorder (APD) and believe that they are above the rule of law and the moral codes by which we are expected to adhere to co-exist within society.

According to Cohen (2004), when discussing the risk-taking behaviour associated with psychopaths, *'Adolescents' brains seem to bias their decision-making capabilities in the direction of favouring short-term benefits, even when these benefits are weighed against potential long-term detriments.'* In short, psychopaths enjoy risk-taking behaviour as they do not inhibit as much fear as a normal functioning member of society. Gacy would have been immature from his dysfunctional upbringing as he would not have reached the required stages of psychological development, and therefore not been able to form a psychological attachment with his father which in turn created an innate and immature psychosis in which he acted out by exhibiting risk-taking behaviour. Fused with his risk-taking behaviour, this also became his confused sexual identity, which was not allowed to develop and flourish. Sexual orientation is not a conscious and voluntary choice that we can just change as we please, and the problem with Gacy, during his formative years, is that he would have undoubtedly been attracted to men or older boys, however, he could not express himself sexually or any other form for that matter due to his father, and this would have led to him being confused sexually and developing feelings of frustration which would ferment from anger to frustration into rage, a rage which would be exhibited outwardly when he matured into an adult with the most tragic of consequences for 33 innocent people and therefore there is growing evidence in psychology that people, when psychologicaly developing, need to be able to express their true feelings, whatever their sexual preference may be, as we need to ensure people do not become tormented with what they are and also in the hope we don't create another monster like John Wayne Gacy and this inner rage and turmoil with Gacy becomes evident in the sequence during the acts of his murders.

The sequence of acts before the killings would involve Gacy somehow coercing the victims into his home. Upon gaining the access to the victim he would proceed to get them drunk, drugged or a combination of the two and show them his handcuff 'trick' after which they would be at his mercy, as Gacy would now be in sole control over whether the victim lived or died. Gacy admitted to the police that he would sexually assault them before gagging them to muffle their screams, and I also believe that Gacy was torturing them during this process as he was deriving sexual gratification, and due to his oversexualised fantasies involving rape and torture Gacy was more than likely to experience multiple sexual climaxes which were heightening his vile crimes. Gacy also admitted that once he had finished sodomising them, he would then proceed to kill them by placing a board against their throats as he raped them one further time, and again this is Gacy transferring his inner rage against the victim, and I believe it was a way of Gacy becoming his father and yet at the same time releasing all his arrested sexual developmental frustrations upon the victims.

After the killings, Gacy admitted to the police that he would keep them in his bed or in his attic for days before burying them, and this is a similar behavioural pattern to Dennis Nilsen. However, Gacy never admitted to the police that he held discussions with them, and unlike Nilsen, Gacy was not retaining the victim out of an excessive paranoid psychological problem of monophobia, Gacy was more than likely committing necrophilia against the deceased victim. Gacy may have left the victims for a few days after, as the actual act of killing could have made him emptier than he initially fantasised, for example, two other serial killers with the same type of behaviours as Gacy admitted that after the murder had occurred, they felt empty again, and this is common with serial killers who partake in this type of behaviour and retain victims within their residence. Dennis Nilsen, who killed Martyn Duffey, proceeded to strip, bathe and take the corpse to bed where he would talk to it, kiss it all over and masturbate over the corpse repeatedly. Jeffrey Dahmer first killed a hitchhiker by the name of Steven Hicks after sexual intercourse and began to gaze upon the corpse with an intense curiosity and a feeling of emptiness. Nilsen explained his action by saying, *'I killed them so they would not leave me' (Greig 2009)* and Dahmer explained his murder of Hicks by stating; *'I simply did not want him to leave' (Montaldo 2012)*. The common denominator with all three killers is a kaleidoscope mixture of confused desires in a warped sexual psychosis of *lust, possession, love, anger, fear, desire, friendship, confusion, loneliness, and rejection*. The three killers in question had experienced a lonely childhood with Nilsen being close to his grandfather who died and left Nilsen feeling alone and Nilsen became sexually aroused at the sight of his body (Greig 2009) which was Nilsen's first sexual experience in his early developmental years. Dahmer's parents were both working long hours before they split up and nobody seemed to notice Dahmer's obsession with dead animals (Greig 2009), and Gacy's father would physically and verbally assault him, and although loneliness in isolation cannot be an excuse for their crimes, I do believe in the examples mentioned that the feeling of isolation and loneliness contributed and fused with other areas led to their crimes later in life.

I believe that due to the warped sexual psychosis of *lust, possession, love, anger, fear, desire, friendship, confusion, loneliness, and rejection*, he may have perceived the victims as there for his own selfish 'pleasures' and he may not necessary have killed them quickly. Although we are not fully aware of how long the acts of rape, sodomy, torture, and murder would have taken, however, due to Gacy's psychology and his obsession with sex, the initial acts prior to the murder could have gone on for minutes or Gacy could even have stretched the torture over several days to heighten his experience and derive pleasure from watching the suffering of the victim.

The testament of Robert Donnelly gives us the insight that Gacy did possibly toy with the victims for a while before the murder occurred, as Donnelly claimed that Gacy brought him in and out of consciousness several times, which is an act of complete control from the killer, and I believe that Gacy was highly sexually stimulated during these instances as he was acting out his fantasy. Donnelly also claimed to investigators that Gacy forced him to watch homosexual films and continued to torture him whilst doing so. It must be remembered that during the era of Gacy committing his murders, homophobia was a widely accepted prejudice and these kids Gacy was killing would have heard the rumours regarding Gacy's deviant behaviours, and I believe that this was Gacy's way of instilling more fear into his victims at the time and it was a perverse way of Gacy saying indirectly, 'I am going to rape you' and by this point, Gacy was gaining a much more hedonistic sense of perverse power. Donnelly also claimed that Gacy made him play Russian roulette with a false round (Donnelly was unaware of this at the time) and again the more fear the victim was showing, the more heightened sense of power and sexual excitement was rising in Gacy. The acts with each murder possibly took longer than the first for Gacy to heighten his sense of power and sexual excitement at each passing stage, as he would have been trying to 'better' his last murder, as he may not have been as psychologicaly fulfilled as he originally hoped for with each of the previous murders and this is a common psychological issue with serial killers, they fantasise about committing a murder and in their mind it becomes 'perfect' and this usually involves a passive victim, however, the fantasy can unravel if a victim fights back or says something that ruins their fantasy. Serial killers don't realise, like most people, that fantasy and reality are two different entities in the sense that in fantasy we are all in control, in reality none of us are all of the time and with a serial killer, once the control element collapses, they become enraged further and need to kill again to 'improve' on the last one and control becomes the means to an end within their ongoing fantasy cycle, fantasies which have fateful consequences for some and Gacy's home became central to this ongoing fantasy of 'improvement' during the series of killings.

The actual acts of murder were perpetrated in Gacy's home as he would have felt safe in the knowledge that he would not have been disturbed and that nobody knew the victim(s) were at his place of residence. There is a psychological factor in the location of where Gacy committed his crimes, and this was the fact that he wanted to retain power and control over his victims as he buried them under his crawl space, and therefore they were 'with him' forever. Another sinister factor which we can attribute to John Wayne Gacy, and we know this from witness testimony, is that Gacy would make his young contractors dig up more spaces in the crawl space as he told them he was dealing with the bad smells, and he was in the process of fixing his drainage and pipes. This act served several purposes for Gacy on a psychological level as firstly he was exhibiting his manifestation of the desire for control, and he knew the victims were there, the young contractors did not.

Gacy, I believe, was already beginning to develop and harbour another fantasy of murder and therefore part of the fantasy was preparing for the next one so it could be 'perfect', and finally, I also believe that he was potentially grooming his young contractors as potential victims and the thrill of the experience was quite literally making them dig their own graves, and this is an area that has not always been considered when we are discussing the crimes of John Wayne Gacy, and this would have suited Gacy's psychopathic personality and risk-taking behaviour as it was providing his psyche with excessive stimulation and a hedonistic belief of his false superiority, which would lead to his arrest because he could not bear the thought of moving the bodies from his home, despite the smell, as he perceived his victims as his 'rightful possessions'.

Out of all of John Wayne Gacy's 33 victims only four of them, Timothy O'Rourke (20), Frank Landigin (19), James Mazzara (20) and Robert Piest (15) were removed from the house after they had been murdered and were found dumped in the Illinois River as he had run out of burial spots in his crawl space beneath his home, and therefore this became a 'means must' scenario for Gacy. Gacy would have loathed the fact that he had to dump the bodies of the victims in the Des Plaines River, not because they were human beings, but because he no longer had 'ownership' and control over them, and this destroyed his fantasies and the whole process of the murder and the original motivations. Gacy was a highly prolific serial killer, and although the FBI definition of a 'cooling-off' period is extremely vague, Gacy once killed two victims within a day of each other when he killed James Haakenson (16) on August 5th, 1976, and then he killed Rick Johnston (17) on August 6th. Even by the low standards of serial murder, this is an extremely rare occurrence. Gacy's last four victims were all dumped in the Des Plaines River, and Timothy O'Rourke was killed in June 1978, with the remaining three being killed over a five-week period in November and December 19. I believe that Gacy was becoming highly frustrated because the fantasy of the complete retention of the victims was dissipating after each murder because he could no longer retain the body under his premises and therefore under his control. If Gacy had not been caught, I believe that his murders would have continued with a highly alarming rate as any remote semblance of control within his psyche and personality had completely vanished and Gacy by now was becoming more enraged as he desired that perfect murder, or in his mind the fulfilment of the perfect fantasy that he had never attained during his murders and this is evident by the initial murder site and body dump sites.

The murder site and discovery sites for most of his crimes were the same, as all the boys had come back to Gacy's home under false pretences where he raped, sodomised, tortured and murdered them. Only four of his victims were removed because he had no more burial spots under his home for them, as referred to earlier in the profile. I believe that Gacy was a highly organised offender, and I will expand on this hypothesis.

After reviewing the crimes committed by John Wayne Gacy, I believe that he was an organised serial killer as he carefully selected his victims for him to pursue his perverse sexual desires, and the victimology was chosen for his own selfish sexual gratification. Gacy showed many other factors that are associated with organised serial killers, and they are as follows:

- *Gacy had an above average intelligence and went to great lengths to avoid detection.*
- *He had strong personal and social skills and was a well-known figure in the community as he was a political activist, entertained sick children and he even managed a Kentucky Fried Chicken (KFC) restaurant where he would have interacted with a variety of people from all walks of life, and this would have included young boys, who tend to work in the fast-food industry, and Gacy may have been inappropriate to some of his employees.*
- *Gacy was able to maintain a normal family life, and this is crucial as it provides a serial killer with a veneer of 'normality', and to those on the outside Gacy was living the 'American dream' and he would appear as mundane and as normal as any other person in the community. The veneer of normality was maintained, at least until he was tried twice and ultimately convicted for sex-related crimes against minors, and on each occasion, this led to his respective wife at the time filing for divorce, which is not surprising.*
- *Gacy appears to have planned his crimes by tricking the victim into the handcuff 'trick' and even posing as a police officer to acquire a form of control over each victim, and again this shows premeditation and not impulsivity that is a trait usually associated with the 'disorganised' sub-category of serial killers.*
- *He operated from a base where he would not have been interrupted and this base of operation was his home. This is important for the motivation for his crimes to occur, as he would have felt in complete control in his hedonistic psyche as he knew he would not be disturbed, and he was 'God' over the victim.*
- *Gacy appeared smartly dressed and this would help produce a 'veneer of normality' to his colleagues and neighbours. This is important*

because Gacy was creating not only a 'veneer of normality', however, he was creating a 'façade of normality' and he just appeared like the average normal hardworking American, when in fact he was committing murders on a prolific scale. Even by the very low standards of a serial killer, Gacy was killing very regularly.
- Gacy also had good hygiene and housekeeping skills, which seem trivial when discussing a serial killer, however, good hygiene shows that there are no underlying signs of a mental illness where more disorganised serial killers show more signs of mental illness.
- Gacy attained white-collar management roles, and this is important when looking at the classification between an 'organised' and 'disorganised' serial killer because the former usually have higher intelligence than the latter and therefore the former usually managed to obtain higher skilled employment. Disorganised serial killers usually have poor work ethic and struggle to maintain and retain employment for long periods, however, Gacy never struggled to gain employment and showed a strong work ethic once employed within his role.
- I believe that Gacy would have been interested with the media and their mentioning of the boys being missing, and I harbour no doubts that he would have followed the investigations without asking the police about an individual/collective case, thus allowing himself to generate suspicion to become a prime suspect in the disappearance of any of the boys. There may be another reason to explain why Gacy never tried to ask the police about their investigations, as some serial killers do this as they like to find out where the police are with their investigations. Gacy never needed to as he knew where the bodies were buried and no suspicion was upon him, and therefore this would have made him feel even more 'powerful' than he already perceived himself to be, as after all who would ever suspect the local politician who did so much for his community? The police had no bodies, eyewitnesses, or forensic evidence and therefore Gacy was smart enough in this respect to avoid the police at all costs.
- Gacy dismembered some of the bodies for them to be buried under the crawlspace of his home – a disorganised serial killer usually kills in a 'blitz' pattern and leaves the body intact. A disorganised serial killer act upon their impulses and they have not planned on what to do next with a victim upon their death, although if we take Dennis Nilsen, I believe that he was a predominately disorganised killer. However, he had to

dismember the bodies so that he could bury them as he had not planned to kill the victims and therefore had to dispose of them somehow. Gacy, however, planned each murder, and he did not want to dump the bodies as burying them under his home served him psychologically as the victims became his possession for eternity as he perceived it within his psyche. I believe that he escalated his killings more frequently towards the end of his series of murders because he had no more burial space within the confines of his home and being unable to possess the victims made him angrier and both psychologically and sexually unfulfilled and had Gacy not been caught he would have killed more than the 33 victims we know of.

- Gacy attacked the victims by use of restraint either by tricking them or using a chloroform rag and again this shows the methodology and planning of his murders as he gained access to the victims by acquiring their trust, and he also created the opportunity to kill them by tricking and deceiving them and he had the murder tools ready for once he had the power over the victim.
- Gacy showed no signs of overkill, which is extremely common with disorganised offenders as Gacy liked to retain the victim in a state that he would have still found sexually attractive, as Gacy would place the dead victim in his bed with him and I believe that he was committing acts of necrophilia, Gacy was creating an elaborate fantasy that the victim was in fact his 'lover' for a short time until putrefaction would have set in.
- Nobody knew that the victims had been in company with Gacy prior to them disappearing, and hence how he got away with his crimes for so long – even though several of the victims had worked for him. Again, this shows organisation and planning and a way to explain the reason why nobody suspected him was because he would convince them to come to his home when he had either seen them around the local community or when he was at work with the working day completed, as people usually inform at least another person where they are going. Gacy was very calculating in every sense of the word and went to great lengths to avoid any suspicion being cast upon him.
- Gacy responded best to direct interview and even admitted to his crimes to the police after several interviews and he also spoke to the FBI agent Robert Ressler on several occasions and even invited him to his execution on May 10th, 1994, which unsurprisingly Ressler turned

down. This shows that Gacy was always in complete control of his crimes, and he was withholding information and releasing information as and when it suited him. More disorganised serial killers can sometimes confess all under intense interrogation, whereas Gacy enjoyed the one-to-one interviews, especially with somebody in high stature and FBI folklore like Ressler, Gacy would have enjoyed the attention he was receiving due to his narcissistic personality, and he would have attempted to outwit or intimidate Ressler with his macabre tales of murder during these interviews. However, Ressler was highly skilled and experienced so it is unlikely that Gacy would have been able to psychologically outwit him.

- Gacy had more diurnal habits than nocturnal habits in the sense that most of his activities were conducted in the day. Although some organised serial killers can slip in what is seen as a mundane action of everyday life, as Ted Bundy's girlfriend, Liz Kendall and her friends had noted that Ted looked like the 'Ted' in the Lake Sammamish disappearance of two young women, and that he slept all day and went out all night without an explanation. Gacy on the other hand was always acquiring his victims in the day and was killing them at whatever the time of the day and in many cases knew the victim or the victims presented themselves to him, whereas Bundy in this example was an organised serial killer. However, he had to work a lot harder to acquire his prey as he was a complete stranger to his victims and had to act under the cloak of darkness on the majority of occasions, otherwise Bundy would have allowed more chances of eyewitnesses providing his descriptions to the police and therefore to acquire his victims, he had no other alternative than to predominately offend at night as his behaviour at Lake Sammamish gave the police a good description of him.

Due to the reasons of analysis as outlined above as to why I believe that Gacy was an organised serial killer as opposed to a disorganised serial killer. Gacy is in fact one of the most organised serial offenders that I have analysed whilst profiling serial killers, as I cannot find a psychological characteristic that puts him into the sub-category of a 'disorganised' offender, and this is extremely unusual. Due to Gacy's highly organised modus operandi, he did not stage any of crimes to mislead the policy.

I do not believe that Gacy tried to stage any of his crimes, as 29 of the 33 victims were found in the crawl space under his house. Misleading the police was never Gacy's intention as it served no psychological gratification or purpose to him, as he killed for sexual gratification and possession. Some serial killers must attempt to mislead the police to avoid capture, however, Gacy was killing in the confines of his own home so there were no bodies being dumped and therefore no forensic evidence and he did not need to 'stage' the murder scene. Gacy did not want to mislead the police and due to his narcissistic personality believed that he would never be caught, however, he was growing in confidence and killing became a compulsion and this was ultimately his downfall and therefore we need to assess his further motivations such as the victims' cause of death, if the wounds left on the victims can provide us with any psychological clues to his psychosis during the commission of the crimes and his behaviour with the bodies after their death.

Gacy claimed that his first murder victim, Timothy McCoy, was stabbed through the chest with a butcher's knife and because of the act of murder, he (Gacy) had experienced an extremely powerful orgasm that he had never attained before. As Gacy experienced possibly the height of his sexual stimulation, he would become compelled by an ever-growing psychological need to heighten that experience time after time in as much the same way a heroin addict would try to reacquire that first feeling from a hit of heroin and will consistently experiment to try to achieve the first 'high' again. Like heroin addiction, serial killing also becomes an addiction to those with the warped personalities who commit these depraved and cruel acts towards another human being. Gacy's later victims were bound, raped, sodomised, tortured, and strangled. Gacy strangled them to acquire 'power' and to heighten his depraved sexual stimulation that he was deriving whilst killing the hapless victim, as Gacy would have felt like 'God' in those moments whilst the victim was struggling and taking their final breaths. According to Greig (2009); *'Strangling is perhaps the most common and certainly the most intimate mode of murder, allowing the killer to literally squeeze the life out of the victim. Its intimacy has a particular appeal for the sexually motivated murderer, who often strangles victims to death whilst raping them'*. Ridgeway, Bianchi and Buono, Bundy, DeSalvo, all experienced heightened sexual gratification whilst strangling their victims and Gacy, I believe, was no different in his intrinsic psychological motivations and hence why he chose strangulation as his preferred method of killing his victims.

The location of the wounds show that Gacy enjoyed the sexual gratification and the feelings of power he derived over his victims whilst in the process of murdering them.

PEN PROFILES OF THE OFFENDERS

The position of the bodies were absolutely crucial to the warped, macabre and perverse psychology of John Wayne Gacy as he buried the victims under the crawlspace of his home as I believe that this was a form of possessing them forever (had he not been caught of course) and this act of 'possession' helped satisfy him sexually for a very short period of time, until the urge to kill again overwhelmed his psyche and became all-consuming and the tension that built and murderous thoughts and rage engulfed his personality.

Organised serial killers such as Gacy usually like to keep the bodies in a place that is 'special' to them for the retention of power, and this is common with organised serial killers. For example, Ted Bundy had the Colorado Mountains, Kenneth Bianchi and Angelo Buono killed their victims above the hills in Los Angeles, California, in the United Kingdom we had Myra Hindley and Ian Brady who killed innocent children on the Saddleworth Moors where they would bury the bodies and proceed to take photographs of each other over the graves of the victims, and this was not only a form or 'power' over the victims, it also acted as an act of 'trophy taking' so that they could relive the memory and possibly both became sexually stimulated by the photographs and therefore the Moors served them in an extremely perverted sense. Staff (2007) quotes Professor MacCulloch whilst reviewing several photographs of the Moors and Hindley and Brady posing over burial sites; *'They (Hindley and Brady) are reviewing what they have done. Either they remember it in fantasy, and that reinforces them, or they have body parts, hair, pictures – through which they are able to relive what has happened'*. As we know that Brady and Hindley kept 'trophies' from their victims, as did Gacy, and the revisiting of burial sites for organised serial killers not only helps relive the memory of the act, but also helps the killer reinforce their belief that they are dominant and superior to others (the others usually being weaker than them in the first instance) serial killing and power are always psychologically intertwined and aid the serial killer's delusional belief that they are 'powerful' and in 'control', however, they are neither 'powerful' as they are killing and harming weaker beings and they are not in 'control' as their sexual urges consume their psyche and their urges cannot be contained and in truth, they are truly pathetic and worthless human beings. This innate hatred would soon be acted outwardly by John Wayne Gacy.

His first offence was committed against a teenage boy, Mark Miller, who was employed by Gacy at his KFC franchise. Gacy, after being indicted by a grand jury in Black Hawk County would ask and pay another boy, Dwight Anderson, to beat up Miller to 'silence' Miller from testifying against him.

Unfortunately for Gacy, Miller held his nerve and Gacy was convicted for ten years and released after two years for good behaviour. At the time of his final arrest, Gacy was thirty-six-years old, so in effect if you take away his two years of incarceration, we know Gacy was an active serial killer for at least a period of ten years, and had he not been incarcerated, I believe that Gacy would have killed even more victims, and this is evident as Gacy was highly prolific and the gaps between each murder was very short and even married life could not control or reduce Gacy's persistent offending as rage, anger, hatred and lust had all become intertwined and fused within his psyche that his sexual deviancy would always find its way to the surface.

Gacy originally married a co-worker by the name of Marilynn Myers, which gave him the chance to work as a KFC franchiser as her parents owned a string of the fast-food outlets. Marilynn divorced him on the grounds that he violated their marriage vows after he was arrested and convicted for sodomising Mark Miller. In June 1972 when Gacy was thirty-years old he married Carol Hoff, a newly divorced mother of two daughters. Gacy courted her when she was at her most vulnerable and she fell for his charm and generosity. She knew about his time in prison but believed that he had changed his life for the better, and sadly for Carole Hoff Gacy was using his psychopathic superficial charm to manipulate her. Carole Hoff fell for Gacy's 'charm' and this is not an uncommon factor when dealing with psychopathic serial killers and psychopaths in general. Many people can fall for a psychopath because they can lie very easily and in a smooth manner, as psychopaths remain cool under pressure and can also concoct implausible stories and do so in a matter-of-fact way that you want to believe them, again this is a part of their personality that even with treatment cannot be altered. In this manipulation phase, psychopaths can distract you from the contents of their words with their charm. They look at you lovingly, stroke your hair or your arm and punctuate their speech with kisses, caresses, and tender words, so that your mesmerised by them instead of focusing on what they are saying (Moscovici 2011). Elizabeth Kendall, who dated Ted Bundy not long after she was divorced, decided to court Bundy, Bundy however, according to Anne Rule in her book, *The Stranger Beside Me*, stated that Bundy would flirt with women whilst Kendall would be at the same party, and she would never confront Ted about his behaviour. Psychopaths such as Bundy and Gacy target these types of women whilst they are in a vulnerable state because for a psychopathic personality it will make them feel important and they can behave how they like without any consequence as these women become reliant upon them as these women have entered a state of emotional flux due to their previous failed relationships. Serial killers can manipulate others than when scoping for a potential partner, however, when discussing serial killers, it reverts to the tenet that consistently exists within their psyche and psychosis – *power and control* and I believe that this obsession with 'power' and 'control' becomes evident in the various types of employment that Gacy sought and achieved.

During the course of John Wayne Gacy's criminal career, we know that he had the following jobs; junior chamber of commerce (voluntary position), the Jaycees (voluntary position), manager of a KFC restaurant, chef in a Chicago restaurant, director of PDM Contractors Inc. Gacy's employment in many of the jobs he worked in gave him access to young boys, for example, in 2012 it was estimated that the average KFC employee was twenty-six-years of age (Thomas 2012) and therefore Gacy would have known even back in the 1970s many young people would have been employed by the fast-food industry and therefore this was where Gacy was gaining access. Gacy's sexual desires were extremely primitive, and I believe that Gacy was employing young boys in his restaurants that he sized up and believed that he may be able to exploit for his own sexual desires and sexual gain. Gacy was very primitive, much like when the lion is watching the wildebeest and she is assessing which one has the limp before striking with lethal intent. I believe that, potentially, Gacy sexually assaulted several of his employees and many have possibly chosen not to speak out to what happened to them possibly because they may have been embarrassed about the episode or they would rather cognitively disown the event that befell them as many of them will have normal family lives and this would undoubtedly be a painful memory that may be best kept buried.

In terms of my hypothesis that Gacy chose employment within the fast-food industry because it gave him access to potential victims as they suited his victimology type and his oldest known victim, Russel Nelson was twenty-one-years old at the time of his demise. Gacy sought out such sectors and employees in order for him to firstly acquire access and secondly opportunity as Professor David Wilson (2008) states, *'all serial killers need to gain access to suitable victims so as to be able to kill and kill again without being detected and the opportunity for them to kill, for example in the case of Beverley Allitt, a lack of vigilance is obvious as is a failure to act when it became clear that somebody on Ward Four was killing patients.'* Gacy would have held a position of power over his employees as their boss, I do believe

JOHN WAYNE GACY

that Gacy was manipulating some of his employees as they would have been younger than him, and Gacy was also a physically imposing figure, and nobody would have expected Gacy of being anything other than a boss of the local fast-food outlet and again this just emphasises how serial killers exist within our midst and reside alongside us and we are none the wiser and therefore we need to delve further into the psychological characteristics exhibited by John Wayne Gacy.

The psychological characteristics of Gacy was that he was a highly organised and sadistic sexual psychopathic serial killer, who I believe killed to satisfy a perverse lust for young men and boys and to provide him with a supreme feeling of 'empowerment'. I believe that Gacy committed his acts because his father never loved him as a father should love a son, and this fermented the seeds of anger. Gacy always yearned to be close to his father and this was a wish that was never achieved or rectified in his life, as his father died whilst he was in prison the first time.

In effect, I believe that when Gacy killed in a sense he was becoming his father and the boys were him, the weaker of the two, and in effect he was killing the part of himself that he loathed all his life. As Gacy's father was a bully with a violent temper who would not listen to the pleas of his family for mercy, I believe that many of the victims would have begged Gacy for mercy and yet Gacy would have derived sexual pleasure from this feeling of empowerment and at the same time seen the victim as 'weak', when in fact Gacy was weak. Gacy had learned this abusive and overpowering behaviour from his father, and he took an already abnormal behaviour to the most extreme levels imaginable. I believe that Gacy suffered from the 'Electra complex' (the opposite from the Oedipal complex) in the sense that although he did not hate his mother, he became in competition with his mother for the love of his father as Gacy craved love and devotion from his father but could never achieve this dream. I believe that Gacy suffered from Electra complex, and this led to Gacy becoming highly confused with his psychosexual development and I believe that Gacy started harbouring early feelings towards men as he began obsessing over love from another male as a substitute of the love that he was not receiving from his father. This led to mass confusion in Gacy's psyche, and this led to Gacy becoming a shy and timid boy who would be bullied by other boys in the neighbourhood and school, I believe that all these factors were manifesting within his psychosis, which would later be transferred upon to his victims, those he killed and those victims he did not kill. Due to these factors, and upon his eventual arrest, I believe that because Gacy was embarrassed about his feelings, he could not cooperate with the police, and he was also desperate to retain information from them. This caused extreme difficulty for the police when trying to obtain information on the missing boys from him.

Gacy was at first was unwilling to cooperate with the police investigation, of course, until Friday 22 December 1978, when the detectives confronted him that they were digging underneath his home, at which Gacy admitted to the police that he had killed at least 30 people and their remains would be underneath his house. Gacy also admitted that he would lure them into being handcuffed and that he would sexually assault them before strangling them. Gacy admitted that he also threw some of the bodies in the river as he was running out of room in the crawl space for further bodies and therefore the police had to search the Des Plaines River for the remaining bodies of the victims. Gacy also aided the police by drawing a sketch of where the bodies were in the crawl space. Although it appears that Gacy was aiding the police, it could have also been a ploy as the media would inevitably become interested in the case and Gacy would receive notoriety for his crimes and this act was a means to an end so that he could hold a form of 'power' of his local community, who understandably would be in shock and outrage that their local politician, friend and businessman could commit such heinous and perverse acts right under their noses and they were not aware at all, however, excavating Gacy's prior criminal records would suggest a dangerous serial sexual predator.

A criminal record check by the investigating officer, Lieutenant Joseph Kozenczak, who led the investigation into the disappearance of Robert Piest (Gacy had offered Piest an interview for a job with PDM Contractors and never returned home), did not trust Gacy when he would not come down to the station for questioning. Kozenczak subsequently conducted a criminal record check on Gacy found that he had a previous conviction and imprisonment for sodomising a teenage boy and this helped Kozenczak to obtain a search warrant for the Gacy residence in which he found 'trophies' that Gacy had taken from the victims.

JOHN WAYNE GACY

Pen Profile

I, Samuel Hodgins, can confirm that I have researched and studied the case and criminal career of the serial killer, John Wayne Gacy, in depth and the crimes he committed to be able to conjure a criminal profile on one of America's most notorious serial killers.

John Wayne Gacy began his murderous career from what we are aware of on 1 January 1972, when he would have been aged 30, and he continued his series of murders up until 11 November 1978, when he would have been aged 36. The crimes committed by Gacy appear to escalate from rape and sodomy and then progress to murder throughout the intervening years. I am therefore classifying the offender, John Wayne Gacy, as a prolific serial killer who was motivated by his own sexual deviancy to commit such acts.

As John Wayne Gacy was executed on the 10 May 1994, I am therefore not trying to offer a psychological profile of an *UNSUB*, in effect I am therefore trying to offer a psychological post-mortem of the offender in question. The pen profile of the offender in question is based upon the information contained here within the above profile sheet and I will try to explain in detail my hypothesis in relation to the psychological motivations of John Wayne Gacy to try to explain the crimes that he committed against many young men whose lives he callously snatched away from them.

1. As established throughout the general profile, the criminal acts committed by Gacy were of a serial nature and had Gacy not been incarcerated between the years of 1968 until 1970, I believe that we would have been talking about even more victims as Gacy was a serial offender and a serial rapist. Gacy even had a charge filed against him in 1972 for forcing a young boy to perform sexual acts on him. He managed to slip through the system when the charges against him were dropped because the victim failed to give evidence in court, possibly through fear of Gacy. The failure of the victim to provide evidence and the failure of the state law enforcement authorities to not keep a close eye on Gacy, unwittingly led Gacy to kill undetected from this period up until his arrest in 1978.
2. Gacy knew several of his victims as they had worked for him at PDM Contractors Inc. and he could easily lure these victims back to his house for the lure of extra cash, booze, drugs or a combination of all three.

Gacy also possessed other methods for him to gain the access and opportunity to a victim and we are aware of these different methods from the surviving victim, Robert Donnelly, who stated that Gacy pretended to be a policeman to abduct him which led to hours of rape and torture.

As we are aware Gacy harboured sexual perversions towards young men as they were his preferred choices of victims to act out his cruel and perverse fantasies. The average age of the victims was 17.7 years and months old and whilst Gacy was in prison, a young budding true crime writer by the name of Jason Moss had struck up a rapport with several serial killers including Richard Ramirez, Charles Manson, Jeffrey Dahmer, and John Wayne Gacy (Ramsland 2011). Moss became almost hypnotised by Gacy to the extent where Moss would read gay novels to learn to pretend that he was a gay hustler so he could offer beguiling descriptions to Gacy. Gacy became the only serial killer to offer Moss a face-to-face visit, which Moss duly accepted and Gacy bribed the guards to leave the two of them alone, which alarmed Moss. Moss wrote a book titled *Last Victim,* as Moss said he felt overpowered by Gacy, and he gained a unique and twisted insight into the warped mind of a serial killer. The experience that Jason Moss gained haunted him for years until his eventual suicide on the 6 June 2006, when he was aged just 31. This may seem a preposterous claim that Gacy had anything to do with the suicide, however, when Moss met Gacy, he was only nineteen-years of age and had no prior training or real knowledge of what to expect when you meet a serious offender. The media and law enforcement should have protected Moss by providing him with some prior training from the prison services of how to deal with a psychopathic personality such as John Wayne Gacy. Gacy would have no doubt used all he had available to endorse his 'power' over Moss, and Moss, being young and inexperienced, would not have expected, and neither would he have been prepared for his meetings with an abnormal personality such as John Wayne Gacy and Gacy would have realised this, hence, he agreed for Moss to interview him. Moss was exactly the type of victim Gacy would have sought had he been at liberty. The State of Corrections should have allowed an older and more experienced person to go with Moss to interview Gacy, as they would have been aware at this point that all Gacy's victims were all young men and sadly this is a failure on the State of Correction's behalf.

3. John Wayne Gacy exhibits the classic signs that we associate with a serial killer in the sense that he lived in a home where at least one parent was abusive, as his father was an abusive alcoholic who would verbally and physically assault the young John Wayne Gacy Jr., he did not have many friends at school and was often bullied (this is not uncommon with serial killers, for example Bundy, Rader, Dahmer et al. were all loners), a family friend who would volunteer to 'look after him' was actually abusing him and forcing Gacy to commit sexual acts upon him. I believe that Gacy may have killed many young victims, as in effect he was killing the very thing he hated, the past and himself. As Gacy was abused by at least two adults in his life who were supposed to protect him, I believe that when Gacy was killing these boys and torturing them prior to their deaths he was using what psychologists call 'transference' in the sense that he was hurting these boys in the same way that his father and his father's friend had hurt him, only this time he was the all-powerful man and they were the hopeless victim, a power that he never held or had during his formative years.

4. I believe that John Wayne Gacy suffered from the 'Electra complex' which is usually associated with a female child who has, according to Sigmund Freud, developed an unconscious sexual desire to possess the parent of the opposite sex. In this case however, Gacy yearned for the love of his father, and I believe that the abuse he received from his father which was mainly physical and verbal and intertwined with the sexual abuse from the family 'friend' that Gacy received during his formative years led to a concoction that sex, rage, violence, abuse and power became intertwined within his psyche which led Gacy to becoming a sexual sadistic serial killer.

It is also believed that Gacy, whilst working as a mortuary attendant, one evening climbed into the coffin of a deceased teenaged male and began kissing and caressing the body (Cahill 1986). I believe that this 'experience' provided Gacy with an intense sexual stimulation that he had never experienced before as Gacy had complete control over the corpse. I believe that during this episode Gacy felt empowered, and although he claimed to be shocked at his actions, I also believe that this was the moment that acted as a catalyst for his future crimes and deviant behaviours as this experience transformed itself into a never-ending fantasy that Gacy would tragically enact onto others to satiate his own fantasies.

5. Gacy was showing dangerous signs of deviancy during his first arrest and after he ordered another boy to beat up his victim, Mark Miller, as the latter had accused Gacy of committing an act of sodomy against him. A judge ordered Gacy to undergo a psychiatric evaluation at several mental health facilities to find if he was mentally competent, after which he was found mentally competent and fit enough to stand trial.

Gacy was considered to have developed an anti-social personality disorder and he would therefore not benefit from any available medical treatment. Gacy is not the first serial killer, and he will certainly not be the last, who did not respond to psychiatric treatment and there are several notable examples of this, for example, Albert DeSalvo did not respond to reform school. Edmund Kemper did not respond to treatment after the murder of his first victims and even learned psychology and psychiatry to convince the psychiatrists that he was ready to be released back into society, which he ultimately was, and Kemper went on to kill eight more victims with the last victim being his mother and her friend. It is known that psychopaths do not respond to treatment and Gacy showed no remorse whatsoever for any of his victims. According to Lynn Scott (2009) Gacy stated that his victims were *'worthless queers and little punks'*.

In the case of Gacy I believe that his psychopathic state was born out of his early experiences and again according to Lynn Scott (2009) the child is usually deprived of nurturing and the parents are detached or absent and there is also inconsistent discipline if the father is stern, and the mother is soft; the child learns to hate authority and manipulate the mother. Gacy did in fact love his mother and older sisters dearly, the problem is that Gacy showed a classic psychopathic trait in relation to this behaviour as he manipulated them into taking him back into their home after his first convictions for rape, when some families would ostracise the child who commits such a heinous act. Gacy would continue to manipulate women throughout the remainder of his life as he managed to convince Carole Hoff into believing that he had reformed when it is obvious now that he was never reformed. Carole Hoff fell for Gacy, but she cannot be blamed for falling in love with him because it is known that psychopaths have superficial charm, and more research is being conducted into this field of psychology at present. Hogenboom (2013) states; *'The ability to empathise with others – to put yourself in someone else's shoes – is crucial to social development to respond*

JOHN WAYNE GACY

appropriately in everyday situations. Criminals with psychopathic characteristics show a reduced ability to emphasise with others, including their victims.' Gacy was a manipulative person in general in the sense that he duped his family, wives, community and even to a degree the then first lady, Rosalynn Carter, who believed that he was acting on the best interests of children in creating his alter-ego, Pogo the Clown. Gacy created a façade of normality, and it is easy to see why he was able to manipulate so many people. After all, who would suspect the local clown and politician to be responsible for the young boys going missing in the area? As Gacy stated to Robert, Ressler, *'Clowns can get away with murder'* and for a long time, Gacy did get away with murder.

6. The mean average of the age of the victims is seventeen years. As the age range shows, Gacy sought out young men with the youngest victims being fifteen years of age and the oldest being 21 years of age. Gacy chose young men as Gacy was homosexual himself and usually serial killers choose victims from their own sexual preference as these sexual preferences usually form the basis for their fantasies and perverse sexual desires. I believe that any young man residing/visiting the Illinois area when Gacy was ready to kill, or if he found an opportunity, then they would have been at severe risk. John Wayne Gacy was a *psychopathic sexual sadist*, and he also was a *power-orientated* serial killer and therefore the victim(s) where exposed to a high level of risk as Gacy had an abnormal sex drive and would have been undisturbed in his home, they would have been exposed to severe cruelty and both physical and mental torture until Gacy was sexually satisfied, upon which they would then be killed. Gacy would have objectified the victim(s) as something that was there for him to fulfil his perverse sexual desires, sex, power, anger, lust, and hatred formed the concoction of evil within his psychosis.

7. In further reference to the above statement, I believe that had John Wayne Gacy not made an error of judgement in the sense that he offered Robert Piest a job, who disappeared outside a pharmacy where he worked, we would have been talking about a lot more victims as Gacy was a prolific serial killer as he was averaging five victims a year. Robert Piest's mother, who had come to pick him up after his shift, was waiting outside for him when he vanished. He told her he would be back in a minute as he was going to talk to a contractor who offered him a job, but he never returned.

Gacy, like many serial killers, was not caught by the intuitive and deductive reasoning by the work of a criminal profiler or a psychologist, Gacy was caught due to an act of impulsiveness and carelessness on his behalf. Although Gacy was an organised offender, they do eventually slip up as they cannot control their behaviour, which is brought about by a hedonistic belief that they are superior to others. For example, Ian Brady brought in Myra Hindley's brother-in-law, David Smith, whom Brady was trying to groom into a life of crime. Smith was brought in against the wishes of Hindley, and Smith watched as Brady killed Edward Evans, aged just seventeen in front of him, Smith, unsurprisingly went to the police after witnessing a horrific crime. By the time of the Robert Piest murder, I believe that Gacy's narcissism was out of control as he was getting away with murder and no suspicion was falling on him. Gacy may have had animosity towards the young boys he was killing but he also made the mistake in the fact that many of them had people who cared for them. The investigating officers quickly established the name of the contractor and therefore the lead investigating officer, Robert Kozenczak, questioned Gacy and did not believe him and therefore conducted a criminal record check on him and this was the first time Gacy had fallen under suspicion.

a. It has been established from records that Gacy began dumping several of his victim's corpses in the Des Plaines River, as he was running out of room in his crawl space beneath his home. I believe that due to the psychology of John Wayne Gacy this act would have ruined the fantasy of the murder for him as Gacy not only wanted to kill these boys for sexual gratification and power, Gacy also wanted to possess them forever. Although this may sound like an exaggerated hypothesis, I do not believe that it is when we analyse Gacy's crimes and delve into his psychology. Gacy's home unsurprisingly had a terrible stench as a dead body will enter a state of putrefaction (decomposition), and Gacy had 26 corpses under his home and even his neighbours complained about the horrific stench of death, and yet Gacy did not attempt to dig them up and dump the body elsewhere as this act would not have served him psychologically.

The perverse desire to possess the victims even after their initial death is not an uncommon trait when dealing with organised serial killers, for example, Ted Bundy had the Colorado Hills, Fred and

Rose West like Gacy had their home, 25 Cromwell Street and Ian Brady and Myra Hindley had the Yorkshire Moors. The other signs of possession that Gacy had shown was the fact that he took 'trophies' from his victims and the items were retained in a jewellery box containing rings and driving licenses, a box containing marijuana, a stained rug, clothing that was too small for Gacy, nylon rope etc. Organised serial killers like to take trophies, for example, Danilo Restivo took locks of hair from his victims (to eventually place them in the hands of other victims); Jerry Brudos took driving licenses, books, clothing, and shoes from his victims; Charles Albright took an even more macabre 'trophy' as he carved out his victims' eyes. The act of taking a 'trophy' from a victim is done for the perverse purpose of the killer to relive the crime over and over and to begin fantasising of the next crime they are planning and how to 'better' it than the last one. I also believe that it serves more than just a chance to relive the crime and become an item to satisfy the killers' sexual stimuli. I believe that it also acts as a form of possession over the victim even after death.

8. Although it has been established throughout the course of the profile that the crimes committed by John Wayne Gacy were of a sadistic sexual and serial nature, that began with rape, sodomy, physical and mental torture which eventually progressed to murder, I believe that the criminal acts committed by Gacy intertwine between different forms of serial murder as outlined by Williams (2005) in the sense that Gacy would fall into the following serial killer categorisations; *hedonistic/ sexual killer and power/control-orientated type killer,* and I will endeavour to provide further psychological analysis in the forthcoming points.

   a. Williams (2005) she describes the hedonistic sexual serial killer as, *'a central part of this crime is sexual. For many of them the sexual pleasure is heightened by the amount of pain and sexual mutilation they can inflict. They often have normal relationships and live normal lives, except that they have a problem with sexual gratification. For most hedonistic lust killers, the lead up to the crime is part of the pleasure, so they fantasise about the crime and then take the time in the selection of the victim, looking for specific traits, perhaps even following the victim for a period before acting. Nonetheless, the victim is a stranger who happens to possess the desired characteristics. The act is usually planned and organised and the sexual assaults and killing parts of the crime are savoured, perhaps even including the disposal of the body.'* I feel that the hypothesis as outlined by Williams (2005) encompasses his psyche and psychosis perfectly in relation to Gacy's acts of criminality. The sexual and deviant nature was central to all of his crimes. Gacy was a sexual sadist and he would have enjoyed inflicting pain and psychological torture on his victims and this was confirmed in his abduction of Robert Donnelly. To a degree, Gacy lived a normal life and was married, and I believe that due to Gacy being a homosexual, a sexual relationship with a woman did not satisfy his sexual stimuli and innate desires for young boys, as Gacy tried all his life to not wanting to be a homosexual, as he loathed them due to surpress his upbringing and he may have linked homosexuality to sexual abuse due to the Gacy's family friend abusing him as a boy and he would have held rancour all his life to surpress his own homosexual urges. I believe that Gacy tried to repress his homosexual desires to not act in what he believed to act in a dishonourable manner against his father's memory, and since his father would call him a *'sissy and a queer'* and therefore Gacy killed them because he hated himself more so than he hated his victims as not all his victims were homosexual. I believe that once Gacy had a young boy in his car or home this is the time he would have become overtly sexually aroused, and his fantasies would have manifested his thoughts above everything else as he sought each victim out on their traits that they were all young men.

Gacy would not have needed to stalk most of them as some of them were in his proximity in the sense that he employed them to work for him, or he knew most of them from the local community. Gacy planned his crimes as he either had a chloroform-soaked rag to subdue them or he would use the handcuff trick to render them useless and, in both instances, the victims would become subservient to him, and they would also be at his mercy. Gacy savoured his sexual acts as he could orgasm on multiple occasions during each criminal act and the disposal of the body acted as another moment of gratification for Gacy as he buried them under his home and took their personal possessions as 'trophies', so in effect he possessed them in their last moments and continued to do so in death. This hypothesis reverts to the central theme associated with many serial killers in the sense that their crimes are committed to have a 'feeling of power' due to the psychological imbalances that manifest themselves within their inadequate psyche.

b. Williams (2005) defines the power/control-orientated serial killer as the following: *'This type of killer is very difficult to distinguish from the thrill-seeking types. Many of the same traits may appear but this criminal acts out a desire to show absolute power over another human by taking ultimate control over life or death. To prove control, he may commit sexual acts, but sex is only a form of power over the victim. The victim will usually tend be a stranger who has specific characteristics, the crime will be organised and planned. The killing is very often sadistic.'* As I have stipulated in previous points, John Wayne Gacy intertwines with several types of serial killer and his 'signature' methods of subduing the victim's shows a form of power in the sense that he tricks them or places a chloroform rag over their faces. The reason that Gacy committed acts of rape, sodomy and torture were done to stimulate him sexually. The victims, however, were not all strangers as some were known to Gacy, and Gacy, I believe, used sex as a 'tool' to mask his own inadequacies and confusion about his sexual identity and his sexual desires towards his own father. Gacy also fits into the final point in the sense that he was a highly organised killer.

c. According to Lane and Gregg (1992) they claim the following about the sexuality of John Wayne Gacy; *'Gacy always claimed that he was not homosexual, and that he indeed hated homosexuals – a fact which if true would account in part for the conscience-free way in which he could kill his sex partners (even though they themselves were not homosexual).'* This preposterous claim made by Gacy was his own cognitive dissonance in which I believed that he managed to separate fact from fiction, or in psychological terms he compartmentalised his sexuality in the same ways he did with the murders as a form of a coping mechanism. Even this claim is a way of Gacy trying to retain power over others, and this is not only central to serial killers but is constantly central to the psychosis exhibited by John Wayne Gacy. The act of killing was the complete form and final form of power, I even believe that the way he used his own home to both hide and retain the bodies was a form of power, and also the fact that he kept lying to neighbours that the smell coming from the floorboards was coming from 'bad pipe works' or 'dead animals', and this served his psychosis more 'power' as he was getting away with murder and nobody suspected anything untoward. Britton (2000) states, *'Against our expectations, we are constantly discovering that these people (serial killers) live blandly amongst us, often unrecognised for years. We look for depraved monsters in Victorian alleyways but don't look for them across the road in places such as Rillington Place and Cromwell Street.'* Gacy also tried to show that he had a 'degree of power'. Even his final words to the executioner were *'Kiss my ass'*; even though Gacy had lost he showed no remorse for his crimes and for the families, as instead he needed to try to retain power to the bitter end.

9. John Wayne Gacy has intertwined with several typologies of serial murder, and I also believe that he fits into all four categories of rape as outlined by Owen (2004); *power-assertive, anger-retaliation, anger-excitation, and power-reassurance.* I believe that Gacy intertwines between each typology since he needed to assert power over those young boys to compensate for flaws in his own personality and psyche. Gacy's innate psychological desires to commit rape, sodomy, mental and physical torture, and murder to reassure himself that he was in 'control' of his own psyche, when he was not as his inner rages drove him to commit his crimes. Gacy also saw those young boys as 'weak', just as his own father and the family friend had once seen him in this light, and therefore Gacy raped and kill them as he was angry with himself and his own relationship with his father, and due to his confused sexual psychosis towards his father, as Gacy had been a victim of molestation as a boy he was taking out all his anger on the boys that he was killing and never took revenge on his father or the family friend who abused him, who were his tormentors over the preceding years.

Even though Gacy was a physically imposing physical man, he could easily have taken revenge on the family friend and his father when they became old, however, the family friend had a hold of Gacy psychologically and his father also had control over Gacy psychologically due to the events in his formative years, and secondly, he yearned for his father's love and respect which was to remain elusive for all Gacy's life.

10. I would class John Wayne Gacy as a 'signature killer' although unlike other serial killers, for example Albert DeSalvo, who posed his victims in crude positions, there are other factors which contribute to Gacy being a

'signature killer' with the first being the type of victims he chose all showed extremely similar traits in terms of age, professions, racial ethnicity, and gender. It must be remembered that in serial murder the victim(s) are highly significant in the cycle of serial murder as the killer's fantasy will begin and end with that type of victim, e.g., Robert Hansen and Ted Bundy chose middle-class professional women as they could not quite attain that level in the class stratosphere as they had flaws in their personalities. Albert DeSalvo chose women due to his misogynistic rage; Harold Shipman chose elderly people for his own monetary benefit and sexual gratification and based upon their vulnerability and his own position of trust. Dennis Nilsen and Colin Ireland chose homosexual men; Ian Brady and Myra Hindley chose children. Gacy displayed other forms of 'signature' in the sense that he would take 'trophies' from his victims and the way that he would strangle many of his victims once his sexual fantasies had expired as they had served his 'purposes' and therefore he could simply discard by killing them.

11. At the time of the arrest of Gacy, modern investigative techniques in police work were beginning to become more common practice within the FBI, and general police work in the sense that forensic science was coming to fruition and being accepted into mainstream policing as an assistance tool in the fight against serious crimes. It was not forensic science that was needed to convict Gacy as there was a plethora of evidence against him in his own home in the sense that there were 26 bodies under his crawl space, all of whom had been alive prior to Gacy residing in the area. There was 'trophies' that Gacy had taken from each respective victim including receipts for a roll of film from the last victim, Robert Piest, which belonged to his co-worker and there is no way Gacy could have been in possession of this item and the police realised this case was bigger than the average missing person case and therefore obtained another warrant to search the Gacy residence. Ironically, the house that became central to Gacy's psychosis, a place where he would have felt completely empowered and in control, helped play a vital role in his downfall.

12. The key problem was with trying to solve the cases of the missing boys in Illinois at the time was that the study of serial murder was in its infancy (Robert Ressler coined the term 'serial killer' after the arrest of Ted Bundy in 1974) and therefore there was not as much text available on the subject as there is today. The other problem is that many people and

groups, including the media, tend to ignore the victims of serial murder and usually intensely focus more on the explanation of why does a serial killer kill and the victims tend to be ignored or at least act almost as a secondary note to the serial killer, when the victim is central to the psychological motivations of the serial killer. If the following investigative tools; *smallest space analysis, offender profiling and geographical profiling* had been used in conjunction with an in-depth analysis of the victims, then Gacy may have been on the police radar much earlier as many of the victims had links to him and many went missing in the surrounding areas around his places of work and residence, this would have led to some areas showing 'inactivity'. Although there were no bodies appearing, it is highly unlikely that 33 (or more) young men just disappear without a trace from several closely linked geographical locations without there being a dangerously organised offender on the loose, and a background check of people within areas of 'interest' may have given the name of John Wayne Gacy to the police earlier as he had several convictions and a criminal history for sexual assaults against young boys.

In further reference to my hypothesis, I believe that my hypothesis was evidenced in the way Lieutenant Joseph Kozenczak conducted a background check after meeting Gacy, and became suspicious and although he could not arrest him at first, he persevered as he believed that Gacy was a serious offender and he bravely persevered because if Kozenczak was wrong, his police career could well have ended as it could have been deemed as harassment and Gacy would simply have continued killing unabated.

13. After studying the case of John Wayne Gacy in great depth, I actually believe that he is possibly one of the most organised serial killers in modern times in the sense that he actually left no evidence (body trail) and nobody had seen anything untoward (until the disappearance of Robert Piest), although it must be remembered that Gacy mainly employed young boys and therefore this would not have aroused suspicion amongst neighbours and friends, when these boys were frequenting his house. It is amazing that nobody recognised one of the boys from the media when they went missing and reported Gacy to the police, and if the police delved into the victims' backgrounds, they would have found the link and connection that they once worked for Gacy. In my opinion Gacy does not show any signs of a 'mixed killer' as

he left no clues for law enforcement to be able to follow up any type of leads and no body trail and therefore the media had no reason to link the cases of the missing boys together, yet had several bodies been found it would have been the main news and would have undoubtedly made the public aware that a killer was on the loose and thus making them more vigilant and wary of their own safety and the safety of their fellow members of the community.

14. To sum up the profile of John Wayne Gacy, I am concluding that he was a sexual sadist and a psychopath and had he not been caught when he was, we would have been talking about many more victims as he was both serial and highly prolific. I believe that Gacy was made into a killer and not born into one due to his early life experiences and the abuse he was subjected to by his father and the family friend led to Gacy becoming sexually confused and angry during his developmental years. Gacy may have always had homosexual tendencies that needed to develop in a normal sexual way through adolescence. However, I believe that due to the sexual abuse he suffered and the verbal and physical abuse from his father, this led him to hate his own sexual identity, and this became a kaleidoscope of confusion in his sexual psychology which caused inner turmoil and rage. I believe that to some degree his psychosis confused paedophilia with normal homosexuality, which in turn, when he later killed, he was taking his anger out on the boys from the abuse that he once suffered as this became his only way that he felt he could have some form of 'control' over his hated sexual feelings and desires and the person he hated the most, himself. Gacy once claimed *'clowns can get away with murder'*, thankfully, Gacy was one clown who never got away with murder as he was executed by the electric chair on May 10th, 1994.

Peter Kurten, the 'Vampire of Dusseldorf'

Peter Kurten was born into a poverty-stricken and abusive family in the Mulheim am Rhein district of Cologne, Germany in 1883. Kurten's adverse start in life would never ever improve and this would result in extremely tragic consequences for the people of Dusseldorf. Due to the abusive imprinting so early in his life, this led to an inner rage developing within his psychosis, which would be shown in the most gratuitous acts of violence.

The primary motive for the murders committed by Peter Kurten was his warped sexual psychosis which manifested and developed itself within his psyche during his formative years. Roland (2007) quotes Berg (1945), *'Stabbing was a sexual act, but it only offered a temporary release. Kurten's voracious sexual appetite could never be satisfied and sooner or later he would feel compelled to seek another victim.'* Peter Kurten was interviewed by Dr Karl Berg, and he admitted that seeing the sight of blood would sexually gratify him. Kurten admitted that once he had committed the murder, the feeling of overriding tension that he felt prior to committing the crimes subsided with each murder and he would feel an overwhelming sense of relief, which is unusual for a sereial killer as they feel empty after commiting a murder.

Kurten once claimed that he was enacting 'revenge' upon society for keeping him incarcerated for long periods in his life to one prison psychologist. However, he admitted to Dr Karl Berg that he deliberately would commit crimes whilst in prison to be sent to solitary confinement so that he could develop his sexual fantasies of violence and murder. Kurten may have tried to use his own grandiose belief that he was exhibiting a form of 'power' over the prison psychologists by changing his story. However, I do believe that the crimes he committed were due to his sexual impulsivity as opposed to wanting to take misguided revenge upon German society, placing men, women, and children in grave danger as Kurten was an indiscriminate killer with absolutely no remorse for his victims.

As Kurten would take them to a secluded place and commit acts of sodomy, strangulation, stabbing and beatings. The victim(s) experienced extremely high levels of risk and violence. It is abundantly evident that the victim(s) experienced high levels of risk from Peter Kurten's statements that he felt tense prior to the murders. There was never any chance of mercy for the victims as any empathy he may have had would have been overtaken in his psyche for complete control over the victim and for his own perverse sexual gratification. Kurten's intertwined obsession with violence and sex manifested itself within his psyche and consumed his cognitive thought processes daily and his mind was so warped with these perverse thoughts that the victims were dead as soon as Kurten became fixated upon them.

The fact that the victim(s) had no chance of survival is evident from Peter Kurten's statement at the trial when responding to the presiding judge's question as to whether he felt any guilt and possessed a conscience. Peter Kurten's response to this question was as follows.

'I have none. Never have I felt any misgivings in my soul; never did I think to myself what I did was bad, even though human society condemns it. My blood and the blood of my victims must be on the heads of my torturers... The punishments I have suffered have destroyed all my feelings as a human being. That is why I had no pity for my victims.' (Peter Kurten, 1931)

Kurten's mind was so engulfed with sexual rage that it controlled him and demanded him to carry out his perverse criminal acts and, as quoted by Osho, *'The mind is a beautiful servant and a dangerous master',* and I believe that this quotation fits Kurten's mindset very aptly as Kurten's mind served all his perverse fantasies and in the end the mind became his master as his fantasies manifested themselves into being acted out as the tension he began to feel became unbearable and ultimately uncontrollable as the mind became his impulsive master, and it was required to be served to satiate its warped sexual fantasies and desires that manifested themselves within Kurten's psyche; Kurten's mind would ultimately become his 'master' and he would take excessive risks in order to obtain a victim.

His first known murder as an adult was the murder of Christine Klein. Kurten took a high level of risk as he broke into an inn and sexually assaulted the young girl whilst her father was still in the house, and he could have been caught at any time. This act already exhibits Kurten's psychopathic personality, as this act corresponds with studies on psychopathic personalities as they take high risks to stimulate their psyche, and this act would have excited Kurten into a frenzied state of euphoria.

Eventually Kurten would ensure that the victims were isolated, and he became more careful until the attempted murder of Maria Budlick, which eventually helped lead to his arrest and execution. Kurten was a very opportunistic murderer and in terms of serial murder, his victim typology was unique as he killed men, women and children and he could easily have been caught. However, I believe that he undertook these risks for two reasons, with the first being it formed a part of his fantasy prior to the murder and therefore heightened the experience of murder for him. The second reason is that once his fantasies became overwhelming, the murders also became very impulsive as he could no longer control himself and resist the urge to kill another person and again his mind had become his master, controlling his innate desires constantly, and this is evident in the sequences of his criminal acts.

The sequence of acts before the murder in most cases was there was that he would usually look for a random victim to kill and this could be men, women or children, Kurten shows the classic symptom of serial murder in killing his victims are 'access and opportunity'. It is known that the victim would suffer from 'overkill', but as he told Berg (1945), *'The number of stab wounds I inflicted differed due to the simple act it took longer to achieve climax.'* Afterwards Kurten went home and to work as normal and nobody suspected him of anything untoward, which again also shows his complete indifference to the suffering that he had just caused his innocent victim, and dependant on how his state of sexual frenzy at the time, the lengths of his criminal acts would vary in the length of time to undertake and the ferocity of the attacks.

The acts could vary in the length of time each took to commit, this would depend upon how sexually satisfied Kurten became with the process of the murder. The acts of murder itself did not take very long to conclude as Kurten attacked usually by cutting the throat of the victim or attacked in frenzy with scissors or a hammer including stabbing one victim (Rudolf Scheer) in the head 45 times with a pair of scissors. Kurten is known to have killed in a 'blitz pattern'.

The murder of Maria Hahn is the only murder that seemed to take longer than an hour, according to Kurten, as he strangled her and stabbed her and then sat alongside her for one hour just waiting for her to die, which sexually stimulated multiple orgasms as he would have derived the feeling of 'supreme power' over the victim because although he could have ended her suffering and he chose not to for his own hedonistic gratifications. Kurten buried the victim in this instance as he was planning to come back later and stage a mock crucifixion to disgust and frighten the public. However, due to rigor mortis setting in, this heinous act became unachievable for Kurten, and I believe that this fantasy was derived in his twisted mind whilst he was watching Maria Hahn take her last breaths.

As mentioned previously during this book, society is always the tertiary victim of a serial killer's murders, and Kurten was planning to shock and terrify society and he knew the media would have given even more attention to his series of murders, which would have psychologically stimulated him further and, although he was already a prolific offender, I believe that he would have escalated his killings had he been able to stage the mock crucifixion of Maria Hahn.

His early assaults occurred in various places where he lived at the time, for example his first attempts at murder were committed as a nine-year-old on two friends who he attempted to drown in the river Rhine in Mulheim, his first known victim as an adult was killed in the city of Koln with the remainder of his crimes (known) occurring in Dusseldorf. Kurten committed crimes wherever he was residing at the time. Kurten committed his first known murder of a young girl, Christine Klein, whom he strangled and slashed with a knife, at a local tavern. Kurten brazenly enough kept returning to the tavern for a series of days to listen to his fellow punters' disgust and outrage at the crime. Kurten admitted that he enjoyed listening to the repulsion of others and he admitted even visiting the child's grave as the sight of it and touching the soil would lead to him ejaculating on several occasions during the 'visit'.

Kurten committed all of his crimes around various areas of the city of Dusseldorf as he was local to the area and he changed his modus operandi on several occasions to throw the course of the police investigation and this led investigators into believing that there were two offenders working in tandem with each other and the method of murder was changed as Peter Kurten became more confident that he was getting away with murder and his psyche was becoming ever more narcissistic with each murder.

Forensic science in the 1930s was non-existent, and out of all of Kurten's ten known victims, from the police records, we are aware that he wanted the police officers to find the bodies of his victims as he grew in confidence as he wanted the media to give him notoriety and to enjoy the public being terrified of his crimes and thus becoming a topic of conversation in Germany. As Kurten acted more on his psychological impulses, moving the bodies of his victims from one site to another (termed as a 'dump site') did not serve him psychologically, and therefore he left the victims in the open as he wanted them to be found so he could revel in his own notoriety.

The only body he buried was that of Maria Hahn, however, this was solely done not to hide the victim or as an act of guilt for what he had done, he buried her because he wanted to come back and dig her up to stage a mock crucifixion as he wanted the media and the public to revile in what he would have done. Kurten reburied the body and kept visiting the grave and he admitted to Dr Berg that he used to feel sexually excited visiting the grave as only he knew what lay beneath the surface and this again was a typical serial killer's obsession with the retention of 'power' over a victim after death. Kurten eventually became bored and sent a letter detailing the events of the death of Maria Hahn and where she was buried, and this was done firstly to taunt the police and secondly, Peter Kurten's perverse fantasy of 'power' over Hahn was wearing off and he needed to acquire new victims to acquire more sexual gratification as by now the tension was building up. Kurten attempted to kill an 18-year-old-girl, a 30-old man, and a 37-year-old-woman during one day in August 1929. During these criminal acts, Kurten exhibited his psychological impulsivity again as he was killing for the sexual 'excitement' as he was not picking a certain victim typology, he was picking them regardless of their sex simply on the basis of 'access' and 'opportunity' and therefore in most of his murders, moving the body would not have entered his mind as he wanted the public to see and read about his crimes, and this is evident when we assess the murder sites and the 'dump' sites when discussing the psychology of Peter Kurten.

All of Kurten's victim's murder sites and discovery sites were the same. Even in the above question and answer, although Maria Hahn was moved, she was moved to a position close to where she was murdered, this was done so Kurten could fulfil his fantasy of necrophilia on the victim as Wilson (2005) states that Kurten would often return to the site of the grave to masturbate on the corpse. Maria Hahn was also sexually assaulted both vaginally and anally before he death, even more alarmingly, Kurten, kept digging up the corpse and lying alongside it as he admitted to Dr Berg that he would have multiple orgasms during this process as he would caress the body and talk to it and as Kurten was sexually repressed and struggled to form normal and meaningful relationships as normal people do, this act shows that Kurten's fantasy was to possess a completely submissive partner, and this is a trait evident with serial killers, most notably Nilsen and Dahmer who was profiled earlier in this book. The pertinent question is what psychological clues are available to us to suggest whether Peter Kurten was an 'organised' offender or whether he was a 'disorganised' offender.

In my opinion, and based on research, I believe that Peter Kurten was a disorganised serial killer as he acted impulsively and struck when the opportunity arose, and there does not appear to be any prior planning which is reflected in the victimology, and this was the only consistency in his modus operandi. The list of victims proves this hypothesis as they ranged from male to female, infant to teenager, teenager to adult. Peter Kurten killed or at least attempted to kill when the 'tension' built up within his psychosis and could not control his primitive impulses any longer. The major signs of Kurten being a disorganised serial killer are as follows:

- *The victim's bodies were not posed and were just left out in the open for members of the public to find. Although it is widely associated with organised serial killers that they pose bodies as this becomes their 'signature', and acts as a psychological taunt to the victim, the police, the media, and the public, I believe that Kurten enjoyed leaving the victims out in the open for all to see and, in effect, this became his 'signature' by accident as opposed to design. Kurten did not have a plan of what to do with the body after the commission of the murder, however, he enjoyed listening to others discuss the murders as evidenced in him visiting the tavern after Christine Klein was murdered, and when he discussed the murder of the 45-year-old mechanic, Rudolf Scheer, with the police officer, in which he claimed he had heard about the murder over the phone. Kurten was enjoying his crimes and the notoriety that they were bringing him; however, he was far from an organised offender.*
- *Kurten did not plan the crime and there was evidence left at the scenes of the crime such as footprints, and there was a lot of blood and Kurten would end up with the victim's blood on his clothes due to his preferred murder method of stabbing, mutilation or beating them to death with a hammer. Organised offenders use more emotive murder methods such as ropes, hands, etc., and they usually bind and gag the victim to acquire complete submission and control. Kurten killed them in a frenzy and a blitz patter as he was highly impulsive, and this was due to his psychological makeup.*

- *Kurten lived alone and he could not form lasting relationships, whereas the more organised serial killers tend to be married and have families.*
- *Kurten was born into an extremely abusive family were both parents were violent alcoholics, and this pattern of violence and warped sexual behaviours would be imprinted within Kurten's psyche for the rest of his life. Kurten would beat his thirteen children and molest his daughters. The Kurten household was perverse in every way imaginable as the father would strip naked and demand the children watch him have sex with their mother in front of them in their one bedroomed flat.*
- *Kurten killed his victims all close to home, whereas more organised serial killers tend to kill or at least begin the phase of murder in three stages which are where they meet their victim, where they kill the victim, and finally where they dump their victim. Kurten on most occasions met the victim, killed them, and left them at one site.*
- *Kurten was sexually inhibited and wilfully sexually adverse and we are aware of this from his own testimony to Dr Berg. Kurten admitted to having a girlfriend at the age of fourteen, where they would kiss, fondle, etc., however, Kurten could not bring himself to have sexual intercourse with her as she was a willing sexual partner. Kurten could not proceed with a normal sexual act with another willing partner as he witnessed his parents having sexual intercourse in front of him and the act of sex more than likely made him feel sick or psychologically extremely peculiar. Kurten would resort to the grotesque act of bestiality so that he could achieve sexual gratification.*
- *The way Kurten killed in a 'blitz' pattern is evidence of his disorganisation as a serial killer as the tension would have built up and manifested itself within his psychosis to the point, he no longer had control of his impulses and killed the victim in a rage and frenzy. At the end of a 'blitz' killing the killer usually leaves the victim in the same place. Prominent examples include Jack the Ripper and the British serial killer Robert Napper, who killed three victims in a frenzy, with one victim being Rachel Nickell, whom he stabbed 49 times. In the case of Napper, he was convicted of manslaughter on the grounds of diminished responsibility, however, with Kurten, although he was a disorganised killer, he was found mentally competent to stand trial.*
- *Kurten had a series of low-skilled jobs, which is common trait in the dichotomy of disorganised serial killers.*

Although I believe that Kurten was a 'disorganised' offender based on the above key facets, during his initial murders, he did not attempt to mislead the police. Kurten took trophies from his victims, e.g., bags, jewellery, money etc., but this act was not done to mislead the police as killers like to take trophies from their victims as this helps prolong, even nourish their fantasy of the crime (Douglas 2012). The crimes Kurten committed were acts of psychological impulsiveness and the murders were extremely savage to comprehend to even the most experienced of investigators, so savage in fact he earned the moniker of 'The Vampire of Dusseldorf' a name that he would have derived satisfaction from as he now held one of the most industrially advanced cities in the world under his cloak of darkness and fear.

The crimes were not initially staged to mislead the police as they did not serve Kurten's psychological aims of instilling mass fear and panic amongst the city of Dusseldorf. Kurten did initially change his weapon from a hammer to scissors and finally a knife, this was done to confuse the police initially to make them believe that there were different offenders operating with the same savagery and violence within Dusseldorf, this actually shows us that the understanding of serial killers and how they operate was virtually non-existent in the late nineteenth and early twentieth centuries and this allowed Kurten to kill at will as he would have believed he was 'intelligent' and the police were 'stupid', as he could throw them off his scent by simply changing his murder weapon. I do believe that as Kurten's own sense of hedonism grew and expanded itself within his psyche, he was progressing to fantasising about becoming a 'signature killer' and this is evident in the murder of Maria Hahn as he was planning to pose the body. In essence, Kurten leaving the bodies of his victims in the macabre states he did became his 'signature'; however, he wanted to progress this perversion and make it more twisted in order so that his crimes would acquire more media attention and he would therefore gain more notoriety and keep a city retained in his grip of fear, and due to this perverse obsession and desire, we need to further psychologically assess him by looking into the cause of death he exhibited against his victims, the locations of the wounds and his behaviours with the dead bodies after the crimes had been completed.

The causes of death varied between either one or a combination of the following methods of murder; *strangulation, excessive stabbing, throat cutting, rape or savage beating.* Many of Kurten's early victims showed signs of excessive violence brought against them which was part of his sexually sadistic fantasies; he said himself he could have multiple orgasms at the sight of blood (Berg 1945). One of the victims, eight-year-old Rosa Ohliger, was stabbed thirteen times in the left breast, stabbed in her vagina and was set alight, and although there was no evidence of sexual assault seminal stains were left on the child's knickers for reasons unknown, however, one can theorise that Kurten could not retain an erection due to his warped sexual psychosis and the act of placing semen inside the victim acted as a substitute for his erectile dysfunction.

I believe that had more academic text been available about serial killers at the time the murders were being committed by Peter Kurten, Kurten would now be categorised as an *anger-retaliatory and anger-excitation rapist/serial killer*, as the offender degraded his victims, and due to his sexual sadist nature, he inflicted pain and fear on the objects of his anger to denigrate them for his own perverse 'enjoyment'. The motive was wholly committed due to his warped sexual psychosis, and this motive helped form a part of his psychosis for power of people and society, which I will expand upon throughout the course of the profile of the offender in question.

The wounds varied, but in most cases, he strangled his victims, and this suggests that his motive was power and control as strangulation is an intimate form of murder compared with shooting another person. I believe that Kurten used this method of murder after slashing or hitting the victim with a hammer to acquire complete control over the victim, as once they were subdued and under his control the strangulation and excessive stabbing was committed as acts to allow him to achieve sexual gratification. Kurten evidently suffered with an abnormal sex drive and from his own testimonies to Dr Berg, once he stabbed the victim excessively and slashed them, he would achieve multiple orgasms. Kurten killed in a 'blitz pattern' and he had no alternative options as he was a disorganised serial killer and killing in this manner helped him achieve both sexual stimulation and sexual gratification.

The bodies of his victims were left in the positions and places he killed them, with the exception of one victim, Maria Hahn, whom he moved from one location to the next as he intended to crucify her to shock passers-by as he knew this would have given him more notoriety, which by this stage in his criminal career was acting as second motivational catalyst for the murders and attempted murders and he was attacking very frequently, including three attempted murders in the space of four days in November 1929. Kurten leaving the bodies of the victim where they were slain could have acted as a way of taking his 'revenge' on society for the earlier 'injustice' brought upon him for committing earlier criminal acts, or so he claimed to Dr Berg; this again reinforces his warped psychosis and a quest for the power he never had over his brutal and abusive father.

Kurten claimed 'revenge' was the catalyst for his crimes, and there may be an element of truth in his claims, however, it must be remembered that serial killers are manipulative and many suffer immaturity problems and Kurten also knew his crimes were wrong as he was mentally competent and he was therefore in effect using psychological *self-justification* as a way to justify his perverse, warped, destructive and sinister actions and to justify to himself from the negative external and internal feedback he was receiving from the acts of criminality that he was committing. Self-justification in psychological terms is another form of *cognitive dissonance* and as bizarre and obscene as it may sound, this helped Kurten rationalise and justify his crimes as he realised that his behaviour was unethical and evil, however, he learned how to live and cope with his crimes and, in effect, he became comfortable with his actions and his own psychosis, as he conditioned his psyche and conscious to be able to do this from an early age as he was already developing antisocial behaviour, whilst most children are still exploring and making sense of the world around them.

Kurten attempted to murder two friends when he was aged just nine-years-old. Kurten admitted to Dr Berg that he first murdered a sheep at this age, and it provided him his first foray of 'sexual excitement'. Kurten was aged just nine-years-old at the time when he befriended the local dog catcher with whom he used to torture and kill the animals that he caught, and this became an obsession with Kurten at a very young and formative age, and this also included bestiality and the unlawful murder of animals that Kurten began partaking in. When we assess the early and formative crimes committed by Peter Kurten, he was doomed to be a serial offender all his life, and due to his psychopathic personality, the chance of becoming reformed was virtually non-existent whilst in prison, as there was no behavioural specialists assessing him psychology at the time. The discipline of psychology did not also understand psychopathy at the time. Kurten even admitted he used to want to be deliberately sent to isolation to enhance his violent fantasies of rape, sodomy, torture and murder as the author, Salmond Rushdie, once claimed; *'It is true that the human body is more vulnerable than the products of the human mind'*. Unfortunately, this quotation can be personified to Peter Kurten as the perverse manifestations and products of his mind allowed the human bodies of others to become his mind's vulnerable prey. The bulk of his murderous career began at the age of twenty up until his capture in 1930. The age range whilst he was committing his murders was between 20 and 40 years of age, and not even marriage would satiate his perverted sexual deviancy.

Kurten was married to a former sex worker named Auguste Scharfe up until his death. Kurten admitted that the only way he could have sex with his wife was by fantasising about committing violent acts whilst doing so, otherwise he would become impotent, and he would never approach his wife for a sexual proposal as normal marital sex did not excite Kurten, and I believe that this formed in his psychosis due to witnessing his parents engage in sexual intercourse and his early trysts of bestiality. Kurten could not develop the normal humane and human emotions of love, feelings, bonding and attachment which could be acted out in a normal and healthy way with a loving partner, and as we delve further into his historical employment, we can begin to see one very sinister role he undertook during his formative years which allowed him to be legally violent and cruel to a weaker species than himself.

During his youth, Kurten was employed as a local dogcatcher, which allowed him to practice bestiality and torture on the animals (as outlined above). Kurten was mainly employed as a moulder, and he also acted as a trade union representative. The trade union representative is again an interesting employment role because the serial killers that I have profiled in the book thus far have had a role with authority. For example, John Wayne Gacy was a local politician, Dennis Nilsen was a police officer and a trade unionist, Harold Shipman was a doctor and again we see the obsession and the lust for power within the psyche of a serial killer and therefore, we need to further assess the psychological characteristics and beliefs of Peter Kurten to build up a more composite picture of him as a serial killer.

The psychological characteristics of Peter Kurten's offending patterns was that he was a predominately disorganised serial killer, as sex and violence became intertwined at an early age due to his father's perversion, and the dogcatcher who lived by him who taught him how to masturbate and torture animals. Kurten killed and committed his crimes for 'lust' and, even when he committed arson, this became for the pursuit of 'lust' and sexual gratification as he once stated to the police and Dr Berg, *'I committed arson for the same reasons (as murder) – sadistic propensity. I got pleasure from the glow of fire, the cries for help.'* (Gilbert 2012) Kurten exhibited at least two of the sides from the MacDonald Triad as he tortured and killed animals and he was obsessed with fire. I also believe that Kurten would have suffered enuresis on multiple occasions past the age five as Kurten was not in control of his mind or body, this is evident when his psychology consumed his psyche, and he became 'tense' at the thought of needing to kill another person, and when he committed the act he could not control his sexual drive and he had multiple orgasms resultant from his crimes. Peter Kurten would fit into several serial killer types as outlined by Holmes and De Burgers (1989), as he was *hedonistic (kills for pleasure)* and he would fit into the *power and control (kills for reassurance of oneself) type*, and he was a *lust killer (kills for sexual gratification)*. With all these psychological alignments fused together with his own inadequacies and rage and his extensive criminal background, and the extensive studies on serial killers, it is quite easy to see why Peter Kurten developed into the monster that he became, and he showed no remorse or sorrow once arrested.

Kurten took two months to confess his crimes to the police, however, he eventually admitted to all his crimes by blaming his childhood and the German penal system, and yet he showed no remorse or emotion for any of his victims. Kurten admitted to the police over 70 crimes which included ten murders and at least 31 attempted murders. Kurten may have been exaggerating some of these claims as the police could not find enough cases to provide linkage analysis or back up his claims. Both terrifyingly and bizarrely, Kurten claimed that on one occasion he strangled a victim and he ejaculated with excitement, and then he felt compelled to apologise to the victim after they were dead and he claimed to the police officer, *'That's what love is all about.'* This is a perversely bizarre way to think of love and the process of expressing it to another human being in the manner that Kurten did, however, I do believe that due to his dysfunctional upbringing, sex, anger, rage and violence became so intertwined he believed or convinced himself that violence and love were the same conflicting emotions and he initially would have convinced himself of this belief as a way of coping with his warped obsessions and outwardly perversions. In short, it was his mind controlling him yet again and his form of 'cognitive dissonance' to cope with his criminal acts.

When we assess love and psychology, there are many theories on the subject. However, if we look at Kurten and apply Professor Robert Sternberg's *triangular theory of love*, we can see the state of flux and confusion as the triangle encompasses, *passion, intimacy, and commitment*. Kurten did not develop correctly in these stages as he was not allowed to develop correctly in any stage, and this applies to his general psychological development overall.

In the *passion* stage of the development of love within a person, the person who begins to feel love will inhibit and exhibit a strong feeling of enthusiasm or excitement about doing something. The person can develop strong feelings such as becoming overemotional (as your feelings can become all consuming) and even anger, which can cause people to act out in dangerous ways (as they are not in control of their emotions). These emotions can develop into strong sexual or romantic feelings for another person. I believe in this stage, Kurten confused love and violence and fused them together to be able to cope with the life predicament he found himself in, and the excitement came about in his elaborate fantasies that he created, and the excitement stage came as he craved sexual gratification. The rage, anger, and tension that he felt towards others allowed him to psychologically drop his moral and social inhibitions and act out his rage and perverse fantasies. Due to Kurten's warped and dangerous personality, the final stage in this part of the *triangular theory of love*, the strong and sexual feelings that he felt were not love they were murderous rage and lust for control and power to reassure his dangerous psychosis.

The second stage in the theory is *intimacy*, which can be described as intense feelings of closeness and attachment to another person. I believe that Kurten could only become 'intimate' in his warped psyche when committing his crimes, and the act of 'intimacy' in his mind was when he was strangling his victims. Intimacy is also an act that is primarily defined as something of a personal or private nature or familiarity. Kurten's 'intimacy' was his perverse fantasies of committing brutal murder to achieve sexual stimulation upon seeing the sight of blood, which in his psyche became extremely personal to him, and again, I believe it shows his completely blurred lines and confusion between love, anger, and rage.

The final stage in the theory is *commitment*. Kurten, although he was married, could not actively commit to his wife and was having a series of affairs, one of which he acquired a conviction of seduction for. Kurten, I believe, may have got married to lie to himself that he could lead a normal life and in the vain hope that being married with a regular sexual partner might quell his perverse sexual desires. However, psychopaths such as Kurten cannot forge long-term commitments as the nature of the psychopath requires constant stimulation and unfortunately, in Kurten's case, the stimulation that he required was brutal murder to satiate himself psychologically, and when we review his criminal record, we can see a plethora of deviant behaviours that suggested he was more than capable of committing his deviant and murderous criminal acts.

Peter Kurten had an extensive criminal record for crimes that included arson, attempted murder, breaking and entering, burglary, theft, seduction, threatening or violent behaviour and murder. Kurten's criminal record also displayed other forms of obsessive behaviour in terms of theft and burglary, and this is not uncommon with serial killers as many commit these types of crimes, for example, Ted Bundy and Ian Brady were also serial burglars. As evidenced in Kurten's murders, he was impulsive, and this is a common psychological factor with people who suffer with kleptomania as they lack any form of psychological controls, and although they know what they are doing is wrong, they cannot refrain from committing the act as it is a psychologically stimulating act for the perpetrator and also, quite possibly in the case of serial killers, helps them to also psychologically play into their narcissistic psychosis that they are 'superior' to the rest of society and it may also provide them with sexual stimulation. However, the latter theory has not been researched in any detail to see if there is a link between their kleptomania and sexual gratification.

His criminal records suggest that there was a mental imbalance due to his comorbidity with pyromania obsession and, therefore, I believe that his records suggested that without treatment his crimes could escalate, yet this was at a time when serial murder was not studied. Pyromania is also one of the sides of the MacDonald Triad, and interestingly psychological studies have shown us that kleptomania and pyromania are both linked as they are both impulsive disorders, and many of those who partake in such acts have also shown anxiety and depression disorders. Although most people with anxiety and depression disorders will not cause others harm, in the case of Kurten, however, I believe that his anxiety and depression were growing when he was getting the urge to kill, and sometimes committing his other criminal acts may have satiated him for a while. However, the urge to kill would overwhelm him and he admitted that the sight of fire caused him to become sexually stimulated. Again, we see the anatomy of sexual violence in all his criminal acts and more research is available to us in the modern era on deviant characters such as Kurten. The frightening aspect is that there will be another Peter Kurten out there somewhere and due to time, resources and capital, the state may allow them to walk freely in society amongst us, and the second alarming factor is that psychopaths such as Kurten do not respond to treatment, and therefore this is why when a serial killer is arrested and we delve into their backgrounds, we keep seeing the same common psychological denominators consistently appear with the psychology associated with the development of serial killers.

Pen Profile

I, Samuel Hodgins, can confirm that I have researched the case and the crimes committed by the serial killer, Peter Kurten. Kurten committed his crimes that we are aware of, between the ages of nine-years of age until the age of 47, before his penultimate incarceration and death by the guillotine on the 2nd July 1931. I am therefore unable to offer a psychological profile of an *UNSUB*, I am therefore in effect trying to offer a psychological post-mortem of the offender in question based upon the information contained here within the above offender profile to try to establish a motive for the criminal acts committed by Peter Kurten.

1. The criminal acts committed by Peter Kurten were of a serial nature and this includes all his previous crimes and not just his acts of serial murder. Peter Kurten began his killing career at the age of nine by attempting to kill two school friends in the river Rhine, which was passed off as a childhood accident at the time of the incident, however, I believe that this was Kurten's first foray into destroying what little social and moral boundaries that he had inside him and this act would be the catalyst for all future murders as he realised that he could take the life of another human being and not feel any remorse for his actions.

   In between this attempted murder and his next known murder at the age of 30, Kurten had already attempted to kill an unknown girl during sexual intercourse, leaving her for dead in the Grafenberg Woods. Kurten committed serial acts of animal cruelty and bestiality as well as a series of arson attacks during adolescence. The known murders occurred between the years of 1913 until 1930, therefore the murders were committed over a period of seventeen years and there was a 'cooling-off' period between each murder. The gap between the known murders could be attributed to the fact that Peter Kurten was called up for military service at the start of the First World War, however, military discipline did not suit him well and he deserted his barracks to commit further arson attacks. He was jailed when captured and remained in prison until 1921, and therefore this 'cooling–off' period could be explainable due to his incarceration as he committed no further murders to fellow inmates whilst in prison but more than likely would have committed more murders if free during this period of his life. In these instances, we are seeing early signs of Kurten's psychopathic tendencies in the sense that he couldn't and wouldn't obey orders or discipline from authority and he loathed this form of control over him, and secondly, being incarcerated he had shown no signs of reform or wishing to reform and as we know from his own testimony that prison was the place he used to develop and enhance his perverse sexual fantasies.

2. The age range of Peter Kurten's known victims is from five years being the youngest, Gertud Hamacher, to 45 years being the oldest, Rudolf Scheer. I believe that Kurten killed for *lust* and sexual gratification and therefore the victim typology did not act to serve a particular fantasy and the act of murder was used as a 'means to an end' to satiate his warped desires and I will expand on this comment and theory in the next point.

3. In further reference to the above statement, I believe that unlike most serial killers who target a vulnerable group of people, for example, Ted Bundy targeted middle-class young pretty women as this was the class of woman he yearned for and the class he aspired to live amongst. Gary Michael Heidnik targeted the African American female group as they were the demographic that he harboured sexual fantasies for. Ian Brady and Myra Hindley targeted children and teenagers, possibly because Brady had no childhood himself and was enraged and harboured jealousy towards the children he and Hindley killed as they had the loving family that he yearned for all his dysfunctional life. Colin Ireland targeted homosexual men as it is believed that he was homosexual himself and he was killing them as he hated them because he was homosexual, and his inner rage was transferred upon them. Harold Shipman targeted the elderly, possibly due to an innate confusion brought on by his domineering mother and I believe his own warped sexual desires.

As there was no general victim typology and the attacks were random and the age and sex of the victims was also random, the residents of Dusseldorf were therefore exposed to a huge risk of extreme violence and not just because Peter Kurten would kill a victim of any sex and age when the opportunity arose, but also because he committed acts of arson and any such act could have led to a crime of 'mass murder' as opposed

PEN PROFILES OF THE OFFENDERS

to a series of 'stranger killings', which are better known today as serial murder. The other reason why I believe the residents of Dusseldorf to be exposed to a high risk of becoming a victim of one of Kurten's criminal acts was because during his incarceration between the years of 1900 to 1904 his feelings of 'injustice' against society had been strengthened and his sexual and sadistic fantasies now involved revenge on society (Wilson 1995). Kurten was a prolific offender and due to his impulsive and psychopathic nature, no citizen was safe, and they could have fallen prey to the 'the Vampire of Dusseldorf'.

4. Although Peter Kurten was tried for a maximum of nine murders, I believe that he has committed many more murders due to his interviews with Professor Karl Berg (1945), who noted that Kurten had astonishing recall. Berg stated, *'Of his own volition he recounted seventy-nine crimes he had committed between 1899 and his arrest in 1931. He described them in order and in detail; they included murder, attempted murder, and assault causing grievous bodily harm, arson and theft.'* In the 79 crimes recalled to Berg by Kurten, at least 30 or more of them were of admittance to the butcher of more than 30 men, women, and children (Roland 2007).

Although it is known that serial killers lie about how many crimes they committed, I do believe Kurten to be guilty of more crimes which include violent assaults and attempted murder and of course the act of murder itself, and the reason that I am inclined to believe Kurten is because of his psychological impulsivity and hyper sex drive and therefore the only ways he could achieve sexual and psychological gratification would have been through his criminal and various heinous and nefarious acts. As with all serial killers, there is a huge chance that Kurten was playing games with Dr Berg, and he may not have committed as many acts as he claimed. Dr Berg admitted that Kurten's memory had *'astonishing recall'* and therefore Kurten could have read about assaults in newspapers and began fantasising that he had committed them himself, and we are aware that Kurten was a serial fantasiser, and this is the element of caution that must be used when dealing with serial killers and psychopathic personalities in general, as they enjoy playing games and misleading figures of authority. In Kurten's instance, he may have been trying to mislead Dr Berg and the Dusseldorf police as he saw it a game of 'cat and mouse' with him being the 'cat' and the police being the 'mouse' as Kurten knew deep down that he would never be a free man again and this would be his final chance at holding a form of nefarious 'control' and 'power' over others.

5. Due to the above statements, I believe that Kurten to some degree was telling the truth and he had indeed committed more crimes than tried for, as its highly unlikely a serial killer begins killing at the age of twenty as their own selfish psychological needs would have needed to be satiated throughout the course of their life. In the case of Kurten, we are aware that he made several attempts at murder prior to his first murder of Christine Klein in 1913, Kurten in the interim was satisfying his criminal needs with an extensive range of crimes and I believe that he would almost certainly have murdered during these periods. Professor David Wilson (2012) states: *'I (David Wilson) believe that a serial killer is guilty of more crimes than they have originally been convicted for'*. Other serial killers such as Ted Bundy confessed to Dr Robert Keppel when he was being asked about the 35 killings. Bundy stated, *'Add one digit to that and you'll have it'* Keppel has stated that he believed Bundy to be telling the truth, however, Keppel never expanded on his reasons as to why to the public. I believe Kurten to have committed many more acts of murder since he was impulsive and he could not control his warped sexual desires as he harboured an innate hatred towards society, a society that he believed had treated him with contempt. I do, however, believe that this was not the overriding psychological motivations in his killings as they were of a sexual nature, and he used his supposed hatred of society to cognitively self-justify his perverted crimes.

Serial killers tend to kill, and the act of the murder is not quite as good as the fantasy as they are not in the complete control of the murder as they originally imagined, due to the differing variables, e.g., killing is stressful, the victim may not be as submissive as planned. Serial killers are known to be complete fantasists and they usually go away and redefine their fantasies to the point where it would never come to fruition once transferred from fantasy into reality. Kurten's crimes originally began with minimal hammer blows or incisions into full blown frenzy attacks, and I believe this was because he needed to experience higher levels of sexual gratification that he was not being able to achieve with just the minimal amount of violence to be able to kill a victim.

Kurten became more frenzied and violent with each attack as he wanted to experience multiple orgasms with each murder, and I believe this to be evident when he stated to Professor Berg throughout the course of his interviews; *'The number of stab wounds I inflicted differed due to the simple act it took longer to achieve climax'*. I believe that from this statement, had Dr Berg pushed for more information from Kurten, Kurten would have admitted that as he progressed with each murder, he found it more difficult to achieve a sexual climax as he was becoming desensitised to the sexual violence he was inflicting upon others. If Kurten had not been caught, he would have undoubtedly killed much more frequently and in shorter spaces of time, because he would have constantly been facing the build-up of psychological tension he felt much more quickly, and the constant need for constant sexual gratification would have intertwined with this psychological tension, which was a cocktail for danger for the public of Dusseldorf.

6. I believe that Kurten's metamorphism from a human being into a monstrous serial killer was largely due to being reared in an impoverished, perverted, and dysfunctional environment in which he was not allowed to develop within the correct stages of *psychosocial and psychosexual* stages of development. I base my hypothesis on the fact that he was born into extreme deprivation and poverty, his father was a brutally sadistic drunkard, who physically and sexually abused his wife and his children in the one-room apartment that they all shared, for the duration of Kurten's childhood. All the sexual acts were conducted in front of all the children. The psychologist, Sigmund Freud, believed that life and sexual development of a person was built around tension and pleasure and due to events in Kurten's home, his sexual instincts almost passed the first stages of sexual development, and his libido grew too quickly for his social, psychological, and sexual development and this led to a manifestation of conflict in his psyche and the psychosis of *love, hate, rage, sex and violence,* became fused together. Kurten was more than highly sexualised by the age of eight years old, and I believe that the attempted murder of his nine-year-old school mates was his first foray into trying to satiate himself sexually and the fault lies with his father's perverted antics at home for Peter Kurten's subnormal development in these formative developmental stages.

Kurten did not appear to integrate or socialise with a person with what could be deemed as a 'normal personality', for example a local dogcatcher who lived in the same building introduced him to the practice of bestiality by showing a young Peter Kurten how to masturbate and torture dogs. At the age of nine, Kurten attempted to kill two young friends and he would frequently commit acts of bestiality on sheep and goats in the nearby stables, and again this is evidence that Kurten had not developed socially, psychologically or sexually in the stages of development as he appears to have bypassed the sexual stage and therefore his 'superego' was controlling his 'ego', which in turn was dominating the social and psychological corners and this became all-consuming with deadly consequences. Throughout the acts of bestiality, Kurten discovered that he achieved his highest sexual gratification when he stabbed the animal whilst he had intercourse with the beast. Peter Kurten was stealing and running away from home, which would lead to his first arrest and the first of 27 prison sentences. Whilst in prison he would commit petty offences to be sent to solitary where he could nurture his sadistic fantasies and where he could achieve multiple orgasms by imagining brutal acts of sexual sadism being committed against another person. To further enhance his warped sexual desires, upon his release from prison in 1889, Kurten began living with an ill-treated masochistic sex worker, twice his age, who enjoyed being ill-treated and abused and we have seen on several occasions that serial killers choose submissive partners as it further feeds their fantasy of 'power', 'control' and 'dominance' and ultimately their perverted egos.

7. The experience with the sex worker, I believe gave Kurten an experience of 'power' and 'control' which he had never really had before due to his father's overbearing patriarchal dominance within the home. The sex worker was, albeit unwittingly, feeding Kurten's ego and fantasy that people were 'submissive' and he had a right of 'control' and 'dominance' over them and as Kurten was a fantasiser, this was affirming a false belief that he held about himself. When Kurten became a runaway and began breaking society's rules and laws he was arrested and detained under the laws of the state. A person like Kurten, who has not been allowed to develop properly socially, psychologically, sexually, and emotionally, allowed violence and sexual encounters to become intertwined in his psyche and I believe that this is not why, long after the experience with the sex worker, he (Kurten) began committing his first known murderous acts. Kurten's sexual and sadistic fantasies also now involved revenge on society (Wilson 1995). However, as mentioned, I do not fully believe that Kurten was seeking 'revenge' upon society as the motivations for murder were purely sexual and with a lust to see blood to

help sexually gratify his psychosis. I therefore believe that Kurten had a psychopathic personality disorder as opposed to suffering from a mental illness disorder.

8. Although it has been established that Peter Kurten's murders and other criminal acts were of a serial nature, I believe that his criminal acts intertwine with the four different types of serial murder as outlined by Holmes and De Burger (1989) as cited by Williams (2005). I believe that Kurten was a *hedonistic serial killer* in the fact that he killed for pleasure as he was a thrill-orientated killer and enjoyed the excitement of killing and killed for the pleasure he derived from it. His victims were strangers chosen mainly at random with no specific characteristic typology. They therefore became victims because they were in the wrong place at the wrong time. A central part of this crime is sexual. For many of these types of killers, sexual pleasure is heightened by the amount of pain and sexual mutilation they can inflict on a victim; for example, Kurten's experience of stabbing the sheep and goats whilst performing sexual acts upon them. Kurten's *hedonistic tendencies* are shown in many of his murders especially in the murder of Maria Hahn in which he beat, strangled and stabbed her with scissors and sexually assaulted her on numerous occasions whilst she lay dying. Grotesquely, Kurten also removed the body from the original burial site to continue to dig the corpse up and masturbate over it (Wilson 1995). This last act was Kurten retaining power over the victim after death and he would do this until the body decayed to such a point, he would have been unable to do so any longer.

   a. Kurten was a *power/control-orientated serial killer*. This type of killer, according to Holmes and De Burger (1989), is very difficult to distinguish from the lust or thrill-seeking types as many of the same traits appear within the two sub-categories. However, this criminal acts out a desire to show absolute power over another human by taking ultimate control over life and death. Kurten's psyche would have required him to be in control to satiate him mentally. I believe that his modus operandi acts as testament to my theory in the sense that in many of his murders, he firstly strangles the victim (which can be an act of sexual gratification in itself) unconscious before raping, stabbing, mutilating, and beating them before sexually assaulting them. If the victim is unconscious or deceased then the victim is under Kurten's control and at his mercy, he also showed signs of the different typologies associated with serial rapists in his criminal act which are as follows; *power-assertiveness, power-reassurance, anger-retaliatory and anger-excitement.* This would ultimately stem from Kurten's sexual inadequacies as we know that he only maintained one consistent sexual relationship with his wife, whom he showed genuine affection for and a caring attitude towards her and showed real joy upon receipt of her letters whilst in captivity (Berg 1945). However, Kurten could not form a natural sexual relationship with his wife due to his psychological problems and his warped sexual psychosis.

b. When we analyse the victimology of Peter Kurten, they were predominately women or young girls whom he would perform perverse acts of sexual sadism upon, yet the victims do not follow the usual victimology patterns whereby they would be of a certain, race, age or sexual preference of the offender. Rudolf Scheer was stabbed in the head from behind with 45 incisions being accounted for at the autopsy of the victim. Although Kurten excessively brutally stabbed several of his victims, Scheer received the most inflicted stabbings of any of the victims, and yet he was not sexually assaulted and therefore the primary motive for this murder would have had an element of sexual gratification for Kurten, as he claimed to Dr Berg, the more excessive stabbings he made was because of him trying to achieve sexual gratification. It must also be recognised that during the murder of Rudolf Scheer, this murder could have also been an act of anger on a man that may have reminded him of his abusive father, although this is speculative as there are no photographs of his father or Rudolf Scheer. However, although this is extremely speculative, I would not rule it out either as Scheer was stabbed in the eyes more than twenty times and this could hold some psychological significance as Kurten may have seen some characteristics in Scheer that he saw in his father and rage took hold over him and the stabbing of the eyes became symbolic as he did not want his father to look at him. Kurten's other known recorded victims were all women.

9. I believe that the crimes committed by Kurten were of a disorganised nature as the victims in many of the cases were victims of opportunity, as opposed to the victims being selected to pursue a generic fantasy based upon a specific victim. This is shown consistently throughout his

criminal career from his first attempted murders of his two friends aged just nine, who he attempted to drown under an overturned raft after one friend tried to save the other friend, right until his last victim, Maria Budlick, who he allowed to survive despite her knowing where he lived as he had taken her there for food, and therefore this shows his disorganisation and that his victims were of an opportunist nature.

All the victims were killed and dumped at one site which suggests impulsiveness, as he had no plan as where to move the body to next, and some organised serial killers move the victims from the attack site to a site where they can be alone with the victim as these warped fantasies build up within their psyche over a period. Although each of Kurten's victims were savagely attacked, the bodies were left intact, e.g., they were not dismembered as Kurten could not always spend a long amount of time with them as he was running the risk of being caught and his impulsivity was not only a danger for his victims, but it was also a danger for him also. The more organised serial killers tend to dismember victims and take limbs as 'trophies', for example, Fred West and Jerry Brudos were known to have taken these macabre trophies. Kurten may have fantasised about committing this heinous act, however, due to his disorganisation, he would not have had the time and the nerve to be able to carry out this act.

Kurten left the crime scenes in a state of chaos and left physical evidence at the crime scene, e.g., seminal stains on Rosa Ohliger. Unfortunately, this was before forensic science was a major investigative tool in the fight against serial offenders. Kurten attacked in a 'blitz pattern' and the victims were killed almost instantly, and they were not kept alive to pursue a particular fantasy or a type of crime committed by *a missionary-type* serial killer. For example, Gary Heidnik planned his crimes of kidnap, rape, torture to the last detail before committing his crimes whereas Peter Kurten acted on impulse alone.

a. Kurten was a predominately disorganised serial killer; however, he did show some signs of being an organised serial killer in the sense that he followed his crimes in the media, and after the murder of Gertude Albermann he sent a map to the communist newspaper *Freedom* detailing her exact position near a factory wall. This act was to gain further notoriety as he was beginning to not only enjoy the attention from the media, but he was also beginning to crave it. In his warped psychosis, Kurten, who had been insignificant all through his life, was now a 'somebody' in his mind and now he had a form of control over society, a society he claimed to loathe, and he would have savoured every story in the newspaper about his crimes, and this would have aided his motivation for his next crimes as he would have fantasised about escalating his crimes further in order to achieve more notoriety from the police, public and the media.

Another example of Kurten being classified within the 'organised' serial killer typology is during the murder of Rudolf Scheer, in which he casually chatted to investigating officers about the murder, and there has been evidence of serial killers deliberately speaking to the police to see how much information the police know. It could also be argued that as he brought his own murder weapons to the scene and did not rely on weapons that formed a part of the scene he was therefore organised in this sense, despite his impulsive nature. In these examples, he was an organised serial killer, and he was not known to suffer from a mental illness, which is a more common occurrence with the disorganised serial killer typology, for example, Richard Trenton Chase committed crimes not too dissimilar from Peter Kurten, however, Richard Trenton Chase suffered from a mental illness and Peter Kurten was found to be sane. I believe that Peter Kurten was indeed on his way to becoming a 'mixed offender' as he was becoming more organised and confident with each murder and he was elaborating his warped fantasies of murder and he was even preparing to 'pose' victims, and I believe with this twisted perversion, he may well have been growing in confidence to what would be classed as a 'signature killer'.

b. In further reference to the above previous two points, I believe that had more research on serial offending and the following investigative tools had been available, *geographical profiling* and *forensic science*, then Kurten may well have been brought to the attention of the police more quickly. I state my previous belief based on the fact that he lived in the area where the murders were occurring and had geographical profiling been an available tool to law enforcement, it would have been known that the offender lived around where the crimes were being committed, and if criminal records had been available at the time coupled with profiling, it could have helped the police focus narrow in their investigations on a 'person or persons of interest', which Kurten would almost certainly have come to the attention of the police. As Kurten left the crime scenes in a chaotic state and forensic evidence at the scenes, Kurten would have been caught and apprehended quite easily as he had been incarcerated on several occasions prior to his arrest for the attempted murder of Maria Budlick, and therefore in the modern era his details would have been stored on a database. This has happened in modern cases of serious offenders, for example, Mark Phillip Dixie, who killed Sally Anne Bowman in Croydon in 2005, was already on the police database for other sexual offences both in the United Kingdom and Australia. Dixie was arrested from a swab taken after he had a fight in a public house during the 2006 FIFA World Cup. In 2017, DNA evidence helped convict Dixie of further rapes and he was sentenced to two further life terms by the Crown Prosecution Service (CPS).

c. In relation to the above points, a check of Peter Kurten's extensive criminal history would have provided an investigation team with more clues to the deviant character they would have been seeking to apprehend. Kurten, like most serial offenders, tend to have an extensive criminal record for previous misdemeanours as a person does not suddenly just develop deviant and criminal behaviour, as this develops over a period of time. For example, Kurten had several convictions for arson, which can relate to serial killers as a form of 'sexual gratification', for example, the 'Son of Sam' serial killer, David Berkowitz, had an obsession with arson and he would achieve multiple orgasms whilst watching the fire service attempting to rescue those in danger, and we know this trait forms a part of the MacDonald Triad with serial killers and serial rapists. Serial killers also tend to have minor criminal records usually stemming back to their pre-adolescent youth. The other factor that could have gone against Kurten if the investigative team had noted Kurten as a 'person of interest' by using an investigative technique such as geographical profiling, is that as one of his surviving victims, Gertude Schulte, was attacked in Grafenberg Woods (near to Kurten's home address), he could have been asked to be a part of an 'identification line up' which could have helped obtain a warrant for his arrest and questioning. Unfortunately, none of these investigative techniques or methods were available at the time and this allowed Peter Kurten to kill unabated.

d. As Kurten killed near his home residence, geographical profiling could have helped narrow the suspect pool down for known offenders with extensive criminal backgrounds that we link to serial offending residing in the areas around where the crimes were committed. Geographical profiling is a useful investigative tool in identifying an *UNSUB*, particularly when they are a disorganised offender as these types of offenders are poor at covering their tracks and deceiving the police. For example, Richard Trenton Chase killed six victims in total and he lived near each crime scene and he left a fortitude of forensic evidence at each, and he was seen by many witnesses near to the crime scenes and these witnesses provided the policy with very accurate descriptions of the offender to the police and the media.

Geographical profiling can act as the tool that helps to unravel both the organised and disorganised serial offender, as they may have been more geographical mobile after one or a series of murders have been committed in one geographical location, as this can then be used against them to link them to their known residence and reasons for being in an area at the time of a murder(s), e.g. Ted Bundy killed in the following states: Washington, Utah, Colorado, Florida, Oregon, Idaho and California (Leslie 2004). Bundy was moving from various university campuses and forms of employment as he had researched the methods the FBI would be using to try to apprehend him. The FBI would eventually conduct an extensive record check on all of Bundy's known residences and connected him to many murders, with some acquiring successful convictions.

10. To conclude the criminal profile of Peter Kurten, I do not believe that he was suffering from any mental disorders, and he was fully culpable and in control of his actions at the time of each attack, rape, and murder. I believe that Kurten committed the heinous crimes that he did due to his rearing in an unstable and dysfunctional environment, where sex and perverse acts to his mother and sisters helped arrest his sexual development, also the dogcatcher that he befriended would have been responsible in part for Kurten's warped psychological and sexual development. I believe that when Kurten stated to Dr Berg that he was going to *'Take revenge on Dusseldorf'*, this was cognitive dissonance and a way of Kurten justifying his crimes to himself and to justify his criminal and antisocial behaviours. I believe that Kurten

had a narcissistic personality and he harboured a complete disregard for the normal social and moral values of society, as he showed his psychopathic tendencies in this regard as he saw the rules and laws to be obeyed by other members of society and not him, and again, I believe this to be linked to his rearing in an unstable environment as if his dad wanted sexual gratification from Kurten's mother he would simply rape her in front of the children, and this act in itself became imprinted on Kurten's psyche that if you want something, simply take it by force, and this is where sex and violence became intertwined within his psychosis.

11. I believe the way that Kurten treated his victims exhibited his psychopathic personality, which was transferred upon them with a complete disregard for the feeling of others. His psychopathic personality was shown to all his victims, and his disregard for the rules of society was most evident with the murder of Maria Hahn in 1929, when he intended to crucify her for passers-by to see. Serial killers in all societies create a *primary victim (initial victim)*, a *secondary victim (family members)* and a *tertiary victim (society)*. Kurten claimed to Dr Berg that he wanted 'revenge' on society and would have enjoyed the notoriety that he was receiving, and this was also evident in the murder of Christine Klein, when he sat in a cafe over the road from the inn when he remarked, *'All the horror and indignation did him good.'* Kurten felt no remorse at all for any crime he committed and due to his psychosis and psychopathic personality. Kurten would never have been able to reform, and he would always have been a danger to society. This is evident when he was in prison and used to be deliberately disruptive to be locked up in solitary confinement to be able to enhance his fantasies of rape and murder, all of which he would act upon on his release back into society.

13. When Berg asked Kurten in 1945 if his conscience troubled him, he answered flatly and candidly: '*I have none. Never have I felt any misgivings in my soul; never did I think to myself that what I did was bad, even though human society condemns it. My blood and the blood of my victims will be on the heads of my torturers. There must be a higher being who gave in the first place the vital spark to life. That Higher Being would deem my actions good since I revenged the injustice. The punishments I have suffered all my feelings as a human being. That is why I had no pity for my victims.*' (Citing Roland 2007) I believe that this quote perfectly provides us with an insight regarding Kurten's psychopathic personality

and his complete disregard for the moral and social rules and laws of society of which its members should adhere to.

13. Peter Kurten was a narcissist and psychopath until the end of his life, when he asked the executioner on July 2nd, 1931, *'tell me ... after my head is chopped off, will I still be able to hear, at least for a moment, the sound of my own blood gushing from the stump of my neck? That would be the pleasure to end all pleasures.'* This quote from Kurten provides us with a final insight into his warped psychosis as even until the bitter end, Kurten, was still trying to retain 'power' over others by showing his complete lack of regard for what was about to befall him, and with a swing of the guillotine the Vampire of Dusseldorf was dead. Peter Kurten was one of the first serial killers after Jack the Ripper to acquire real notoriety on a grand scale and his crimes have allowed psychologists to be able to delve into a completely warped personality, and helped aid psychological investigations into the motivations of serial killers, and as Bram Stoker once said; *'It is only when a man feels himself face to face with such horrors that he can understand their true importance.'* Peter Kurten left the world with the horrors of his crimes; however, we harbour a duty to his victims to study warped individuals such as Kurten in the hope that we can intervene and treat these individuals so that these crimes do not repeat in the future.

Thomas Hamilton, the Dunblane Massacre

Thomas Hamilton was born in Glasgow on the 10 May 1952, and he would eventually become one of Britain's most notorious spree killers.

As Thomas Hamilton managed to take the lives of one adult teacher and seventeen children in the Dunblane Primary School massacre on March 13th, 1996, and Hamilton left countless of others injured and psychologically scarred, the crimes committed by Thomas Hamilton are classed as 'spree killing'. The massacre, along with the 1987 Hungerford Massacre and the 2010 Cumbria Massacre, was one of the most single deadliest criminal acts committed in the United Kingdom by a single perpetrator involving firearms. I am therefore classifying Thomas Hamilton as a *'spree killer'*, as a I believe that he fits in with the following FBI definition of a *spree killer:* '*Two or more murders committed by an offender or offenders, without a cooling-off period; the lack of a cooling-off period marking the difference between a spree murder and a serial murder'* The act of this murder undoubtedly shocked Great Britain and the world and would act as the catalyst for change in the way firearms could be purchased in the United Kingdom. To be able to understand the psychological motivations of Thomas Hamilton, we need to firstly evaluate his modus operandi as this may provide us with the first insights into his warped personality and psyche.

The criminal acts committed in Dunblane by Thomas Hamilton was a spree killing as outlined in greater detail in the first point. The modus operandi of Thomas Hamilton, due to the isolated nature of the criminal act, was to walk into a school that was full of children, teachers, visitors, and support staff in which he proceeded to indiscriminately open fire on anybody who was unlucky enough to walk within his path and he would proceed to shoot them without remorse for any life that he may take or ultimately leave scarred by his acts of criminality. The modus operandi of a spree killer will differ from that of a serial killer in the sense that spree killers usually take multiple lives at once (it can happen in serial murder, but this is extremely rare) and the pattern with a spree killer is that they will take their own lives after the event(s) as it is a final act for them to enact revenge against a perceived 'injustice' that they have faced, and a final chance for them to release all their rage against their supposed 'tormentors', and this pattern is common for spree killers, for example, Michael Ryan after the 1987 Hungerford Massacre shot himself after killing seventeen people including his own mother. Adam Peter Lanza, who committed the Sandy Hook Elementary School shooting in Connecticut, USA, in 2012 also shot himself after killing 28 victims which also included his mother. Serial killers will differ in their psychological motivations as they usually select victims for a specific psychological purpose, whether that be for monetary gain, e.g. John George Haigh, who killed victims to inherit their estates and personal belongings; Ted Bundy, who killed young middle-class women to enhance the fallibility within his psyche and to enact 'revenge' upon the women as he could not achieve their class stratosphere; or Denis Nilsen, who was a sexual inadequate and killed young men for 'company'. Spree killers usually aim to kill as many as possible in one single incident, whereas serial murders usually kill and then go back to their normal mundane diurnal habits and activities and they do not intend to die after the incident. I also believe that the psychology of a serial killer is more in control of his mind during the commission of his crimes, whereas a spree killer in many cases perceive society to have 'wronged' them; they feel let down badly by society that their mental state becomes too fragmented that their inner rage becomes the precursor to their ultimate crimes.

I believe that Thomas Hamilton, like most serial offenders (Hamilton had prior criminal convictions) harboured a narcissistic personality and he did not take any responsibility for his previous actions. Hamilton was previously expelled from being a scout master and running several boys' sports clubs due to gross negligence and for inappropriate behaviour towards the boys. For example, his odd behaviour of asking the boys to rub lotion on his skin whilst writhing and groaning in ecstasy (Russell 1996). During an incident in the winter of 1973, Hamilton took a scout trip of a dozen boys to Aviemore in the Scottish Highlands and upon arrival their van broke down. With no accommodation close by, Hamilton and the boys spent the evening in the freezing cold vehicle huddled together, and weeks later Hamilton made the boys complete a 'survival course' which was beyond the criteria of the activities of a scout's brigade and was more akin to the army, such a course recklessly endangered the boy's lives and thus several of the boys came down with a mild form of hypothermia. Naturally, Hamilton's strange behaviour towards the boys was beginning to raise alarms and the district chief commissioners of scouts and the boys' parents questioned Hamilton's decisions and he was told to resign by the board. Hamilton was furious that his leadership abilities were questioned and incensed and enraged, he wrote several letters of complaints to Scotland's Scout Association (SSA) Headquarters demanding an enquiry into the events, upon which he was told to tender his resignation immediately. A narcissist such as Hamilton would not have been able to deal with this rejection at all, and his own rage and sense of injustice would begin to manifest itself within the quagmire of his psyche.

Prior to the appalling events of March 1996, the rumours began spreading around Dunblane that Hamilton was in fact a depraved paedophile and the former head of the Central Scotland Police Child Protection Unit wrote a damming report in which he recommended that Hamilton's gun licence be revoked because of his unsavoury character and unstable personality. Hamilton was enraged by the accusations and faced with this 'injustice', Hamilton wrote letters to authority figures within the community and even to the Queen protesting of his 'unfair treatment'. This behaviour provides us with an insight into a highly delusional and narcissistic criminal personality, as he believed that he was above the laws of the land and the moral laws of society, as he was actively refusing to recognise that he was committing serious criminal acts against minors. Hamilton refused to accept that his perverted behaviour was the very reason why he was ostracised by his local community. The ostracization helped feed Hamilton's paranoid constitution that everybody was against him and wanted to see him fail, when in fact the community were keeping their children safe from the clutches of a sexual predator.

The teachers of Dunblane primary school urged the parents to not use his sports clubs and Hamilton sent letters to parents, the school and its teachers complaining of his 'mistreatment', and I believe that due to his psyche and his criminal tendencies, and also following on from a failed business in the area, Hamilton had nowhere to go and he was finished as a member of the community of Dunblane, and therefore, as Hamilton took no responsibility for his criminal acts, his failed business ventures were the fault of the community of Dunblane and Hamilton's paranoid constitution would vow to take 'revenge' on his perceived 'tormentors'. His heinous crime would be taken out against the school and the parents who he perceived to have turned their backs on him. I will mention more in due course and outline why I believe that his psychology enabled him to commit the heinous acts that he ultimately enacted against one of society's most vulnerable groups.

The crime scene was one of horror and carnage as Hamilton burst into the assembly hall, where a class of five and six-year-olds were having a P.E. lesson, where he opened fire indiscriminately upon them, which resulted in the murder of sixteen children and a teacher. Hamilton deliberately targeted the teachers first to ensure that the last and only bastion of protection the children may have had was extinguished. After Hamilton had killed the teacher, he then mercilessly began shooting at the children as they desperately tried to hide in cupboards or under chairs in what undoubtedly would have been a horrific moment in their short lives.

Hamilton then left the gym and entered the hallway and indiscriminately opened fire again, in which several more people were injured. He entered the gym again and began firing one final time. After discharging more than 100 rounds of ammunition, he put a pistol in his mouth and took his own life, thus leaving so many questions unanswered. The crime scene of a spree killer will differ from that of a serial killer in the sense that a serial killer, if they were an organised offender, will try to remove any forensic evidence and hide the bodies of their victims as they do not aim to get caught. A spree killer on the contrary, will inhibit differing psychological motivations as they aim to take as many lives as possible as they believe that they are enacting 'revenge' on those who caused them 'misery' at some point in life.

Although Hamilton had left a chaotic crime scene, there is evidence to suggest that he planned the attack for at least a year. The Lord Cullen Enquiry (1996) found that Hamilton had spoken to a pupil on several occasions and questioned the boy about the daily routine and layout of the school hall, including how many exits there were, what classes entered the hall at certain times and periods of action throughout the course of a normal school day. Hamilton's own corpse would eventually form a part of the crime scene; however, this was his final act of 'power' over the community and the United Kingdom as we are left to theorise about his motivations and his desires as we will never truly know because we could not study him in depth after the commission of his crimes, however, based on reports we can ascertain that as the victims were aged between only five and six years old (with the exception of the teacher, Gwen Mayor), Hamilton callously targeted the community of Dunblane as he believed that they had 'shunned' him, and he targeted the primary school children as the ultimate and most terrible act of 'revenge' that he could have inflicted upon the community of Dunblane and general society. Hamilton was a prolific paedophile and believed that he was the 'victim', and therefore we need to delve into his formative years to understand this psychosis in a more comprehensive way.

Thomas Hamilton had a very confusing and unstable childhood, which may have borne early resentment within his psyche from an early age. His father, Thomas Watt, and his mother, Agnes Graham, were already divorced by the time he was born on May 10th, 1952. Watt left his family for another woman and started a new life. When Hamilton was two years old, his grandparents adopted him and convinced him to believe that they were his natural mother and father and that his mother was in fact his sister, a story that he believed until 1974 when he was aged 22. This would have ultimately led to resentment and anger within his psyche and been an ultimate stressor upon his psychosis.

Hamilton, I believe was truly evil. However, I do believe that he did suffer from a paranoid constitution and this incident would have contributed a lot more to an already unstable psychosis. Millon, Simonsen, Davis et al. (1998) cites the works of Meissner (1979); *'Paranoia has its roots in the desperate attempt to maintain self-esteem, to control the self, and to master an environment that is viewed as hostile and chaotic.'* Meissner is discussing his works on *Evil Intent: Violence and Disorders of the Will*, and Hamilton was told the devastating news at the time when rumours began circulating of his strange and weird behaviour and he had not long been struck of the staff at the Regional Scotland Boy Scouts Association Movement all through his own failings, however, in his warped psyche this would have provided further precedence that people were out to 'get him' due to his *psychosis of paranoia*.

I also believe that Hamilton suffered with a narcissistic personality disorder (NPD), and I will elaborate on my beliefs as to why I state this hypothesis. Hamilton was obsessed with his own issues of personal adequacy, *'power'* and *'prestige'* and *'vanity'* that his positions of leading the boy scouts' clubs and sports clubs gave to him. In the sense of his 'power' according to Jonathan Russell (1996) writing for the *Daily Mirror*, Russell claimed: *'Hamilton enjoyed disciplining the boys and expected them to obey his every command. One of the boy's mothers complained that they were forced to rub suntan oil all over Hamilton's naked body as he withed and groaned in ecstasy.'* Hamilton exploited his position of 'power' and the trust that the parents had instilled in him to look after and care for their children whilst in his custody. Hamilton shows many other symptoms associated with a narcissistic personality disorder in the sense that he always wanted to be recognised as superior and special, without achieving any superior accomplishments; he envied others (this formed a part of his *psychosis* of paranoia) and he believed they envied him and thus were 'against' him; he lacked the ability to emphasise with the feelings and desires of others – which is evident in his early paedophilic criminal acts and the Dunblane Massacre; Hamilton was arrogant and expected special treatment – this is evident when he recklessly endangered the lives of the boy scouts in his care and could not recognise his own failings; Hamilton expected special treatment – in the sense that he could not understand his 'authority' and 'leadership skills' were being questioned, so much so he even wrote to Queen Elizabeth II to complain. The fact that Hamilton wrote to Her Majesty the queen is an absurdity that the queen would focus on what at the time would seem a very trivial issue. However, this may seem innocuous and laughable, but there are others out there who exist amongst us today who harbour these delusions of grandeur and somebody with Hamilton's personality. I believe this type of grandiose behaviour in a person shows that they are either (i) at harm of hurting themselves, or (ii) they are in danger of harming another person, as they are both a result of an unstable personality. The writer of such letters is creating an even more elaborate and delusional fantasy world for themselves and if allowed to continue, the spiral into the descent of madness will continue unabated this can have tragic consequences.

In terms of clinical psychology, I also believe that Thomas Hamilton suffered from OCD and again, I will elaborate on my hypothesis as to why I believe he suffered from this alignment. Hamilton showed early symptoms or at least a form of OCD when as a teenager he became obsessed with guns and the boy's clubs that he was a member of at the time. This fascination carried on into his adult life and his hobbies transformed into an obsession. The NHS website classifies OCD as the following: *'obsessive compulsive disorder (OCD) is a mental health condition where a person has obsessive thoughts and compulsive behaviour(s). An obsession is an unwanted, unpleasant thought, image or urge that repeatedly enters a person's mind, causing them anxiety.'* I believe that Hamilton was obsessive by nature and due to other natures of his personality and within his *psyche*, all the factors fermented within him in overtime as he never sought professional psychiatric help and I believe that he created a fantasy world due to his narcissistic personality, where he existed as a 'special being' in the realms of

PEN PROFILES OF THE OFFENDERS

his fantasy, when he was nothing more special than the next person. The danger is when we are dealing with delusional people such as Thomas Hamilton, their elaborate fantasy worlds and their real world collide, and the two worlds begin to collate within their psyche so much that they become one as the realms of both fantasy and reality became intertwined and the two cannot be differentiated.

Hamilton began to believe his own lies that he was innocent of any wrongdoings. This may sound a bizarre concept to those who exist within a rational and healthy mind, however, there have been instances where the realms between fantasy and reality become so blurred that the fantasy takes over reality and therefore the initial fantasy becomes the new reality. I believe that the most prominent and tragic example of what I am referring to is the 1999 Columbine Massacre, in which the perpetrators, Eric Harris and Dylan Klebold, were societal outcasts at their school and became ostracised and they found solace in each other and solace in the computer game, *Doom*, in which they began to fantasise that the monsters they were shooting on the screen were actually their own schoolmates and the fantasy and reality became more blurred with each passing week, until of course, the fantasy became *their* reality, and this ended in brutal and tragic consequences on April 20th, 1999, in which they killed thirteen students, injured fifteen more and proceeded to take their own lives.

Therefore, I believe that some of these delusional musings of the 'oppressed' may seem almost comical at first, however, it may mean that they require mental and psychiatric professional help before they commit serious criminal acts against others or injure or kill themselves. Society can be dismissive and prejudiced against those who suffer from mental health issues, and it is a stigma that needs to end because it can end with tragic consequences for the initial sufferer, the families of the sufferer, another person and wider society, and therefore in the case of Thomas Hamilton we need to conduct further analysis in order to attempt to establish the motives for his crimes away from solely his misguided belief about enacting 'revenge' against the community of Dunblane, as there will be undoubtedly more psychological factors at play that led to the commission of his crimes.

I believe that the psychological motivations for the criminal acts of Thomas Hamilton were borne out of plethora reasons as opposed to a single contributory factor. I believe that Hamilton committed his crimes firstly out of a financial motive, since he became obsessed with the boy scouts' clubs and the sports clubs from his formative years, and he would never acquire a

THOMAS HAMILTON, THE DUNBLAME MASSACRE

paid position within them again after his crimes in 1995. The reason I believe that this to be the case was Hamilton could not find and he also did not want to find any other line of work, firstly because the boy scouts became his obsession from an early age and the other factor was a sexually driven motive, as employment with the boy scout's organisation would have given him ready access to young boys. Hamilton was willing to abuse his position of trust to pursue his warped sexual fantasies.

I believe that Hamilton, although he suffered from mental health alignments during the commission of his crimes committed in Dunblane, was genuinely evil due to his paedophilic acts on children as he was a narcissistic control freak and children are one of the most vulnerable demographics in society and they are easy to control. I believe that Hamilton was evil; in the crimes he committed at Dunblane his disintegrated mental state were a contributing factor in the build-up to the commission of his crimes, and although it sounds a contradictory statement, Hamilton did have an underlying form of mental illness, the details of which have been outlined recently, which in itself was not a sole factor for his crimes, but was one of many contributing factors that enabled the commission of the crimes to occur.

Due to his desire for power and his obsession, I believe that the Dunblane Massacre became personal to him, as he could not strike back at the adults who he saw as causing him his misery as they actually held the power over him, which would have caused further anger and enragement within his psychosis; the easiest and most cowardly way to hurt them was to strike at the children whom they strove to protect from his perverted acts of evil in the first instance. I believe that Hamilton would have known this would be the cruellest act of revenge possible and the lead up to the commission of the crime would have undoubtedly satiated his psyche and helped him cope and possibly soothed him with the thoughts of what he was about to do. Hamilton also blamed the school for encouraging the parents to not use his sports clubs due to the accusations and the police interest, and again, this would have been a key motivational factor in his decision to destroy so many lives and a community on that fateful day in March 1996, and it goes without question that anybody who crossed paths with Thomas Hamilton that fateful morning could have easily become a victim and they would have been at great risk.

Due to the advanced degree of diagnosis of the personality of Thomas Hamilton and the disorders associated within that personality as outlined

PEN PROFILES OF THE OFFENDERS

previously, I believe that the victims experienced a high level of risk and coupled with the fact that they were completely defenceless against him and had no chance as he was older and armed, he could physically overpower them. Hamilton would have known that he could have caused as much destruction and carnage as possible without recourse. Hamilton could easily have chosen the parents or another place of public congregation in the community, e.g., the local pub, church etc. where the adult population gathered, however, there would have been too much risk for him in doing so as an adult, knowing they will more than likely die, may be more inclined to put up some form of final resistance when facing certain death. There have been recorded stories where adult victims have escaped from serial killers, for example, Carol Da Ronch escaped from Ted Bundy when he tried to handcuff her; the former nanny of Fred and Rose West, Caroline Roberts, talked herself to freedom by also being compliant with their sadistic behaviours. The victims with Hamilton could not have put up any resistance, and this became the *raison d'etre* for him to be able to carry out his crimes.

Thomas Hamilton took low risk in his choice of victims because the victims were all young or professional teachers, who would not have expected anything out of the ordinary on what should otherwise have been another mundane school day. The children, parents, and the staff in the school on that fateful day would have been completely defenceless against the personification of evil with the amount of weaponry Hamilton was carrying. Hamilton could have ceased the killings at any point and showed at least some form of empathy upon hearing the screams of the children, however, Hamilton had already made the conscientious decision to kill as many children as possible and take his own life as the penultimate act of 'retention of power' over the local community, and therefore in Hamilton's warped psychosis the risk was minimal to him as he knew he was never going to be arrested and he had no intention of surviving after the crime was concluded, and therefore he did not associate any risk with the crime.

Hamilton had been planning the Dunblane Massacre for weeks before and he began to send letters to higher authority figures within the community claiming that he was 'victimized' and again, as I mentioned earlier, it's very simple to dismiss these musings as the ramblings of a 'madman', however they should be passed to the authorities, particularly in the cases of people like Hamilton. The former head of the Central Scotland Police Child Protection Unit had already noted that Hamilton had an 'unsavoury character', who was flagged as a potential risk. If a figure of authority had intervened, then we may not be discussing this case now and those children and their teacher would have lived their lives as they should have been allowed to live.

The Lord Cullen Inquiry (1996) found that Hamilton had spoken to several children about the layout of the hall, the timetable of classes etc. up to one week before the Dunblane Massacre, and we know he had a high degree of planning leading up to the commission of his crime because he was armed with this 'intelligence'. He proceeded to cut the telephone wires adjacent to the school to cripple all communication with the police; this act indicates that he wanted to cause as much carnage as possible in a short space of time. After the killings, his final act of 'power' was to take his own life so we can only ever guess or theorise as to why he committed the dreadful acts that he did.

Hamilton could have easily taken his own life, but he planned the atrocity for weeks, maybe even up to a year, and this is what separates him from two other British *spree killers*, Michael Ryan (Hungerford, 1987) and Derrick Bird (Cumbria, 2010), both of whom had been suffering with a mental breakdown for a long period of time and acted impulsively without any real plan of action, and this is what differentiates Hamilton from Ryan and Bird and thus in my opinion makes him pure evil. The psychosis of Bird and Ryan slowly degraded over time; however, Hamilton convinced his own psyche that he was the 'victim', and Hamilton was in control of his mind and actions as we will see from the timeline of events.

According to W Douglas Cullen (1996), Hamilton was seen by a neighbour at around 08:15am scraping ice of his white van at number 7 Kent Road, Stirling. The neighbour and Hamilton held a conversation before he drove off in the direction of Dunblane. At about 09:30am he parked his van besides a telegraph pole in the lower car park of Dunblane Primary School and cut the wires with a pair of pliers to try to destroy all lines of communication to and from the school. In effect he only managed to destroy communication lines to a few adjoining houses (again this shows that he had planned the massacre). Hamilton knew once he had done this, the police response would be delayed even further, and this would have given him enough time to perpetrate his crimes and kill himself in the process. Hamilton entered the school at around 09:30am and began shooting at roughly 09:35am and the commission of the crime was estimated to be concluded later at 09:40am and the first call to emergency services was recorded at 09:43am. Hamilton took roughly around a mere total of five minutes to take seventeen lives and destroy countless many more with his depraved acts of criminality. Hamilton's criminality had always centred around children, and regretfully, if more action was taken against him, Dunblane may never have happened due to his prior deviant behaviour around children.

In terms of Hamilton's record as a predatory paedophile, these crimes had been taking place since the early 1970s when he was scout leader and a sports coach and shortly prior to the Dunblane Massacre as the accusations began to amass and the police became interested in his strange behaviour, which was the catalyst for the Dunblane Massacre all those years later. In terms of the massacre itself, it was mainly confined to the school assembly hall, although Hamilton did indiscriminately fire in the playground first and the hallway before returning to the assembly hall and indiscriminately firing off several more rounds of ammunition before killing himself. Hamilton had planned the massacre, and the sports hall was central to his psychological aims as he had premediated his crime and he had planned to undertake his shooting in the sports hall as he was aware that this area of the school would achieve the most fatalities and he had envisioned the hall as the place where he could enact his ultimate act of 'revenge' against a society that he had deemed to abandon him for all of those years. Are there any more psychological clues to Hamilton's warped psyche and psychosis and can we assess this by reviewing his behaviour towards his dead victims after the commission of his crimes?

Hamilton did not need to move the bodies as this served no psychological purpose for him to do so, and as mentioned in above point the sports hall was central to his psychological aims as this is where he knew he had complete control and he would achieve a high victim count. In terms of organised serial killers, these type of criminals usually move the bodies of their victims from the original kill site to a dump site to serve a psychological purpose and to be able to spend more time with the victim without being disturbed, as Ted Bundy used to take the girls from one place such as a shopping mall or a university campus to a secluded area so he could return to the body for the purposes of perverse sexual gratification on several occasions; Angelo Buono and Kenneth Bianchi would leave the bodies on the Hollywood hillside after they had tortured the victims in Buono's garage. Spree killers usually leave more carnage and a less controlled crime scene than a serial killer, and whereas spree killers kill in an extremely short space of time, they have no inclination or psychological motivations to move the bodies of their victims. The murder site and the discovery site were the same for all the victims of the Dunblane Massacre and just to reiterate, a spree killer has no inclination or psychological motivation to move the bodies of their victims, in fact, spree killing also tends to become their final living act as well.

Although Hamilton did not move, pose or defile any of his victims after his initial crime, this is not a common psychological factor associated with spree killers, and the only common denominator when assessing spree killers and serial killers is that one must always assess the crime scenes as these areas form a part of the killer's fantasies, and therefore there may be more psychological clues as to the thoughts and rage within their psyche during the commission of their heinous criminal acts.

Although the crime scene was chaotic and macabre, I believe that Hamilton both premeditated the murder and he was also suffering from a psychotic episode that had been manifesting itself for quite some time, and I believe that this is evident from his letters to figures in authority. I believe that the murders were predominately organised, and I have outlined my reasons for this hypothesis below:

- *Hamilton had an above average IQ and had always done well academically, and this level of intelligence helped him plan the murders and this is evident when he was gathering 'intelligence' about the sports hall and the times it was in use and where the exits were situated.*
- *He was geographically mobile, and I believe this formed a part of his planning.*
- *He had diurnal (daytime) habits and I believe that he was actively watching the school for several days prior to the murders as he had been seen in the vicinity of the area and this would have been a part of the 'game' for him as he wanted to ensure that he could kill as many people as possible, because in his psychosis, the more people he killed, the more 'revenge' against the Dunblane community he achieved.*
- *He did not experiment with either self-help or professional medical help for his problems due to his narcissistic and paranoid personality, and believed that everybody else was against him, despite his acts of criminality. People who are unfortunate to suffer various mental health alignments usually attempt to acquire help when possessing dangerous thoughts. Hamilton allowed his dangerous thoughts to consume his psyche and he could have sought help at any time; however, he allowed*

his rage to control him and take the lives of the most innocent of victims.
- I believe that due to the findings by Lord Cullen in 1996 Hamilton had conclusively planned the murders. I even believe that he had no intention of being caught after and suicide was his final act of 'power' as he knew that the community of Dunblane would be left asking that awful question, 'Why?'
- Hamilton had taken enough ammunition and weaponry for four classrooms and therefore this is another sign that he had planned the commission of the crime. I believe that because of how heavily armed he was, the fantasy leading up to the crime was manifesting itself and growing in his psychosis as he was fantasising about killing those in the sports hall and then killing another classroom. However, a mass shooting is inevitably carnage, yet Hamilton's fantasies did not factor this in and as I have mentioned the lines between fantasy and reality became so blurred that the former became the latter. Hamilton, prior to the killings, was spending increasingly more time at the gun club and again, this is an indicator that he was preparing for the final commission of his crime.

Hamilton, it could be argued, did show some signs of being a disorganised killer (they usually suffer from mental illness and are prone to psychotic episodes). In terms of being a disorganised killer, Hamilton shows the following symptoms:

- He was socially inadequate and he did not date and there are no records of marriage. Hamilton was socially awkward and spent all his time around children, with one of these reasons for his own perverted desires, and secondly, I believe that he felt more comfortable in their company as children probably took him more seriously than adults ever did or ever would.
- He lived a few miles from the actual crime scene, however, this hypothesis is more consistent with 'disorganised serial killers' as a opposed to 'spree killers' as disorganised serial killers travel less due to their own impulsive and psychotic episodes as opposed to an 'organised serial killer'; a spree killer usually targets a group or community known to them because they blame that group or community for causing them misery, or their misguided belief that they are being targeted by this group they begin to hate, for example, in the 2015 Charleston Massacre,

USA, the perpetrator, Dylan Roof, became obsessed with white supremacy and a dysfunctional belief that Black people were 'taking over the world'. He ended up killing nine innocent people in a local gospel church and is currently on death row.
- Hamilton killed at one site and considered the 'mission' over. Again, this is more common with organised and disorganised serial killers as opposed to a spree killer, some of whom kill at one site e.g., Thomas Hamilton and Eric Harris and Dylan Klebold in Columbine High School in 1999. Others will stay in a similar geographical area and move around, e.g., Derrick Bird in Cumbria 2010 and Michael Ryan in Hungerford 1987.
- To conclude this part of the profile, I believe that Hamilton does show some signs of a 'disorganised' offender, however, they are too few and oblique to be considered within this classification and I believe that the arguments for him being an 'organised' offender are much stronger as he showed a high degree of planning, I am therefore deeming Thomas Hamilton to be a highly organised offender and spree killer.

The crime at Dunblane Primary School was not staged to mislead the police and I believe that Hamilton's intention all along was to kill himself after the carnage as he would have become and been aware that he would have become Britain's most reviled prisoner and man, therefore in any prison he would have become a 'trophy' prisoner whereby the other inmates, if they attacked or killed him, would increase their rank, and therefore he did not need to stage the crime scene to mislead the police as he would not have had the time to do so, and it served his psyche no psychological purpose. The commission of the crime took roughly between ten and fifteen minutes to complete. We still need to delve further into how he killed his victims: did he inflict any 'signature' wounds, and did he pose the bodies as a way of taunting the victims or to act as his 'signature?' With serial and repeat offenders, which Hamilton was, these are key areas that can provide us with further insight into his warped psyche and psychosis during the commission of his crimes.

The cause of death was from gunshot wounds, which would cause the victim to severely bleed and usually enter a state of *hypovolemic shock*, which causes an inadequate delivery of oxygen to the vital organs due to blood loss. The strange psychological factor associated with the case of the Dunblane school massacre and the perpetrator, Thomas Hamilton, is that the use of a gun in criminological theory usually means that the murder is less personal and to a degree in this case the hypothesis remains true as Hamilton's gripe and rage was against the parents and the teachers mainly. However, he was too cowardly to confront either of the two groups and therefore his act became 'personal' by proxy as he targeted their children instead. The cause of death from gunshot wounds was to create as much carnage, death, and destruction in a short space of time, and sadly Hamilton achieved his aims.

The location of wounds to each victim was either a single gunshot wound or multiple gunshot wounds, and he wanted to kill as many people as possible in a short space of time.

Not one of the victims was moved from their original position of where they were slain. Hamilton had no psychological motivations to move the bodies as I believe that he knew that anybody entering the scene after would have been truly horrified and disgusted by the sight that awaited them, and although Hamilton would not be alive to witness this, he would undoubtedly have taken pleasure from the mere thought of this occurrence. The other reason of course why Hamilton did not move the bodies was because of the question of time, and he may not have wanted to in the first instance as spree killers aim to cause carnage and death. I believe that in Hamilton's warped *psyche* this was another way of him trying to exert his 'power' over the community of Dunblane, who he perceived to have caused him so much grief over the past 22 years of his life, however, the individual that was causing the problems in the community of Dunblane was indeed Thomas Hamilton himself, and this was spanning over 23 years at least.

When Hamilton began committing acts of paedophilia in 1973, he was 21 years old, and Hamilton committed the Dunblane Massacre at the age of 43. I believe that Hamilton was always a criminal. However, I believe his descent into madness occurred over a longer period and this descent all led up to the Dunblane Massacre.

Thomas Hamilton was unmarried and there are no records to suggest he was at the time of the offence. As I have mentioned previously in the profile, I believe that Thomas Hamilton, was a predominately 'disorganised offender', and disorganised offenders usually suffer from mental health alignments and find social situations extremely difficult, and they also struggle to form normal emotional attachments required to be able to fall in love with another human being. I do believe the story of him believing his sister was in fact his mother destroyed his psyche, and he may have harboured misogynistic rage, however, when we assess his victim typology, they were all young boys and therefore Hamilton may not have found women attractive due to harbouring the hatred for his mother.

Hamilton was more than likely homosexual, however, it needs to be remembered that attitudes to homosexuality in the 1990s in Britain were still in the process of societal change and if Hamilton was suffering mental health issues, coupled with his own sexuality being repressed, this could have led to more frustration and angst, which could have in turn propelled his mental descent even further into the quagmire of his own internal frustrations, and again I believe that this was evident in his writings. The report concluded to take away his gun licence due to his mental imbalance and should have piqued the authorities interests as a precursor to act, which was a serious error of judgement which led to one of the most tragic mass shootings in British criminal history. Even when we assess Hamilton's employment history, the warning signs are evident that he was a serial and repeat offender. When profiling serious criminals, it is always important to review their employment history, as there are clues as to their future behaviour as it is always said that the best predictor of future behaviour is past behaviour, and when discussing the crimes of Thomas Hamilton, a phrase could not be truer.

Thomas Hamilton had a varied employment history including being employed as an assistant scout leader up until 1973 (voluntary/part-time is not clear). Hamilton in 1972 also created a DIY workshop, 'woodcraft', which collapsed due to decreasing sales. He then set up a series of boy's clubs in and around Stirling and Dunblane, which would be his preoccupation for the remainder of his life.

Hamilton set these clubs up deliberately after being sacked from the Scottish Boys Scouts Movement (SBSM), and after his business venture failed again, we see his narcissism in this act as he is almost goading the SBSM by saying, *'You can sack me, but you will never ever stop me.'* It is alarming to think at that time he could set the clubs up, however, there are more child protection services available in the modern era to deal with child abuse than there would have been in the 1970s, and had this been the modern era, Hamilton would never have been allowed to pursue these types of ventures. In terms of serial murder, according to Professor David Wilson, for a serial killer to be able to kill the 'access and opportunity' needs to be there. In terms of Thomas Hamilton, to gain the 'access' to the boys he needed to put himself in a position of authority, trust and a position which would interest the young boys, e.g. sports coaching, outdoor activities; all of these activities in the 1970s attracted predominately boys, the types of victims Hamilton desired. The 'opportunity' phase arose when he had the boys alone, and therefore Hamilton sought out the employment that he did to satisfy his own perverse sexual desires, and therefore we need to delve even further into Hamilton's psyche and character to build a more composite picture of him as an offender.

I believe that Thomas Hamilton was a *narcissistic control freak* who could only obtain 'power' by harming those weaker than himself and he loathed the children in his care as more than likely many of them came from stable and loving families, which was the diametric opposite of his childhood, and this caused unforetold jealousy in his psyche. The most controlling aspect was that Hamilton sought roles in which he had a form of power over the boys as rules were more lackadaisical in the 1970s. Hamilton would have had complete control over the boys and I believe that if any boys complained about their mistreatment, many adults would have simply told them to 'get on with it', as the UK in the 1970s was still very much a patriarchal and macho culture and this allowed many to unwittingly turn a blind eye to Hamilton's absurd behaviour, and it was an era in which the old mantra would have been used that *'children should be seen and not heard'* which allowed a predatory paedophile such as Hamilton to continuously get away with his perverted crimes.

I believe that instances such as when Hamilton made the boys complete a 'survival course' are testament to the macho culture that existed of simply 'getting on with it', and I also believe that Hamilton perversely enjoyed the mental and physical exertion he held over the boys and these acts formed a part of his 'game' when he was assessing which of the boys was 'weak', as he was assessing which boy he could potentially groom, and this 'survival' course was allowing him to look for the access and ultimately the opportunity to a potential victim that he was preparing to abuse.

Hamilton also suffered from an *obsessive compulsive behavioural* (OCD) disorder, and he had a deeply disturbed and paranoid personality. Due to his psyche and his criminal acts prior to the Dunblane Massacre, he came to believe that he was a 'victim' and everybody was out to 'get him', and this is not an unusual psychological trait with *spree killers* as they usually suffer from a form of paranoia prior to the actual spree killing itself. Hamilton committed the act he did because he wanted 'power' over the parents and teachers as well as the community and wider society, ironically his name has become synonymous with 'evil' and he was not heard of in life and yet in death he has left many scarred since that awful day of March 13th, 1996, and as Hamilton committed suicide after the massacre the police never had the opportunity to question him, and Hamilton had no desire to ever allow himself to be captured at the end of the crimes as he went to his grave believing that he had the final act of 'power' over the community of Dunblane, and therefore suicide after the commission of the crime was his plan all along and formed part of his premeditation of the crimes. As mentioned, with serial and repeat offenders it is always important to check their employment history as there will be psychological clues as to their personality and potential future behaviours, it is also important to check their criminal records as this will provide us with an insight as to whether they can commit their heinous acts that they ultimately become reviled for around the world.

Hamilton did not have a criminal record prior to the Dunblane Massacre, which I find quite astonishing despite the number of accusations made against him and the fact that Detective Sergeant Paul Hughes, the former head of the Central Scotland Police Child Protection Unit, wrote a damming report to have Hamilton's gun license removed, due to the dangers he posed to others, which tragically turned out to be prophetic. I believe that had Hamilton been previously arrested, tried and convicted, he may have been given a form of treatment to help him, and if he also had a criminal record, and had thorough checks been conducted against him, then he would never have had the chance to become a sports instructor (no qualifications he held allowed him to get to this position in the first instance) and then the Dunblane Massacre may have been avoided. Although Hamilton never had a criminal record, I do believe that his past and his obsessive personality, paranoid constitution and psychosis was enough of a warning sign to suggest that he could commit such an act under the correct circumstances.

Pen Profile

I, Samuel Hodgins, can confirm that I have researched and studied the case and the criminal career of the spree killer Thomas Hamilton in depth, including the crimes he committed prior to the infamous Dunblane Massacre in 1996, which remains as one of the single most deadly acts involving firearms in the history of the United Kingdom.

The criminal career of Thomas Hamilton began with strange advances to young boys under the jurisdiction of his care from 1972 onwards, when Hamilton would have been aged 21, and his criminal career ended on March 13th, 1996, when he shot himself in the mouth upon the completion of the Dunblane Massacre, Hamilton was aged 43 at the time of his death. Since the Dunblane Massacre, many adults have gone on record to speak about Hamilton's strange and perverse behaviour, however, as Hamilton was never convicted of any of these crimes that appear to be of a *serial nature* I am therefore predominately profiling him mainly on his ultimate crime, the Dunblane Massacre, and I am therefore classifying him as a *spree killer* who was motivated by several key factors which I will outline during the pen profile of Thomas Hamilton.

As Thomas Hamilton took his own life, I am therefore not trying to offer a psychological profile of an UNSUB, I am therefore in effect trying to offer a psychological post-mortem of the offender in question. The pen profile of the offender in question is based upon the information contained within the above profile sheet and I will try to explain in detail my hypothesis as to the motivations of Thomas Hamilton to try to explain why he committed one of the most horrific crimes in the annals of British criminal history.

1. As established thus far on several occasions throughout the course of the general profile, the criminal act committed by Thomas Hamilton can be defined as a *'spree murder'*. I believe that Hamilton fits into this categorisation as he killed seventeen people in one single incident and injured many more during the commission of his criminal acts. I believe that Hamilton would have killed or at least injured many more had he somehow managed to maintain his *stress response levels* whilst committing his crimes, as we know after firing into the hall, he entered the hallway and fired a few rounds that thankfully hit nobody, and yet there were more classrooms he could have entered whilst in the hallway and he bypassed all these as he was transfixed on entering the sports hall.

    The other hallmark with Hamilton being a spree killer was that he killed himself, and this act usually happens after the offender has had the time to calm down after the initial violent act and take stock of what they have done and what will face them afterwards, if of course they surrender. With spree killers rage can dissipate over a few hours or over the course of a number of days, for example, Michael Ryan in Hungerford took his own life on the same day after calming down and Raoul Moat decided to take his own life around seven days after the initial criminal acts, whereas others can be within a matter of minutes or seconds, for example Eric Harris and Dylan Klebold in Columbine fired their last shots at 11:43am before eventually turning their guns on themselves at 12:08pm; whereas Hamilton committed suicide immediately after and the whole event took no longer than fifteen minutes. It is highly unlikely that a spree killer is captured alive, although there are rare in recorded cases of spree killings, for example, Anders Breivik who massacred 69 teenagers in Norway in 2011 awaited the police to capture him so he could tell the world his 'story'. Breivik's motivations were more political as opposed to Hamilton, who was enraged at his perceived 'tormentors'.

2. In terms of the actual criminal act of the Dunblane Massacre, the crime scene was one of carnage and destruction. However, I believe that Thomas Hamilton had planned this for a while and there was spontaneity within the criminal acts, according to McLaughlin (1996), when she cites the findings of the Cullen report (1996); *'Evidence also emerged which suggested that Hamilton had planned the school massacre well in advance. Less than six months prior to the shooting, Hamilton had purchased more guns and ammunition than ever before. His attendance at gun clubs dramatically increased and he spent countless hours trying to improve his shooting accuracy.'* We also know that Hamilton cut the telephone wires near to the school to cut all communication and he had asked an anonymous boy for the layout of the school prior to the murders. Hamilton was a criminal with a warped psychosis and wanted to enact 'revenge' upon the community of Dunblane on the weakest members of its body.

3. Having extensively analysed Thomas Hamilton, I do believe that Thomas Hamilton was an evil person long before the Dunblane Massacre occurred. I do believe that due to his own criminal acts and strange behaviours, where young boys were concerned, any parent would be concerned about sending their child to a class or club where the teacher behaved in the way that Hamilton was acting towards the young boys. The incidents were all his own creation and thus triggered several forms of *psychosis* within his *psyche*. I firstly believe that Hamilton had an obsessive personality disorder, and this was evident from an early age when he acquired a fascination with guns. I believe that prior to the Dunblane Massacre, Hamilton had convinced himself that the community of Dunblane was 'against' him as his narcissistic

personality would not allow him to comprehend that he was the problem and his warped misconceptions that the community was 'against' him were vehemently not true.

Due to these warped beliefs, Hamilton began to develop a paranoid constitution and excessive delusional beliefs. It was a classic case of staring into the abyss and the abyss staring back, however, the abyss was not only staring back, but the abyss was also manifesting itself in all of Hamilton's manic and delusional psychosis. Grinnell (2012) states, '*a paranoid delusion is the fixed, false belief that one is being harmed or persecuted by a particular group of people. It involves the persons belief that he or she is being conspired against, cheated, spied upon, followed, poisoned or drugged, maliciously maligned, harassed or obstructed in the pursuit of long-term goals.*' This is evident when Hamilton wrote to higher figures of authority including the highest authority of the realm, Queen Elizabeth II.

From conducting a psychological autopsy on Thomas Hamilton, I believe that Hamilton believed that he was above the community of Dunblane, and this is a completely unfounded school of thought brought on because of his narcissistic personality. I believe that Hamilton had a 'delusion of grandeur' in relation to himself and his capabilities. Due to his narcissistic personality and other factors within his psychosis, the rage, hatred, resentment, anger, lust, paranoia, stress all fermented and fused together over time and as Hamilton was in control of his actions, he did not once seek professional help. This is what led to the terrible malevolent act of March 13th, 1996, at Dunblane school.

The pathologist Professor Anthony Busuttil oversaw the post-mortem on Hamilton's body as he looked for evidence of drugs, alcohol, a brain tumour, viral infection, and lead poisoning, without any conclusive results on any of the factors mentioned. He concluded that there were no physical causes for Hamilton's behaviour and therefore the crime could only have been committed due to psychological factors.

4. I fully concur with the pathologist, Professor Anthony Busuttil, that Hamilton's crime could have only been committed due to psychological factors which we can only theorise about as Hamilton's last act of power was to take these dark secrets to his grave and this becomes a forensic and pathological issue as they tend to take their own lives, psychologists don't have the opportunity to study them and their psychological motivations whereby there could be more information acquired to

hopefully help them before they commit their crimes, or force public policy to change to provide them with the help some of them will ultimately require.

During his formative years, however, Hamilton did have a loving mother who tried to overprotect her son from being stigmatized by a very staunch Christian community whilst Hamilton was a young boy, as his parents were already divorced at the time of his birth and this would have been frowned upon by society during the early 1950s. Hamilton's mother, Agnes, could not afford to really look after the young Thomas and therefore sent him to live with his grandparents until he was twelve years old. Thomas Hamilton was led to believe that his grandparents were in fact his paternal mother and father and his mother was his sister, a story which he would believe until the truth was revealed in 1974 when he would have been aged 22. So how could all these circumstances of his formative years account for his later criminal career?

a. Brain (2009) cites the work of the psychologist and psychoanalyst John Bowlby (1946 and 1956) when he produced his *theory of attachment* when he stated, '*Children deprived of their mother – their attachment figure – would have problems later in life. The psychoanalytic theory suggests that problems can arise from fantasies about relationships with parents and problems can arise from real relationships with parents can also be the cause of later problems in life. The child's mother or main caregiver acted both as ego and super-ego, before they (problems) can develop.*' I believe that the *attachment theory* as outlined by Bowlby, is very accurate in the case of Thomas Hamilton because Hamilton's circumstances are extremely like that of Ted Bundy, in the sense that both men were relatively intelligent, and I believe that both men always knew that their 'sister' was in fact their mother. I believe that Hamilton knew from an early age that he was living a lie, and this began to fester within his psyche and may have induced his foundation state of a paranoid constitution that people were 'against' him, and nobody 'cared' about him, as he would have known that his maternal father had never bothered with him.

The problems in this case did arise once he had formed a real relationship with his mother, as the fantasies that he inhibited previously had now become a reality and there was probably no real bond as there should be within a normal mother and son relationship. Brain (2009) cites Bowlby's *maternal deprivation hypothesis* when she states, '*Bowlby believed that such problems in adulthood are permanent and irreversible, meaning that once there are problems nothing can be done about them. Maternal deprivation means having an attachment broken through separation, and the first two years of life are very important. By 'deprivation' Bowlby seems to have intended both not having formed an attachment in the first place and having an attachment broken through separation.*' Hamilton's was sent to live with his grandparents at the age of 18 months and by the time he was 22 he had discovered the truth; there are reports and records that this was when he began committing his strange and perverted acts against young boys. I believe that Hamilton was annoyed with his community and his family and therefore the young boys entrusted within his 'care' were the easy targets for him to enact 'revenge' on and to try to rectify his feelings of inadequacy within his psyche and to try to achieve the feeling that a range of serious offenders wish to achieve, the feeling of excess power over another human being.

b. Hamilton was an inadequate person who I believe due to his upbringing and his mother living in a world in which she feared ostracization was the early foundation of Hamilton being suspicious of the outside world and the community that he lived within, and over time as he felt he was not really part of his community, he began to not only mistrust them, he actively loathed them and he would eventually blame them for his own failings and therefore he would go on to commit a crime so terrible that his name would be remembered for all the wrong reasons and this would be his final 'act' of power.

Winch (2011) cites the work of Cattaneo and Chapman (2010) when they spoke about *personal empowerment* within an individual; '*The first step is to identify a power orientated goal. The idea is to increase our level of influence at any level of social interaction, either with another person, a group, or a system. Winning the battle by attaining the result we want is a significant demonstration of our social influence.*' Although they are referring to general empowerment, I believe that this comment and study can be transferred from the subject of general psychology to criminal psychology when psychoanalysing Thomas Hamilton. Hamilton took his first steps prior to his crime, and he identified a 'goal' and there has been evidence to suggest that he had planned the crime for a while according to Lord Cullen report (1996).

Hamilton wanted to increase his level of influence within the community by pretending to be altruistic to the needs of many young boys, however, this provided Hamilton the opportunity to both pursue and enact his perverted desires. Becoming a scout master and a sports coach, firstly gave him access and opportunity to young boys so that he could enact his perverted fantasies against them, and secondly, he could impose his perverse perception of 'power' over the boys and according to Russell (1996), Hamilton enjoyed disciplining the boys and expected them to obey his every command. Russell further stated that one boy's mother complained that they were forced to rub suntan oil all over Hamilton's naked body as he writhed and groaned in ecstasy. This shows that Hamilton loved the feeling of 'empowerment' and that he also had acquired the access to pursue his perverse sexual desires. Hamilton managed to achieve the result he had wanted and took so many lives and left many others shattered through the course of his actions.

In chapter 7 of the Cullen report (1996), Lord Cullen suggested an outright ban on handguns and tighter gun controls in the United Kingdom which was eventually implemented by the New Labour government under Tony Blair's premiership when Parliament bound the following act: *Firearms (Amendment) (N.02) Act 1997*, into UK statue, an act which virtually banned all guns with a few notable exceptions, for example somebody with a license can legally own an air pistol. I believe that if Hamilton had not taken his own life, then he would have taken satisfaction that his crime had enforced the UK government to change the law due to something that he had perpetrated, after all high figures including the local member of Parliament and the queen never responded to his ramblings about being treated 'unfairly', and therefore in his psyche I believe that he would have felt a grandiose sense of 'achievement' and 'empowerment'.

5. As mentioned previously during the profile, upon Hamilton's death Professor Anthony Busuttil performed a post-mortem on Hamilton, conducting extensive tests to find any clues as to why Hamilton committed such a ghastly crime. Busuttil looked for evidence of a brain tumour, alcohol, drugs, a viral infection and even led poisoning, yet he

was unable to find any explanation for the commission of such offences. It is therefore clear that Hamilton's problems were committed due to his warped psychological factors. I believe that Hamilton had a very complex psychological motivation for his crimes and his crimes were not committed as an act of impulsivity, it has been established that the crimes were planned to a degree of detail, and neither was his crime a psychotic episode, and therefore he probably would not have been detained under the then Mental Health Act 1983. We need to ask the following question in the Dunblane case, *'Can a single psychological theory attempt to explain why Hamilton committed the horrendous crime that he did?'* As we are aware that Hamilton was, to a degree, rejected by his mother at a young age (although she did love him), therefore the research conducted by Bowlby (1946 and 1956) may help explain why Hamilton became a criminal in later life. McLeod (2007) cites Bowlby's work when he notes that the long-term consequences of maternal deprivation might include the following *psychoses* in later life, delinquency, reduced intelligence, increased aggression, depression, and affectionless psychopathy. McLeod (2007) also cites Bowlby (1946 and 1956) when he states, *'Affectionless psychopathy is an inability to show affection or concerns for others.'* I believe that due to Hamilton's early experiences and his family background that he did not develop, and this would later turn him into a perverse psychopath which would inhibit him to look outward and only emphasise with his own internal anguishes and ignore the suffering he was causing to others.

6. In further reference to the theories outlined above, I believe that Hamilton, had he not been dismissed by the scouts and had many children kept silent about his strange and perverse behaviour at the sports clubs, then I do believe that Hamilton would have committed many more perverse acts against minors in his care. Hamilton, according to the police was said to have had pictures of boys in swimming trunks in his house when they searched it whilst he was still alive, and unfortunately they could not charge him with any crimes as they were not deemed to be of a pornographic nature and they could not find any further evidence of any wrongdoing, which sounds perversely absurd as he was in possession of indecent images of a minor and these were not the only problems associated with Hamilton and young boys, and the police should have arrested him on other serious charges which had been reported to them by concerned parents.

Hamilton was known to whip the boys and be overtly disciplinarian with them. I believe that although there is no evidence or conviction charge against Hamilton for actual sexual contact, it should not be ruled out in its entirety as not all victims of sexual assault report to anybody due to a plethora of reasons, e.g., embarrassment, fear, anger etc. It is commonly known that many serial killers and serial rapists take a 'trophy' from their victims, e.g. Jerry Brudos took shoes and he also took nipple casts of the victims, whereas John Wayne Gacy took the victim's driving licenses and other items of personal effects, and these 'trophies' are there to serve as a psychological purpose so they can relive the crime and relive the commission of the act whenever they wish to sexually gratify themselves. The 'trophy' is more than just an item taken from a victim by the offender; they transfix upon the item after the crime has been committed and it aids them in building up the next fantasy and acts as a precursor to their next crime. Psychologically, items in general life can be used as a motivational tool and strictly speaking in a psychological sense, there is nothing untoward about this, for example, a businessman may strive to get their next big contract to acquire another car; a person may solely collect antiques and reminisce how they felt when they acquired the item and use it as a motivation in the quest for the acquisition of the next one; a sports person may have eighteen winner's medals and yet still crave their nineteenth. Why does this occur? It occurs to help psychologically stimulate the mind and helps a person focus upon their next goal and aim and this form of psychological motivation is no different when dealing with serial offenders, the only difference is the psychological acquisition is perverse with a serial offender from the groups of people mentioned.

7. Since the now infamous day of March 13th, 1996, there have been robust changes in UK law with the most notable being the ban on handguns, and adults working with children and vulnerable people now must be aware of child protection procedures and are all instructed to go through the process of a Criminal Records Bureau (CRB) check. Although all laws are put in for protection and to maintain law and order, no law is fool proof as criminals will still commit crimes as they are trying to satiate their internal psychological motivations, for example, although guns were banned after the Dunblane Massacre, criminals will still commit gun crimes for a variety of reasons (mainly drug related and gang related). Casciani (2008) cites the following Home Office figures on

UK gun crime for the years 2006/2007: 'According to Home Office figures, there were 59 firearms-related homicides in 2006-2007 compared with 49 in the previous year. That is an increase of 18% in just one year.' Britain, on the other hand, has thankfully only had one massacre thus far since the Dunblane Massacre, the Cumbria Massacre in 2010. Whether this is solely down to legislation is debatable. The CRB checks are not perfect, but it minimises the risk to children posed by a would-be serious sexual offender and all the changes in terms of law and procedure have become the legacy of Dunblane.

As Hamilton was a deviant sexual offender, I believe that he fits into the following two types of sexual offender: *power-assertive* and *power-reassurance*. I believe that Hamilton was an overt disciplinarian with the boys in his care and he would strike them to assert his power and secondly to 'reassure' his psychosis that he was still 'powerful', both of which helped his psychosis to believe that he was still 'powerful' and still in 'control' of his life, and he was also transferring his internal anger onto the children. According to Groth (1979) when he claims that the two mentioned typologies of sexual offender both take trophies or souvenirs from the victims to relive their crimes, I believe that all the pictures of the boys was Hamilton's form of trophy-taking to serve himself both sexually and psychologically.

8. To sum up the profile of Thomas Hamilton, I believe that he may have had some forms of mental disturbance within his psychology, however, Hamilton was a sexual predator and a psychopath and as there was evidence to suggest he planned the Dunblane Massacre, he is therefore far worse than Britain's other two spree killers, Michael Ryan, Hungerford, 1987 and Derrick Bird, Cumbria, 2010, as the crimes committed by both Ryan and Bird were heinous, but there is evidence to suggest that their mental states had completely disintegrated and the crimes were psychotic episodes rather than organised premeditated murders. The name of Dunblane will be forever seared into our memories for the events of that terrible morning of March 13th, 1996, and yet we wish it could only be synonymous for the first British men's singles Wimbledon champion since 1936, Andy Murray, who in a bizarre twist of fate was in the school on that day and hid in the headmaster's office whilst the shootings were taking place. Unfortunately, we will never be able to change the past and neither do the British public ever want to forget the victims of Dunblane, and rightly so as an event like Dunblane must never ever be allowed to happen again.

Derrick Bird

Derrick Bird was born in Cumbria to Joseph and Mary Bird in 1957. He would live a normal life and was a popular member of his community, which makes his crimes even more shocking as to why a seemingly upstanding member of society would go on to commit one of Britain's worst ever mass murders.

The types of murders and criminal acts perpetrated by the offender in question, Derek Bird, ties in with the FBI spree killing definition:

'Two or more murders committed by an offender or offenders, without a cooling-off period; the lack of a cooling-off period marking the difference between a spree murder and a serial murder.'

Derrick Bird also shows striking similarities with two other British spree killers: Michael Ryan, who shot dead sixteen people on the streets of Hungerford, Berkshire, in the summer of 1987, and Thomas Hamilton, who walked into a primary school in his hometown of Dunblane, Scotland, killing sixteen children and their teacher (Leigh C. 2010, pages XI – XII). The other similarity is that all three offenders committed suicide after the commission of their crimes, and this is quite a common occurrence with spree killers. To try to understand the psyche and psychosis of Derrick Bird, it is important to evaluate his modus operandi and to begin working backwards from there, as I believe that this will be the best method to build a composite psychological profile of the offender in question.

Derrick Bird's modus operandi was simply to shoot all his victims at random, and there was no dialogue between the offender and the victims, and this is because Bird's mental state had denigrated into its own abyss that there was no psychological desire or need to converse with the victims as the act of shooting itself was all Bird required to satiate his own psychological imbalances. In terms of serial offenders, dialogue and conversing with the victim is key to their fantasy. For example, serial rapists at the start of their series of crimes use minimal dialogue with victims because they are nervous and are shocked that they are capable of such acts, however, as their crimes progress, the dialogue becomes more assertive and aggressive as they are becoming more confident in their criminal behaviours, and they are enacting out their fantasies in a greater reality. Spree killers usually have no dialogue as most of these types of crimes are spontaneous and they aim to cause as much destruction as possible in a short space of time.

The first three victims of the twelve dead and eleven wounded were targeted for a purpose which we can only theorise about, as Derek Bird took his motive to the grave with him. According to the BBC News website on 3rd June 2010, it was believed that Bird was in a dispute with his brother, David Bird, and that is why he killed David, and their solicitor, Kevin Commons, within the space of 35 minutes of each other. Leigh (2010) states that, 'After Joe (father) died in 1998 his net estate was just £10,000. Debts and taxes had reduced his worth considerably. As his widow, Mary, would, along with the house in Ennerdale – which was hers for her lifetime – receive the money – Brian (the other brother) and Derek were left with nothing.' The problem here was those days after the murder, according to Leigh (2010), 'The Probate document shows that Joe, in 1997 gave David a sum of £25,000 on the condition that the sum be deducted from his share of the estate upon his death.' The problem is that there was nothing left of the estate to divide between them. I do not believe that this was the overriding psychological factor for the crimes that Derrick Bird ultimately committed, however, I believe that this was part of the myriad of problems that would accumulate within his psyche over the ensuing years and lead to the complete denigration of both his psyche and psychosis and I will expand on this statement throughout the profile.

Another theory that arose at the inquest in Lillyhall, near Whitehaven, according to Bird's best friend, Neil Jacques, Bird was obsessing about his tax problems and had already resigned to being jailed for not declaring income for the past fifteen years. Jacques also stated that Bird kept repeating that his twin brother, David, and the solicitor, Kevin Commons, were in 'cahoots' against him (Carter 2011).

The truth is that we will never know the real reason behind Derek Bird's motives for committing the atrocities he did on the day of June 2nd, 2010, as all we have been left with is a plethora of different theories as to why, when dealing with serious offenders, the crime scene can provide us with psychological clues as to why a person may have committed the crimes that they did. However, with a spree killer this is not always as easy to do because their psyche is so fragmented, and the attacks can appear as 'random'. Yet this is an easy assumption as a spree killer begins to blame a community e.g., Thomas Hamilton with Dunblane, or a place e.g., Eric Harris and Dylan Klebold blamed the students at Columbine High School for their own inner frustrations, and I will evaluate the crime scenes committed by Derrick Bird to ascertain if he has left us within any psychological clues that could have led to the commission of his crimes and the Cumbria Massacre.

Derrick Bird did not attempt to contaminate the crime scenes of any of his 23 victims as he left the bodies of the twelve people that he murdered in view of the public and the wounded where he shot them on the streets. There was no time between each murder and there was no psychological motivation for Bird to contaminate the crime scenes as I do not believe that he was in any form of a rational state of mind during the spree.

Bird did not try to hide any evidence, as spree killers such as Michael Ryan (Hungerford), Thomas Hamilton (Dunblane) and the Columbine killers, Eric Harris, and Dylan Klebold, after the commission of spree killings usually calm down from their frenzy and end their life. Spree killers know that they will also be apprehended and don't go to any length to contaminate a crime scene, whereas a serial killer would contaminate the crime scene because they want to evade capture and they actively enjoy the acts of killing and enjoy playing a 'game' with the police, for example, the 'Green River killer', Gary Ridgeway, would deliberately contaminate crime scenes with discarded items of other people such as chewing gum, items of clothing, cigarette butts and written materials to confuse the police as he was an organised offender and he was also forensically aware of police procedures. Ridgeway believed that he was 'outwitting' the police and it became another form of his 'power' as he knew this would be wasting police time as they were looking for DNA that wasn't in the system or, if lucky, a perpetrator from a previous crime whose DNA data was in the system would have been questioned, thus wasting more police time and police resources, whilst Ridgeway just carried on with his normal mundane life and his spate of serial murders unabated whilst the police were confused because of the plethora of forensics from each crime scene.

I believe that a spree killer knows that they will get caught, whereas a serial killer will go to great lengths to not get caught; the FBI and Morton and Hills (2005) believe that the public and police have formed a conceptual myth that a serial killer wants to get caught. On the contrary they don't as they would spend the rest of their lives in a jail cell and be hated by all people including other prisoners, who see them as 'trophy kills', whereby they would rise in the rank of prisoners for such a scalp. The other factor is that serial killers want to continue to kill due to their warped psychosis and the psychological need to keep killing. Even if they want to stop, their primitivity will not allow them to stop and they will always be a danger to others and there is no chance of reforming them whilst they are incarcerated as the psychological and sexual drive is too far imprinted within their psyches. As with serial killers, sometimes spree killers will kill a demography of victims due to their own inner rage and therefore it is important to assess the victimology of a spree killer as much as a serial killer as both will hold the victim as the contributing source to their internal anger and frustrations.

Derrick Bird killed indiscriminately, and he did not appear to pick a victim based on sex, race, and political preference or fit any other preference, and the victim's age range varied as well, for example the youngest victim was the 23-year-old estate agent, James Clark, who was simply driving through the area of Seacastle, when Bird shot him once in the head and killing him instantly. The oldest victim was the 71-year-old retired security worker, Kenneth Fishburn, who was found shot on a bridge just 50 yards from his home in Bridge End according to BBC News. Derrick Bird did target the first three victims and the police have established this from their investigations as I believe that he felt these victims were to blame for his problems in life. As mentioned, there is no single motivational factor for why Bird targeted the other victims, however, his mental state was completely denigrated and due to a series of events that occurred over the years, he may have felt psychologically compelled to continue his rampage as the denigration in his psyche felt complete after the initial targeted killings, and there is a possibility that his rage consumed him and he may have wished for a chance of suicide from 'death by cop', which would have been the armed police shooting him as opposed to him taking his own life. Due to the degradation in the psyche and psychosis of Derrick Bird, it is important to assess the psychological characteristics of the offender in greater detail to ascertain the psychological motivators to be able to commit the crimes that he ultimately did on that fateful day in Cumbria.

Professor David Canter is an expert in criminal psychology, and he pioneered 'geographical profiling' in the United Kingdom, which aided the investigation that led to the arrest and capture of the serial killers and rapists John Duffy and David Mulcahy. Professor Canter theorised that people in general enact their daily acts based upon their own geographical locations or in line with their employment, or where relatives live for example, and he applied this hypothesis to serial offending which helped him build a very accurate profile on the then unknown railway rapist suspect based on several criteria, one of which included that the offender was employed to work on the railway lines as they felt comfortable and knowledgeable about the crime scenes, whereby they could act without getting caught. Eventually, upon his arrest, John Duffy was found to be an employee of British Rail during the time of the offences.

If we apply Professor Canter's model to the offender in question, Derrick Bird, the offender's characteristics in relation to Professor David Canters theory of geographical profiling and offending are as follows: Derrick Bird was a local man who knew the areas that he killed in well, and he would have possessed a good geographical knowledge of the area, and this could have been acquired through his occupation as a taxi driver. In terms of the occupation of Derrick Bird, as people we begin to recognise areas, roads and landmarks that allows us to navigate round places with ease. In short, we create 'mental maps' within our minds and due to Bird's occupation, he would have known Cumbria extremely well. Bird was aged 52 at the time of the shootings and he did not possess an extensive criminal record, other than a misdemeanour for theft of wood from Sellafield Nuclear Plant in 1990, in which he was subsequently convicted and given a twelve-month suspended sentence, which is a petty crime and was twenty-years before the Cumbria Massacre. Derrick Bird's sexual activity was normal and there is no record of a warped sexual psychosis; he lived a seemingly normal life and, truth be told, the psychological motivations for the commission of crimes associated with spree killers are never sexual, as these crimes are the psychological motivations associated serial offenders such as rapists, predatory paedophiles and serial killers, and Bird's previous and later crimes do not fit a sexual pattern.

In terms of his general characteristics many people liked Derrick Bird according to Leigh (2010), who states, *'To those who knew him Derrick Bird was kind and affable, friendly and sociable man, the kind of man who would stop and greet you in the street when you passed him by.'* Another neighbour told BBC News that Bird was *'very approachable'* and therefore Bird was not exhibiting any signs of psychological abnormality that would have made his neighbours to be wary of him. In terms of the criminal act committed, Bird was a 'disorganised killer' as he was out of control and he left several chaotic crime scenes, and he also made no attempt to hide any of the bodies and he did not feel the perverse need to take any trophies from the victims. The other disorganised criminal characteristics that put Derrick Bird into this category is the fact that the victims were targets of opportunity and he attacked them by surprise at the scene. None of the victims dead or alive was forced, bound, or controlled by him, and he did not make any attempt to hide the bodies. I therefore believe Derrick Bird falls into the 'disorganised killer' category, and I will expand on this hypothesis during the profile of the offender in question.

Derrick Bird was divorced with two sons and had become a grandfather in the weeks before the shootings on 2nd June 2010 and was said to be overjoyed at the birth of his grandchild, which makes the acts that he would commit only two weeks later even more difficult to comprehend and to fully understand.

As mentioned, it is not fully clear as to why Derrick Bird committed the atrocities he did in Cumbria, and we are left with a plethora of theories as to why he committed such a barbaric act against his own community. The police, community, media et al. believe that he may have committed his crimes because of his financial decline which intertwined with his own personal vendetta as he convinced his own psyche and psychosis that the family solicitor, Kevin Commons, and his brother, David, were in 'cahoots' against him and he mentioned this to several people on several occasions.

Derrick Bird was also the subject of a Her Majesty's Revenue and Customs (HMRC) tax inspection, and I believe that as his mental state was degrading piece-by-piece, Derrick Bird quite possibly believed that his brother and Kevin Commons were colluding with the HMRC to cause him more angst, and this was leading to further stress within his psyche and psychosis. During the inquest of Derrick Bird, the findings within the inquest returned a verdict of unlawful killings and suicide. The inquest heard from a psychologist, Dr Adrian West, who stated that he believed that all the events such as the financial, the paranoia, the Thai 'girlfriend' taking his £1,000 and never speaking to him again, which also led to his colleagues 'joshing' (as he called it) him unwittingly, and this continued to feed his paranoid constitution as Derrick Bird was more than likely psychologically on the edge after the culmination of these events. Dr West told the inquest, *'That bitterness, resentment and depression led Bird to enact vengeful, retaliatory fantasies, believing that people would never forget him and that he was also heard to say, Whitehaven will be as famous as Dunblane'* (Wainwright 2011). I do believe that Derrick Bird was becoming enraged and harbouring vengeful thoughts, however, I believe that originally, Bird intended to only target those individuals that caused him angst and I will expand on my hypothesis for this during the profile.

As I have previously stated, I do not believe we will ever know the true motivations for the crimes committed by Derrick Bird and whether he was 'evil' or began to suffer from delusional paranoia due to the series of events occurring in his life. Undisputedly, his criminal acts were evil and there is evidence to suggest that he was not as his mind had degraded to such a degree that he was no longer in control of his emotional and psychological state as he his psyche and psychosis had entered a state of rage due to his perception of his own perceived egregious injustices that he suffered that he felt killing his 'oppressors' was the only way he could find some psychological semblance within his fragmented mind, and anybody in Cumbria on that day would have been exposed to a great risk as ultimately Derrick Bird would be himself once his psychosis had re-entered a state of equilibrium.

The victims and anybody within the area on the day of June 2nd, 2010, experienced vast levels of risk as Derrick Bird had completely lost control of his psyche and his senses and his emotional state was completely despondent to the suffering and pain that he was inflicting upon others. Spree killers, unlike their serial counterparts, usually choose victims indiscriminately, whereas a serial killer may choose them to fulfil a particular fantasy. For example, Professor David Wilson (2009) recognises that in Britain there are five groups most vulnerable to fall victim to a serial killer: *the young, women, sex workers, homosexual men, and the elderly*. The examples of Wilson's hypothesis in Britain that relates to serial killers are the following prominent examples: Jack the Ripper' (sex workers), John Christie (women), Brady and Hindley (children/young people), Kenneth Erskine (elderly) and Colin Ireland (homosexual men). Bird shot at random strangers of all ages and gender whilst on foot and from his taxi indiscriminately, except for the first three victims who he targeted as these people were the source of his initial rage. The first three victims were all heterosexual men, a victim typology that is rarely at risk from falling prey to a serial killer, however, it highlights how indiscriminate a spree killer is when 'choosing' a victim, and if a person is unlucky enough to be in the wrong place at the wrong time. Sadly, this could be the biggest and last mistakes of their life.

Derrick Bird took a high level of risk in murdering the victims as he was seen by many people and was also a well-known and liked member of the community and was of course at risk of being shot by an armed police unit. However, due to his fragmented mental state, and as he had entered a state of rage, I don't believe that he was concerned that he had been seen as he may have already been planning on committing suicide and the possibility of a 'death by cop' suicide, as he may have been prepared to allow the police to shoot him as he knew he could never have a normal life after the commission of his crimes.

The Cumbria police force was criticised at the inquest for not responding quickly enough and not working well with the ambulance service, however, the inquest may criticise the police, but places like Cumbria have very low crime rates and the most serious crimes tend to be teenagers playing up in the local park or a few speeding offences, and were more than likely not well-equipped to deal with a spree killing like major cities such as Manchester, Birmingham, London et al. would be due to exponential threat of terrorism.

If the police responded 'better' to an incident unheard of in Cumbria, then they could have called an armed response unit from outside the area, which could have posed a significant risk to Derrick Bird if he intended to survive. It is known that Derrick Bird called his family to say goodbye before shooting himself, therefore he did not wish to live any longer and I believe that by this state, his mental process had calmed down and his psychosis had left the state of rage as he passed others and allowed them to live, and was even polite to people as he was now beginning to realise the true extent of the nature of what he had actually done to others. The mental state of Derrick Bird before the occurrence of the shootings was fragmented to say the least, and the inquest should have mentioned what mental health services were on offer in the area and how these were functioning at the time, because such a service may have helped Derrick Bird and saved the lives of so many others on that fateful day. Unfortunately, the psyche of Derrick Bird had become so degraded, confused, and enraged to the point of committing murder, it is important to assess the sequence of the acts before, during and after the killing to assess his psychology further, as there will be clues to his psychosis within this area.

The sequence of acts before the commission of the crimes was what one can only define as extremely mundane and normal, for example Derrick Bird would visit and have dinner with his elderly mother. According to Leigh (2010), Bird patronised his local pubs the Stork Hotel in Rowrah, and the John Paul Jones Pub in Whitehaven and again this is normal that it could be attributed to routine behaviour of any resident of Cumbria. I do, however, believe that although externally these acts appear to be normal, even during these routine and mundane acts Derrick Bird's mental stability was disintegrating at an alarming rate and he would have needed help, and nobody appeared to recognise that his mental stability was highly imbalanced, and Bird was becoming a danger to himself and others.

The alarming quote that he said to his best friend, Neil Jacques in April 2010, over a row about a speedboat, *'I am going to make Whitehaven as famous as Dunblane'*, should have been taken more seriously in hindsight as Derrick Bird was suffering mentally at this point and his friends should have asked him to seek professional help, as this wasn't just a comment borne out of anger or 'out of the blue', as Bird may have recently seen or read something on the Dunblane Massacre and he was possibly beginning to want to exact 'revenge' against those he perceived had caused him pain and also upon his community that he felt was 'betraying' him.

It has also been rumoured that Bird was planning to flee the country the day before the murders. Bird was planning to withdraw his money and flee to Thailand (Sims 2011). Bird had also made comments to friends and family that he would not get to see his grandson be born as he would be in jail. We can see from these comments that his psyche was in a complete state of flux as he fantasised about running away and beginning a new life in Thailand, and again this would have given his psychosis a 'false dawn' as he believed internally that such an act would rectify his problems. The other part of this is the confusion where he was emotionally torn about not seeing his grandson and potentially ending up in jail, which was adding to his state of flux, confusion, and depression even further, and these emotions were causing him excessive internal grief. The events after the killings have left only theories after the inquest as Derrick Bird shot himself and so many other people, however, I do believe that Derrick Bird was suffering from a severe mental illness which did sadly and ultimately lead to the commission of his crimes.

Derrick Birds rampage, in which twelve people were killed and eleven were left wounded, was estimated to have occurred been between 10:01am and 13:20pm (The Telegraph article, 3rd June 2010). Each malicious act may have only taken a matter of seconds to commit, including Bird's own act of suicide, yet Derrick Bird has left a trail of destruction and misery upon a small town as the radius that his crimes were committed in was relatively small geographical, however, for a spree killer this area was also quite big as they usually kill in a single location.

Derrick Bird committed his murder in his own area, Lamplugh, Rowrah, Frizington, Whitehaven, Egremont, Carleton, Gosforth and Seascale. The distance between these areas from Lamplugh to Seascale is 12.55 miles and therefore based on this route Derrick Bird committed an act of criminality every 0.54 miles. Derrick Bird was committing his crimes frequently and at random, which is expected with spree killers. When assessing killers, as the victims are always the central facet to their murders, we need to delve further into the victimology. Did they pose or move the body from the spot where they were originally slain? As this may provide us with more psychological clues as to their motivations.

Derrick Bird did not move or make any attempts to move the bodies of any of his victims and he left them to die in the place upon which he had shot them, for example, he left a victim, who would later survive his wounds, in his Range Rover and was later saved by the emergency services. Derrick Bird possibly considered that he had killed the victim and he just continued his spree without giving any second thought to the victim.

Spree killers, unlike a psychopathic serial killer such as Ted Bundy, do not usually move their victims from one location to another, as a spree killer does not select a victim to fulfil a particular fantasy, whereas a prolific serial killer such as Bundy would render the girls he targeted into becoming helpless by using his modus operandi of pretending to be injured and then striking them over the head and later transporting them to the Colorado Hills to 'play' with his victims and to later commit acts of necrophilia, as Bundy was enacting and living his perverted fantasies that had manifested themselves prior to the commission of his crimes in order to attempt to fulfil his psyche, to be able to feel a semblance of 'completeness', which he never attained as the act of killing made him feel more depressed. However, he craved the excess power that murder provided for his psychosis on the short-term basis. Bundy once spoke to the FBI agent, Robert Ressler; *'You feel the last breath leaving their body. You are looking into their eyes. A person in that situation is God!'* The difference between Bundy's victims was that they fulfilled a misogynistic hatred of woman, for example many of his victims were from a middle-class background, they were all attractive and well-educated and had parted hair. Rule (2001) believes that this was due to being rejected by his girlfriend Stephanie Brooks, whereas Bird shot, killed and wounded victims indiscriminately of all ages and gender orientation as his rage that built up and manifested itself for possibly years was being outwardly expressed indiscriminately in the most violent way possible.

DERRICK BIRD

As outlined above, the victims that were murdered by Derrick Bird were not moved or tampered with at all, as with spree killers there is an issue of time between the commission of each criminal act and moving the bodies does not serve their psyche for any psychological purpose.

The classic assumption with spree killers from the media and the public is that they simply 'lose it' and go on a rampage, which of course is random. However, this is so far from the truth as we have seen with the Columbine Massacre in 1999, the perpetrators planned this for weeks and their fantasies built up and became more elaborate. There is evidence to suggest that Thomas Hamilton had planned the Dunblane massacre, and therefore a spree killer, just like a serial killer, can be classed as an 'organised' and 'disorganised' offender and so it is important to assess each spree killer as individuals within this classification area.

The murders committed in Cumbria by the offender in question, Derrick Bird, were not committed in an organised manner and I have outlined several psychological traits that are associated with these types of killers. Derrick Bird was a disorganised killer based on the following:

- *Derrick Birds crimes were the indiscriminate killings of random civilians that served no sexual obsession, religious or political hatred towards a demography of people; they were his own friends, family, and members of his local community. Derrick Bird put himself and the public in grave danger. There was no plan as he just shot indiscriminately, and he was not choosing a victim to attempt to solve his own psychological crises.*
- *All the sites where he committed his criminal acts were left in a chaotic state with eyewitnesses and a multitude of forensic evidence.*
- *His attacks were spontaneous and showed very little evidence of planning other than the first three victims. However, I believe that all the latter victims became victims due to opportunity as Bird's psyche after the initial killings had allowed his psyche to release all his inner rage against a community that he perceived to have all 'conspired' against him.*
- *His victims were not selected to fulfil a psychological purpose, e.g., a sexual fantasy, a symbolic killing or a cult killing, and victims differed in various terms and traits such as age, gender, profession, educational levels, etc.*
- *All the victims were targets of opportunity and just happened to be in*

- the wrong place at the wrong time.
- The victims would have been surprised at the events and they were killed or wounded at the scene where Bird struck. There is no evidence or witness testimony that Bird had any dialogue with the victims.
- Bird made no attempt to conceal the bodies, hide evidence or tamper with the scene of the crimes. The motives of a spree killer differ to a serial killer as the former are not attempting to hide their crimes as their psychosis has entered such a fragmented state, once the rage within them subsides many just decide to take their own life, with a few notable exceptions such as Dylan Roof after he committed the Charleston Church Shootings in 2015.
- No trophies were taken to fulfil any twisted psychological purpose as Derrick Bird did not wish to relive his crimes as he perceived them as a final act of revenge; a serial killer takes 'trophies' from their victims to relive the fantasy and the commission of their crimes repeatedly as there is a psychological sexual element to this kind of warped behaviour.
- Derrick Bird lived alone and near to the scenes of his crimes. This is a common trait with more disorganised killers due to their mental imbalance. In this case, however, the offender committed his crimes locally because he was committing them against his own community as he had convinced his psyche that an entire community had conspired against him to set him up to fall.
- His hygiene and appearance had been rumoured to be falling weeks before the criminal acts and again this is an important physical trait with a disorganised offender as their mental imbalance begins to outwardly manifest itself in another form, as bad hygiene indicates that they have stopped caring and they have 'given up', and again it is another reason why I believe that Derrick Bird was suffering from mental illness during the lead up and the commission of the crimes.
- Derrick Bird's employment as a taxi driver at the time of the murders and as a joiner in a factory previously can be classed as 'unskilled' work, which is generally a common feature with disorganised killers as they tend to seek lower skilled employment as it is less stressful upon their psyche.
- It is believed that he was suffering from a psychological disturbance and paranoia before the criminal acts were committed and I feel that this is all evidenced in the above points.

- *Derrick Bird had a psychotic (impulsive) episode as opposed to psychopathic personality disorder. Psychopathic killers are usually more 'organised'; Bird's acts were more psychotic as he calmed down after the initial state of rage and allowed others to live without harming them.*

I believe the only real factor in the commission of Derrick Bird's crimes that shows a degree of planning and organisation is when he used statements such as *'I am going to make Whitehaven as famous as Dunblane'*. This does show he was either planning the commission of the crimes, or at least fantasising about committing them. I believe that Derrick Bird suffered a psychotic episode brought on by his mental state as opposed to planning the crimes. I believe that as his mental state had completely disintegrated, on the actual day of the murders he planned to kill his initial three victims and possibly take his own life after, however, his rage that had been restrained for so long was allowed to be released from its own mental prison and Bird had no control over his emotions and he continued to kill at random against a community that he perceived had 'conspired' against him. Following on from all my research on the offender, I cannot find any further evidence of planning on the commission of such crimes, and we need to delve even further to ascertain whether the offender staged any of the crimes to mislead the police, and whether this became a part of the fantasy before the commission of the crime itself.

The crimes were not staged to mislead the police as Derrick Bird left chaotic crime scenes and there was no apparent motive at the time for the commission of such crimes. The theorisation as to the psychological motivations by Derrick Bird would only materialise upon further investigations by the police. Spree killers do not tend to mislead the police as this is not their psychological motivation during their crimes. It is always important to assess the cause of death of the victims, the types of wounds inflicted against the victim and whether they posed the bodies to taunt the victims, the police or society, as these key areas will provide us with a further psychological insight into their psyche and psychosis that ultimately led to the commission of their crimes.

The cause of death or injury to all of Derrick Bird's victims was a gunshot wound. The act of killings committed by Derrick Bird appear to be of an impulsive nature and the act of shooting a victim is usually an impersonal act, however, this is the oddity in the crimes committed by Derrick Bird. I have unequivocally stated that I believe that his first victims were targeted and this was a very *personal* act of revenge, however, due to his fragmented mental state, I believe that the remaining shootings and killings were of a random nature and were not personal, however, this is where we are led to another conundrum in these crimes as I believe that the acts in Derrick Bird's psychosis became personal during the commission of the crimes as he believed the residents of Cumbria were 'conspiring' against him.

Derrick Bird shot his victims sometimes more than once so the location of wounds differed. Once Bird had shot a victim, he would immediately proceed to drive or walk to the next location to continue his killing spree. The location of the wounds when conducting an autopsy will differ between the victims of a spree killer. Spree killers may shoot a victim more than once and move on quickly, which is in complete contrast when analysing the victim of a serial killer; their chosen victim will usually show signs of 'overkill' and can provide us with a psychological autopsy of how the killer's mind was cognitively working during the process of the murder. For example, Lisa Levy, a victim of Ted Bundy's, was bludgeoned, bitten and had her left breast mutilated (the bite marks would later convict him) (Rule 2012) and this excessive rage exhibited against the victim shows that the killer was releasing all of his misogynistic rage and sexual frenzy against the victim and any sense of rational and controlled thought the killer had previously held within their psyche had completely dissipated. The same applies to serial killers such as Gein and Dahmer, who would kill their victims and excessively stab, mutilate, experiment, and flay (removal of the skin). All these acts show complete power and control over a victim and the act of stabbing can act as a highly sexually stimulating experience for a serial killer. Serial killers can fall into various categories, and they are not usually mentally disturbed, and they choose a victim typology to fulfil a fantasy or to enact their inner rage against a weaker being, and extensive studies always appears to show similar results.

A spree killer may suffer mentally, and as events in their lives spiral out of their control, their own dysfunctional and fragmented psychosis become wedded to a delusional belief that people are 'against' them. In the case of Derrick Bird, there have been unconfirmed reports that he sought mental health treatment weeks prior to the shootings (Herald Sun Article – 4th June 2010). And therefore, the location of the wounds did not show that Derrick Bird had any 'psychological' fantasy to fulfil with each victim judging by the location of their wounds. If these reports are true, then I believe that Derrick Bird was harbouring these thoughts of committing an atrocity and he was trying desperately to fight his mental imbalances, and this is another reason why I believe that although the criminal acts committed by Derrick Bird were of an evil nature, Derrick Bird was not an evil person and he suffered from both a mental and psychotic breakdown which led to the commission of his crimes.

Derrick Bird did not move any of the bodies as this act would not have been a psychological motivator for him after his crimes. As we delve more into Derrick Bird's past, we can see that he led a relatively normal life. However, there are some issues in this normal life that one could argue began to add to his already imbalanced mental state that would ultimately snowball and lead to the complete degradation of his mind over a period.

Derrick Bird was previously married with two sons; however, he was divorced since 1995 and Derrick Bird, I believe, was actively looking for a long-term relationship, hence the Thai 'girlfriend' stealing £1,000 off him and thus ending his dream of emigrating to Thailand. Derrick Bird was ageing; he possibly began to convince himself that he could only find a long-term relationship by leaving Britain. I believe that as he could not acquire a long-term partner and he did not wish to really emigrate, this caused his psyche and psychosis more angst and pain, in particular the 'girlfriend' stealing the money would have further convinced him that everybody was 'against' him and there appears to be an accumulation of problems for Derrick Bird which snowballed over time and eventually avalanched to the commission of his crimes in Cumbria. As with all serious offenders, it is important to assess their employment history as this provides us with psychological clues as to whether there are indications that they could commit such crimes. For example, it has been established that many serial killers undertake employment practices where there is a form of authority because they are obsessed with 'power', and this is a central facet to their psychological fascination and fantasies that ultimately lead them to the commission of their crimes.

Derrick Bird was a taxi driver at the time of the offences, and he was previously a joiner and manual worker at Sellafield Nuclear Plant in Cumbria, from which he was sacked for theft and given a twelve-month suspended sentence, however, although this was a petty theft, Derrick Bird appeared to be a normal law-abiding citizen until the events in Cumbria in June 2010. If Derrick Bird's employment history shows us no clues that he could be capable of committing such a crime, then we need to look further into his character to ascertain the psychological motivations as to why he committed the crimes that he did, as by all accounts he worked and never bothered another soul.

The psychological characteristics of Derrick Bird before he committed the killing spree were, according to the forensic psychiatrist Dr Mark Swinton, stated at the inquest, *'Derrick Bird had a mental illness characterised by his delusional beliefs'* and this was evident when he began to believe that his brother and their solicitor, Kevin Commons, were 'conspiring' with HMRC to send him to jail for a 'very' long time, when in fact they were trying to help him rectify his financial problems, and they paid with their lives for it. Derrick Bird lived a very mundane life other than the crimes he committed, he was a popular member of his community and a committed grandfather who loved his sons and grandchildren dearly. Other than his criminal acts you could easily say his beliefs and values were as normal as the next person in Cumbria and we will never know his true motivations for the crimes as he took his own life afterwards.

As Derrick Bird took his own life by a gunshot to the head, the police never had a chance to question him about the underlining motives for his crimes, however, I believe that if they did have the chance, it would have changed the way the United Kingdom looked at the issue of mental health at the time because of the dangers and the emotional torment a sufferer has to face whilst going through the endless nightmare. I believe that the then new coalition government would have looked further into the issue of mental health at taking office had Derrick Bird survived and been interviewed, because there was still a stigma around mental health and secondly the media and the public would have put pressure on a new government to deal with the hidden problem in society. As we will never fully know the true motivations for the crimes committed by Derrick Bird, and having researched his employment history, reports etc., I have checked his previous criminal record history to ascertain whether there are any psychological clues contained within them as to whether his past misdemeanours could provide us with clues that he would be capable of committing the tragic events in Cumbria.

Derrick Bird had a previous misdemeanour for theft from a previous place of employment. Other than a minor driving offence, there was no possibility to suggest the commission of the offences that Derrick Bird committed. After viewing his criminal records history, you would not have thought that he would commit such acts of malevolence. This contrasts with Thomas Hamilton, who committed the Dunblane Massacre, who had been investigated by the police during his time as a scout leader for having an unhealthy interest in young boys and photographs of naked young boys kept in his home. Jonathan Russell (1996), writing in *The Mirror*, claimed Hamilton enjoyed disciplining the boys and expected them to obey his every command. One of the twisted commands was for the boys to rub suntan oil on him whilst naked as he writhed and groaned in ecstasy. Many of the complaints came from the parents of Dunblane school and it was known that Hamilton was obsessed with guns, yet Bird seemed normal whereas Hamilton was anything but normal. I feel that the more we delve further and further into the history of Derrick Bird, we begin to see that he was mentally ill, and his illness and paranoid beliefs became intertwined and wedded together in his excessive state of confusion and this became the protagonist for his crimes.

Pen Profile

I can confirm that I have researched to some great depth the crimes committed in Cumbria on the 2nd of June 2010, by the offender Derrick Bird, aged 52 (male, Caucasian) at the time of the incident. The offender died on the same day as an act of suicide. I am therefore not trying to offer a psychological profile of an *UNSUB*, in effect I am trying to offer a psychological post-mortem, based on the information contained within the above profile to try to establish a motivation for the criminal acts committed by Derrick Bird.

1. The offender, Derrick Bird, committed his crimes in the county of Cumbria between the areas of Lamplugh to Seascale, which is a total distance of 12.55 miles, committing a criminal act averaging every 0.54 miles. As human beings our mental processes register places, we become familiar with, the brain registers them as areas of comfort and we create 'mental maps' e.g., places we know how to navigate around with ease. Although in criminological terms we associate mental maps with areas of comfort and familiarity, these 'mental maps' in the minds of 'serial killers' use these areas to not get caught and to enact out their perversions upon their victims, for example, Ted Bundy killed mainly in the Colorado Hills, Jeffrey Dahmer killed in the privacy of his flat, spree killers usually kill either in one location or an area of familiarity and do

not kill a single victim typology and they kill indiscriminately within the area or the place where they are committing their crimes. Derrick Bird would have been familiar within these areas as he had grown up in Cumbria all of his life, and he would have known that people are around at the time of the day that he committed the shootings and the killings, and therefore in his warped psychosis, he would have believed during his state of rage that he was enacting 'revenge' upon the people of Cumbria, a community that he began to hate as he had delusions that they were all 'against' him.

Bird's occupation as a taxi driver would have also familiarised him with the areas in which his criminal acts were committed, and this allowed him to navigate quickly between the areas within the districts, whilst the community and the police were trying desperately to make sense of the horrors that were befalling them on that morning of June 2nd, 2010.

2. The crimes committed by Derek Bird on that fateful day in June 2010, in which he killed thirteen people and injured eleven other falls into the category of a *'spree' killing'* and the FBI definition of this type of criminal act is as follows: *'two or more murders committed by an offender or offenders, without a cooling-off period; the lack of a cooling-off period marking the difference between a spree murder and a serial murder.'*

3. Derrick Bird's crimes were of an extremely disorganised nature in the way that he chose victims at random, and he shot them on sight. If the victims did not die from the first shot, he would leave them where they were shot (except for his brother, whom he shot eleven times) and therefore the crime scenes were of a chaotic nature, which strongly suggests Derrick Bird was not of a sane mind and all sense of rational thinking from his thought process had been eradicated throughout the criminal acts. The chaotic crime scenes resembled his own fragmented mind and thought processes and the crimes became a way of releasing his anger, frustration, inner turmoil, and rage. Derrick Bird, like all spree killers, do not intend to cover evidence as even though their cognitive and emotional responses to the suffering of others have evaporated from their mind, they still know that their crimes are wrong and usually move on quickly to commit their next criminal act before the rage dissipates. However, it's too late then as they have left a series of tragedies in their wake.

4. The overall victimology from the Cumbria Massacre represents Derrick

Bird's irrational mind during the commission of the crimes as the victims did not fit a specific victimology type to pursue any fantasies, and solely acted as an attempt to restructure his destroyed psyche and excessive feelings of rage. The innocent victims had a mixture of gender, ages, ethnicity, appearance, and careers. Bird did not try to hide his victims, and neither did it serve him psychologically to corrupt the crime scene, which does suggest a form of mental illness is manifested within the criminals psychosis and this has been seen in both spree offenders and serial offenders, e.g. Richard Trenton Chase, who in early adulthood developed hypochondria (health anxiety) where he believed drinking the blood of humans and animals would keep his heart 'beating'. Chase never tried to hide bodies or contaminate the crime scenes, and likewise with spree killers, for example, Michael Ryan (Hungerford Massacre perpetrator) was described by Dr John Hamilton of Broadmoor Hospital as suffering from 'acute schizophrenia', and Ryan committed crimes of a similar nature to Bird, albeit 23 years apart. The other striking similarity of all three mentioned perpetrators is that they all committed suicide, which is common with a variety of types of mental illness and depression.

The act of killing is extremely stressful; the difference between Chase in contrast to both Bird and Ryan is that Chase could cope with his guilt over a longer period, until he could not cope anymore living with the hell, he had created for himself within his psyche and, coupled with the fact he would never be released, he believed it was better to be dead than to exist in his own created hell. I believe that Bird and Ryan, once they had left their psychological state of rage, began to take stock of what they had done, and the feeling of rage quite quickly became replaced with a feeling of shame and guilt and depressed them even further as both committed murder against their own family. Michael Ryan committed matricide by killing his own mother and Derrick Bird committed fratricide by killing his brother. Once in a state of calm this would undoubtedly have eaten away at both men's psychosis and they would have hated themselves for it and seen suicide as the only option, as their disintegrated mental state would have spiralled further out of control once they had begun to come to terms with what they had done.

We can only theorise about Derrick Bird as to whether he felt an overriding sense of guilt and shame about his act of fratricide. However, Michael Ryan did ask the police about his mother. He was told directly that he had killed her, to which he cried uncontrollably and shortly afterwards he committed suicide. As the act of killing causes PTSD, I believe that with spree killers such as Ryan and Bird, unlike a serial killer, the guilt does not build up over several days after the event as a serial killer can compartmentalise their acts and unfathomably rationalise their twisted behaviours by 'promising' themselves to never do it again. However, a spree killer, once in a calmer state of psychosis, becomes instantly repulsed at what they have done and as many are already severely depressed and suffering from various mental ailments, they can't cope with their criminal deeds and actions, and they perceive the only way out for them is suicide as they can't compartmentalise their guilt.

5. The crime scenes and the types of crimes involved provide further psychological evidence that Derrick Bird was not of a sane mind at the time of the acts and his psyche and psychosis had entered a complete state of psychological rage. By expanding on point 4, the sites where he committed the crimes were left in a chaotic state as Bird made no attempt to conceal the bodies. No trophies were taken from any victims, which can be a trait when analysing an 'organised' serial killer (usually to remind them of their criminal act), which is a common trait amongst spree killers who are suffering from a form of mental disturbance, e.g., Michael Ryan (Hungerford Massacre), Eric Harris and Dyan Klebold (Columbine Massacre) and more recently Adam Peter Lanza (Sandy Hook Elementary Massacre). The other common denominator with these perpetrators is that they had suffered a loss in the family either through bereavement or through a family dysfunction, recently or a few years prior to their criminal acts. Therefore, I believe Derrick Bird was not of rational or sane mind at the time of the murders and Bird was suffering from an extreme psychotic episode.

6. The events that led up to the events of 2 June 2010 in Cumbria also show Birds mental state had disintegrated, and the paranoid constitution that engulfed his psyche and psychosis became wedded with a state of 'intermittent explosive disorder' (commonly referred to as 'rage'). Bird perceived the whole of Cumbria and Whitehaven to be 'conspiring against' him, which to a healthy and functional mind is a completely absurd chain of thought, due to these internal feelings of anger and suspicion. I believe that Bird began harbouring violent fantasies of 'revenge' within his psyche, and this became evident when he stated to

his friend during an argument that he was going to *'Make Whitehaven as famous as Dunblane'*, which is not a rational comment under any normal circumstances. There is further physical evidence of his mental disintegration as his hygiene and appearance began to fall and deteriorate several weeks prior to the commission of the crimes, and therefore I believe this was a manifestation of his multitude of psychological disorders.

7. Derrick Bird did not have an extensive criminal record prior to the Cumbria Massacre, other than a theft from his place of employment in 1990 and a driving conviction for speeding, and therefore nobody could have foreseen the heinous and destructive acts that he would bestow upon Cumbria on the 2nd June 2010.

    Bird's criminal acts in part may be attributed to many factors that could have led to him suffering depression, which transformed to him suffering from a combination of a paranoid constitution which fermented into a psychosis of paranoid schizophrenia, all of which metamorphosised themselves into excessive rage and turmoil, deluded in his beliefs that the only way he could rectify his psychological pain would be to firstly undertake an act of 'revenge' against his first three victims and then commit further shootings against random people as the ultimate act of 'transference'. However, as mentioned previously, Derrick Bird, suffered PTSD soon after the events and took his own life.

8. Bird believed that his brother and David Commons (the Bird family solicitor) were both in a partnership conspiring against him with HMRC to have him 'locked up for a very long time', as he was the subject of a tax investigation. It is also believed that he was in dispute with his brother over the will of their father's estate. A few weeks before the shootings, a girl that Bird had met in Thailand, whom Bird had given a substantial amount of money to, decided to break off their relationship, which resulted in Bird becoming angry and resentful. After the 'breakup' Bird's colleagues began taking the 'mickey' out of him and Bird did not enjoy their acts of ridicule. The combining factors may have attributed to Bird's psychosis of paranoid delusional schizophrenia, which turned into bitterness, resentment fuelled by his depression that could be a form of an explanation for his motivations to commit such heinous acts. There is an element of tragedy here as well in the sense that people could not recognise that Derrick Bird, who by all accounts was popular and well-liked, suddenly had a change in behaviour and became outwardly

unfriendly, unsocial, irritable, and upset at the slightest 'joke'. As society has become more understanding about mental health and the effects it has upon an individual in the years since the Cumbria, had there not been a stigma in the late 2000s, somebody may have recognised that Derrick Bird was suffering mentally and they could have quite possibly alerted others to cease their antics due to the distress being caused to him at the time.

9. Both the offender and the victims were exposed to great risk and the risk factors involved provide us with an insight into Derrick Birds mental state. Any person in Cumbria on 2 June 2010 was a potential victim due to Bird's unbalanced mental state, and therefore everybody was at risk as he was not killing a certain type of victim to fulfil a fantasy. Bird also placed himself at risk as he gradually made his way to Sellafield Nuclear Plant, which is maintained by the government of the United Kingdom, and therefore if Bird had been spotted by an armed response team who patrol this site, he may well have been killed before having the opportunity to take his own life.

10. I will conclude my profile of the offender Derrick Bird by stating that although his criminal acts were pure evil, I do not believe that Derrick Bird was an evil person, as I believe that he was suffering from a psychotic personality disorder brought on by depression and paranoia, which without correct treatment created the downfall within his psychosis, which turned him into a paranoid schizophrenic as he showed the classic symptoms. The classic symptoms that Derrick Bird exhibited for him to be classified as a 'paranoid schizophrenic' are as follows: he became aggressive prior to the crimes; he believed people were cheating him, e.g. his father and brother with the estate; he believed there was a 'plot' against him, e.g., Kevin Commons and his brother, David, were going to turn him into the HMRC; his social skills, along with his personal hygiene, waned prior to the crimes. Derrick Bird, like most spree killers, took his own life at the end of his acts and we know from medical research that suicidal thoughts or actual suicide are the psychosis of a mental disorder.

11. I believe if Derrick Bird would have 'opened' out to somebody a family member or sought professional help from a psychiatrist, the criminal acts he committed in Cumbria on 2 June 2010 could have been avoided. We will never know why he committed such acts as we can only theorise his motivations as he will never be questioned by professionals or stand

trial/be committed to a mental institute for further examination. I will close the profile on Derrick Bird by unequivocally stating that although his acts were heinous, savage, wicked and vile, Derrick Bird was not an evil person and we must do more as individuals and as a collective society to end the stigma of mental health that hundreds of thousands of people suffer, as it is our moral and humane duty to do so and as the writer Shannon L. Alder once stated, *'When "I" is replaced by "we", illness becomes wellness.'*

Raoul Moat

Raoul Thomas Moat was born in Durham, Newcastle in 1973, into a very dysfunctional family, as his father was absent, and his mother spent time in mental hospitals. Moat and his younger brother, Angus, were predominately raised by their grandmother and Moat would become one of Britain's most notorious rampage killers in the annals of British criminal history.

According to Howard (2010), '*The police operation was the largest in British policing history. Hundreds of officers from 15 police forces had been recruited for the hunt, specialist advice had been sought from the British Army, the Police National Search Centre, and even the heat-seeking technology of a £20m RAF Tornado jet had been deployed. The final cost of the operation would amount to more than three million pounds: All for just one man.*' Raoul Moat only actually killed Chris Brown, aged 29, who was the partner of his ex-girlfriend, Samantha Stobbart. Moat also attempted to kill Samantha Stobbart and PC David Rathband, 42, the latter victim was left blinded and would eventually take his own life in 2012 because of the incident that befell him. Although, Moat did only manage to end up killing one person during his rampage, he attempted three murders and I believe that his type of crime was of a '*spree*' nature as three people could easily have been killed during his rampage.

As Moat killed one person and could quite easily have killed two or more people in the space of a few hours, which he attempted to do, I believe that Raoul Moat fits into the FBI definition of a spree killer: '*Two or more murders committed by an offender or offenders, without a cooling-off period; the lack of a cooling-off period marking the difference between a spree murder and a serial murder.*' I believe that Moat would have initially, during his state of rage, wanted to have a suicide in a 'death by cop' method, as he would have been fantasising about a gun fight with the police and taking out as many police officers he could before his eventual death. Moat may have only killed one victim; however, I do believe that in the nine days between the shootings, Moat's goading of the police eventually subsided, and he realised that his life was effectively over and hence why, like most spree killers, his mental state had degraded to the point where suicide became his only option, as a lifetime in prison would have ultimately awaited Moat, who had already been in prison. We need to evaluate and assess the criminal acts committed by Moat further and establish his modus operandi during the commission of his crimes as this will give us further insight into the psychological motivations for his crimes, and this will allow for me to work backwards to establish a composite profile of the offender in question.

The criminal act was a failed *spree killing* (see below for full details). As a spree killer, Moat's modus operandi differs significantly of that of a serial killer as a serial killer may bind or gag a victim and usually strangle them in order to acquire that feeling of power and to make the murder more 'personal' against a complete stranger, e.g. Ted Bundy, Jerry Brudos and Dennis Rader et al. all strangled their victims in order to try to make them submissive and to control them in order for their psychosis to achieve a grandiose feeling of 'power'. Moat shot his victims as he saw this as an act of revenge on his ex-girlfriend and a declaration of war on the police, and he even believed that Chris Brown was a police officer (based on what Samantha Stobbart had previously advised him whilst in prison), when in fact he was a karate instructor. Samantha Stobbart was trying to warn off Moat with this ploy as she believed it would 'protect' her against his obsessive behaviour towards her, however, Moat's psyche was already beginning to decline at a rapid state, and he already hated the police for putting him in prison and taking away his freedom.

According to Howard (2010), Moat's psychological motivations for his crimes was because he wanted 'revenge' on firstly his ex-girlfriend, who he felt had betrayed him, and it generated a rage in his psychosis when she informed him that she was dating a 'police officer' as a method of protecting herself from him to warn him off from her and their daughter. The fact that Moat would have seen his perceived 'enemy', a 'police officer', raising his daughter would have enraged his psychosis even further and done nothing to warn him off as it antagonised him more. I believe that the crimes committed by Moat were the end of a lifelong process of mental instability that was not recognised and therefore could not be treated professionally, all of which would lead to tragic consequences in 2010.

Moat's early life was not exactly the picture of the perfect family as his parents never lived together and he never saw his father, who deliberately exonerated himself from the young Raoul Moat's family life. Moat was raised predominately by his grandmother, and the young Moat brothers had a poor relationship with their mother and stepfather, Brian Healy (Whelan 2010). Moat's mother, Josephine Healy, reportedly suffered from bipolar disorder, and Howard (2010) quotes Angus Moat (Raoul Moat's brother); *'Our mother's presence was erratic, and she was absent for periods of time, although I accept that due to her diagnosis of bipolar disorder accounted for her spells in hospital.'* Howard (2010) talks about children being around parents who suffer from bipolar disorder; *'Children who have a parent who suffers from bipolar disorder can witness a parent stare absently in a trance-like state for hours, or find them possessed by excessive energy, making plans that are totally impractical and even running up serious debt as they pursue them. Not knowing what state, a parent will be in each day, whether high and excitable or low and depressed, can cause stress and ongoing upset in a child.'* Due to Raoul being the younger of the two brothers and not being mature enough to understand, I believe that this had a detrimental effect on his development process and his psychosocial development as Moat also developed bipolar disorder in later life, and he would have several problems with the law throughout the years.

The psychologist and psychoanalyst John Bowlby believed that mental health problems could be attributed to early childhood. Bowlby (1969) also believed that attachment behaviours are instinctive and will be activated by conditions that seem to threaten the achievement of proximity, such as separation, insecurity, and fear. Moat could not psychologically develop within the confines of the psychosocial stages of development as he had an absent father and an absent mother for the majority of his early life, and I believe this is the period where his *psychosis* began to suffer developmental problems, as Raoul Moat had no attachment and the people who should have cared for him and provided the love and attention were not there; this would have left Moat feeling alone throughout his formative years.

It has been reported by other prisoners that prior to Moat's release from prison, during the period when he found out that Samantha Stobbart no longer wanted him in her life, Moat became depressed and would rant in prison that Sam had 'betrayed' him, and these rants were often of an irrational nature. Moat did not sleep properly for days and nights for several weeks. I believe that Moat was suffering from depression as these feelings did not pass for weeks. Usually many people feel depressed, down or anxious, but these feelings pass, however, Moat's feelings did not, and I believe that he had begun to give up on life. According to Howard (2010), *'Moat asked to speak to the prison's priest, he talked of suicidal feelings, and it seemed that his rage when not aimed at others turned inwards and made him question whether he wanted to live or die.'* I believe that due to the breakdown of his relationship with Samantha Stobbart, and the isolation of prison life, Moat began to psychologically look inward at himself, as opposed to looking outward to solve his own mental crises, and his sensitivity began to be directed towards himself only and he therefore could not empathise with the feelings of Samantha Stobbart and also the fact that Moat was in prison for assaulting a minor, which was a child of his from another relationship.

According to White (2012), *hypersensitivity* occurs during the breakdown of a relationship and effects the individual's life dramatically; *'People with self-loathing suffer from intense feelings of inadequacy, like those suffering for depression, often take things said to them in the worst way possible. They process other people's comments in a way that filters out any positive content or implications, leaving only the negative, which then becomes part of how they think other people see them. This is particularly hard on those who deal with self-loathing in romantic relationships.'* I believe that Moat was driven to commit his crimes as he believed that others began to see him as weak and the fact that he had lost complete control of his life and he was not mature enough to handle the situations due to suffering from the effects of *maternal deprivation* in the formative years of his life. Moat even showed his psychosis of *hypersensitivity* during his six-hour stand-off with police marksmen in Rothbury, Northumberland.

Moat shot himself in the head with a sawn-off shotgun after declaring: *'I've got no dad, and nobody cares about me.'* This quote and final act of Raoul Moat again shows that he was self-loathing and he could only focus innately on his own internal pain, and even in his final moments of life could not accept that he had caused misery to three different families and left several communities in Northern England in fear for several days.

Is it also possible that due to *maternal deprivation* during the formative years of his life Moat's brain did not develop correctly, and therefore a chemical reaction could be part of the reasons why he committed such crimes in later life? Maternal deprivation will have severe detrimental effects on the brain, according to Marco, Valero, Borcel et al. (2012), when they state, *'Data from both human and animal studies suggest that exposure to stressful life events at neonatal stages may increase the risk of psychopathology during adulthood. Both maternal and postnatal depression has been associated with persistent neurobehavioral changes like those present in developmental psychologies such as depression and schizophrenic-related disorders.'* It is believed that if children, boys, do not receive enough consistent care and attention during the formative years then the amygdala mass nuclei of the brain, which is located deep in the temporal lobe, can become damaged. It is a limbic system structure that is involved in many of our emotions and motivations, particularly those that are related to survival (Bailey 2014). Howard (2010) also states, *'If boys do not receive enough consistent care and attention that area of the brain that processes empathy can be damaged. It can affect the amygdalae, the part of the brain that processes memories that are connected to emotional events; and if the child has not learned that their needs are met, it can lead to an oversensitive reaction to stress. Emotional neglect has also been linked to the fall in the production of hormone serotonin that induces calm, whilst the production of corticosterone, the stress hormone is increased.'* I believe that all the neglect that Raoul Moat experienced fermented in him over time and, as he was inward looking, it imbalanced his *psychosis* even further with devastating results.

Durham Prison was in the news in 2003 due to its high suicide rates, and therefore we could question was enough done in the sense that were the staff trained enough to recognise prisoners showing the symptoms of problems arising that are consistent with mental health? The other side of the argument is that in 2002 a total of six prisoners committed suicide at Durham Prison, (BBC News) which in October 2006 had a population of 981 inmates, and therefore this figure is relatively low. I believe that Moat committed the crimes that he did due to personal grievances and a general mental imbalance within his psychosis, as opposed to a failing by the Her Majesty's Prison Services (HMPS) for England and Wales.

When we begin to analyse the crime, scenes committed by Raoul Moat, these become personifications of the psychological manifestations of the confused psychosis within his mind as each crime scene was one of chaos and anarchy as Moat was not too interested in hiding his identity from the media, public and authorities. On the contrary, Moat was enjoying goading the police and courting the media in the ensuing days after his crimes. Raoul Moat's victims at these crime scenes were all deliberately targeted, which is unusual for a spree killer as they target their victims based on a single demography, or a single location, however, Moat's victims were targeted against those people who he perceived had caused him an 'injustice', and I will expand on Moat's victim typology to provide further psychological analysis for the motivations of his crimes.

A spree killer's choice of victims differs heavily from that of a serial killer.

For example, Colin Ireland aka 'the Gay Slayer' targeted gay men, as I believe that he felt by killing them he was killing a part of himself. A spree killer such as Raoul Moat's choice of victims will differ from a mass murderer due to firstly mass murderers operating under the guise of a political party or organisation that are murdering for the 'greater good' on behalf of their people or chosen ideology, and these type of crimes can be enacted by more than one person for Adolf Hitler's Nazi Party and their quest to eradicate the Jewish people from Europe which lead to the outbreak of World War Two in 1938. Raoul Moat began attempting or killing those people who he perceived as his 'enemy' or who were causing his depression. Moat did not kill random members of the public after his initial crimes as he may not have perceived them to have caused him harm or distress, and he may felt a grandiose sense of self-achievement as there was sections of the public that elevated him into a 'hero' status, something which would have reaffirmed his belief that he was in fact right in his actions as the public 'supported' him and again this delusional belief fed into his already warped psychosis.

Raoul Thomas Moat suffered with several severe psychological issues and disorders, and I believe that the main protagonists to his mental disorders were formed early in his childhood experiences. Moat had an unbalanced childhood due to his mother suffering from bipolar disorder and she would disappear for long periods of time, and love and discipline was also inconsistent in the Moat household. Raoul Moat did not develop though the stages of *psychosocial development* as theorised and studied by the German-born American developmental psychologist and psychoanalyst, Erik Erikson (1902–1994).

Erikson proposed eight stages of *psychosocial development*, and one must complete each stage before being able to successfully complete another. Having previously studied the work conducted by Erikson, I believe that Raoul Moat's developmental problems began at the following stage of the psychosocial development process: *psychosocial stage three – initiative vs. guilt*; this is the stage where children begin to assert power and control over the world through directing play and other social interactions. Children who are successful at this stage feel capable and able to lead others. Those who fail to acquire these skills are left with a sense of guilt, self-doubt, and a lack of initiative. Due to his mother suffering from bipolar disorder and his older brother, Angus, in part trying to raise him, I believe this led to Moat developing self-doubt within his *psyche* and he began feel powerless from a very early age. When we assess Moat's psychological behaviours as he became older, his only way of asserting power and control was through acts of violence as he had not developed socially within the normal stages of development, and this was because of the inconsistent discipline from his mother and I believe that Angus Moat, being a child himself, could not control Raoul Moat, who would have been already exhibiting signs of an antisocial personality disorder.

As Moat did not complete the above stage in the *psychosocial development* model, he may have to some extent reached the other stages in the psychosocial developmental process. However, due to not completing one stage correctly, he could not successfully complete the remaining stages that a person progresses through in the normal stages of development to make sense of the world around them and exist within the expected social norms within it.

The following stage, *psychosocial stage four – industry vs. inferiority*, is the stage that covers the early school years (ages five–eleven). In this stage children develop through social interactions with others, and they begin to develop a sense of pride in their accomplishments and abilities. Children who are encouraged and commended by parents and teachers develop a feeling of competence and belief in their skills. Those who receive little or no encouragement from parents, teachers or peers will doubt their abilities to be successful. Moat could not develop at this stage due to his mother being absent and his relationship with his stepfather, who Moat loathed, was wholly dysfunctional based upon a mistrust of each other. As Moat could not complete the previously stipulated stage, he would not have been able to successfully complete the next stage; *psychosocial development stage five – identity vs. confusion*; in this stage the child will explore their independence and develop a sense of self. Those who receive proper encouragement and reinforcement through personal exploration will emerge from this stage with a strong sense of self and a feeling of independence and control. Those who remain unsure of their beliefs and desires will feel insecure and confused about themselves and the future. Erikson believed that completing this stage successfully would lead to 'fidelity', which is the ability to live by society's standards and expectations. There is varying evidence that Moat did not live by the expected standards of society and held the rule of law in complete disregard – even before the shootings and the ensuing manhunt. Moat had several convictions and many of them were for violence or threatening behaviour, including his incarceration for the assault against a minor. It is evident from the two mentioned stages that Moat had developed an inferiority complex, so he reacted to stressful situations and rejection in a childlike way with the use of violence. Moat was confused by his identity and did not develop a *'sense of self'* and he could only look inward when external problems would arise. Moat would have saw himself as a *'unique case'*, and yet many people will face such problems throughout their lifetime, Moat could not as he was almost childlike in his understanding of such external problems.

As we delve further into the psyche and psychosis of Raoul Moat, it becomes more transparent that Moat had developmental issues as the respective stages of the *psychosocial development* progresses. *Psychosocial development stage six – intimacy vs. isolation,* covers the period of early adulthood when people are exploring personal relationships. This is the stage where it becomes vital that people develop close, committed relationships with other people. Those who are successful at this step will form relationships that are committed and secure. As Moat did not develop correctly at the previous stages, he could not form intimate relationships, this is evident that he had several live-in partners, all of whom left him due to the persistent and consistent acts of violence he committed against them. Moat could not develop meaningful and lasting relationships with women because he was inward looking due to failing to develop at previous stages; children when developing through the *cognitive stage* will be egocentric and they tend to only see the world through their beliefs and values, which are not necessarily the beliefs of society and others. As Moat could not pass through the stages in the normal developmental procedure, he looked inwardly as a child would and could not recognise the pain he was causing to others, and he could only feel his internal anger and inner frustrations due to the inadequacies within his *psyche*. Moat had several partners who left him, and I feel that when Samantha Stobbart finally left him, the inadequacies and rage within him became personified as he had failed as a partner and a father, the latter he was incarcerated for as he assaulted one of his children.

The next stage in the *psychosocial development* is *stage seven – generativity vs. stagnation*; this is the stage where, during adulthood, we continue to build our lives, focusing on our career and family. During this stage, a person who is successful will feel that they are contributing to the world by being active in their homes and community. Those who fail to attain this developmental skill will feel unproductive and uninvolved in the world. This stage is imperative in understanding Moat's *psychology*, in the sense that he felt that the way he treated his partners and family was of a 'caring' nature, and prior to his incarceration, his tree surgeon business began to fail as he could not do the work due to his own criminal behaviours. As I have mentioned, Moat looked inward and had an almost childlike egocentric view of the world around him; children will very rarely blame themselves for their failings due to their egocentric view of the world and Moat blamed the police for the failing of his business (he mentioned this on his Facebook page prior to the commission of his crimes) and he blamed Samantha Stobbart for the breakup of their family life, despite his acts of violence towards his family. In psychological terms, Moat was showing elements of *cognitive dissonance* as a mental process for a way of coping for the inadequacies within his *psyche*.

The final stage of the *psychosocial developmental stages* is *integrity vs. despair*; this is the stage that occurs during old age and is focused on reflecting on life. Those who are unsuccessful during this stage will feel that their life has been wasted and will experience many regrets. The individual will be left with feelings of bitterness and despair. In a bizarre and strange way, I believe that this is the only stage of *psychosocial development* that Moat managed to achieve in his short life, and instead of embracing integrity, he embraced despair and he created a *victim mentality* for himself and this developed throughout his childhood and carried on later in life when he was the abuser, and when people began to abandon him because of his actions he turned himself into the 'victim'. Raoul Moat exhibits the psychological symptoms of what Colin Wilson (1984) defines as the *'right man'*. Moat had to be the *'alpha male'* in terms of his everyday activities including the gym by being stronger than others in there, and this is different to simple competition. People with the *'right man'* syndrome act as tyrants in home, at work, or in public to others for the most minor transgressions and explode with rage towards anybody who 'dares' to cross them. This type of behaviour is brought about by an extremely low sense of self-esteem, and they always tend to harbour feelings of excess jealously within their psyche.

Testament to my statements above, I believe that this becomes evident during Moat's crimes and the ensuing manhunt, as Moat believed that he was engaging in a 'moral' reaction to an 'immoral world', as he believed that he had been singled out for persecution by the state, his family and the authorities and he was therefore enacting his 'justified' revenge on these manifested feelings that controlled his psychology. I believe that at the end of his life in those last few hours in the rain, Moat realised that he had failed at everything he had ever done or attempted, and he was experiencing many regrets and feelings of emptiness, and I believe that this was one of the reasons he took his own life as a final act of power to not be seen as 'weak' in the eyes of the public if he surrendered and sought help from the authorities, which he needed, and this was evident when he spoke to the priest whilst in prison before his crime spree. As Moat was suffering mentally, we need to establish the exact motivations for the commission of his crimes, as I believe that there was an element of sexual, financial and a 'personal' factor, all of which became intertwined in his mental imbalances that led to him committing the horrific crimes in 2010.

I believe that the primary motive for the offences were of a financial nature in the sense that he blamed others for the failure in his tree surgeon business, which was naturally not acquiring customers during his incarceration as this failure played into the psyche of Raoul Moat that he was the 'victim'. I also believe that Moat had developed a paranoid constitution and a paranoid personality disorder, and all these ailments constantly fed into his victim mentality when other failures and events in life began to occur. Moat, not having developed within the normal stages of psychosocial development, could not cope mentally and rationally with the stresses that can occur in normal life. I believe that there was an element of mental disturbances within his *psyche* due to the failings in his relationships and general family life and business and all these became a cocktail of rage mixed within his psyche and psychosis, and without treatment these mental disturbances would end in tragic circumstances for all involved including Raoul Moat.

Moat took a high level of risk in killing his victim and attempting to kill two more, because, firstly, once a gunman is on the loose the police will issue specialist armed police officers in order to attempt to counter and neutralise the threat posed to them and the general public and, secondly, the fact that Moat attempted to murder a police officer in the line of duty would have helped to intensify the search even further, and thus became the most expensive police manhunt in British criminal history. I do however, believe that Moat during this period had lost all sense of reality and I believe during the time that he was hiding, he was psychologically looking inward again and assessing his life and how dysfunctional it truly was, and this was evident in the stand-off with the police and his final comments that 'nobody cared about him' showed that his psychosis was still in a state of hypersensitivity, and I believe that in part this is one of the reasons he took his own life as he had lost everything, the other being an act of power, in the sense that nobody would ever control him again and in psychological terms, Moat had finally developed *self-realisation* and he possibly accepted that his life had been an abject failure and faced this dawning reality. Moat in his depressed state and the declinature from his state of rage could no longer cope and he did not wish to function for what was to await him if he surrendered.

Professor David Wilson has also theorised that Moat committed suicide as it would act as a 'final act of control', Wilson (2010) states; *'There was a chance Moat would try to commit suicide by "cop" an American phenomenon in which the perpetrator goes out of the way to be shot by the police. Instead, he took his own life, his final act of control.'* This behaviour is not uncommon with spree killers for a variety of reasons; firstly, they have lost all sense of reality and know that life as they knew it is over and therefore it is their final act of control; secondly, they will remain in control and will take their motivations to the grave and leave others theorising as to 'why' such acts of gratuitous violence were committed, and thirdly many of them create a fantasy world, e.g. Moat made reference to the Incredible Hulk in his 49-page statement left for the police. The Columbine High School killers Eric Harris and Dylan Klebold became obsessed with the 1995 video game, *Doom*, and these fantasies are born out of their narcissistic personalities. Wilson (2010) states the narcissistic personality (when referring to Moat) as: *'He (Moat) is a classic case of a violent narcissist with a dangerously twisted view of humanity and a childish determination to impose his will on the world around him.'* As mentioned, I believe that Moat did not develop in the correct psychosocial stages of development and therefore the outward acts of violence were his way of regaining 'control'. Children, whilst developing, enact this behaviour because their minds are still formulating the correct moral and socially acceptable ways of behaviour as their minds and psyche are still in a stage of primitiveness and I believe that Moat's mind and psychosis was still very primitive.

I believe that spree killers pose a huge risk to victims and potential victims as they create an elaborate fantasy world to almost justify their acts of violence. In short, Moat was never going to surrender or be captured and there would always have been one of two outcomes which were the option of suicide or a shootout with the police, and therefore the 'risk' that Moat took in his crimes can be debatable based upon this premise.

Due to Moat's dangerous psychosis and his inner belief system that he was the 'victim', those people he attacked on that fateful day were at extreme risk, and despite the fact that many people still believe he was an 'antihero', he may well have turned on them also if the conditions were right or he perceived them to have transgressed him in any way shape or form, as Moat was adamant on 'revenge', and he was never likely to turn himself over to the police, and due to the imbalances within his mental state, the victims experienced extremely high levels of risk and the sequence of acts before, during and after the criminal acts provide weight to this statement.

The sequence of acts before the killings was that Moat was suffering from depression and hypersensitivity that was brought on because of failings in his personal life and business, and these mental alignments wedded his paranoid constitution and feelings of 'injustice' led to Moat believing that the only way he could regain control is through the only way he knew how, which was to commit extreme acts of violence. It has been documented that Moat even tried the help of the prison priest to help him through this period, and this act proves that Moat knew he had psychological inadequacies and this is another reason why I don't believe that he surrendered to the police as he didn't want others to perceive him as 'weak', as all these previous mental alignments and his failure to develop within the normal context of psychosocial development meant that these psychological problems developed into narcissistic personality disorder.

Moat was also telling fellow prisoners that *'People were going to pay'* for crossing him. According to Camber, Sims, Brooke and Dolan (2010), Moat even posted on Facebook that he had lost everything, and he had even published an extraordinary 'hit list' of his next targets on Facebook, in which he vowed to execute 22-year-old Miss Stobbart's family and gun down any police officers that 'get in the way'. It has since transpired that Moat had two accomplices; Karl Ness, 26, and Qhuram Awan, 23, helped him plot the plan of chaos and destruction. Ness, it has been believed, helped Moat commit the shooting at the first crime scene and Awan acted as a getaway driver whilst originally pretending to be hostages of Moat. Ness was sentenced to a minimum 40-year tariff and Awan must serve a minimum of at least twenty years (BBC News, 15 March 2011).

Moat killed himself and therefore could not be studied or questioned to gain more psychological clues to his full motivations, however, in the case of Moat, although we can only speculate, I do believe that the psychological motivations for the commission of his crimes are clear. As *spree killers* kill themselves, we can only theorise to their motives and innate desires, despite all the psychological clues on offer, it would be easier to assess them if they surrendered and talked to the police and psychologists.

Anders Breivik, who killed 77 people at a Workers Youth League (AUF) camp on the island of Uotya, Norway, on the 22nd July 2011 explained all his motivations for the commission of his crimes to the police and it's easy to assume without empirical research that all *spree killers* are insane, yet Anders Breivik was found legally sane by the courts and therefore we will never be fully aware to their true motivations. In the case of Raoul Moat, there is evidence to suggest mental health issues, however, there is evidence to suggest that he was in full control of his actions as he planned the crimes to the full extent, including picking his accomplices and goading the police afterwards, and he was organised and prepared to even survive in the wild for several days. This degree of planning does show a controlled train of cognitive thought processes, which is not associated with a psychotic episode, and it does suggest that Raoul Moat was in complete control, and was very calculating in his actions during the course and commission of his crimes.

Each criminal act of shooting each victim only took a matter of minutes if not seconds as Moat quickly fled each scene. Moat killed Chris Brown (29) and shot his ex-partner, Samantha Stobbart (23) on Saturday 3 July 2010 at 02:40. Moat shot PC David Rathband (42) on Sunday 4 July 2010 at 00:45. If Moat had of been successful in killing Stobbart, and later been successful in the attempted murder of PC Rathband, then Moats case as a 'spree killer' would have been unique as this type of murder usually kills in a small geographical location, e.g. Michael Ryan in Hungerford in 1987, and in one place, e.g. Thomas Hamilton in Dunblane school in 1996. These types of killers also usually commit their acts in a matter of minutes or hours and not usually 24 hours apart. The other thing that makes Moat's case unique is that he was willing to kill more police officers until he was killed, and the manhunt could have been worse had Moat not eventually been cornered and taken his own life (Source – BBC News, 2011).

The crimes were committed in the Newcastle area of England, and this city of England was central to his psychological motivations as the people who he perceived had 'mistreated' him and caused him an 'injustice' were all residing in Newcastle at the time of the events, and therefore further assessment is warranted on the victims' bodies, i.e., did he move them, did he stab or repeatedly or shoot them afterwards, which suggest overkill? His behaviour if any towards his victims' bodies after the kill may provide us with more psychological insight into the commission of his crimes.

Moat did not move the body of Chris Brown, 29, and he did not attempt to move the body of PC David Rathband, 42, as this act would not have served any psychological purpose to the criminal motivations of Raoul Moat. Moat left each victim where he had slain them and this is a common occurrence with a spree killer; serial killers usually move their victims from one site to another, usually to fulfil a psychological purpose (usually to derive an intense feeling of 'power') and to sexually gratify themselves, whereas the psychosis of a spree killer has entered an enraged state of mind and they believe that they are enacting 'revenge', and therefore do not move the bodies of their victims as it serves no psychological purpose to their imbalanced psyche.

As with both serial killers and spree killers, there will be killers in each of these classifications that will fall into the sub-classifications of 'organised' and 'disorganised' offenders, and I will outline the psychological traits for Raoul Moat in this respect as I believe that he will fall into the classification of a 'mixed' offender, as there is evidence of organisation and disorganisation and I will outline both areas to explain my hypothesis.

There are certain elements to the crimes committed by Moat and there are certain psychological traits within his personality to suggest that he was an 'organised offender' and the key characteristics have been outlined below:

- *There is evidence to suggest that he was plotting his crimes whilst still in prison (Durham Prison had raised concerns with the local Probation Service) and this included his 'kill list' and the fact that he had told other inmates of his intentions upon release. Moat had also threatened his ex-girlfriend, Samantha Stobbart, which provides enough unequivocal evidence to conclude that Moat was planning his criminal acts for some time.*
- *He was sexually competent, had several sexual partners and he fathered at least four children prior to his incarceration. Usually, disorganised offenders cannot form relationships with others due to their dysfunctional and strange behaviours and patterns, however, Moat had multiple relationships, and this is where the juxtaposition occurs between him being an 'organised offender' based on the premise that he had formulated long-term relationships, he could flit in this psychological trait between the two as his relationships all faltered and this is where his mental imbalances could have led to the commission of his crimes as they appeared chaotic. Although the crime scenes may have*

been chaotic, as Moat was a 'spree killer' and spree killings are always chaotic, I believe that Moat was organised overall and in control during the commission of his crimes as they had been planned for some time.
- Moat had inconsistent discipline as a child (mainly due to his mother's mental illness and mental deterioration) and this is a common theme amongst 'organised offenders'.
- Moat was in control of each crime and controlled his mood, and he targeted those he believed to be the 'source' of his internal anger and frustrations. Moat's crimes contrasted with other spree killers, who once they begin their rampage kill indiscriminately. Moat attacked those who he perceived to be at the source of his psychological problems.
- Moat's psyche was 'precipitating situational stress' as he had planned the attacks by asking two accomplices to help him gain access to a car (this makes him geographically mobile as well – another common factor with organised offenders), and he had also accumulated enough weaponry and packaged food to survive in the wilderness for several days. Moat knew that there was going to be mass public interest when he was on the run from the law and would have followed this in any way he possibly could. The last act is playing into Moat's self-created fantasy that he was the 'hero', and the public would support him, it was to be the last fantasy of a destructive mind and personality.

There are certain elements to the crimes committed by Raoul Moat, when we combine this within his personality, to suggest that he was a 'disorganised offender', and the key characteristics have been outlined below:

- Moat had a below average intelligence, and this is common with disorganised offenders as they do not have the mental capacities and mental intelligence to hide their crimes.
- Moat had a variety of unskilled jobs on his CV, such as a panel beater and a bouncer, and this is not an uncommon trait with disorganised offenders.
- Moat was suffering from a plethora of mental health conditions such as hypersensitivity, paranoia etc. during the crimes and again this is common with disorganised offenders as they have mental health problems that combine to allow for the commission of the crimes, organised offenders do not always suffer from these alignments and are in much more control of their psyche and the world around them.

- During his incarceration, Moat was known to have significant mood changes and this would have been brought on due to the decline within his mental state as Moat began to suffer from insomnia when he found out his girlfriend had a new partner, and again this event would have imbalanced his mental state even further and over time this anger would have fermented into a state of 'revenge' and the fact he was incarcerated would have led to more frustration in his psyche as he could not act out on his internal feelings.
- The first shootings of Brown and Stobbart were planned as they were the initial source of his psychological angst and internal frustrations, however, the shooting of Police Constable Rathband was an 'opportunity' for Moat to begin his 'war' on the police.
- He held no conversation with any of his victims prior to the commission of his crimes, which is another common trait of a disorganised offender as dialogue forms a part of the fantasy of an organised offender as they use it to instil fear in the victim and gain their complete submission and control.
- The crime scenes were chaotic, and no evidence was tampered with or moved from one location to another.
- No victims were restrained, and no hostages were taken during the manhunt. A hostage could have been of use to an offender like Moat for use as a 'bargaining tool' with the authorities or to flee the area, however, this was not Moat's intention and I believe that after several days alone in the wild, his initial rage cooled, and he just wanted to end the whole saga without harming anybody else other than the police and himself.

Moat did not stage any of the crime scenes to mislead the police as the offences committed by Moat vary from that of a serial killer or serial rapist, as these classifications of criminals may be trying to destroy evidence or leave their 'signature' to ensure that they take 'credit' from the media for the crime. Moat, on the contrary, did not stage the crime to mislead the police, public or the media; he wanted everybody to be aware that the crimes were committed by him and him alone as he was in effect trying to rationalise his behaviour after all those years of pent-up frustration. If we look at the methods, he used to bring about the victims' demise, and this includes the wounds that he inflicted before and after death and whether he moved or defiled the bodies of his victims, they will provide us with further insight into the criminal mind and criminal motivations of Raoul Moat.

The cause of death of Chris Brown, and the attempted murder of two other victims, Samantha Stobbart and PC Rathband, showed that within Moat's psyche he believed that he was enacting 'revenge' as each victim was shot with a shotgun, and he wanted them killed as quickly as possible.

As a spree killer, Moat's chosen weapon to inflict death is different from the choice of weapons chosen by a serial killer during the commission of their crimes. A serial killer may commonly use strangulation as a method of murder for example, as they can 'bring the victim back to life' and they can repeat this action several times, and this type of act will serve their psychosis as it will provide persistent sexual stimulation whereby, they will ejaculate on multiple occasions during this abhorrent procedure. In terms of serial murder, the victim is usually a stranger and strangulation is the most intimate form of murder, even though the victim is a complete stranger. The fantasies that dwell in the abysses in the minds of a seral killer manifest within their psyche and psychosis and when acted out they are transforming the acts from an impersonal one to a very personal act and they use aggressive and demeaning dialogue towards their victims during their crimes to make the act interpersonal. However, spree killers target those that they believe have caused their downfall initially and usually random strangers and use guns as the act becomes more impersonal and the choice of weapon is used to an end as they attempt to resolve their inner psychological crises.

Each victim had differing wound locations. The first victim, Chris Brown, died instantly from a gunshot wound from close range. After Moat had killed Brown, he fired into the living room and hit Samantha Stobbart in the left arm and abdomen. Moat shot PC David Rathband in the upper body and the resultant shards of glass caused head injuries as well which in turn resulted in blindness. The location of wounds vary other than the fact they were all from a shotgun, Moat wanted to kill the victims almost instantaneously as he saw them as the external cause of his internal pain, and therefore set about killing them in the vain and desperate final hope he may find some form of psychological 'closure' due to the inadequacies within his psychosis; in terms of psychology this is an act known as 'transference' as Moat was projecting all the years of pent-up psychological frustrations and psychological inadequacies onto the victims.

Moat did not want to hide the bodies and he did not wish to pose them either as this served no psychological purpose for him. Moat, on the contrary, was quite happy for the bodies to be found as they were slain and the motivation for such an act lies within his narcissistic personality. Moat knew that the shootings would have gained him mass media and public interest and he had left a 49-page letter declaring war on the police. At 01:35am on Sunday, 4 July 2010, Moat called the police and confirmed that he had shot PC David Rathband and advised the police and stated, *'You are not taking me seriously enough.'* I am therefore led to believe that Moat wanted all the bodies to be found by others. As Moat planned to declare 'war' on the police, in his own self-created fantasy I believe that he almost saw himself as a 'soldier' taking on a corrupt and unjust police force in something almost akin to a real-life Rambo as Moat fantasised that he was the 'hero' of his own creation and he had an almost warped childlike imagination, this may be evident in the fact that he planned to survive in the wild for several days. As with all serious and dangerous offenders, it is important to review their past employment to ascertain whether there are any psychological clues as to why they may have committed the crimes that they did, and I believe that Raoul Moat did have some past employment practices that do show he is more than capable of committing acts of violence against other people for minor indiscretions.

Raoul Moat's known employment history was as follows, panel beater, bouncer, and a tree surgeon. All employment was within the Newcastle upon Tyne area. Moat was a self-employed tree surgeon, and it is believed that he blamed Samantha Stobbart and the police for his business failing and therefore this 'blame' shows us an insight into his narcissistic personality in the sense that he blames others for his own failings, and he is showing cognitive dissonance as he was exonerating and absolving himself from his own actions as he went to jail for the assault of a minor. Moat was to blame for his business failing because his answer to everything was to resort to violence to gain 'control' of the slightest of the most adverse situations.

Moat's other job as a bouncer is an interesting career choice for somebody with his psychological traits and characteristics. Although most bouncers are there to do a job to retain and restore order at premises, I believe that due to the psychological makeup of Raoul Moat, he chose this profession as it gave him a chance to commit acts of violence in a 'semi-legal' fashion. As I have established, Moat's psychological understanding of regaining control of a situation was to resort to the use of violence and intimidation brought on due to Moat not being able to complete the stages of psychosocial development. Moat did not have the articulate social skills of reasoning as he was not intelligent enough, and therefore he was extremely primitive in his social behaviours.

According to reports by the BBC on 11 July 2010, Moat posted the following statement of his Facebook status page; *'Just got out of jail, I've lost everything, my business, my property and to top it all my lass has gone off with someone else.'* This completely unfounded belief was another catalyst for the motivation for him to commit his criminal acts. If we apply the discipline of *forensic linguistics* and apply it the Facebook post from Raoul Moat, we can see from his wording that he has created a victim status and as we are aware from social media, people will read a post and simply 'like' it and provide sympathy comments below it without understanding the context of the statement or what has happened previously to bring the author of the post to this stage. I believe that this happened to Raoul Moat after posting the above statement, he would have read other comments and these sympathetic comments were convincing his psyche and psychosis that his forthcoming actions were indeed justified and 'moral' as he was of course the 'victim' about to fight back against the 'unjust' and this was an early foray for his psyche and fantasies that he was about to become the 'hero'. This misguided belief that he was the 'hero' was a creation fuelled by the media, and he simply played into their narrative. However, there must be more psychological underlining that were already manifested within his psychosis for this to psychologically occur after the commission of his criminal acts.

Raoul Moat suffered with a narcissistic personality disorder, brought on due to the developmental issues and mental imbalances from his developmental years, which were due to his dysfunctional and strange upbringing. Wilson (2010) states; *'Raoul Moat is a classic case of a violent narcissist with a dangerously twisted view of humanity and a childish determination to impose his will on the world around him. Typical of his eagerness to remain the centre of attention was the 49-page letter he sent to the police, trying to explain his monstrous actions. This rambling document, full of dark threats and shallow self-pity, provides a graphic insight into his mentality in all its explosive fury, with incoherent passages in which blame-passing is mixed with righteous indignation. A strong streak of sentimentality usually shines through the text, as the brute declares his devotion to his children or his ex-girlfriend. But these self-obsessed maniacs have no genuine concern for others. All that matters to them is their own impulses.'* I believe that Moat, judging from the above quote by Professor David Wilson, shows a *self-serving bias*, whereby he would completely absolve himself of all responsibility of his actions and place the blame onto others, in this case his ex-partner and the police, and this is a classic symptom associated with those individuals who suffer from a narcissistic personality disorder.

Wilson (2010) elaborates further on Moat's psychology by labelling him a *'control freak and a fantasist.'* In terms of Wilson labelling him a fantasist, Wilson states; *'Like many narcissists, he (Moat) had a puerile, cartoon view of the world, seeing himself* as *a hero battling malign forces. In this case, he has taken the cartoon imagery to a literal conclusion. Again, in absolving himself of responsibility, he says his rages are like 'the Incredible Hulk taking over'.* Tellingly, the Hulk, as portrayed in comics and Hollywood movies, was a force for good, using his supernatural powers in the quest for justice. Furthermore, Moat even tried to turn himself into a real-life version of the Hulk. An extreme bodybuilder, he is said to have indulged in heavy steroid abuse, which not only artificially expanded his muscles but also warped his mind, making him extremely paranoid. Wilson was referring to the contents of Moat's 49-page letter and offering his expert opinion on the *psyche* of Moat.

At this point in the profile, I must reiterate again that Moat had not successfully completed the *psychosocial stages of development* and he saw the world from his own egocentric childlike myopic vision. Moat would have also realised the drama that he was creating through the media, and he would have no doubt been aware due to reports that some members of our society empathised with him and saw him as an anti-hero taking on a totalitarian establishment, which Moat was not.

These types of reports would have fuelled his fantasies even further. Over the years we have seen the media not so much reporting the news as opposed to 'making the news', and I believe that although in the case of Moat they were not 'making the news', they were spinning the narrative that was playing into Moat's psyche that he was the 'anti-hero' and this was fuelling Moat's psychosis, and apart from fuelling Moat's psyche and psychosis, it was also filling the bank accounts of a morally bankrupt media as one person had died and two were critically injured in hospital. The most prominent example of the media playing into this narrative that Moat was the 'anti-hero' was evident when MPs asked Facebook to remove a Raoul Moat 'fan page' which had 29,500 followers in the week after Moat's death, and their excuse was that the information was in the public domain and was being debated and discussed up and down pubs, offices, and factories in breadth of the country. We have seen the double standards associated with

Facebook, who have censored the American ex-president, Donald Trump. However, surely as the then leader of the free world, President Donald Trump would have been discussed and debated by normal people, which lays bare the hypocrisy associated with the media as it was glorifying a serious criminal at a time whilst the media were proclaiming to be 'fed up' with the disintegration of law and order in the United Kingdom, and even labelling the problem as *'Broken Britain'*, which shows the lack of morality and the use of a catchy phrase and an emotive bandwagon for the public to jump on and get on board with. The sad reality of claiming Britain was 'broken' was the media creating a mass sense of fear to sell papers and gain clicks on news sites, whilst of course making editors and journalists wealthier with every story that could have been attributed to the *'Broken Britain'* moniker. Raoul Moat summed up *'Broken Britain'* during his crimes as he showed how morally bankrupt the press and some members of society were, however, as he helped to sell papers and advertising space, the media desperately needed him for a short time without considering the risks posed to the public and Moat himself as he had severe mental imbalances within his psyche, and the fact Moat also required correct and professional psychological help.

Unfortunately, we will never fully understand the psyche and criminal motivations of Raoul Thomas Moat as he was never questioned by the police as he shot himself at approximately 01:15am on Sunday 10 July 2010 and was pronounced dead in Newcastle General Hospital at 02:20am. As always with all serial offenders, it is imperative that their criminal records are thoroughly checked as there could be evidence for the commission of such crimes based on their previous acts of criminality, as the American Sociologist, Carol Tavros once stated that *'nothing predicts future behaviour as much as past impunity'*, and with Raoul Moat's extensive criminal record, Carol Tavros so easily could have been referring to him when she made this statement.

Gammell (2010) in her article for the *Daily Telegraph* on 5 July 2010 states in detail Raoul Moat's known criminal history: *'He split her (Samantha Stobbart) head open one night and threw her to the ground and jumped on her stomach; he had used threatening behaviour towards the Stobbart family in the past; he was in prison for assaulting a younger family member; he was remanded in court in 2005 for possession of an eight-inch serrated steel knuckle duster and a 5ft long Samurai sword; in 2003 he was arrested for threatening council staff after his then two-year-old daughter, Chantelle, fell out of an unsecured window at home.'* Writing in the *Daily*

Telegraph in 2010, Robert Mendick and Ben Leach state the following: '*Moat had been arrested twelve times since 2000; in 2000 he was arrested on suspicion of conspiracy to murder in relation to a gangland killing. He was released without charge.*' Moat's convictions have not all been disclosed by the authorities, however, judging by his arrest record, there is one common denominator in his criminal history – violence. I am therefore stating that a criminal record check of the offender in question, Raoul Thomas Moat, did heavily suggest the possibility of the commission of such offences later in his life as Moat's psychological responses to stress was always the use of violence.

Pen Profile

I, Samuel Hodgins, can confirm that I have researched and studied the case and criminal career of the spree killer, Raoul Thomas Moat in depth, which ultimately lead to the largest single manhunt in the annals of UK criminal history.

The criminal career of Raoul Moat spanned several years, which was swiftly followed by numerous arrests and convictions for violence or intending to commission acts of violence, all of which would ultimately end in the rain in Newcastle, England, during the early hours of Saturday 10th July 2010. Moat appeared to be a serial violent offender due to his previous convictions for violent behaviour, however, I am mainly more concerned with his penultimate crime, the 2010 Northumbria police manhunt, and I am therefore classifying Moat as a *spree killer* who was motivated by several key factors which I will outline during the *pen profile* of the offender, Raoul Thomas Moat.

As Raoul Moat took his own life, I am therefore not trying to offer a psychological profile of an *UNSUB*, I am therefore in effect trying to offer a psychological post-mortem of the offender in question. The pen profile of the offender in question is based upon the information contained here within the above profile sheet and I will try to explain in detail my hypothesis as to the motivations of Raoul Moat to try to explain as to why he committed the crimes in 2010 that shocked a nation, and at the same time showed an underlying social problem in the very moral fabric of our country.

PEN PROFILES OF THE OFFENDERS

1. In terms of spouse abuse, you could argue that the crimes by Raoul Moat were of a serial nature as he committed them against several partners (and even minors in some cases) and there was a 'cooling off period' between each act of malevolent abuse, however, for the purpose of this criminal profile, I will focus mainly on the crimes and events committed between Saturday 3 July 2010 – Saturday 10 July 2010. Moat's crimes were committed within the space of a few hours and although he only killed one person, I am still classifying Moat as a *'spree killer'* as he attempted to kill at least two others and it was down to extreme good fortune that the victims survived, however, PC David Rathbone took his own life after the initial events and this was because of Raoul Moat's criminal actions, because had Raoul Moat not shot PC Rathbone, he would have more than likely lived his life until he died of natural causes.

   After studying Raoul Moat to some depth, I believe that these criminal acts that occurred were a culmination of not being reared correctly and thus failing to pass through the *psychosocial development stages* as theorised by Erikson and through maternal and patriarchal deprivation through not having the normal family life that he craved through his formative years, and this caused him internal misery through both his formative and later years. I believe that Moat was immature, and he could only look internally at his own pain, and he had a childlike selfishness which engulfed his psyche, and he could not see the anguish of others that he was primarily causing with his own selfish actions.

   As we are aware, Raoul Moat divided the moral ethics of British society and showed what was already there but denied vehemently prior to the 2010 general election by the left-wing media, and most notably the Labour Party, that there was an undercurrent of a *'social underclass'* becoming more prevalent within society, and I will discuss this societal issue throughout the profile. The other issue that must be addressed is that Moat was no 'hero' taking on an elite totalitarian ruthless empire or dystopian state, he was a criminal that caused distress to so many other people throughout the course of his life before the crimes committed in 2010. From Raoul Moat's behaviours, including attacking women and children, he can only be defined as a bully. The question that must be addressed is as follows: *'Is Raoul Moat evil, mentally ill or neither?'* I will provide my hypothesis again throughout the course of the profile on the offender in question as to where Moat's psychology and psyche sits within the confines of this question.

2. As we are aware from the profile Raoul Moat, although not reared in the usual environment of what we would define as a 'stable family' to the best of our knowledge, did not suffer from physical or sexual abuse by any members of his family, and he was loved and even protect by his older brother, Angus. Moat would have realised this from an early age that his family was 'different' from other families and this realisation would have continued throughout the course of his life, and when he began to form relationships they broke down because he had not experienced and been shown the behaviours of the way a normal family functions, and due to his emotional states this led to problems in his homes and living arrangements with his later partners. I believe that he began to internalise an anger, resentment, and rage about this issue because he never had the normal upbringing that he was seeing his children and stepchildren were enjoying and I believe that his own internal rage caused him to attack the minor that he was eventually incarcerate for.

   Moat hated and loathed his stepfather, and he despised the fact that his dad had never been around when he was growing up. This was clearly never far from Moat's thoughts as he exhibited his internalised frustration in his final hours when he shouted with the gun to his head: *'I've got no dad; nobody cares about me.'* Moat may have also realised that like his father, he too had failed his children as he had several children by different partners and left them to be reared in one-parent families, just as he had, and I believe that Moat may have seen his own inadequacies in this act and over the course of the days in the wilderness prior to his death, as during this time in the wilderness, whilst he was leaving his enraged psychological state, he would have had ample time to reflect on his life and his behaviours.

   I believe he began to look back and reflect on his life and as he suffered from a victim mentality, he would have cried for himself and his own failures and the psychological problems that he was already facing and the forthcoming problems he would have faced upon his arrest, all of which led to him seeing no future at all, the future was to be bleaker than his past and this left him with only one option in his psyche, which was to commit suicide.

3. I believe that Raoul Moat bore a form of misogynistic hatred towards women and yet he still craved women, possibly brought on by the early rejection by his mother. These feelings towards women caused

confusion in his psyche for one of two reasons, firstly, he wanted to dominate them as they would be weaker than him and this would have gratified the inadequacies within his own psyche, and secondly, as Moat's thought processes and outward behaviours were primitive, he required these women to breed with him and again this is a form of control as they would be tied to him forever; the second psychological motivation in this process were also his fantasies of becoming the father that he never had, the role which he would fail spectacularly in doing as all of his children would eventually be reared in one-parent families and he even violently assaulted one of his children.

I believe that Moat was a misogynist who loathed women because of the way his mother treated him during an early age, and his mistrust of women that manifested itself within his psyche and this innate belief would be reinforced later in life when his partners all left him, albeit due to his aggressive and violent nature towards them and the children. As Moat was inward looking, he would never accept that these women left him to protect themselves and their children from Moat's violent temper. Moat's interpretation of these abandonments would have been that all women were untrustworthy and deceitful, and each rejection would have led to him becoming more dominant and controlling with his next partner, and I believe that it would have been an extremely violent household.

A narcissist such as Raoul Moat can never see their own fallacies and they will always blame others for their own shortcomings and failings; in psychological terms this is known as a *self-serving bias*. Professor David Wilson (2010) comments about the misogyny of Raoul Moat in Moats own 49-page handwritten letter which he left for the police whilst on the run; *'In a 49-page handwritten letter, he claimed to have shot his partner, Samantha Stobbart, so she could claim compensation for her and their daughter. This is what is known as neutralisation. Moat was trying to underplay the fact that he shot his ex-girlfriend. Then he said (in the letter) that he shot her in the stomach to stop her from wearing a bikini. That shows the misogyny, the need to control a woman, perhaps even more so when she was no longer his.'* I would even argue that to a degree in terms of the type of employment that Moat sought there was an element of power to all work that he sought, for example he was a bouncer, and in this type of work he could have power over who enters a club/bar/pub and reinforces his 'power' by brute force when a drunk punter acts out of turn. His other employment was as a tree surgeon, a company which he owned and in which he could have the final say over anything that happened under or to the respective business. Although not all bouncers and tree surgeons are using their employment to suit their 'God-complex', I am merely stating that in terms of the psychology of Raoul Moat, that this type of employment is a small but relevant part in helping to understand his psyche. The reality is due to his childish view and perception of the world. Moat was a control freak in everything he did, from work to home life, and if he could not, then violence was his only answer to the slightest of adversities.

4. As Raoul Moat suffered with a narcissistic personality disorder and innately harboured a misogynistic hatred towards women, combined with the underlining issues of not being able to develop through the correct psychosocial developmental stages during adolescence, this created a myriad of problems within his psychosis, all of which would be outwardly enacted with violent episodes throughout his life. We also know that Moat was a fantasist, in which he would talk about characters such as the Hulk and paint himself as an anti-hero of the establishment.

In all the previous mentioned psychoanalysis of the psychology of Raoul Moat, I believe that he developed a paranoid delusion initially which would later intertwine with an elaborately created fantasy world for him to make some sense and justification of his actions. Moat developed a paranoid constitution whereby he convinced himself that everybody was against him and that the police and his ex-partner, Sam Stobbart, had somehow colluded in his downfall and the collapse of his business. Moat shows that by his actions his delusions, fantasies and paranoia all became intertwined with deadly and tragic consequences to all those involved during that week in July 2010.

I believe that Moat suffered from a *bipolar disorder*, with the sub-categorisation of *manic-depressive disorder*. I believe this was the case because whilst in prison, Moat was severely depressed and even sought the help of the Durham Prison priest to try to find solace within his internal sadness. Whilst in prison, Moat showed all the symptoms associated with the *depressive phase* of bipolar disorder, which include the following mental alignments: persistent feelings of sadness, anxiety, anger, isolation, or hopelessness, disturbances in sleep and appetite, fatigue, loss of interest in normal activities, problems on concentration, loneliness, self-loathing, apathy, or indifference, lack of motivation and morbid suicidal thoughts.

There is another symptom associated with the *depressive phase* of *bipolar disorder* and that is the feeling of guilt. I believe that Moat did not inhibit this feeling all through his suffering due to his narcissistic personality and thus him looking internally at his own pain and not the pain that he caused to others. The question I have had to ask is whether Moat could have acquired *bipolar disorder* genetically through his mother and whether it was brought about due to environmental factors or a combination of both? The classical adage that poses up the same conundrum of problems when discussing the psychology of serious offenders whilst trying to find a cause and reason for their crimes.

a. According to the American Medical Association (AMA) in a white paper on bipolar disorder they state, '*Bipolar Disorder is a complex disorder caused by both genetic and environmental factors. It is thought that heritability of bipolar disorder is approximately 80%. Identification of the genes associated with bipolar disorder has been difficult, likely because there are multiple genes that each contributes small effects to the phenotype. Nevertheless, several genes that are promising candidates for bipolar disorder have been identified through linkage and association studies. The findings implicate several different signalling pathways, such as the serotonergic, dopaminergic, neural development, cell growth maintenance, and circadian pathways, in the control of bipolar disorder. This suggests that bipolar disorder is likely to be controlled by several different biological processes interacting with each other.*' Dopamine plays a very important role inside the brain in terms that it plays important roles in motor control, motivation, arousal, cognition, and reward. The ventral tegmental area (VTA) contains the largest group of dopamine neurons in the human brain and the VTA dopamine system is strongly associated with the rewards system within the brain. Dopamine is released in areas such as the nucleus accumbens, and most notably the prefrontal cortex which makes us aware of rewarding experiences such as food, sex and neural stimuli that have become associated with them (Arias-Carrion and Poppell, 2007). If Moat did inherit the condition from his mother and being reared in an imbalanced environment, e.g., broken home and bad relationship with his stepfather, could these external factors have caused internal damage to the development of his frontal lobe?

b. The frontal lobe consists of a right and left lobe or hemisphere, which is the hub of *'who you are',* your emotions and personality. Both lobes deal with social, emotional, motor, and sexual behaviour, as well as problem-solving, decision-making and memory. Damage or lack of development within the frontal lobe can severely affect your conscious and emotions, motivation, judgement, mood, behaviour, personality, and organisational capacity according to the Brain Injury Institute website (2012). The other external environment to consider when trying to conclude whether he was mentally ill or just bad is that we know that he was addicted to anabolic steroids, which have several detrimental health effects. Moat took these because again he had inadequacies within his psyche and many people do take these drugs to increase athletic performance to increase performance levels in sport. Many others take anabolic steroids for cosmetic purposes and these people, according to the NHS choices website, usually suffer from body dysmorphia (an anxiety disorder where the way someone thinks about their body does not match the way it looks). Teenage boys and young men may take the drugs because they have *'reverse anorexia'*. This is when they do not see themselves as being physically big or strong enough. Moat needed to become big and strong as a way of being able to intimidate and control people due to his inadequate psychosis, however, prolonged use of any drugs over a period will have negative effects, especially for somebody suffering from a mental disorder. The prolonged use of anabolic steroids can cause several psychological or emotional side effects which include the following: aggressive behaviour, mood swings, manic behaviour, hallucinations and delusions, depression and apathy, feelings of anxiety, lack of concentration, insomnia, sadness. Moat was already suffering from depression and the drug use would have contributed further to the decline within his mental state.

c. I believe that a lot more in-depth research would need to be conducted because there are too many questions left unanswered. For example, Raoul Moat's brother, Angus Moat, seems to have lived a normal life in comparison to his brother. If Raoul Moat did indeed suffer from *bipolar disorder* due to genetics, then it does not explain why Angus Moat did not inherit the same condition, and likewise if it was environmental factors whilst growing up it does not explain why Angus Moat did not become a criminal whereas Raoul Moat did. Although it is difficult to establish whether Moat even did have bipolar or his violent personality was a combination of his innate psychological traits, even then the 'nature vs. nurture' question will always arise, for example, did the use of anabolic steroids (external factor) cause Moat to become a *spree killer* or did Moat genetically inherit the *bipolar disorder (internal factor)*, as Serriti and Mandelli (2008) state, *'Bipolar Disorder (BP) is a complex disorder caused by a number of liability genes interacting with the environment. Evidence suggests that environmental factors playing a significant role in the development and cause of bipolar disorder, and those individual psychosocial variables may interact with genetic dispositions.'* I feel that trying to explain the crimes committed by Moat on the old psychological conundrum of 'nature vs nurture' is a difficult one at best, as a *spree killer*, like a *serial killer*, will have their own unique personality traits and thus the motivation between each criminal will differ entirely from those of another as the psychological makeup from one person to another will differ due to several variables.

5. Professor David Wilson stated he believed that Raoul Moat was a narcissist and a fantasist who created an elaborate world in which he was the 'hero', and in his 37-page statement to the police, he branded himself as 'the Hulk'. Moat, when and where possible, would have followed the media coverage of his actions and he would have undoubtedly seen some of the 'positive' reaction that he was acquiring from a small but vocal demographic section of society. As Moat would have been labelled by some in society as a 'hero' he would have ignored the views of the vast majority that were disgusted and repulsed by his actions, as this did not fit his own *confirmation bias* of how he perceived himself to be.

Raoul Moat was no 'hero'. As Moat was in fact a fantasist, he would have believed that he was in fact a 'hero', and this intertwined within his psyche that he was fighting a 'just war' with the police and this belief became a *self-fulfilling prophecy*. Raoul Moat should have listened to the heartfelt pleas of his brother, Angus Moat, and surrendered to the police as he would have been able to get the psychological help he needed and would still be alive today.

In British law and British society, if Moat had been found mentally ill by the legal definition, then he would have received the same rights and clinical treatment as others who have been in trouble with the law due to their mental conditions. The small demographic of society that backed Moat fuelled his fantasy of being the hero or a real-life Rambo. This demographic of British society did not really care of the consequences for the outcome for any party involved, and this included the fate of Raoul Moat as they only wished to satisfy their own innate desires and lawless behaviours by proxy through another party, which in this case was Raoul Moat, who was completely mentally unstable and was a danger to himself, which would only become evident upon his eventual suicide and the eventual investigations into his crimes and his personality.

6. There have been several instances over the past years in Great Britain that have shown there is a social underclass that is prevalent and exists and politicians (particularly those on the left) either pretend do not exist or do not realise how lawless this demographic class of society can be, or class this demographic as the same as the working class for their own intents and purposes, which they are not, or a combination of all factors. The incidents that have occurred in Britain over the past few years since the change in government in 2010 (when the Conservative and Liberal Democrats gained power from New Labour) have shown a prevalent underclass actually started with Raoul Moat, followed by the English riots in 2011 showing that there is a criminal underclass who existed in the shadows of society, and they were actively encouraged by the New Labour government and their lackadaisical approach to law and order.

    a. The German philosopher, economist, socialist, historian, revolutionary socialist and journalist Karl Marx, is famous for his writings about creating a communist state and is also seen as the deity for left-wing parties and politicians worldwide in the same sense that Christ is revered in Christianity, Marx is seen as the 'bastion' of truth. However, Marxism has wilfully created poverty and a Confucian system whereby people cannot rise, and this causes a plethora of social problems. Any society or government that actively pursues and implement this ideology usually ends up with a destroyed economy, a worthless 'education' system which is used to peddle ideological doctrine as opposed to the basics of education such as English, maths and science, and criminals become the 'victims' as opposed to the 'victimiser' and this was evident in New Labour's Human Rights Act 1998, which was borne from a cultural Marxist theory of *'victim precipitation'* whereby the victim supposedly plays a part in their own 'victimisation' as the perpetrator is acting out against the internal frustrations due to the 'unfairness' of society. This in effect becomes a secondary victimisation process for the victim and the British legal system has been actively pursuing this school of thought for the past two decades. All these issues once combined had devastating effects on the moral fabric of British society that only became prevalent in the riots of 2011.

Marx has produced several radical theories on criminology. Williams (2005) cites Marx (1904); *'Human nature itself is not criminal. Capitalism causes people to become criminal. Capitalism teaches individuals to be greedy, self-centred, and exploitative. The law and legal systems are the tools of the owners of the means of production and are used to serve their interests in keeping their activities legal even if they are harmful, brutal, and morally unacceptable. They are also used to control the activities of the people, so that they do not challenge the position of the owners of the means of production. The people are made to compete for an inadequate number of jobs, pushing them towards self-interest to survive. Some turn to crime as a means of survival.'* Karl Marx wrote that during his life in the 1800s and was later published in 1904.

The problem is that when Marx wrote this theory, the social politics and societies of Europe were different to what we have today, and political ideologies were firmly rooted in idealism. However, many parties have moved to a more 'central' position of government. Marx tended to ignore the fact the Industrial Revolution in Britain was in full swing and was shaping Britain, and the world's technological future and therefore this employed many more people and increased wages for the otherwise poor. The Industrial Revolution is a very capitalist revolution and it helped Britain become the most civilised and advanced country in the world during this era. The problem we have today is left-wing elites pretend to be altruistic to the working classes and yet still follow Marx in believing that the criminal is acting out against the inequalities of a capitalist society and is thus as much of a victim as the victimised. The implementation of Marx's criminological theories allowed the lawless to become the victim and the law abiding to become the 'criminals' and those supporting Moat would have undoubtedly been in the belly of the undercurrent of Britain's criminal underclass.

b. The left-wing governments, association and movement in Europe and Britain, including the last Labour government, followed the doctrines of Marx and Engels' teachings and they were (and still are in some cases) trying to slowly but surely implement them into not only law, but wider society, and the indoctrination of Marxist philosophy is deeply rooted within the education system, health system and the civil services including the ideologies of the Marxist view of criminality into the courts, and these Marxist indoctrinations were trying to be forced upon the population to adhere to them and Britain was, for thirteen years, sleepwalking into a Marxist state where law and order was slowly being strangled and we was becoming ruled by decree from a 'top-down' form of government. During this period in British history, the criminal underclass were becoming more prevalent and powerful without any deterrent because of the Human Rights Act 1998, which was implemented by Tony Blair's government in New Labour's first term, has shown the left has a warped sense of morality when dealing with serious criminals and there was no desire by New Labour to protect the rights of the innocent members of the public as the rights were extended to criminals under the New Labour government. As mentioned earlier in the profile of Raoul Moat, this warped sense of morality acted as and is a second victimisation process for the already victimised. There have been several notable cases of the Human Rights Act 1998 and its fallacy and its affront to an already civilised law system and country. Hitchens (2013) provides some stark examples; *'Career criminal, Stuart Blackstock, who shot and crippled unarmed PC Phillip Olds, was paid over £7,000 for minor delays for his prison release ... Mustafa Abdi, a Somali child rapist was awarded £7,237 for being 'wrongfully detained' as he resisted deportation. On and on goes the list of terrorists, murderers, rapists and child abusers handed thousands of pounds by British taxpayers after justice-defying rulings by the European Court of Human Rights (ECHR).'* The working classes hold fears of crime and being exploited by others and yet the party that this demographic group predominately elect to protect them were wilfully being ignored by them for an ever-growing and more prevalent demographic social underclass.

The *Daily Telegraph* newspaper (6 December 2008) stated the growing rise of the underclass in society in their article by stating; *'The failure to tackle the underclass despite – or because of- the annual expenditure of about £150 billion on welfare, is an indictment of Labour's period in office. Astonishingly, welfare spending continued to grow despite a period of high unemployment and 80 per cent is still paid out on a something-for-nothing basis. When Labour left office in 1951 after laying the foundations of the post-war welfare state, about 4 per cent of the population relied on the principal means-tested benefits national assistance. Today (2008) nearly 17 per cent rely on its successor, income support. If other benefits for housing and council tax are included, one in four is in receipt of a state payment.'* Not all claimants are criminals, that would be a wholly unfair, unjust, and immoral view as people fall on hard times. Labour deliberately created a reliance on welfare for votes and created a social underclass for votes for them to pursue their Marxist ideological fantasies and, of course, a criminal underclass ultimately rises from this ill-thought type of policy. Labour actively encouraged a feckless lifestyle for votes at the expense of the law-abiding majority, e.g. Gary Newlove who was beaten to death outside his home by thugs were protected originally by the law and none of the three arrested and later convicted had ever been employed, and all three had a long list of prior convictions, these would be the same type of people who have elevated Raoul Moat into a 'hero', as Moat shared their criminal beliefs and primitive behaviours.

Although the demographic group of Britain's criminal underclass cannot be blamed directly for the criminal actions of Moat, I do believe that their encouragement through the media and social networking helped fuel his fantasies and psychosis, which had tragic and devastating consequences for all involved, including the United Kingdom as a whole as it showed that a country that is respected around the world and is seen as the bastion of law and order, was indeed quickly becoming the Marxist lawless society, although for the militant left in society that harboured fantasies of what a Marxist state truly is with its dystopian outlook, the near realisation of a Marxist state for the remainder of society away from the left-wing intelligentsia and chattering classes was quickly turning into a dystopian nightmare for the lower middle and working classes within society.

7. To conclude the criminal profile of Raoul Moat, although his acts were evil and cannot be justified, and he is certainly no hero or a romanticized outlaw, I do believe that the final weeks of his life that lead up to the events of July 3rd – July 10th 2010, could have been brought on due to imbalances within his mental psyche and psychosis. The issue I have is that the earlier crimes committed by Moat were violent and spiteful acts that violated the rights of others. In view of these acts, the earlier criminal acts can only be attributed so much to being raised in a broken and dysfunctional home, however, it must be remembered that many other children suffer with this experience and yet many of them grow up to become law-abiding members of society. Raoul Moat's crimes have not left a legacy as much, however, his criminal actions did show that the moral fabric of British society is waning: a country that was once proud of law and order. There is no way Moat can be classed as a hero as Moat left many people victimised by his selfish acts of brutality. Moat left a man dead and his ex-partner in a critical condition and left a police officer for dead, who later committed suicide due to the events of July 3rd, 2010.

The reaction to Moat's death even prompted the then prime minister, David Cameron, to speak out after flowers were left at the scene of Moat's death and at his home in Newcastle. David Cameron reacted to this act in Parliament by stating; *'It is absolutely clear that Raoul Moat was a callous murderer, full stop, end of story. I cannot understand any wave, however small, of public sympathy for this man. There should be sympathy for the victims and the havoc he wreaked in that community. There should be no sympathy for him.'* (BBC News – 14 July 2010). Although Moat cannot be blamed entirely for the actions of the social underclass, he has shown that this demographic group do indeed exist and are an entity that are completely different from both the values of the working and middle classes and despite what left-wing commentators, politicians, academics et al. state, this demographic group do not respect the laws of the land and they aspire to a state of anomie as opposed to a moral and law-abiding society. Journalists David Randall and Jonathan Owen, when writing for the *Independent* newspaper in 2010 state the following and ask a question, '*He was a violent, jealous man who murdered one and left two more fighting for their lives before, finally turning the gun on himself. Yet, with police facing criticism over their handling of the affair, floral tributes placed outside his (Moat) home portrayed him as a victim. What does this story say about Britain today?*' (Randall and Owen) Indeed, what does the story tell us about Britain today? I believe that it warns us that if the left continues to appease the innate wills and desires of the criminal underclass and continue to treat them as victims rather than the victimisers, then we will continue to see more states of anomie in the forthcoming years within our society with more devastating consequences as cultural Marxism and its destructive doctrines are firmly embedded within out organisations from the police, law courts, law society, education, etc., and the so-called 'right wing' 'conservative' government that has been in power for eleven years at the time of writing has not made any changes to root this dangerous indoctrination out of our institutions and I am afraid to say nothing will change in the near future.

Conclusion

During this book, we have assessed the psychology of some of the worst and most prolific offenders that the world has been unfortunate to have endured as its own custodians at some point or another throughout the last hundred years since criminal and offender profiling began to achieve mainstream precedence as a psychological discipline and an investigative tool. The aim of criminal profiling is to aid investigators to have a better understanding of how the offender or offenders may be psychologically motivated and how they may react if they are facing the prospect of arrest, the dangers that both officers and psychologists may face when they inevitably must deal with them throughout the ensuing interviews to delve into their warped psyches and psychosis.

It must be remembered that criminal psychology and offender profiling is still in its relative infancy, and it is a discipline that has only gained more interest in the past 30 years due to media influence on the subject. The public's fascination on the subject began with the 1991 Hollywood film, *The Silence of the Lambs*, which led to many people wanting to pursue a career in criminal and offender profiling. Following on from the success of the film, the FBI had a surge in female applicants to become agents and criminal profilers as the actress, Jodie Foster, portrayed the heroine of the film, Clarice Starling, and her portrayal helped women achieve a more prominent and equal role in law enforcement. The irony is that when Robert Ressler first termed the label *'serial killer'* in 1974, following on from the arrest of Ted Bundy, there was a female police officer who was working on the Bundy case. The officer in question provided a psychological profile of Ted Bundy (an unknown offender at the time) from his age, mannerisms, use of speech, looks and demeanour, all of which would turn out to be highly accurate and regretfully the officer was derided, and her profile dismissed by her colleagues due to the patriarchal culture that existed in law enforcement during the 1960s and the 1970s. The protagonist and serial killer, Buffalo Bill, was influenced by several serial killers with one of them being Ted Bundy and this is portrayed when 'Bill' pretends that he is injured to snare

CONCLUSION

his prey. If the female officer in question had provided her psychological deduction after the release of *The Silence of the Lambs*, then I have no doubt it would have received much more attention and acclaim. It could have been used to make women on the university campuses much more vigilant and may have slowed Bundy's patterns of serial murder downwards as he would have undoubtedly had to alter his modus operandi or risk being apprehended, and therefore this could have saved more lives in the process as Bundy was actively researching how to evade capture, a point which was made in the report as one of his behavioural traits used to evade capture by moving from state to state to throw law enforcement off his trail.

Hollywood may have helped bring criminal and offender profiling to the forefront of the public's attention, however, it must be remembered that a psychological profile only aids the police in reality once they have the suspect in their custody, and there is no great reason of deduction where everything in the 'jigsaw moment' in a Hollywood film falls into the place and the detective suddenly realises that the serial killer they have chased for so long was known to them all along; this is vehemently never the case and is purely the work of Hollywood, which misleads the public. To the best of my knowledge and my years of extensive research into criminal psychology and serial killers, I am yet to find a case where a psychological profile of an unknown offender has solved a case, hence why criminal profiling is dismissed in a court of law as it is actually not classed as science, and therefore it cannot be used in evidence against a defendant as it can be prejudiced, for example, an offender may have the psychological characteristics on the profile, however, it does not mean that they are guilty of any crimes as many people share similar psychological characteristics. It also does not prove a person or defendant has committed a crime. The most prominent example of when the police used a psychological profile of an offender was when the British psychologist, Paul Britton, provided the police of a profile of an offender in the case of Rachel Nickell, who was stabbed in a frenzied attack on Wimbledon Common in 1992.

The police pursued a local man by the name of Colin Stagg, solely because he fitted the offender profile provided by Paul Britton. This led to the police using an undercover officer to entrap Colin Stag. The case would be later thrown out of court and Colin Stagg would be awarded £706,000 in 2008 due to the behaviour of the police, and this nearly brought down the whole discipline of criminal profiling in the United Kingdom. The behaviour of Paul Britton and the police force brought not only the law and the reputation of the police force into disrepute, and nearly ruined criminal profiling as a respected psychological discipline, it prejudiced the police investigation against an innocent party as Robert Napper, a local schizophrenic who had a history of serious sexual assault and violence against women, would be detained indefinitely at Broadmoor Hospital in 2008 for the murder of Rachel Nickell and two other female victims (one being a child). The police more than likely wanted a quick arrest to satiate the public and allay their fears, however, their behaviour, which was against all the police ethics of the United Kingdom, took the investigation off course and allowed Napper to kill again and commit further sexual assaults and therefore it is imperative that offender profiling is used as an investigative aid and not to be used as 'evidence' of a person's perceived 'guilt', real or imaginable.

It is to the horror and fear of each society that these monsters exist and dwell amongst us, and no criminal profile will suddenly solve a series of grisly murders, and as it stated in Peter 5:8, *'Be sober, be vigilant; because your adversary the Devil walks about like a roaring lion, seeking whom he may devour.'* Serial killers are society's very own modern 'devils' and they exist amongst us with no distinguishable features, and this is what makes them so terrifying as we can be as 'vigilant' as we may wish, however, serial killers are extremely manipulative and human nature and human psychology causes us to drop our initial guard and defences to these monsters. Despite all the media attention on serial killers, and although it is a rare crime as it accounts for less than 1.00% of all murders in the USA, anybody can become a victim of a serial killer or a prolific offender as we have seen throughout the duration of this book.

The terrifying embodiment of a serial killer is that once they have a potential victim in their sights, they usually go to great lengths to snare their prey and it becomes the most primitive of acts, and due to their primitive urges a serial killer will not stop until they have snared their prey, the same way a lion will remain patient until they have their prey in the wild. However, a lion is killing for survival whereas a serial killer is killing for a plethora of psychological motivations which include lust, rage, anger, resentment, excessive sexual desires and urges, frustration, desire etc., and therefore an animal possesses more human qualities as opposed to these devils that appear on the outset at least to be just like you and I.

At the time of writing, due to the current procedures in criminal psychology and the discipline of criminal profiling, I don't believe that a singular profile of an *UNSUB*, apprehending and detaining serial killers and

CONCLUSION

potentially prolific offenders, will change dramatically, however, as criminal psychology and investigative methods advance, it may help the processes involved in catching these offenders. The downside to this is that serial killers can also alter their methods and react to the methods which the investigators are employing as they desperately attempt to stop them, and therefore the truly terrifying aspect of this is that any advancements in investigative and criminal psychology could be negated in their entirety and therefore we could exist in a state of constant continuum and the constant struggle between the forces of good and the forces of evil could be doomed to co-exist.

I do believe, however, that in the end, criminal psychology and offender profiling will eventually lead to a more open and inclusive application for the vacancies in these areas within universities as the jobs will need the best brains possible in this field to counteract the dangers society and individuals face with the menace of serial killers and prolific offenders. These brilliant minds will ultimately have to stare into the abyss, and they will have the abyss staring straight back at them as their work may ultimately save the lives of others and spare families the pain and torment of losing a loved one and spare the society the fear of evil living within their midst. There is still much more work and study to be conducted in the field of offender profiling, however, one can only find the light after travelling through the darkness, and as Carl Jung once stated; *'One does not become enlightened by imagining figures of light, but by making darkness conscious.'*

Sam Hodgins
Sutton Coldfield, West Midlands,
May 2021.

Further reading and research used for the commission of this book

CAYETANO SANTOS GODINO

NCC Home Learning Course Folder – *Diploma in Psychology of Criminal Profiling (2010)* – Copyright NCC Asset Management Ltd 2010 – ISBN No 978-1-907937-04-0.
Chapter 2: Cayetano Santos Godino
(Pages 23 -38)

NCC Home Learning Course Folder – *Diploma in Forensic Psychology (2010)* – Copyright NCC Asset Management Ltd 2010 – ISBN No 978-1-906281-94-6 –
Module 4: Serial Killers
(Pages 55-65).

TRUTV (2012) *Serial Killer Myths Exposed: Myth Number 7 – Signature is the mark of a serial killer.* (Brown 2008))
Available at: http://www.trutv.com/library/crime/criminal_mind/profiling/s_k_myths/index.html
(Accessed 9th January 2013)

CBC News (2006). *Why do Serial Killers target sex workers?*
Author: Professor Steven Egger
Available at: http://www.cbc.ca/news/background/crime/targeting-sex workers.html
(Accessed 11th January 2013 at 18:25).

FURTHER READING AND RESEARCH

Book: *The Shocking True Story of One of America's Most Notorious Female Serial Killers! - Lethal Intent (2002)*
Author: Sue Russell (Page 511)
ISBN Number: 0-7860 – 1518-7
Publisher: Pinnacle Press

Author: *McLeod, Sam*
Website: *Simply Psychology*
Article: *Erik Erikson Developmental Psychology*
Available at: http://www.simplypsychology.org/Erik-Erikson.html
Published and Last Updated: **2008 and Updated 2013**
References to: *Mcleod 2008*
(Accessed on Saturday 19th July 2014)

Author: *McDermot, David Dr*
Website: *Decision Making Confidence and Psychology*
Article: *Sexual Psychopaths*
Available at:
http://www.decision-making-confidence.com/sexual-psychopaths.html
Published and Last Updated: **2006**
References to: *McDermott 2006 citing the works of Cleckley 1941*
(Accessed on Saturday 19th July 2014)

Author: *Wade, Lisa PhD*
Website: *The Society Pages*
Article: *U.S. Racial/Ethnic Demographics: 1960, Today and 2050*
Available at:
http://thesocietypages.org/socimages/2012/11/14/u-s-racialethnic-demographics-1960-today-and-2050/
Published and Last Updated: *November 14th, 2012 at 11:01am*
References to *Lisa Wade*
(Accessed on Saturday 19th July 2014)

Author: *Morton, Hilts, Johns, Keel et al*
Website: *Federal Bureau of Investigation*
Article: *Serial Murder: Mutli-Disciplinary Perspectives for Investigators*
Available at: http://www.fbi.gov/stats-services/publications/serial-murder
Published and Last Updated: *Friday 2nd September 2005.*

References to *Morton, Hilts, Johns, Keel et al*
(Accessed on Saturday 19th July 2014)

HAROLD FREDERICK SHIPMAN

NCC Home Learning Course Folder – *Diploma in Psychology of Criminal Profiling (2010)* – Copyright NCC Asset Management Ltd 2010 – ISBN No 978-1-907937-04-0.
Module 10- Case Study 9: Harold Frederick Shipman
(Pages 151 -186)

Author: **Williams, Katherine S.**
Book Title: **5TH Edition Textbook on Criminology**
Chapter 2: **Public conceptions and misconceptions of crime**
Sub-Section: **3.4.2 White-collar crime**
References to: (*Williams 2005 page 55*)
Publisher: *Oxford University Press*
ISBN 0 19-926440-6

Author: **Leslie, David**
Book Title: **Serial Killers: Harold Shipman – Doctor Death**
Chapter 1: **Introduction**
References to: (*Leslie 1999 page 7*)
Publisher: *Chameleon Press Group*
ISBN 9 772044 0306017

Author: **Cherry, Kendra**
Website: **Education Psychology**
Article: **Stages of Psychosocial Development**
Available at:
http://psychology.about.com/od/psychosocialtheories/a/psychosocial_2.htm
Last Updated and Published: April 7th, 2013
References to: (*Cherry 2009 citing Erikson*)
(Accessed on Friday 4th October 2013 at 10:40)

FURTHER READING AND RESEARCH

Author: *Lynn Scott, Shirley*
Website: *Crime Library*
Article: *What Makes Serial Killers Tick*
Chapter 12: *Lustmord*
Available at:
http://www.trutv.com/library/crime/serial_killers/notorious/tick/lust_7.html Last Updated and Published: April 2011
References to: *(Lynn Scott 2011)*
(Accessed on Tuesday 8th October 2013)

Author: *Sarah Scott McCready B.A.*
Report: *Serial Killing Myths Versus Reality: A Content Analysis of Serial Killer Movies Made Between 1980 and 2001*
Available at:
http://digital.library.unt.edu/ark:/67531/metadc3228/m2/1/high_res_d/thesis.pdf Last Updated and Published: August 2002
References to: *(McCready and McCready cites Rossmo 1995)*
(Accessed on Tuesday 8th October 2013 at 19:04)

Author: *Connor, Steve*
Website: *Psychological Profile of a Narcissistic Control Freak – Shipman: The Murder*
Available at:
http://tonymusings.blogspot.co.uk/2008/03/harold-shipmans-motivation-trauma-or.html
Last Updated and Published: Saturday 6th January 2001
References to: *(Connor 2001)*
(Accessed on Wednesday 9th October 2013 at 18:52)

Author: *BBC News*
Website: *BBC News*
Article: *In Depth: Profile of a killer doctor*
Available at:
http://news.bbc.co.uk/1/hi/in_depth/uk/2000/the_shipman_murders/the_shipman_files/611013.stm
Last Updated and Published: Monday 31st January 2000 at 21:35 GMT
References to: *(Badcock 2000)*
(Accessed on Thursday 24th October at 18:41)

FURTHER READING AND RESEARCH

Author: **Wilson, David**
Website: **The Guardian Newspaper**
Article: **Shipman's Grim Legacy**
Available at: http://www.theguardian.com/uk/2006/jan/13/shipman.health
Last Updated and Published: Friday 13th January 2006
References to: *(Wilson 2006)*
(Accessed on Friday 25th October 2013 at 18:30)

Authors: **Putwain, David and Sammons, Aidan**
Book Title: *Psychology and Crime*
Chapter 2: *The Nature and Measurement of Offending*
References to: *(Putwain and Sammons 2002 cite Rotter 1966)*
Publisher: *Routledge Modular Psychology Series*
ISBN 0-415-25300-4

Author: **Lane, Brian and Gregg, Wilfred**
Book Title: *The Encyclopaedia of Serial Killers*
Chapter 1: *Introductions*
References to: *(Lane and Gregg 1992)*
Publisher: *Headline Book Publishing*
ISBN 0-7472-0461-6

PETER SUTCLIFFE, THE YORKSHIRE RIPPER

NCC Home Learning Course Folder – **Diploma in Psychology of Criminal Profiling (2010)** – Copyright NCC Asset Management Ltd 2010 – ISBN No 978-1-907937-04-0.
Module 7: Case Study 6 – *Peter Sutcliffe – The Yorkshire Ripper*
(Pages 99-122)

NCC Home Learning Course Folder – **Diploma in Forensic Psychology (2010) –**
Copyright NCC Asset Management Ltd 2010 – ISBN No 978-1-906281-94-6 –
Module 4: Serial Killers
References to: *(NCC Dip FPsy, Page 58)*.
(Pages 55-65).

FURTHER READING AND RESEARCH

Author: *Mackay, Mark*
Website: *The Mirror Online*
Article: *'I Couldn't Breathe at All': How Terrified Young Woman Talked Murderer Out of Strangling Her*
Available at:
http://www.mirror.co.uk/news/real-life-stories/talked-murderer-out-strangling-me-1788850
Last Updated: 28th March 2013 at 02:00
References to: *(Mackay 2013)*
(Accessed on Saturday 25th May 2013 at 11:46)

Author: *Wilson, Colin and Damon*
Book Title: *The World's Most Evil Murderers*
Article: *Peter Sutcliffe the 'Yorkshire Ripper'*
References to: *(Wilson and Wilson, 2006, page 70).*
Publisher: *Parragon Publishing*
ISBN-13 978-1-0454-8828-0

Author: *Canter, David*
Book Title: *Inside the Mind of The Serial Killer: Criminal Shadows*
Chapter: *Criminal Maps*
References to: *Canter (1994, page 116)*
Publisher: *Harper Collins Publishing*
ISBN 0 00 2552159

Author: *Cawthorne, Nigel*
Book Title: *The World's Greatest Serial Killers*
Chapter 18: *The Yorkshire Ripper (Pages 99 – 111)*
References to: *(Cawthorne, 2000, page 101 and 102).*
Publisher: *Chancellor Press*
ISBN 10: 0-753700-89-1

Author: *Steel, Fiona*
Website: *Crime Library*
Article: *Peter Sutcliffe*
Available at:
http://www.trutv.com/library/crime/serial_killers/predators/sutcliffe/epilogue_13.html

FURTHER READING AND RESEARCH

Last Updated: May 11th, 2012 at 01:51am
References to: *(Steel, 2012)*
(Accessed on Thursday 13th June 2013 at 19:07pm)

Author: *Greig, Charlotte*
Book Title: **Evil Serial Killers: In the Minds of Monsters**
Chapter: **Ruthless Rippers Pages 140 – 160 (Peter Sutcliffe – 156 -159)**
References to: (*Greig 2009, Page 156*)
Publisher: *Arcturus Press*
ISBN 978-1-84193-460-0

Authors: *Egger, Steven and Boyd, Neil*
Website: **CBC News – in Depth**
Article: **Why Serial Killers Target Sex Workers**
Available at: http://www.cbc.ca/news/background/crime/targeting-sex workers.html
Last Updated: December 19th, 2006
References to: *(Egger and Boyd, 2006)*
(Accessed on Tuesday 18th June 2013 at 17:36)

Authors: *Siddique, Haroon*
Website: **The Guardian Newspaper**
Article: **Mother Didn't Know Suffolk Murders Victim Was a Prostitute**
Available at:
http://www.guardian.co.uk/uk/2008/jan/22/ukcrime.haroonsiddique
Last Updated: Tuesday 22nd January 2008 at 17:24 GMT
References to: *(Siddique, 2008)*
(Accessed on Tuesday 18th June 2013 at 17:49)

Authors: *Goodchild, Sophie*
Website: **The Independent Newspaper Online**
Article: **Yorkshire Ripper 'Has Admitted More Attacks'**
Available at:
http://www.independent.co.uk/news/yorkshire-ripper-has-admitted-more-attacks-1353965.html
Last Updated: Sunday 24th November 1996
References to: *(Goodchild, 1996)*
(Accessed on Tuesday 18th June 2013 at 18:09)

FURTHER READING AND RESEARCH

Author: *Lane, Brian and Gregg, Wilfred*
Book Title: **The Encyclopaedia of Serial Killers**
Chapter: **Peter Sutcliffe: The Yorkshire Ripper**
References to: *(Lane and Gregg, 1992).*
Publisher: *Headline Book Press Publishing*
ISBN-0-7472-0461-6

Author: *Canter, David, Professor*
Book Title: **Mapping Murder**
Chapter: **Marauding Criminals – 12 Criminal Gravity**
References to: *(Canter, 2003 Page 159).*
Publisher: *Virgin Books*
ISBN 978 0 7535 1326 2

Author: *Wilson, David (Professor)*
Book Title: **A History of British Serial Killing**
Chapter 7: **'It sounds a bit evil now': Prostitutes**
References to: *(Wilson 2009, page 161)*
Publisher: *Sphere Press*
ISBN 978-0-7515-4100-7

Author: *Steel, Fiona*
Website: **Crime Library**
Sub-section: **Sexual Predators**
Article: **Peter Sutcliffe – Red Herring**
Available at: http://www.trutv.com/library/crime/serial_killers/predators/sutcliffe/herring_10.html Last Updated: January 17th 2001 at 10:02 am
References to: *(Steel, 2001)*
(Accessed on Wednesday 3rd July 2013 at 18:16)

ALBERT DESALVO, THE BOSTON STRANGLER

NCC Home Learning Course Folder – **Diploma in Psychology of Criminal Profiling (2010)** – Copyright NCC Asset Management Ltd 2010 – ISBN No 978-1-907937-04-0.
Module 6: Case Study 5 – *Albert DeSalvo the Boston Strangler* (Pages 81–98)

FURTHER READING AND RESEARCH

Author: *Morton J, Robert*
Website: ***The FBI (Federal Bureau of Investigation)***
Article: ***Serial Murder: Multi-Disciplinary Perspectives for Investigators – Behavioural Analysis Unit National Center For the Analysis of Violent Crime***
Available at:
http://www.fbi.gov/stats-services/publications/serial-murder#content
Last Updated: September 2nd, 2005
References to: (*Morton, J Robert, 2005*)
(Accessed on Saturday 4th May 2013 at 09:06)

Author: *Bardsley, Marilyn*
Website: ***Crime Library: Criminal Minds and Methods***
Article: ***The Boston Strangler – Chapter 1: Controversy***
Available at:
http://www.trutv.com/library/crime/serial_killers/notorious/boston/index_1.html
Last Updated: August 21st, 2012
References to: (*Bardsley, Marilyn*)
(Accessed on Saturday 4th May 2013 at 09:48)

Author: *Lynn Scott, Shirley*
Website: ***Crime Library: Criminal Minds and Methods***
Article: ***What Makes Serial Killers Tick?***
Available at:
http://www.trutv.com/library/crime/serial_killers/notorious/tick/1b.html
Last Updated: March 21st, 2012
References to: (*Lynn Scott, 2011*)
(Accessed on Saturday 4th May 2013 at 10:43)

Author: *Vernon J Geberth M.S., MPS.*
Website: ***Practical Homicide***
Article: ***Psychopathic Sexual Sadists: The Psychology and Psychodynamics of Serial Killers***
Available at: http://www.practicalhomicide.com/articles/psexsad.htm
Last Updated: 4th April 1995
References to: (*Geberth 1995 cites Meloy 1992*)
(Accessed on Saturday 4th May 2013 at 11:28)

FURTHER READING AND RESEARCH

Author: *Roland, Paul*
Book Title: ***In the Minds of Murderers***
Chapter 4: ***Profiling in Practice***
References to: (Roland, 2007, Pages 125-125)
Publisher: *Arcturus Publishing Limited (2007)*
ISBN 978-0-572-03376-7

Author: *Montaldo, Charles*
Website: ***About.com: Crime and Punishment***
Article: ***Characteristics of the Psychopathic Personality***
Available at: http://crime.about.com/od/serial/a/psychopaths.htm
Last Updated: 2013
References to: *Cleckley (1941) as cited by Montaldo (2013)*
(Accessed on Tuesday 7th May 2013 at 18:36)

Author: *Ainsworth, B. Peter*
Book Title: ***Offender Profiling and Crime Analysis***
Chapter 9: ***Current Developments and Future Prospects: Sub-Heading 3 – Stalking***
References to: *(Ainsworth, 2001, Page 171)*
Publisher: *Willian Publishing*
ISBN 978-1-903240-21-2

Author: *Johnston E. Joni*
Website: ***Psychology Today***
Article: ***The Human Equation: Female Serial Killers***
Available at:
http://www.psychologytoday.com/blog/the-human-equation/201205/female-serial-killers
Last Updated: May 29th, 2012
References to: *(Johnston, 2012)*
(Accessed on Wednesday 8th May 2013 at 19:21)

Author: *Sycamnias, Evan*
Website: ***Uplink Law Library, Australia***
Article: ***Evaluating a Psychological Profile of a Serial Killer***
Available at:
http://www.uplink.com.au/lawlibrary/Documents/Docs/Doc5.html

Last Updated: May 29th, 2012
References to: *(Sycamnias, 1998)*
(Accessed on Wednesday 8th May 2013 at 19:37)

Author: *Ramsland, Katherine*
Website: **Crime Library: Criminal Minds and Methods**
Article: **The Fetish Killer: Jerry Brudos**
Available at:
http://www.trutv.com/library/crime/serial_killers/predators/jerry_brudos/8.html
Last Updated: January 20th, 2013
References to: *(Ramsland, 2012)*
(Accessed on Thursday 9th May 2013)

Author: *Ramsland, Katherine*
Website: **Crime Library: Criminal Minds and Methods**
Article: **The Fetish Killer: Jerry Brudos**
Available at:
http://www.trutv.com/library/crime/serial_killers/predators/jerry_brudos/18.html
Last Updated: March 28th, 2006
References to: *(Ramsland, 2006)*
(Accessed on Saturday 11th May 2013 at 09:50)

NCC Home Learning Course Folder – **Diploma in Criminal Psychology (2010)**
ISBN –No. 978-1-906281-71-7
Module 12 – Violence, Psychopathy and Anti-Social Personality Disorder
References to: *(NCCHL DipCPSY, Page 174)*
(Pages 172 – 193)

Author: *Brain, Christine*
Book Title: **Edexcel A2 Psychology**
Chapter 2: **Child Psychology – Methodology**
References to: *(Brain, 2009) cites Bowlby (1953)*
Publisher: *Hodder Education*
ISBN 978-0340-96684-6

FURTHER READING AND RESEARCH

Author: *Johnson, J*
Website: **National Justice Education Programme**
Article: **Intimate Partner Sexual Abuse: Adjudicating This Hidden Dimension of Domestic Violence Cases**
Module XII: **Orders of Protection, Pre-trial Release, Determinations and Dispositions**
Sub-Article: **Psychopaths are Not Good Candidates for Any Type of Treatment**
Available at:
http://www.trutv.com/library/crime/serial_killers/predators/jerry_brudos/18.html
Last Updated: March 28th, 2006
References to: *(Ramsland, 2006)*
(Accessed on Saturday 11th May 2013 at 09:50)

Author: *Golgowski, Nina*
Website: **Daily Mail**
Article: **'I May Have Eaten a Body Part': How Serial Killer and Cannibal Jeffrey Dahmer Still Haunts Survivors and His Neighbours Decades Later**
Available at:
http://www.dailymail.co.uk/news/article-2279444/I-eaten-body-How-Jeffrey-Dahmer-haunts-survivors-neighbors-decades-later.html
Last Updated: 15th February 2013 at 23:03
References to: *(Golgowski, 2013)*
(Accessed on Thursday 16th May 2013 at 18:32)

JOHN GEORGE HAIGH, AKA THE ACID BATH MURDERER

NCC Home Learning Course Folder – **Diploma in Psychology of Criminal Profiling (2010)** – Copyright NCC Asset Management Ltd 2010 – ISBN No 978-1-907937-04-0.
Module 5: Case Study 4 – **John George Haigh: The Acid Bath Murderer** (Pages 65 – 80)

FURTHER READING AND RESEARCH

AOL News (2010) Article: ***Expert, No Surprise Cleveland Victims Strangled***
Author: Lohr, David
References to (Safarik, 2010)
Available at:
http://www.aolnews.com/2010/04/04/expert-no-surprise-cleveland-victims-strangled
Last Updated: April 4th, 2010 at 06:15pm
(Accessed Friday 29th March 2013)

Author: Cawthorne, Nigel
Book Title: ***The World's Greatest Serial Killers***
Chapter 14 – Jeffrey Dahmer: The Milwaukee Cannibal (Pages 81 -88)
Published by *Chancellor Press (2000)*
ISBN 10: 0-753700-89-1

Crime and Punishment Website Article: ***Why killers target sex workers***
Author: *James Alan Fox*
Reference Used: (J.A. Fox, 2011)
Available at: http://boston.com/community/blogs/crime_punishment/2011/04/why_killers_target_sex workers.html
Last Updated: April 15th, 2011 at 12:00pm
(Accessed Wednesday 10th April 2013 at 17:49)

Crime Library Article: ***What Makes Serial Killers Tick?***
Author: *Shirley Lynn Scott*
References Used: (Scott 2012) and Ressler (1988)
Available at:
http://www.trutv.com/library/crime/serial_killers/notorious/tick/5b.html
Last Updated: April 27th, 2012 at 14:33
(Accessed Wednesday 10th April 2013 at 18:43)

NCC Home Learning Course Folder – ***Diploma in Criminal Psychology***
Copyright NCC Asset Management Ltd 2009 – ISBN No 978-1-906281-71-7
Chapter 13 – *Crime and Psychology*
References Used: *Alison et al (2002) and* (NCCHL – Dip in CPsy, Page 199).
Published by NCC Resources Ltd

FURTHER READING AND RESEARCH

Internet Article: ***How to get in the mind of a serial killer***
Author: Dvorsky, George (2012)
Available at:
http://io9.com/5954476/how-to-get-inside-the-mind-of-a-serial-killer
Last Updated: 24th October 2012 at 09:52 am
(Accessed on Sunday 14th April 2013 at 11:09)

Author: *Litchfield, Michael*
Book Title: ***The Cutter***
Chapter 1 – *Shattered Lives*
References to: (Litchfield, 2011, page 16)
Publisher: *John Blake Publishing (2011)*
ISBN 978-1-84358-358-5

Internet Article: ***What Motivates Serial Killers to Kill***
Author: *Blake, J. (2007)*
Available at:
http://twistedminds.creativescapism.com/psychological-disorders/motives/
Last Updated: 2007
References to: (Blake 2007)
(Accessed on Sunday 21st April 2013 at 09:48)

Author: *Owen, David*
Book Title: ***Criminal Minds: The Science and Psychology of Profiling***
Chapter 3 – *At the Crime Scene*
References to: (Owen, D, 2004, Page 52)
Publisher: *New Burlington Books*
ISBN 1-86155-421-4

Author: *Lane, Brian and Gregg, Wilfred*
Book Title: ***The Encyclopaedia of Serial Killers***
Chapter – *Introductions*
References to: (Lane and Gregg, 1990, Page 13)
Publisher: *Headline Press*
ISBN 0-7472-0461-6

FURTHER READING AND RESEARCH

Internet Website: *The Psychopath's Relationship Cycle: Idealize, Devalue and Discard*
Author: *Moscovici, Claudia (2010)*
Available at: http://psychopathyawareness.wordpress.com/2010/12/22/the-psychopaths-relationship-cycle-idealize-devalue-and-discard/
Last Updated: December 30th, 2011 at 08:51
References to: (Moscovici, 2010 and Hare and Babiak, 2007)
(Accessed on Monday 22nd April 2013 at 18:36)

Internet Article: *Randy Kraft, The Freeway Killer*
Author: *Newton, Michael (2012)*
Chapter 1: *Moving Violation*
Available at: http://www.trutv.com/library/crime/serial_killers/predators/kraft/1.html
References to: (Newton, 2012)
Last Updated: October 11th, 2012 at 10:13
(Accessed Tuesday 23rd April 2013 at 18:48)

About.com Website – Crime and Punishment Article: *Characteristics of the Psychopathic Personality*
Author: *Montaldo, Charles*
Reference Used: (Montaldo, C 2013 citing Cleckley, 1941)
Available at: http://crime.about.com/od/serial/a/psychopaths.htm
Last Updated: 2013
(Accessed Tuesday 24th April at 18:08)

Author: *Wilson, Colin and Seaman, Donald*
Book Title: *The Serial Killers: A Study in the Psychology of Violence*
Chapter 7: *The Roman Emperor Syndrome*
References to: (Wilson, C and Seaman, D, 2007)
Publisher: *Virgin Books*
ISBN 978-0-7535-1321-7

Author: *Wilson, David, Professor*
Book Title: *A History of British Serial Killing*
Chapter 1: *Society's biggest plague*
References to: (Wilson, D, 2009, Page 20)
Publisher: *Sphere Media*
ISBN 9 780751 541007

FURTHER READING AND RESEARCH

Author: *Lambert, Timothy (2012)*
Article: ***A Brief History of Life Expectancy in Britain***
Available at: http://www.localhistories.org/life.html
Last Updated: 2012
References to: (Lambert, T, 2012)
(Accessed on Saturday 27th April at 11:28)

Author: *Bell, Rachael*
Article: ***Ted Bundy: Chapter 3 – A Time of Change***
Available at:
http://www.trutv.com/library/crime/serial_killers/notorious/bundy/3.html
Last Updated: October 2nd, 2012 at 09:53pm
References to: (Bell, R, 2009)
(Accessed on Monday 29th April 2013 at 17:44)

Author: *Ramsland, Katherine*
Article: ***The Fetish Killer: Chapter 8 – Troubled Teens***
Available at:
http://www.trutv.com/library/crime/serial_killers/predators/jerry_brudos/8.html
Last Updated: January 20th, 2013 at 08:39am
References to: (Ramsland, K, 2013)
(Accessed on Monday 29th April 2013 at 18:10)

DENIS NILSEN

NCC Home Learning Course Folder – ***Diploma in Psychology of Criminal Profiling (2010)*** – Copyright NCC Asset Management Ltd 2010 – ISBN No 978-1-907937-04-0.
Module 9: Case Study 8: Denis Nilsen
(Pages 139 – 150)

Author: *Greig, Charolotte*
Book Title: ***Evil Serial Killers: In the Minds of Monsters***
Chapter 8: ***Sadistic Stranglers***
References to: (*Greig 2009 Pages 153 – 156*)

Publisher: *Arcturus Press*
ISBN 978 – 1 -84193-460-0

Author: *Cawthorne, Nigel*
Book Title: **The World's Greatest Serial Killers**
Chapter 13: **Denis Nilsen**
References to: (*Cawthorne pages 73-81*)
Publisher: *Chancellor Press*
ISBN 13: 978-0-753700-89-1

Author: *Wilson, David, Professor*
Book Title: **Serial Killers: Hunting Britons and their Victims, 1960 -2006**
Chapter 6: **'To kill undetected:' Gay Men.**
References to: (*David Wilson, 2009, page 136 -163*)
Publisher: *Waterside Press*
ISBN 978 1904380 33 7

Author: *Wilson, David*
Website: **The Scotsman Online**
Article: **A Life of Crime: Professor David Wilson – Trying to Understand Why Serial Killers Kill**
Available at:
http://www.scotsman.com/lifestyle/books/a-life-of-crime-professor-david-wilson-trying-to-understand-why-serial-killers-kill-1-816044
Last Updated and Published: 4th July 2010 at 20:47
References to: (*Wilson 2010*)
(Accessed on Wednesday 7th August 2013 at 19:02)

Author: *Kocsis, Richard N. PhD*
Book Title: **Criminal Profiling: International Theory, Research, and Practice**
Chapter 4: **Murder by Manual and Ligature Strangulation: Profiling Crime Scene Behaviour and Offender Characteristics**
References to: (*Kocsis 2007 page 75*)
Publisher: *Human Press inc.*
ISBN 978-1-60327-146-2

FURTHER READING AND RESEARCH

Author: *Strack, Gael B and McClane, George*
Report: **How to Improve Your Investigation and Prosecution of Strangulation Cases**
Available at: http://www.ncdsv.org/images/strangulation_article.pdf
Last Updated and Published: October 1998 and Updated May 1999
References to: *(Strack and McClane 1998)*
(Accessed on Tuesday 13th August 2013 at 19:02)

Author: *Cowling, Emma*
Internet Site: **The Scotsman Newspaper**
Article: **Denis Nilsen: The Making of a Serial Killer**
Available at:
http://www.scotsman.com/news/dennis-nilsen-the-making-of-a-serial-killer-1-769305
Last Updated: 24TH November 2009 at 09:11
References to: *(Cowling 2009)*
(Accessed on Friday 15th August 2013 at 18:32)

Author: *McCready, Sarah Scott*
Report: **Serial Killing Myths Versus Reality: A Content Analysis of Serial Killer Motives Made Between 1980 and 2001**
Available at:
http://digital.library.unt.edu/ark:/67531/metadc3228/m2/1/high_res_d/thesis.pdf
Published: *University of North Texas, USA, August 2002*
References to: *(McCready 2002)*
(Accessed on Saturday 17th August 2013 at 08:27)

Newspaper: *The Mail Online*
Report: **Serial Killer Dennis Nilsen Confesses to First Murder**
Available at:
http://www.dailymail.co.uk/news/article-415443/Serial-killer-Dennis-Nilsen-confesses-murder.html
Published: 9th November 2006
Last Updated: 12:00 9th November 2006
References to: *(Daily Mail Newspaper Article 2006)*
(Accessed on Saturday 17th August 2013 at 08:50)

FURTHER READING AND RESEARCH

Author: *Wilson, David, Professor*
Book Title: ***Serial Killers: Hunting Britons and their Victims, 1960 -2006***
Chapter 6: ***'To kill undetected:' Gay Men.***
References to: (*David Wilson, 2009, page 136 -163*)
Publisher: *Waterside Press*
ISBN 978 1904380 33 7

Author: *Williams, Katherine S.*
Book Title: ***5TH Edition Textbook on Criminology***
Chapter 8: ***Psychological Theories of Crime***
Sub-Section: ***8.2.2 Formation of the super-ego***
References to: (*Williams 2005 page 173*)
Publisher: *Oxford University Press*
ISBN 0 19-926440-6

Newspaper: *The Guardian Online*
Report: ***Margaret Thatcher: A Life in Quotes***
Available at: http://www.theguardian.com/politics/2013/apr/08/margaret-thatcher-quotes
Published: Monday 8th April at 13:38 BST
Last Updated: 13:38 Monday 8th April 2013
References to: (*Thatcher 1987 – cited in the Guardian Newspaper 8th April 2013*).
(Accessed on Friday 13th September 2013 at 18:19)

Website: ***Psychology Today***
Section: ***The Legacy of Distorted Love***
Article: ***Why Am I So Afraid of Being Alone?***
Available at:
http://www.psychologytoday.com/blog/the-legacy-distorted-love/201109/why-am-i-so-afraid-being-alone
Published: September 3rd, 2011
Last Updated: September 3rd, 2011
References to: (*McBride 2011 cites Falk 2007*)
(Accessed on Saturday 14th September 2013 at 18:19)

FURTHER READING AND RESEARCH

JOHN WAYNE GACY

NCC Home Learning Course Folder – *Diploma in Psychology of Criminal Profiling (2010)* – Copyright NCC Asset Management Ltd 2010 – ISBN No 978-1-907937-04-0.
Module 8: Case Study 7: John Wayne Gacy
(Pages 123 – 138)

Author: *Wichita Eagle News Archives*
Website: *Wichita Eagle Kansas*
Article: *BTK suspect's minister reacts in sermon* (Published Monday March 12th, 2007)
Available at: http://www.kansas.com/2005/02/27/16529/btk-suspects-minister-reacts-in.html
Last Updated: Wednesday 10th July 2013 at 07:42 am
References to: *(Wichita News Article, 2007)*
(Accessed on Thursday 11th July at 17:53)

Author: *Lynn Scott, Shirley*
Website: *Crime Library*
Article: *What Makes Serial Killers Tick?*
Chapter 1: *Monsters or Victims? What they are and who they kill*
Available at:
http://www.trutv.com/library/crime/serial_killers/notorious/tick/victims_1.html
Last Updated: February 16th, 2012 at 10:08 am
References to: *(Lynn-Scott, 2010)*
(Accessed on Thursday 11th July at 18:10)

Author: *Ainsworth, Peter.B.*
Book Title: *Offender Profiling and Crime Analysis*
Chapter 6: *Early Approaches to Profiling: Further Classifications of Rapists*
References to: *(Ainsworth 2001, page 106).*
Publisher: *Willan Publishing*
ISBN 978-1-903240-21-2

FURTHER READING AND RESEARCH

Author: *Moscovici, Claudia*
Website: *Psychopathy Awareness*
Article: *Dangerous Mind Games: How Psychopaths Manipulate and Deceive*
Available at: http://psychopathyawareness.wordpress.com/2011/09/13/dangerous-mind-games-how-psychopaths-manipulate-and-deceive/
Last Updated: 13th September 2011 at 01:04pm
References to: *(Moscovici 2011)*
(Accessed on Thursday 11th July at 19:06)

Author: *Thomas, Natalie*
Website: *The Telegraph*
Article: *KFC boss offers food for thought with a degree course*
Available at:
http://www.telegraph.co.uk/finance/newsbysector/retailandconsumer/9418980/KFC-boss-offers-food-for-thought-with-degree-course.html
Last Updated: 09:30 BST 22nd July 2012
References to: *(Thomas 2012)*
(Accessed on Monday 15th July 2013 at 18:08)

Author: *Wilson, David, Professor*
Book Title: *Serial Killers: Hunting Britons and their Victims, 1960 -2006*
Chapter 6: *Children (Pages 147 – 171)*
References to: *(David Wilson, 2008, page 167)*
Publisher: *Waterside Press*
ISBN 978 1904380 33 7

Author: *Cohen, Jonathan*
Website: *Science Daily*
Article: *Brain Differences in Adolescents, Psychopaths, Lend to Their Impulsive Risk-Taking Behaviour*
Available at:
http://www.sciencedaily.com/releases/2004/10/041030131905.htm
Last Updated: November 2nd, 2004
References to: *(Cohen 2004)*
(Accessed on Tuesday 16th July 2013 at 17:51)

FURTHER READING AND RESEARCH

Author: **Greig, Charolotte**
Book Title: **Evil Serial Killers: In the Minds of Monsters**
Chapters **2 – Crazed Cannibals and 10 – Ruthless Ripers**
References to: (*Greig 2009 Pages 22 and 153*)
Publisher: *Arcturus Press*
ISBN 978 – 1 -84193-460-0

Author: **Montaldo, Charles**
Website: **About.com Crime and Punishment**
Article: **Profile of Serial Killer Jeffrey Dahmer**
Available at: http://crime.about.com/od/serial/a/dahmer_2.htm
Last Updated: 2012
References to: (*Montaldo 2012*)
(Accessed on Tuesday 16th July 2013 at 18:32)

Author: **Staff, Duncan**
Book Title: **The Lost Boy: The definitive story of the Moors murders and the search for the final victim.**
Chapter 4: (Chapters in this text do not have subchapter titles)
References to: (*Staff 2009 Page 149*).
Publisher: *Transworld Publishers*
ISBN 978-0-593-06078-0

Author: **Ramsland, Katherine**
Website: **Crime Library**
Article: **Serial Killer Groupies: Male Bonding**
Available at:
http://www.trutv.com/library/crime/criminal_mind/psychology/s_k_groupies/9.html
Last Updated: May 8th, 2013 at 16:06
References to: (*Ramsland 2011*)
(Accessed on Friday 26th July 2013 at 18:36)

Author: **Cahill, Tim**
Book Title: **Buried Dreams: Inside the Mind of a Serial Killer**
Chapter 6: ***(Chapters are not provided with a sub-title)***
References to: (*Cahill 1986, page 184*)
Publisher: *MC Productions inc.*
ISBN 0-553-25836-2

Author: **Lynn Scott, Shirley**
Website: *Crime Library*
Article: *What Makes Serial Killers Tick*
Chapter 10: *Psychopaths? Twisted Rationalizations*
Available at: http: http://www.trutv.com/library/crime/serial_killers/notorious/tick/psych_6.html
Last Updated: July 15th, 2013 at 2:06pm
References to: *(Lynn Scott, 2009)*
(Accessed on Saturday 26th July 2013 at 10:36)

Author: **Hogenboom, Mellisa**
Website: *BBC News Science*
Article: *Psychopathic Criminals have empathy switch*
Available at: http://www.bbc.co.uk/news/science-environment-23431793
Last Updated: 25th July 2013 at 01:59
References to: *(Hogenboom 2013)*
(Accessed on Saturday 26th July 2013 at 11:02)

Author: **Britton, Paul**
Book Title: *Picking Up the Pieces*
Chapter 23: *Chapters are not sub-headed.*
References to: *(Britton 2000 page 493)*.
Publisher: *Corgi Books*
ISBN 0-552-147187

Author: **Owen, David**
Book Title: *Criminal Minds: The Science and Psychology of Profiling*
Chapter 6: *Power and Anger*
References to: *(Owen 2004 pages 103 -106)*
Publisher: *New Burlington Books*
ISBN 1-86155-421-4

FURTHER READING AND RESEARCH

PETER KURTEN, THE VAMPIRE OF DUSSELDORF

NCC Home Learning Course Folder – *Diploma in Psychology of Criminal Profiling (2010)* – Copyright NCC Asset Management Ltd 2010 – ISBN No 978-1-907937-04-0.
Module 3: Case Study 2 – *Peter Kurten – The Monster of Dusseldorf* (Pages 39 – 52)

Author: *Roland, Paul (2007)*
Book Title – *In the Minds of Murderers*
Chapter 1 – *Footsteps in the Fog*
ISBN 978-0572-03376-7
Published by Arcturus Publishing

Author: *Douglas, John (2012)*
Mindhunters Website Article – *Why Killers Take Trophies*
Available at: http://mindhuntersinc.com/?s=trophies
(Accessed 17th January 2013 at 18:09 – Last updated October 6th, 2012)

Author: *Gilbert, Alexander (2012)*
Article – *Peter Kurten: The Vampire of Dusseldorf*
Chapter 6 – *Inside the mind of a psychopath*
Available at: http://www.trutv.com/library/crime/serial_killers/history/kurten/psychopath_6.html
(Accessed 24th January 2013 at 18:18)

Author: *Williams, S. Katherine*
Book Title – *5th Edition Textbook on Criminology*
Chapter 8 – Psychological theories of criminality (Pages 186 -187 – De Burgers and Holmes 1989)
Published by Oxford University Press (2005)
ISBN 0-19-926440-6

Youtube Website Video – *Killers Behind Bars: Series 1 – Peter Tobin*
Produced by Professor David Wilson
Available at: http://www.youtube.com/watch?v=1AT-VKsyDA0 (Time of reference – 44:02)
(Accessed on Wednesday 27th February 2013)

True Crime TV Article on Richard Trenton Chase – *The Making of a Vampire*
Last updated in 2013
Available at: http://www.trutv.com/library/crime/serial_killers/weird/chase/vampire_5.html
(Accessed on Wednesday 27th February 2013 at 15:42)

Book and DVD – *Ted Bundy: Beneath the Mask*
Author of book – David Leslie (2004) and Producer of AandE DVD Biography – Andrew Rothstein (2010)
ISSN 2044-0367
Publisher: Paper view Europe Ltd.

THOMAS HAMILTON, THE DUNBLANE MASSACRE

NCC Home Learning Course Folder – *Diploma in Psychology of Criminal Profiling (2010)* – Copyright NCC Asset Management Ltd 2010 – ISBN No 978-1-907937-04-0.
Chapter(s): *Module 1: An Introduction to Profiling Criminals (Pages 1-22) and Module 11: Case Study 10: Thomas Hamilton: The Dunblane Massacre (Pages 187-198)*
References to: *(NCC Dip PSYCP, Page 7)*

Author: **The Rt. Hon Lord Cullen**
Website: ***The Public Inquiry into the Shootings at Dunblane Primary School on 13th March 1996***
Chapter 3: *Timeline of Events*
Available at: http:
http://www.archive.official-documents.co.uk/document/scottish/dunblane/dunblane.htm
Last Updated and Published: *16th October 1996*
References to: *(W. Douglas Cullen 1996)*
Report ISBN No: 0 10 133862 7 Cm. 3386
(Accessed on Wednesday 27th November 2013 at 12:17pm)

FURTHER READING AND RESEARCH

Authors: **Millon, Theodore; Simonsen Erik; Birket-Smith, Morten and Davis D., Roger**
Book Title: **Psychopathy: Anti-social, Criminal and Violent Behaviour**
Chapter 5: **Evil Intent: Violence and Disorders of the Will**
References to: (*Millon, Simonsen, Davis et al cite Meissner (1979)*)
(*1998 page 79*)
Publisher: *Guildford Press*
ISBN 1-57230-344-1

Author: **Russell, Jonathan**
Website: **High Beam Research**
Article: **'Sick Lord of the Flies'** – *Daily Mirror News Article – March 15th, 1996*
Available at: http: http://www.highbeam.com/doc/1G1-61324064.html
Last Updated and Published: *March 15th, 1996*
References to: (*Russel, J. 1996*)
(Accessed on Thursday 28th November 2013 at 12:44)

Author: **NHS Website**
Website: **NHS Choices – Your Health**
Sub-Website: **Health A-Z**
Article: **Obsessive Compulsive Disorder (OCD)**
Available at:
http://www.nhs.uk/conditions/obsessive-compulsive-disorder/Pages/Introduction.aspx
Last Updated and Published: 30TH September 2013
References to: (*NHS Website*)
(Accessed on Thursday 28th November 2013 at 16:15)

Author: **Grinnell, Rennee**
Website: **PsychCentral**
Article: **'Paranoid Delusion'**
Available at: http://psychcentral.com/encyclopedia/2008/paranoid-delusion/
Last Updated and Published: *24th January 2012*
References to: (*Grinnell 2012*)
(Accessed on Thursday 5th December 2012 at 18:36)

Authors: **Brain, Christine**
Book Title: **Edexcel A2 Psychology**
Chapter 2: **Child Psychology**
References to: (Brain 2009 cites Bowlby 1946 and 1956)
Publisher: Bookpoint Ltd and Hodder Education
ISBN 978-0-340-96884-6

Author: **Winch, Guy (Ph. D)**
Website: **Psychology Today**
Article: **The Squeaky Wheel: How to Attain Real Personal Empowerment**
Available at:
http://www.psychologytoday.com/blog/the-squeaky-wheel/201101/how-attain-real-personal-empowerment
Last Updated and Published: *January 11th, 2011*
References to: *(Winch 2011 cites the work of Cattaneo and Chapman 2010)*
(Accessed on Monday 23rd December 2013 at 18:08)

Author: **McLeod, Saul**
Website: **Simply Psychology**
Article: **Bowlby's Attachment Theory**
Available at: http://www.simplypsychology.org/bowlby.html
Last Updated and Published: September 2007
References to: *(McLeod 2007 cites Bowlby 1946 and 1956)*
(Accessed on Sunday 12th January 2014 at 12:02)

Author: **Groth, A.N.**
Website: **Rapist Typology**
Article: **Men Who Rape**
Available at:
http://www-psychology.concordia.ca/fac/Laurence/forensic/rapists.pdf
Last Updated and Published: January 1979
References to: *(Groth 1979)*
(Accessed on Sunday 12th January 2014 at 12:24)

FURTHER READING AND RESEARCH

Author: **Casciani, Dominic**
Website: **BBC News**
Article: **Analysis: UK Gun Crime Figures**
Available at: http: http://news.bbc.co.uk/1/hi/uk/6960431.stm
Last Updated and Published: *Thursday 31st January 2008 at 16:42GMT*
References to: *(Casciani 2008)*
(Accessed on Sunday 12th January 2014 at 12:56)

DEREK BIRD

NCC Home Learning Course Folder – **Diploma in Psychology of Criminal Profiling (2010)**. Copyright NCC Asset Management Ltd 2010 – ISBN No 978-1-907937-04-0.

Leigh, Claire (2010) – **Massacre in Cumbria** – John Blake Publishing Ltd – ISBN No 978-1-84358-294-6.

BBC News (2010). **Family dispute theory over Cumbria rampage**. (Updated 3 June 2010 at 12:59)
Available at: http://www.bbc.co.uk/news/10222188
(Accessed 27th December 2012 at 18:36)

The Guardian Newspaper. **Derrick Bird talked of suicide before Cumbria shootings, inquest told**. Author: Helen Carter (Wednesday 2nd March 2011 14:56).
Available at: http://www.guardian.co.uk/uk/2011/mar/02/derrick-bird-cumbria-shootings-inquest
(Accessed 27th December 2012 at 19:02)

NCC Home Learning Course Folder – **Diploma in Forensic Psychology (2010)** – Copyright NCC Asset Management Ltd 2010 – ISBN No 978-1-906281-94-6 – Module 4: Serial Killers (Pages 55-65).
BBC News (2010). **'Lucky escape for intended victim' of Derrick Bird**. (Updated 6th June 2010 at 14:59)
Available at: http://www.bbc.co.uk/news/10222161
(Accessed 28th December 2012 at 19:03).

FURTHER READING AND RESEARCH

BBC News (2010). ***Profile: Cumbria gunman, Derrick Bird.*** (Updated 2nd November 2010 at 15:00)
Available at: http://www.bbc.co.uk/news/10216923
(Accessed 28TH December 2012 at 19:22)

The Guardian Online. ***Derrick Bird inquest returns verdict of unlawful killings and suicide.*** Author: Martin Wainwright (2011). (Updated Friday 25th March 2011 at 16:30 GMT)
Available at: http://www.guardian.co.uk/uk/2011/mar/25/derrick-bird-inquest-unlawful-suicide
(Accessed 28th December 2012 at 20:02)

Author: *Wilson David (2009).*
Book Title: ***A History of British Serial Killing: The shocking account of Jack the Ripper, Harold Shipman and beyond.*** –
Publisher: *Sphere Press Publishing – ISBN No 9 780751 541007.*

BBC News (2010). ***Derrick Bird police 'weakness' criticised.*** (Updated 28th March 2011 at 18:24)
Available at: http://www.bbc.co.uk/news/uk-england-cumbria-12884612
(Accessed 29th December 2012 at 12:29)

Daily Mail Online (2011). ***'I'll make Whitehaven as famous as Dunblane': Derrick Bird's sick boast just weeks before the Cumbria Massacre.*** (Updated 3rd March 2011 at 01:18)
Available at:
http://www.dailymail.co.uk/news/article-1362177/Derrick-Bird-inquest-Ill-make-Whitehaven-famous-Dunblane-Cumbria-gunman-said.html
(Accessed 29th December 2012 at 12:59)

The Telegraph Online (2010). ***Cumbria shootings: timeline of Derrick Bird's rampage.*** (Updated 3rd June 2010 at 3:26AM)
Available at:
http://www.telegraph.co.uk/news/uknews/crime/7799723/Cumbria-shootings-timeline-of-Derrick-Birds-rampage.html
(Accessed 29th December 2012 at 13:10)

FURTHER READING AND RESEARCH

Rule, Ann (2012) – *The Stranger Beside Me*
Publisher: Time Warner Paperbacks (1986 – Reprinted 2012) – Chapter 29
ISBN 978-07515-0818-5

Herald Sun Article: *Taxi gunman Derrick Bird goes on killing rampage in Cumbria, in the lake district of England, killing 12 and injuring 25.*
Available at: http://www.heraldsun.com.au/news/victoria/gunman-goes-on-killing-rampage-in-lakes-district-of-britain/story-e6frf7lf-1225874762500
(Accessed 5th January 2013)

Mirror Online Article: – **Killer Derrick Bird was bitter, resentful and depressed, psychologist tells inquest.**
Available at:
http://www.mirror.co.uk/news/uk-news/killer-derrick-bird-was-bitter-resentful-117897
(Accessed 5th January 2013 at 14:20)

RAOUL MOAT

NCC Home Learning Course Folder – *Diploma in Psychology of Criminal Profiling (2010)* – Copyright NCC Asset Management Ltd 2010 – ISBN No 978-1-907937-04-0.
Chapter(s): *Module 1: An introduction to Profiling Criminals (Pages 1-22)*
References to: *(NCC Dip PSYCP, Page 7)*

Author: *Howard, Vanessa*
Book Title: *Raoul Moat: His Short Life and Bloody Death*
Chapter: *Prologue*
References to Howard *(2010 page viii)*
Publisher: *John Blake*
ISBN 978-1-84358-324-0

Author: **Whelan, Andy**
Website: **The Mail Online**
Article: **'I'm to blame': Revealed for the first time, the horror and remorse of killer gunman Raoul Moat's missing father**
Available at: http://www.dailymail.co.uk/news/article-1307130/Im-blame-Revealed-time-horror-remorse-killer-gunman-Raoul-Moats-missing-father.html
Last Updated and Published: *01:32 29th August 2010*
References to: *(Whelan 2010)*
(Accessed on Saturday 18th January 2014 at 10:42)

Author: **White, Mark D.**
Website: **Psychology Today**
Article: **Maybe, It's Just Me, But ... Hypersensitivity Cuts Both Ways**
Available at:
http://www.psychologytoday.com/blog/maybe-its-just-me/201210/hypersensitivity-cuts-both-ways
Last Updated and Published: *19th October 2012 by Mark D. White, Ph D.*
References to: *(White 2012)*
(Accessed on Saturday 18th January 2014 at 12:00)

Authors: **Marco, E.M., Valero M, De La Serna, O, Aisa B, Borcel E, Ramirez, M.J., Viveros, MP**
Website: **US National Library of Medicine National Institutes of Health**
Article: **Maternal Deprivation Effects on Brain Plasticity and Recognition Memory in Adolescent and Female Rats.**
Available at: http: http://www.ncbi.nlm.nih.gov/pubmed/22939999
Last Updated and Published: *24th August 2012.*
References to: *(Valero, Marco et al)*
(Accessed on Saturday 18th January 2014 at 12:34)

Author: **Bailey, Regina**
Website: **About.com Education: Biology**
Article: **Amygdala**
Available at: http://biology.about.com/od/anatomy/p/Amygdala.htm
Last Updated and Published: *January 2014.*
References to: *(Bailey 2014)*
(Accessed on Saturday 18th January 2014 at 12:48)

FURTHER READING AND RESEARCH

Author: **BBC News**
Website: **BBC News: England**
Article: **Durham Prison tops suicide table**
Available at: http://news.bbc.co.uk/1/hi/england/2645303.stm
Last Updated and Published: *Sunday 12th January 2003*
References to: *(BBC News 2003)*
(Accessed on Saturday 18th January 2014 at 12:59)

Author: **BBC News**
Website: **BBC News: England**
Article: **Shot PC David Rathband 'bears no malice' to Raoul Moat**
Available at: http://www.bbc.co.uk/news/10513994
Last Updated and Published: *11th July 2010 at 09:10am*
References to: *(BBC News Reports 11th July 2010)*
(Accessed on Saturday 18th January 2014 at 13:28)

Author: **BBC News**
Website: **BBC News: England**
Article: **Timeline of Raoul Moat Shootings**
Available at: http://www.bbc.co.uk/news/10583120
Last Updated and Published: *26th September 2011 at 14:56*
References to: *(Question 11 – Source BBC News 2011)*
(Accessed on Thursday 13th February 2014 at 19:10)

Author: **Gammell, Caroline**
Website: **The Telegraph Online**
Article: **Raoul Moat's history of violence**
Available at:
http://www.telegraph.co.uk/news/uknews/crime/7871393/Raoul-Moats-history-of-violence.html
Last Updated and Published: *06:30am BST 5th July 2010*
References to: *(Gammell 2010)*
(Accessed on Thursday 13th February 2014 at 19:42)

FURTHER READING AND RESEARCH

Author: *Mendick, Robert and Leach, Ben*
Website: *The Telegraph Online*
Article: *Raoul Moat: 'I've no dad, no one cares about me'*
Available at:
http://www.telegraph.co.uk/news/uknews/crime/7883742/Raoul-Moat-Ive-no-dad-no-one-cares-about-me.html
Last Updated and Published: *09:00am BST 11th July 2010*
References to: *(Mendick and Leach 2010)*
(Accessed on Thursday 13th February 2014 at 20:03)

Author: *Wilson, David, Professor*
Website: *The Mail Online*
Article: *Violent narcissist who thought he was Rambo*
Available at:
http://www.dailymail.co.uk/debate/article-1293954/Raoul-Moat-Violent-narcissist-thought-Rambo.html
Last Updated and Published: *08:11am on July 12th, 2010*
References to: *(Wilson 2010)*
(Accessed on Friday 14th February 2014 at 16:22)

Author: *Camber, Rebbecca, Sims, Paul, Brooke, Chris and Dolan, Andy*
Website: *The Mail Online*
Article: *'I'm at war with the police and I won't stop until I'm dead: Killer fugitive's chilling letter after shooting three on murderous rampage'*
Available at: http://www.dailymail.co.uk/news/article-1292320/Raoul-Moat-puts-hit-list-Facebook.html
Last Updated and Published: *09:35 7th July 2010*
References to: *(Camber, Sims, Brooke and Dolan)*
(Accessed on Saturday 15th February 2014 at 12:40)

Author: *BBC News*
Website: *BBC News: England*
Article: *Raoul Moat accomplices get minimum 40 and 20-year terms*
Available at: http://www.bbc.co.uk/news/uk-england-tyne-12742868
Last Updated and Published: *15th March 2011 at 14:28*
References to: *(BBC News 15th March 2011)*
(Accessed on Saturday 18th January 2014 at 13:05)

FURTHER READING AND RESEARCH

Author: *Lyall, Sarah*
Website: *The New York Times*
Article: *Norway Killer Gets the Maximum: 21 Years*
Available at: http://www.nytimes.com/2012/08/25/world/europe/
anders-behring-breivik-murder-trial.html?_r=0
Last Updated and Published: *August 24th, 2012*
References to: *(New York Times)*
(Accessed on Saturday 18th January 2014 at 13:09)

Author: *Wilson, David, Professor*
Website: *The Mail Online*
Article: *Twisted Mind of a Maniac*
Available at: http://www.dailymail.co.uk/debate/article-1292668/
Raoul-Thomas-Moat-Twisted-mind-maniac.html
Last Updated and Published: *07:44 7th July 2010*
References to: *(Wilson 2010)*
(Accessed on Saturday 15th February 2014 at 15:00)

Authors: *American Medical Association*
Website: *American Medical Association Resources*
Article: *Genetics of Bipolar Disorder*
Available at:
http://www.ama-assn.org/resources/doc/genetics/bipolar-disorder.pdf
Last Updated and Published: 2008
References to: *(American Medical Association AMA)*
(Accessed on Monday 3rd March 2014 at 11:48)

Authors: *Arias-Carrion, O and Poppell E*
Website: *NCBI Us National Library of Medicine National Institutes of Health*
Article: *Dopamine, learning and reward-seeking behaviour*
Available at: http://www.ncbi.nlm.nih.gov/pubmed/18320725
Last Updated and Published: 2007
References to: *(Arias-Carrion and Poppell 2007)*
(Accessed on Monday 3rd March 2014 at 12:08)

FURTHER READING AND RESEARCH

Author: **Brain Injury Institute**
Website: **Brain Injury Institute.org**
Article: **Frontal Lobe Damage**
Available at:
http://www.braininjuryinstitute.org/Brain-Injury-Types/Frontal-Lobe-Damage.html
Last Updated and Published: 2011
References to: *(Brain Injury Institute Website)*
(Accessed on Saturday 18th January 2014 at 12:26)

Authors: **NHS Choices Website**
Website: **NHS**
Article: **Anabolic Steroid Misuse**
Available at:
http://www.nhs.uk/conditions/anabolic-steroid-abuse/Pages/Introduction.aspx
Last Updated and Published: 2014 March 3rd
References to: *(NHS Choices Website)*
(Accessed on Monday 3rd March 2014 at 12:46)

Author: **Serretti, Alessandro and Mandelli, L**
Website: **Molecular Psychiatry**
Article: ***The genetics of bipolar disorder: genome 'hot regions', new genes, new potential candidates and future directions***
Available at: http://www.nature.com/mp/journal/v13/n8/full/mp200829a.html#aff1
Last Updated and Published: *11th March 2008*
References to: *(Serretti and Mandelli, 2008)*
(Accessed on Tuesday 4th February 2014 at 13:59)

Author: **Williams, Katherine**
Book Title: ***5th Edition Textbook on Criminology***
Chapter 14: ***Conflict theories and radical criminology's***
Sub-Section: *15.3.2 Early radical criminology*
References to *Williams (2005, page 410) cites Marx (1904)*
Publisher: *Oxford University Press*
ISBN 0-19-926440-6

FURTHER READING AND RESEARCH

Author: ***Hitchens, Peter***
Website: ***The Daily Mail Online***
Article: ***Human rights and an affront to justice***
Available at: http://www.dailymail.co.uk/debate/article-2449247/Human-rights-affront-justice.html
Last Updated and Published: 7th October 2013 at 23:14
References to: *(Hitchens 2013)*
(Accessed on Thursday 13th March 2014 at 19:08)

Author: ***Telegraph Comment Page***
Website: 44***The Daily Telegraph***
Article: ***Karen Matthews and the Underclass That Thrive on Labour's Welfare State***
Available at: http://www.telegraph.co.uk/comment/telegraph-view/3645067/Karen-Matthews-and-the-underclass-thrive-on-Labours-welfare-state.html
Last Updated and Published: *12:01 am GMT 6TH December 2008*
References to: *(Telegraph Article)*
(Accessed on Thursday 13th March 2014 at 19:17)

Author: ***BBC News***
Website: ***BBC News: England***
Article: ***Raoul Moat: Prime Minister criticises public sympathy***
Available at: http://www.bbc.co.uk/news/uk-england-10633297
Last Updated and Published: *14th July 2010 at 18:51pm GMT*
References to: *(BBC News – 14TH July 2010)*
(Accessed on Friday 14th March 2014 at 10:23)

Author: ***Randall, David and Owen, Jonathan***
Website: ***The Independent UK***
Article: ***The strange life and death of Raoul Moat***
Available at: http://www.independent.co.uk/news/uk/crime/the-strange-life-and-death-of-raoul-moat-2023987.html
Last Updated and Published: *Friday 14th March 2014*
References to: *(Randall and Owen 2010)*
(Accessed on Friday 14th March 2014 at 10:41).

www.ingramcontent.com/pod-product-compliance
Lightning Source LLC
Chambersburg PA
CBHW030212170426
43201CB00006B/65